# Vikings of the Steppe

This book explores the relationship between Vikings, Rus' and nomadic (mostly Turkic) steppe dwellers during the course of the Viking Age (c. 750–1050) in a geographical area stretching from Eastern Scandinavia through the Kievan Rus', Byzantium, the Islamic world to the Western Eurasian steppes.

The primary focus is the steppe influence on the development of Scandinavian-Rus' culture. It illustrates the effects of Turkic (nomadic) cultures on the evolving Scandinavian-Rus' communities in their military technology and tactics, as well as in everyday customs, ritual traditions and religious perceptions, whilst paying attention to the politico-commercial necessities and possible communication channels tying these two cultures, normally considered to be distinct, together. The arguments are supported by a multi-disciplinary analysis of diverse historical and archaeological materials occasionally supplemented with linguistic evidence. The result is a comprehensive evaluation of the relations of the Scandinavians active in the 'East' with Turkic groups and brings the (so far neglected) steppes into Viking studies in general.

The book will fill a serious scholarly gap in the field of Viking studies and will be read by both academics and students interested in the archaeological and historical sources concerned with the traditions of the 'Eastern Vikings'.

**Csete Katona** earned a PhD in History at the University of Debrecen. Currently, he is a PhD candidate at Central European University and employed as a research assistant at Pázmány Péter Catholic University. His research interest is the Vikings in the East, on which he has several publications in English and Hungarian.

**Routledge Archaeologies of the Viking World**

Series editors: Neil Price, Charlotte Hedenstierna-Jonson, and Ben Raffield

THE VIKING PHENOMENON

The editorial management of this book series is supported by the Swedish Research Council project *The Viking Phenomenon* (2015–00466).

Vikings are a perennially popular topic across a broad audience spectrum, from the general public to academics at all levels, but there are comparatively few book series dedicated to the steady flow of Viking-related archaeological texts. *Routledge Archaeologies of the Viking World* showcases the latest outputs of the profession's brightest scholars, including established names but particularly acting as an outlet for the new generation of early career researchers.

The archaeological investigations of the Viking world within the series have a direct focus on the Scandinavians but also on the zones of cultural interaction that characterised their broad diaspora. The editors have particular interests in the eastern Viking Age, from European Russia to the Asian Steppe, the Arab world and beyond to the Silk Road and the Far East. This region is significantly under-represented in new English-language publications, and books on this theme will become a hallmark of the series alongside western studies.

**Viking Silver, Hoards and Containers**
The Archaeological and Historical Context of Viking-Age Silver Coin Deposits in the Baltic c. 800-1050
*Jacek Gruszczyński*

**Monarchs and Hydrarchs**
The Conceptual Development of Viking Activity across the Frankish Realm (c. 750-940)
*Christian Cooijmans*

**A Viking Market Kingdom in Ireland and Britain**
Trade Networks and the Importation of a Southern Scandinavian Silver Bullion Economy
*Tom Horne*

**Viking-Age Trade**
Silver, Slaves and Gotland
*Edited by Jacek Gruszczyński, Marek Jankowiak, Jonathan Shepard*

**Vikings of the Steppe**
Scandinavians, Rus', and the Turkic World (c. 750–1050)
*Csete Katona*

For more information about this series, please visit: https://www.routledge.com/Routledge-Archaeologies-of-the-Viking-World/book-series/RAVW

# Vikings of the Steppe

## Scandinavians, Rus', and the Turkic World (c. 750–1050)

**Csete Katona**

Routledge
Taylor & Francis Group
LONDON AND NEW YORK

Cover image: Henryk Siemiradzki – Warriors Battle Silistria. Artefact/
Alamy Stock Photo

First published 2023
by Routledge
4 Park Square, Milton Park, Abingdon, Oxon OX14 4RN

and by Routledge
605 Third Avenue, New York, NY 10158

*Routledge is an imprint of the Taylor & Francis Group, an informa business*



*British Library Cataloguing-in-Publication Data*
A catalogue record for this book is available from the British Library

ISBN: 978-0-367-48075-2 (hbk)
ISBN: 978-1-032-34075-3 (pbk)
ISBN: 978-1-003-03785-9 (ebk)

DOI: 10.4324/9781003037859

Typeset in Times New Roman
by Apex CoVantage, LLC

# Contents

# Figures

# Tables

# Preface and acknowledgments

This book deals with the interactions of Scandinavians, Rus' and the inhabitants of the steppes during the Viking Age (c. 750–1050 CE). As these labels indicate, the geographic boundaries of the topic encompass (mostly) Eastern Scandinavia, Eastern Europe, the Baltics, European Russia and in a few cases even territories beyond. It is an immense challenge to present even parts of the history of roughly three centuries over such a vast territory and among such varied people, especially when the available evidence is so complex and exists in both material and written forms, the latter in a wide variety of ancient languages, including Arabic, Persian, Old Church Slavonic, Old Norse, Latin and Byzantine Greek. No researcher can be equally knowledgeable in all these types of sources; thus, it is necessary to explain my position and outline my intentions in writing this book.

Such a subject could have been addressed (and has previously been addressed by others) based on just one type of surviving evidence, from the viewpoint of various disciplines, or within a specific framework of Scandinavian, Russian or steppe history. Here, as a historian, I have aimed for a synthesis and attempted to establish a basic narrative. The primary goal was to bring the Western Eurasian steppes onto the horizon of Viking studies. This corresponds to my original background as a history student in Hungary, where studies of the steppe people occupy a prominent position in curricula, also to my training in Old Norse studies in Iceland and Denmark. Accordingly, the book presents a 'steppe perspective' on the Viking diasporas and introduces this world to scholars working in related fields. This naturally means that some facts receive more attention than others in order to familiarize the reader with the situation. A reader coming from a different background may also find some useful information. The impact the steppe had on neighbouring cultures should appeal to scholars and students working on early Russian or Turkic steppe history. The various types of contacts among these groups deserve systematic treatment. The book admittedly has a Hungarian bias in the archaeological material, not only because I know this material the best and it is accessible to me but also because I feel able to extend the picture drawn by previous works on this topic, which were mostly case studies.

Keeping the audience in mind, I have tried to provide easily accessible translations of sources written in languages other than Old Norse, Latin or Greek. These are mostly Arabic and Slavic sources that are fortunately accessible in English translations. In some cases, the reader will not find 'dual' references to sources (that is, a translation and an original edition), as I have used bilingual editions. When these were unavailable I used the original editions, and for the Persian sources, which I am unfortunately unable to read, I have relied on translations. Since I am not equally familiar with all the source languages, I received great help from specialists in cases when sources' terminologies required deeper analysis.

One of the most difficult tasks was to decide on a principle of transcription for foreign words. Given the wide variety of source languages, I felt it would be disturbing to leave everything in the original, but anglicizing everything also raised problems. I have to confess I did not opt for consistency. Geographical names are mostly anglicized unless they appear in quotes. I preferred the simpler forms (e.g. in case of Russian names: Gnezdovo instead of Gnëzdovo), but left the original expressions intact (e.g. Staraya Ladoga instead of Old Ladoga, Rurikovo Gorodische instead of Rurik's stronghold). Arabic personal names remained in the original, but geographical names are replaced with the English equivalents. Arabic letters are transcribed with the simplest possible combination of Latin letters in which long vowels are indicated with a dash. Since I expect many readers to come from Viking studies, Old Norse names appear in the original with a few exceptions. They are not inflected if they come from a source that is not written in Old Norse (e.g. Asmund instead of Ásmundr). To accommodate other readers, it somehow felt odd to use Haraldr Gormsson instead of Harald Bluetooth or Knútr inn ríki instead of Cnut the Great, therefore rulers' names appear in anglicized forms. Byzantine and Latin names are also anglicized, as similarly it felt more natural to refer to Constantine Porphyrogenitus (the Latinized version) than to Kōnstantinos Porphyrogennētos. In the case of ethnonyms or geographical names that have multiple spellings in the literature, I resorted to options depending on the situation. Thus, Bulghars denotes the Volga Bulghars, but Bulgar refers to their town or applies to the Danube Bulgars to avoid confusion. The word Rus' is used with an apostrophe throughout, denoting both singular and plural.

The basic structure of the book is based on my PhD dissertation, defended in 2019 at the University of Debrecen (Hungary). This book, however, is a re-conceptualized and elaborated version that has been partly developed at Central European University (Vienna), where I am enrolled in further studies. It also evolved thanks to comments from colleagues on various parts of the manuscript that were published or presented at conferences. I am grateful to all who contributed to its completion. Financial support for the writing of this book was provided by research scholarships from Central European University, the "Our Eastern Heritage Interdisciplinary Historical- and Archaeological Research Group of Pázmány Péter Catholic University" (TUDFO/51757–1/2019/ITM) and the "Legends of the Eastern Vikings" research group, who generously funded my research stay in Iceland in 2020.

Here I express my gratitude to a wide range of people who contributed to this work in some way. First, I am most indebted to my supervisors at the University of Debrecen and Central European University, Attila Bárány and József Laszlovszky. My dissertation benefited from detailed comments by István Vásáry, Márta

Font and Szabolcs Polgár, all of whom I am immensely grateful for pointing out my inaccuracies. Although the text has developed and been restructured, their constructive criticism remains decisive. Earlier drafts of individual chapters (some in the form of a previous MA thesis) have also been read by Judith Jesch, Neil Price, Terry Gunnell, Jonathan Shepard and Sverrir Jakobsson. I thank all of them for suggestions or concerns expressed about some of my argumentation. The first draft of the entire manuscript was read by Péter Langó, whose expertise in archaeology is evident in corresponding parts of the manuscript. I also thank Heinrich Härke for a thorough reading of a later version of the manuscript and Sven Kalmring for suggesting literature. The editors of the *Routledge Archaeologies of the Viking World* series, Charlotte Hedenstierna-Jonson, Neil Price and Ben Raffield, have always responded to queries during the submission process. I thank them for their utmost patience with me and also for their extremely valuable comments on the manuscript, which made the final version of this book much more nuanced and hopefully more attractive to readers. The submission process also became much smoother due to the always quick and efficient assistance of Roy Manas, the editorial assistant for the series. Gratitude also goes to Attila Türk for corresponding on my behalf with Ukrainian and Russian institutes and scholars in order to obtain images and secondary literature. These colleagues, especially Sergei Kainov and Oleksiy Komar, as well as the museums that supplied images, also merit my gratitude. Credit for drawing the maps and images in the book goes to Béla Nagy and Krisztián Balla respectively. Other scholars helped me with languages, István Lánczky and László Tüske for the Arabic sources, István Kovács for Byzantine Greek and Judith Rasson for correcting my English. Naturally, all remaining errors are my own.

I also thank the colleagues with whom I have conducted fruitful discussions about academic life and the writing of this book in general: Zoltán Véber, László Szabolcs Gulyás, Dorottya Uhrin, David Rockwell and Daria Segal. Lastly, I thank my family and my friends all over the world, without whom this book would never have been finished. Sorrowfully, I dedicate this work to the memory of three friends, Gyuri, Gabi and Ádám, who passed away tragically in traffic accidents. This is a modest recompense for their friendship.

Csete Katona
Budapest, 2021

My research was conducted within a project framework entitled Archaeology Research on the Contacts between Hungary and the East (Our Eastern Heritage, PPCU History and Archaeology Interdisciplinary Research Team; TKP2020-NKA-11), with the support of Thematic Excellence Program, National Research, Development and Innovation Office.

# 1 Introduction

Around the year 1000, Norse ships were rowing the sea towards an unfamiliar land in the west, the Americas. Groups set sail from settlements established recently on the coast of Greenland, a place already considerably distant from Scandinavia, where they originated. An Icelandic source, the *Grœnlendinga saga* – a heroic tale committed to parchment only in the fourteenth century and one of the chief sources for the American voyages – states that on board one of the ships was a man named Tyrkir – "Turk" in the Old Norse language (Sveinsson and Þórðarson 1935a, 248–53). Although personal names are not always definite indicators of ethnic origin, it is not unlikely that a later medieval saga drawing on substantial oral tradition faithfully maintained the memory of a foreigner called "Turk" sailing to America with the Scandinavians. Who was he? Was he really a Turk? If so, what was he doing on board a Viking ship? If not, why was he called that? He was clearly a stranger within the group. As the story relates, when the expedition arrived, Tyrkir was sent out as a scout to explore the countryside. Returning in a strikingly good mood, he starts to speak in *þýzku*, a language completely unintelligible to his Scandinavian companions. Tyrkir then switches back to Norse and explains that he found grapes, which reminded him of his homeland. Scholars have postulated that Tyrkir was in fact a German. On the one hand, *þýzku* is usually translated as 'German', and on the other hand, because he is labelled as a *suðrmaðr*, a 'southerner', which is also a term for a Saxon merchant near the end of the saga (Sveinsson and Þórðarson 1935a, 268), and finally because the closest grapes to Scandinavia grew only in Germany (cf. Piványｙ 1903; Hermansson 1954; Hreinsson 1977, 23; Wallace 2008, 606). Questions arise about whether the vague term 'southerner' could refer to someone from other than Saxony (as it was at the time) and whether it might be the expression of a later saga writer to make sense of a character known from earlier oral traditions. Equally, grapes could grow elsewhere in lands the Scandinavians knew, and it is hard to believe that a Germanic language (which would have been closely related to Old Norse in the period) would sound incomprehensible to a group of Scandinavians around the year 1000. This identification still lacks a reason for calling a German a Turk. The same designation occurs in various genres of medieval Old Icelandic documents from different eras, but in meanings that vaguely associate the 'land of the Turks' with Asia (Klingenberg 1993; Beck 1994; Jakobsson 2016a), and have nothing to do with Germans or Germany.

DOI: 10.4324/9781003037859-1

Of course, being a Turk or Turkic was not the same in and around the year 1000 and in the fourteenth century, when the saga was recorded. Turkic is originally a linguistic term that gained a foothold as a cultural marker (see Chapter 2). It is a vague category, however, and early medieval sources are usually more specific when calling these people by their tribal affiliations. The only contemporary exceptions are the Magyars, a semi-nomadic tribal group that inhabited the grasslands of the Black Sea steppes at the time, who are explicitly called 'Turks' in both Byzantine and Muslim documents of the period (Moravcsik 1983, 320–27; Zimonyi 2001). In contrast, to a fourteenth-century saga writer, Turks could easily have meant the Ottomans, his contemporaries. Of course, one can never be sure that the composer of the saga meant the Turks of the era of the story rather than projecting his own knowledge back to earlier times, an otherwise common practice with any historic source material, especially sagas. Still, a Turk with the Vikings in America would certainly be an unconventional image. But who were the Turks and what, if anything, did they have to do with the Scandinavian Vikings?

The Turks originated somewhere in Central Asia, probably around the third millennium BCE. The region where they emerged was ruled by groups speaking Indo-European language(s) who, from the second millennium BCE, practised mobile pastoralism characterized by seasonal migrations, a lifestyle often called nomadism. Various branches of Turkic-speaking people still followed this way of life (to varying degrees) in 1000 CE, when the *Grœnlendinga saga*'s actions take place (Findley 2005, 21–55; Golden 2011, 8–21).

It is a popular cliché to call the Vikings "the nomads of the sea" (e.g. Pritsak 1977, 256; Bell-Fialkoff 2000, 171; Kennedy 2002, 175–76; Chaliand 2005, 49). The label is based on the mere similarity between long-distance movements, migrations, attacks and plundering, a lifestyle that typified Scandinavian sea-marauders – the original meaning of the word 'Viking' – in the period between c. 750 and 1050 CE, as well as contemporaneous mounted horsemen of Central Asia and Eastern Europe (Golovnov 2009, 209–310). The symbolic juxtaposition of Vikings with nomads also draws on images of the geographical terrain. The unending horizon seen from the sea strongly resembles the view from the steppe as recognized in Chekov's novelle *The Steppe*: "Of the sky's unfathomable depth, of its boundlessness, you can judge only at sea and on the moonlit steppe by night. It is frightening and picturesque, yet kindly. Its gaze is languorous and magnetic, but its embraces make you dizzy" (Chekhov 1992, 29). The flat area of unforested grasslands stretching to infinity brings to mind a 'grassy sea'. This geographical unit, extending from the northern borders of China to the Pannonian plain in present-day Hungary, was home to many nomads (and Turks) throughout history.

A first-glance similarity of the worlds of Vikings and nomads is indeed inescapable; terrain, movement and means of transportation were inherently linked in both ways of life. The sea and the ship are a typical image of the Viking Age, while the steppe and the horse equally evoke the nomadic world. Perhaps we can even detect an unconscious recognition of this in the contemporary mindset of Viking Age poets, who skilfully forged kennings (metaphors with highly complicated rhyme structures) and often described their primary means of transportation, the ship, as the "horse of the sea" (Jesch 2001, 34). There is, however, much more to the steppe nomads in relation to Vikings than a superficial parallel between them implies. The 'nomads of the sea' and the 'nomads of the steppe' not only look familiar from a cursory glance, they were frequently in contact during historic times. How did these encounters come about?

The Scandinavian voyages to America related in the Vinland sagas are seen today as one of the major achievements of Scandinavian maritime expansion during the Viking Age. It has been argued recently that they connected the trading systems of the globe for the first time, at least theoretically (Hansen 2020, 25). The short-lived Scandinavian settlements – confirmed by archaeological research in L'anse aux Meadows in New Foundland (Canada) – were the westernmost edges of a network of Scandinavian settlement today referred to as a diaspora based on shared identities and interconnections (Abrams 2012). Scandinavians also made important voyages in the other direction: East. People embarking on such a journey stepped on the *austrvegr*, the 'Eastern Road', which in general meant a territory encompassing the Eastern Baltic region, today's European Russia, Belarus and Ukraine, as well as the Black Sea region, Byzantium, the Caucasus and even beyond. The Eastern edge of the Scandinavian diaspora stretched to somewhere in modern-day Uzbekistan, evidenced by a runestone inscription (Vs 1) found in Västmanland, Sweden, commemorating a man named Slagvi, who died in the East in *karusm*, an Old Norse transliteration of the Middle Turkic name for Khorezm in Central Asia (Jansson 1964, 8–9; Gustavsson 2002, 145–49).

Scandinavian traders in the east were actively linked to the system of Silk Roads, the Eurasian highways that transported goods, knowledge, ideas, people and sometimes even diseases. They mostly maintained long-distance exchanges with the Islamic lands; the Abbasid caliphate in the ninth century and the Samanid regimes in the tenth. Central commercial hubs of the latter, such as Samarkand, Bukhara and Merv, were instrumental in producing and sending silver (in the form of coins), exotic products and raw materials, most importantly textiles, gold and gemstones, from Central Asia towards the north (Michailidis 2013; Hedenstierna-Jonson 2020a). The steppe was an integral part of this network, an intermediary between the 'oriental' routes and the so-called Fur Road, a northern branch of the Silk Roads where Scandinavians were active.

America and Central Asia thus constituted the geographic boundaries of the Viking world, where people of Scandinavian origin maintained contacts and shared a common language, a similar religion and a sense of belonging (Jesch 2015). The question is the degree this cohesiveness exerted. Is it even a possibility that there was communication of information between the extremities of the known Scandinavian world besides direct contact?

The relevance of steppe contacts for the Viking diaspora as a whole is apparent in the example of Tyrkir. As implausible as it sounds at first (and of course one is allowed to be sceptical), individuals in this period could cover huge distances, and it is possible that someone from the steppe travelled to America. As seen from the excerpt, individuals travelled with a linguistic and cultural package – in Tyrkir's case, a non-Germanic language and a knowledge of grapes. So did objects.

In Lundur (Vestur-Skaftafellsýsla district), Iceland, a strap-mount for horse harnesses was found which belongs to a wider horizon of similar objects found elsewhere in Scandinavia (Jansson 1975–77; Figure 1.1; Figure 1.2).

They are often connected to items that originated in the East, a wide array of raw materials, everyday as well as luxury artefacts (scales, weights, jewellery, clothes, textiles, glass, weapons and horse equipment), found mainly in Sweden. Some of these came directly from the caliphates, Byzantium or the steppes, but their manufacture sometimes includes the curious addition of Eastern cultural

*Figure 1.1* Belt mounts from Lundur, Vivallen, and Shestovitsa

Source: Redrawn after Jansson 1975–77, 384, fig. 1; Hedenstierna-Jonson and Olausson 2006, 32; Arne 1931, 288, fig. 17

traditions (Arbman 1942; Hägg 1984; Jansson 1987, 1988; Hedenstierna-Jonson and Olausson 2006; Hedenstierna-Jonson 2012). Since T. J. Arne's (1914) first famous collection of such finds, *La Suède et l'orient*, archaeologists term them vaguely as 'oriental'. The strap-mounts found in Scandinavia originated in the

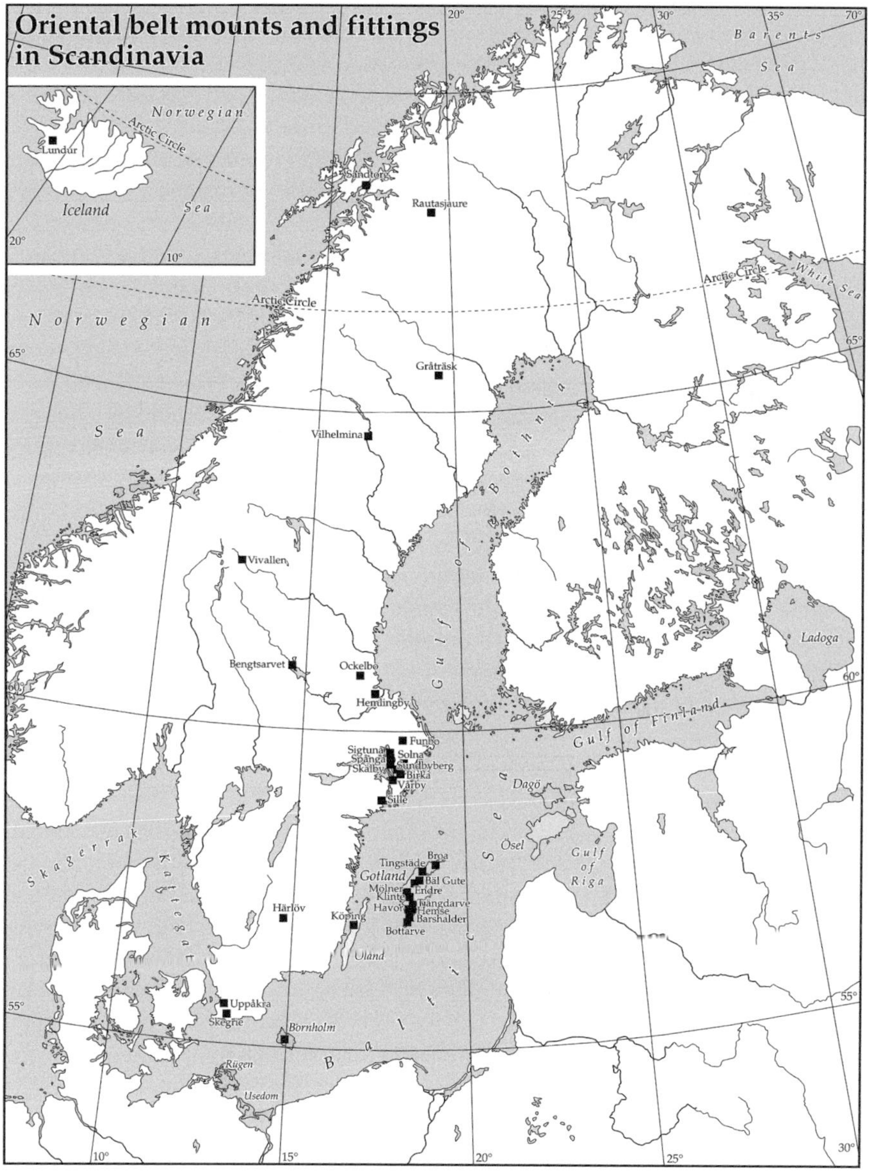


*Figure 1.2* 'Oriental' belt mounts and fittings from Scandinavia

East; they were one of the most prestigious personal items of mounted warriors of the steppes. The steppes were home to many (culturally) Turkic polities and loosely knit groups in the Viking Age, some of whom are the protagonists of this book, most notably the Khazars, the Volga Bulghars, the Magyars and the Pechenegs. Naturally, a single object does not necessarily signal a direct connection; the mount found in Lundur could easily have been trickle-traded. The lack of exact analogies for some strap-ends and belt mounts also suggests that the tradition stemmed from common roots but developed in different directions in Scandinavia, Russia and the Baltics and was in fashion until the late eleventh century (Mikhajlov 2007). Nevertheless, the Lundur find certainly implies a network through which objects, information and know-how could flow between remote parts of the Viking diaspora. A statue of Buddha found in the Swedish site of Helgö (a rural settlement dating just prior to the Viking Age) is a comparative example (Gyllensvärd 2004).

Tyrkir might not have been a real Turk, and the Lundur strap-mount or the process of its production might not have been transferred directly from a Turkic owner to a Scandinavian, but the possibility is more than there. Plenty of evidence, all pertaining to close interaction in Eastern Europe, shows that Turkic–Scandinavian commercial, military and cultural (as well as personal) networks developed.

Scandinavian groups venturing to the East were called by different names. Most frequently they appear as Rus' in contemporary documents (Obolensky 1982; Hraundal 2013). This designation, however, is not without controversy as it evolved slowly to mean a hybrid ethnic group of Scandinavians, Balto-Finns, Slavs and even Turks who merged in Eastern Europe and later established a medieval polity with a centre in Kiev. Despite its ethnic inclusiveness, the Rus' elite maintained its Scandinavian links throughout the Viking Age, not only in expressive cultural features communicated through rites and material elements (Hedenstierna-Jonson 2017) but also in terms of physical contacts. New groups coming east directly from Scandinavia also joined this network. A new designation could perhaps be 'Scandinavian Rus'', to imply the Scandinavian background or attachment of (rather eclectic) Rus' groups.

Some Scandinavians and the Rus' cooperated closely with the steppe dwellers. Eastern Europe was the stage for the meeting of these two (originally) distant cultures, one predominantly Scandinavian, the other mainly Turkic in character, more precisely, the territory encompassing present-day European Russia, Ukraine and Hungary. Scandinavian and Rus' traders, warriors, settlers, men and women interacted with various people of the Western Eurasian steppes in an intricate web of migrations, politics, warfare and trade, which all paved way for the development of eclectic identities. Some of these ties were so close that they had visible cultural effects whose resonances could be felt even in Scandinavia. Strap-mounts found in Scandinavia are only the tip of the iceberg; the most distant example, Tyrkir (if he existed), would have been just one among many steppe people living in the company of Scandinavians during the Viking Age. In a sense, Tyrkir could have been a 'true nomad of the sea', a man originating in the steppe but rowing with a Scandinavian crew on the other edge of the world. Individuals and groups with similarly complex travel stories were not without precedent in the early Middle Ages. Moreover, contacts persisted in the other direction, too, and scenarios the reverse of Tyrkir's also occurred; some Scandinavians and Rus' also spent considerable time in the company of steppe people and were affected by them. Some adopted customs or modified their beliefs based on their Turkic experience or started to mount horses and shoot arrows like nomadic warriors. If Tyrkir, or people with a similar life path, qualify as Vikings, some of these Rus' would certainly deserve to be called the 'Vikings of the steppe'. The goal of this book is to illuminate how interactions in various places and contacts through channels such as warfare, trade, religious thought and communication facilitated the rise of new, culturally hybrid identities.

The task here is to integrate the findings of various disciplines and data from various written and archaeological sources into a coherent macro narrative. It should be emphasized that the aim is not to investigate contacts strictly between Scandinavia and the steppes, but to assess the interactions of various groups comprehensively within the regions in between, contact zones between these originally distinct cultural spheres. Gaps and uncertainties about the details of this synergy naturally surface, but, besides the contact zones, the contact spheres – military, commercial and cultural – can safely be reconstructed. Thus, the structure of this book reflects conflict, trade, military co-operation and cultural interaction, illustrating the potential of studying the steppe as a relevant factor for the identities of intertwining groups and individuals during the Viking diaspora.

It is worth returning to scholarly terminologies for Scandinavians in the East, most importantly the Rus', and another term, Varangians. The origin of the Kievan Rus' state and the Scandinavians' role in the formation of a Rus' ethnic identity was long in the centre of politically motivated debates in the framework of the "Normanist-controversy" (Stender-Petersen 1953; Schmidt 1970; Klejn 2013). One bloc of scholars postulated that the different variants of the term Rus' in contemporary Latin, Muslim, Byzantine and later Slavic sources refer to Scandinavians, others maintained the Slavic origin of the designation and denied any connections to a Germanic population which finally gave its name to modern Russia. Although the unequivocal merging of the Rus' with Slavs or with purely Eastern Scandinavians is now outdated, antagonistic scholarly attitudes are not entirely gone (see, for instance, Mel'nikova 2012). There is still no consensus on the precise meaning of the term 'Rus'' or on the development of Rus' identity in general (Androshchuk 2004–05; Schramm 2007; Urbańczyk 2014).

The term is best situated within modern theories of ethnic identity. As treated in modern scholarship, ethnicity is a practiced and chosen, rather than inherited, identity that changes and is renegotiated constantly (Bentley 1987). Ethnic groups in history were not necessarily stable entities sharing cultural norms, language or biological ancestry. Rather, they developed around emerging power centres or dominant elites of culturally mixed groups brought together by conquest or common goals in a shared geographical space (Pohl 1998). Ethnicity worked as a situational construct, where the (re)negotiation of common cultural practices and norms (including fashion, laws, beliefs and even language), as well as notions of kinship could be merged to forge new identities (Geary 2012).

The term 'Rus'', similar to 'Viking', best describes a way of life and refers to martial groups incorporating people of varying biological origins engaged in warfare, craft production and long-distance trade along the rivers (Golden 1995; Melnikova and Petrukhin 1990–91). Not all medieval authors used the term in the same meaning, and they often adopted earlier historiographic traditions by copying designations without illustrating the changes that occurred in the identity of a given group (Montgomery 2000, 2010). Hence, the designation Rus' should denote a population initially of predominantly Scandinavian origin, including women and children, mixing with the local Slavic, Balto-Finn and Turkic inhabitants of Eastern Europe. In later periods they should perhaps better be termed 'northern foreigner'.

In the ethnic connotations of the word Rus', the Slavic component (at least in the Kievan Rus' principality) became more decisive over time, and sources refer to 'northern foreigners' as Varangians from the eleventh century onwards (Shepard 2008, 509). This slightly different term has a Scandinavian connotation with a reference to professional warrior groups or associations operating in the East as pillagers, hired mercenaries or bodyguards (Stender-Petersen 1931–32; Androshchuk 2004–05). Nevertheless, the term clearly developed only in the eleventh century and was re-purposed, and later medieval authors projected it back in time (Jakobsson 2020, 63–74, 84–87, 175–76). This in no way rules out that Scandinavian mercenaries were present in various courts of the East during the ninth and tenth centuries, but caution is perhaps warranted about an anachronistic use of the term 'Varangian'. In the following, I will only employ it when it seems relatively safe to assume that ninth- and tenth-century Scandinavians were present in situations where later records describe them as Varangians.

The field of Scandinavian/Rus' steppe contacts is definitely not new, although less attention has been devoted to it than to the Western spheres in Viking studies. International scholarship, dominated mainly by Scandinavian and Russian scholars, however, has dealt with the issue in several regards. The field seems to have received an impetus in recent years from new trends in medieval studies, especially "cross-cultural" and "global" histories of the Middle Ages.

Trade is a well-covered area of Scandinavian-steppe contacts. Scholars dealing with Scandinavian history, not without justification, often incorporated their results on the Volga Bulghar– and Khazar–Scandinavian trade into their research on Scandinavian–Islamic or just 'oriental' connections generally (Piltz 1998; see also the other references above about 'oriental imports' into Scandinavia). Contemporary dirham deposits (hoards), found in great numbers in Scandinavia, Russia, Ukraine and the Baltics shed light on the intensity of trade flowing through the steppes and sometimes even on political events that occurred among the Scandinavians, Rus' and steppe dwellers (Noonan 1990, 2000–01; Kovalev 2000–01, 2011, 2013). Rus'–Turkic commercial relations have been discussed under Slavic–Turkic contacts in general, resulting in less treatment of Scandinavians among the Rus' population in these processes (Marquart 1903; Boba 1967; Noonan 1992; Nazmi 1998).

The political relations of the emerging and expanding Kievan Rus' polity with the nomads has received detailed attention on the basis of written sources

(Vernadsky 1939; Kaplan 1954; Franklin and Shepard 1996, 71–91, 139–51; Petrukhin 2009, 2015 with further references; Tolochko 2017). Other (mainly earlier) works put the weight of argument on the later, better documented, periods of Cuman and Mongol relations, and sometimes interpreted earlier periods of clearly Scandinavian ventures in a specific framework of early Russian expansion (Golubovskiy 1884; Rasovskiy [1933] 2012; Mavrodina 1983; Gumilyov 1989).

Military relationships have been treated extensively, especially by archaeologists. Scandinavian and steppe military equipment is often found in both Rus' settlements and the Scandinavian Birka, evincing close contacts among groups. These, the related relics of a blended material culture, and the question of evolving identities have been mentioned in general works on the Scandinavians in the East and the Rus' in general (Mel'nikova 1996; Kazanski et al. 2000; Duczko 2004; Callmer 2008; Androshchuk 2013, 213–26; Makarov 2017) and recently also in relation to Rus' contacts with nomads (Komar 2018). Targeted studies have also dealt with the spread of the so-called *druzhina* culture, Rus' retinue equipment especially in the case of Eastern weapon imports to Scandinavia, such as axes, sabres, bows and related artefacts, belts, sabretaches, quivers and other horse tack (Kirpichnikov 1970, 1977; Hedenstierna-Jonson and Olausson 2006; Lundström, Hedenstierna-Jonson, and Olausson 2009; Hedenstierna-Jonson 2009a, 2012, 2015). Archaeologists in Ukraine, Russia and Belarus have accumulated an immense amount of material from steppe territory connected to the Kievan Rus', such as nomadic weapons – especially bows and arrows, helmets, axes and sabres – and exotic items from far beyond the steppes that were transmitted through the nomads and sometimes even reached Scandinavia (Eniosova and Murashova 1999; Mikhajlov 2011, 211–13; Mikhailov and Kainov 2011; Murasheva 2006, 2016; Pushkina 2020). From the textual side, the sphere of Scandinavian engagement with steppe cultures is a speedily emerging field, mostly taken up by Arabists (Montgomery 2000, 2010; Hraundal 2013, 2014).

These studies fill in important gaps in our understanding of the social and ethnic make-up and far-reaching contacts of ninth- and tenth-century populations and their intricate and perhaps overlapping social, ethnic and religious identities. I aim to integrate these in a wider context, sometimes in contrast to the 'Western experience' among members of the Viking diaspora, in order to situate the steppe as an important factor within this network. Before proceeding to the early contacts among the Scandinavians, Rus' and steppe dwellers, it is necessary to discuss how we know what we know about the nomads and the Vikings of the steppes.

## The sources

### *Muslim sources*

Contemporary accounts of steppe territory and the Scandinavian Rus' derive largely from Arabic and Persian historical and geographical works. Building on earlier traditions of Greek, Indian and Persian geographical knowledge, Islamic scholars during Abbasid times in the ninth century invented something akin to human geography. This genre cannot be delineated as a separate science in the sense of the modern times. It rather integrates scientific observations (of various disciplines) with travelogues and also histories of the different regions of Islamic lands and their border zones (Krachkovskiy 1957; Hopkins 1990). These works often take a viewpoint of keen inspection of the outside world, something akin to modern anthropological descriptions, although without following a systematic representation or well-worked-out methodology.

Regarding the source value of these accounts, both *pro* and *contra* arguments can be formulated. For the pros, one could highlight that several of the early Muslim writers served state purposes by reporting on the lands of Islam and their surroundings; thus their accounts rarely tend to misguide the reader, as the intended audience was the Islamic courtly elite. In addition, many of the classical 'geographical' authors bear witness to a change in epistemological attitude towards scientific data by emphasizing direct observation and personal experience. Acquiring knowledge through travelling became a fitting method of scientific inquiry, condemning previous armchair historians who gathered their information from books (Heck 2002, 94–98). Despite this sound methodology, however, even the keenest observers scanned the outside world through their own cultural filters and terminology. They distorted indigenous customs of non-Islamic people, employed stereotypes and expressed their views from an ethnocentric perspective (Al-Azmeh 1992; Hermes 2012). Also, even widely travelled authors consulted previous works, which sometimes led to uncritical copying that makes it hard to distinguish between misnomers and the different chronological layers of the information in later accounts. Most of what we know about the authors of individual works derives from the works themselves. It is also apparent that each author grew up in a different political and ideological environment and received a different education. Codicological problems (manuscript divergences) also present themselves in the study of Islamic geographical literature.

The information in Muslim sources on the Scandinavians and Rus' has been treated extensively (Birkeland 1954; Montgomery 2000, 2008, 2010; Hraundal 2013). Accounts vary on using the term 'Rus'' to pertain to ethnicity (e.g. Urbańczyk 2014) even though, for the most part, Arabic sources separate it from another ethnic term, *Ṣaqāliba*, a common designation for the Slavs (Goehrke 1992, 124–27). This ambiguity is connected to the nature of the sources themselves since none of the Muslim authors from the eastern caliphate ever visited Scandinavia; Aḥmad ibn Faḍlān got the farthest, and he only reached the Middle Volga area. In contrast, Muslim authors' awareness of the steppe region was on firmer ground, although also having some of the fallacies noted previously.

The first extensive mention of the Rus' in Arabic sources comes from the *Book of Roads and Kingdoms* (*Kitāb al-Masālik wa-'l-mamālik*) by Abu 'l-Qāsim ʿUbayd Allāh b. ʿAbd Allāh ibn Khurradādhbih, an officer of the Baghdad postal system. The work was originally written in 850 CE and revised some 30 years later; it describes a curious itinerary of Rus' merchants in a passage that has figured in philological and manuscript-related debates (Pritsak 1970).

Most of the source material related to the history of the steppe region and the Rus' comes from two collections of geographical treatises, both going back to lost individual works. The first group of works builds on an early tenth-century compilation by Abū'Abdallāh al-Jayhānī, the Persian vizier of the Samanid Empire, whose lost work, with the same title as that by ibn Khurradādhbih, describes conditions in Eastern Europe in the ninth century (Göckenjan and Zimonyi 2011). Later copyists used his material extensively, such as the Samanid traveller Aḥmad ibn Rusta in his *Book of Precious Objects* (*Kitāb al-A'āq al-nafīsah*) dated between 903 and 913 CE. He also preserves another piece of important testimony, that of Hārūn ibn Yaḥyā, a Syrian traveller and Christian captive in Constantinople at the turn of the ninth century (880–912 CE), who noted the presence of various steppe people in the imperial capital. Other works building on Jayhānī include the anonymous Persian world geography roughly translatable as *Regions of the World* but most widely known by its original name as the *Ḥudūd al-'Ālam*, composed in 982 CE. The list goes on with the work of the Persian Abū Sa'īd Gardīzī's *The Ornament of Histories* (*Zayn al-akbār*) from the eleventh century and that of an eleventh-century Muslim author from al-Andalus, Al-Bakrī's dictionary of often-misspelled place names (*Mu'am mā 'sta'am*). The 'Arab Herodotus', Abū'l-Ḥasan'Alī al-Mas'ūdī, also consulted Jayhānī's material when writing his *Meadows of Gold and Mines of Precious Stones* (*Murūj aḏ-Ḏahab wa-Ma'ādin al-Jawhar*) on the history of the Abbasids, finished in 934 CE.

The other important cluster of sources are known as the al-Balkhī tradition. This tradition, named after the Khorasanian geographer Abū Zayd Aḥmad al-Balkhī (d. 934/954? CE), is a reworking of lost commentaries on a world map (Tibbets 1992). The first to use this material was Ibrāhīm ibn Muḥammad al-Iṣṭakhrī (d. 961 CE), who followed tradition in naming his book *Roads and Kingdoms* (*Kitāb al-Masālik wa-'l-mamālik*). Another contemporary copyist was Abū'l-Qāsim ibn Ḥawqal (d. c. 990 CE), who personally met al-Iṣṭakhrī and decided to revise his work. The result was that ibn Ḥawqal preserved details of history which al-Iṣṭakhrī omitted (de Goeje 1871). The most sophisticated follower of al-Balkhī was Muḥammad ibn Aḥmad al-Muqaddasī (d. after 988 CE), whose *The Best Divisions in the Knowledge of the Regions* (*Aḥsan al-taqāsīm fī ma'rifat al-aqālīm*) provides invaluable details on contemporary commercial traffic. A Persian work called *The History of Derbent* (*Ta'rīkh Bāb al-abwāb*) probably nearly contemporary to the events, was written by an anonymous Arab writer, probably in the eleventh century, and preserved in the later work of the Ottoman writer Münejjim-bashī. It supplies valuable information on the Rus' in the Islamic lands at the end of the tenth century.

Other authors, writing later, also mention the Rus' and may have used earlier well-informed sources. A thirteenth-century Iranian historian, Bahā' al-Dīn Muḥammad b. Ḥasan ibn Isfandiyār, compiled his *History of Tabaristan* (*Ta'rīkhi Tabaristan*) from earlier records and mentions several Rus' raids in the region, as did the Arab geographer Ibn Abī Ṭālib al-Dimashqī, who completed his work, entitled *Cosmographie*, in 1300 CE.

Other authors also supply important information on steppe people and the Rus'. Probably by far the best known is the Arabic diplomat ibn Faḍlān, sent on a mission to the Volga Bulghar court in 921–22 CE by the Baghdad caliph Al-Muqtadir (908–29 CE). Upon his return, he recorded his journey through the lands of the steppe to the mid-Volga capital of the Bulghars, where he encountered the Rus'. There is an immense literature on the credibility and problems of his ethnographic-style report (Montgomery 2004a, 2004b; Zadeh 2017). For a time, his work was only known through excerpts preserved in the thirteenth-century lexicon of the Islamic scholar ibn Yāqūt, but later a more complete manuscript was discovered in Mashad and published by Zeki Validi Togan (Togan 1939). There is, however, a chance that later copyists, such as the sixteenth-century Safavid geographer Amīn Rāzī, might have been working from an edition that was even more elaborate than the Mashad text (Wikander 1978).

Miskawayh, a Persian philosopher and historian said to have lived an exceptionally long life (c. 930–1030 CE), is the foremost authority on the Rus' in the Caspian Sea region around the mid-tenth century, which he describes in his book *Experiences of Nations* (*Tajārib al-Umam*). As a chancery official and librarian to various viziers, he had access to primary materials, knowledgeable informants and even eyewitnesses when compiling his history, making his observations on the Rus' among the most detailed recorded by Islamic historiographers (Arkoun 1993).

Another area of Rus' activity is noted by a Jewish traveller from al-Andalus, Ibrāhīm ibn Ya'qūb al-Ṭurṭūshī, who made a round trip to Eastern Europe in 965 CE. He passes on important information on the commercial activities of Rus' and other steppe people, notably the Magyars, who were present in Bohemian and Polish markets, and a description of the Danish town of Hedeby. Ibn Ya'qūb's work only survives in excerpts in Al-Bakrī's *Book of Roads and Kingdoms* (*Kitāb al-Masālik wa-'l-mamālik*) (Mishin 1994–95). Besides these key texts, I will make occasional references to other authors who are less important here.

Works by later medieval authors may be referenced to provide analogies for issues that affected the region. One of these is the Iranian polymath Abū al-Rayḥān Muḥammad ibn Aḥmad al-Bīrūnī, who wrote his geographical work *Determination of the Coordinates of Places for the Correction of Distances Between Cities* (*Taḥdid nihāyāt al-amākin li-taṣḥīḥ masāfāt al-masākin*) around 1030 CE. The other is Abū ʿAbd Allāh Muḥammad ibn ʿAbd Allāh al-Lawātī al-Ṭanjī ibn Baṭṭūṭah, a famous Moroccan scholar and traveller who visited the northern parts of the Volga area and recorded his visit in his *Travels* (*Riḥlah*).

### *Byzantine sources*

Byzantine historical works are another important cluster of contemporary documents about the Rus' and steppe people. In terms of historiography, the tenth century in Byzantium saw a new wave of interest in historical writing, greatly surpassing that of the previous hundred years. A new narrative style emerged, centred around an individual rather than chronology, as had been the fashion previously. This new style of rhetoric makes the modern historian's work harder because it blurs facts with heroic scenes or constructed dialogues. Despite these tendencies, Byzantine historiography developed from the personal styles of individual authors rather than through genre clichés (Markopoulos 2003; Kaldellis 2010; Efthymiadis 2013). The historical value of these works is immense because with the loss of the imperial archives they basically form the backbone of information on political events in the empire.

Historical works that present ample data on the steppe people, Scandinavians and Rus' have received much attention from researchers (Moravcsik 1983; Blöndal 1978; Obolensky 1982; Scheel 2015). For this book, they are the only contemporary documents to corroborate the Muslim sources and supplement their accounts. Despite their usefulness, source criticism reveals that the Byzantine sources are not without fallacies. In accordance with a classicizing Greek and Roman heritage, they often replace foreign peoples' names with Classical ones. The Magyars, for instance, are equated with the 'Turks' in Byzantine works, the Rus' became 'Tauroscythians', and the Slavic tribe of the Drevljanes became 'Germans' (Moravcsik 1983, 303, 320–27; Ditten 1984). Textual criticism is also required because they tend to generalize ethnographic details and are embedded with Classical *topoi*; furthermore, most authors copied from previous chroniclers and the origins of specific passages might determine the authenticity of the information (cf. Ljubarskij 1998).

Due to the individual character of each work, a short review of the authors in this period is necessary (a useful summary is found in Treadgold 2013). In the mid-tenth century, Emperor Constantine VII Porphyrogenitus (945–59 CE) and the circle around him produced two immensely informative accounts that regularly mention foreigners in and around the Byzantine Empire. One of these, the *De administrando imperio* (henceforth DAI), is a didactic book for Constantine's son and successor, Romanos II (959–63 CE). The book was assembled by the emperor and/or educated men under his supervision between 948 and 952 CE, although parts of its information derive from earlier periods. The DAI discusses the diplomatic and external relations of the empire with foreign powers and peoples and offers guidance to a young prince on how to handle affairs with cunning policy. Among the groups adjacent to the empire, the work notes specifically the inhabitants of the Pontic steppes and nomadic people, such as the Khazars, Magyars, Pechenegs and Rus'. It is regarded as largely authentic; its sources were intelligence reports, oral accounts by foreigners, foreign ambassadors who visited the Byzantine court, official documents and eyewitnesses. The work's chronology, however, is problematic; most of the information is impossible to date precisely and likely refers to various periods in the early or mid-tenth century (Howard-Johnston 2000; Mel'nikova 2016). The other account, commissioned by Constantine slightly later than the DAI (probably around 956–59 CE), is a ceremonial book on Byzantine court culture (*De cerimoniis aulae Byzantinae*), most often referred to simply as the *De ceremoniis*. It addresses Byzantine religious festivals, courtly practices and customs and includes sporadic mentions of foreign people on official duties in Constantinople, such as nomadic and Rus' mercenaries and guards and the visit of a Rus' princess, Olga.

Another mid-tenth-century author is Leo the Deacon, a chronicler whose *Historia* is closely associated with the *Synpopsis historiarum* (Synopsis of histories) of a later author, the eleventh-century John Skylitzés. The two authors provide a common account, although differing in some details, on the Bulgarian campaigns of John I Tzimiskes (969–76 CE) against the Rus'. How the two texts are related is central for evaluating their passages on the Rus' and their nomadic allies. For some time it was thought that Leo was an eyewitness in the campaign and that Skylitzés copied Leo's work, inferring some information not found in the *Historia*. Now it has become more likely that both authors were referring to a common source and each copied or omitted certain passages according to his agenda (Kaldellis 2013a). Since they were both building on an eyewitness description, their works, after removing Classical and heroic *topoi*, complement each other well (McGrath 2007).

Other texts are pertinent, such as the so-called Byzantine–Rus' peace treaties that were concluded after the Rus' attacks against Byzantium in 907, 911, 944 and 971 CE. The Byzantine originals of the treaties are lost, but they were preserved in the *Russian Primary Chronicle* in Old Church Slavonic. Although that is the only existing version of the texts, the phrasing and the structure of the treaties show indisputably that the Slavic versions are translations of a Greek original (Malingoudi 1994). The legal instructions in the text clearly parallel Scandinavian law and thus support the authenticity of the information on customs, norms and legal matters (Stein-Wilkeshuis 1991, 2002; cf. Lind 1984).

Other contemporary authors also mention Rus' or nomadic attacks on the empire or mention Rus' people in Greek service. Theophanes the Confessor's *Chronicle* covers events until 813 CE, and an anonymous writer (labelled Theophanes Continuatus) continued his work until 961 CE. Photius, patriarch of Constantinople in the ninth century, lamented in two letters about the devastation of Rus' attacks against the empire at the time. The hagiographic life of the eighth- or ninth-century saint George of Amastris also mentions an early Rus' raid, but the account was only written in the tenth century. Brief notice of the Rus' and steppe people in Byzantine service is mentioned in eleventh-century sources, such as George Cedrenus's *Synopsis historion*, a military manual compiled by a (probably) Georgian-Armenian author whose family name was Kekaumenos, and an anonymous annal compiled in Bari, Italy (*Annales Barenses*). These sources, although not used specifically here, will nevertheless provide trustworthy chronologies for political events (such as foreign attacks and military service) connected to the Scandinavian Rus' and steppe people.

### *Old Norse-Icelandic sagas*

Old Norse literary texts provide additional information. The Old Norse-Icelandic sagas, or 'stories' as the word itself indicates, are heroic late medieval tales narrated in prose with occasional insertions of poetry. These sources are notorious for their controversial portrayal of events in the Viking Age and even earlier. Although Icelandic sagas evidently drew on a common pool of knowledge preserved in oral tradition, they were written down later than the events they describe, mostly during the thirteenth and fourteenth centuries. The original stories, originating in the Viking Age, were altered by anonymous scribes or saga authors (only a handful known by name), usually driven by a mixture of Christian ethics, fantasy and current political agendas. Thus, the sagas' depiction of events and the extent to which they can be used for historical investigations of the Viking Age have been hotly debated (Sigurðsson 2004; Bibire 2007). Source criticism of their information is critical for any study that tries to use them; nevertheless, I share the opinion that certain aspects of the sagas hold enlightening material for the history of Scandinavia and Eastern Europe during the Viking Age (e.g. Glazyrina 1991; Lönnroth 2008; Jackson 2019). Political events in the sagas are not taken at face value unless confirmed by other sources and their stories mostly just shade the argument. When like accounts based on analogies allow, however, saga episodes will be presented as 'potentially believable', whether or not the specific events occurred exactly as described in the narrative (Ólason 2007). Analogies with saga accounts also help read the archaeological evidence of the Viking period, a successful practice in recent decades (e.g. Price 2002; Raffield, Price, and Collard 2017).

Icelandic tales set exclusively in Eastern regions are referenced here most often. They fall into different sub-genres, such as family sagas (*Íslendingasögur*) that relate the histories of Icelandic families, their local struggles and the travels of some of their members abroad. The kings' sagas (*konungasögur*) are more important here. Mostly recorded by Snorri Sturluson in his *Heimskringla* from around 1230 CE, they deal with the histories of Norwegian kings. Some of the legendary sagas (*fornaldarsögur*), tales of by-gone heroes set in unspecific times, sometimes earlier than or during the Viking Age, although historically somewhat less reliable, are still important for events in Eastern Europe.

Some sagas feature here more frequently than others. Two of the most important ones belong to two quite different sub-genres; these are *Eymundar þáttr Hringssonar*, a short story incorporated in a longer saga, and *Yngvars saga víðförla*, a legendary account of a trip to the mysterious East. Both sagas were written down in the fourteenth century. Despite flaws of literary conventions and borrowings, both offer details unprecedented in other sources and contain serious elements of historical truth that are supported by other historical documents or, in the case of *Yngvars saga*, by archaeological evidence in the form of runic inscriptions (Shepard 1984–85; Cook 1986). The Vinland sagas are unique in telling far-away adventures about Scandinavian expeditions to America around the first millennium. The story of these ambitious undertakings was narrated in two slightly variant forms, *Grænlendinga saga* and *Eiríks saga rauða*, probably at the beginning of the thirteenth century, although they were only written down a century later. The stories evolved from a common source building on the oral statements of the original travellers. Some of the episodes in the Vinland sagas will be used here as parallels mirroring the 'Eastern experience'.

Sporadic mention will be made of saga episodes dealing with travelling and experience in the East, from the *Orkneyinga saga*, *Játvarðar saga*, *Magnússona saga*, *Óláfs saga hins Helga*, *Knýtlinga saga*, *Haralds saga Sigurðarsonar*,

*Snegluhalla þáttr* (a short story incorporated into a saga), *Laxdæla saga* and *Örvar Odds saga*. Apart from the common theme of the episodes, only the style of writing connects these accounts, as they cover diverse sub-genres of saga writing and were composed at different times from the late twelfth to the fourteenth century. Those relating events in the eleventh century are closest to the events; they might be more trustworthy than the family sagas (like *Laxdæla*) or legendary sagas (like that of *Örvar Oddr*), but they are not accurate historical accounts either. Thirteenth-century sagas are similar in occasionally using diverse terms that hint at pre-Christian pagan practices: *Hákonar saga Góða*, *Kormáks saga*, *Egils saga Skallgrímsonar*, *Ragnars saga loðbrókar* and *Guta saga*. Religious rituals and customs recorded there might have been known by later authors of Christian sagas from earlier oral tradition. Despite possible distortions or misinterpretations, they are unlikely to have survived as pure fantasies.

Even though literary in nature and recorded later, many of these sagas fit in with multiple lines of evidence from other (external) contemporary and less biased sources. That being said, saga accounts are secondary to the investigation here, but will serve as analogies or background pictures for understanding events in Eastern Europe. They will help decipher situations witnessed in the East related to issues of communication, customs, religion and the identity of warrior groups.

### *Other sources*

Discussions about early medieval Rus' are usually built on the information in the so-called *Povest' Vremennykh Let* (henceforth PVL), the 'Tale of the Bygone Years', more commonly known as the *Russian Primary Chronicle*. The PVL, written in Old Church Slavonic, describes the beginnings of the Kievan Rus' polity and the history of its dynasty, the Rurikids. Although opinions vary about the exact dates of its composition and author, it can be safely said that its first versions were produced at the beginning of the twelfth century, probably by a monk in the Kievan monastery (Tolochko 2011; Gippius 2017).

The PVL does not exist independently, however; it is not a chronicle in the sense of its medieval counterparts. The *Primary Chronicle*, as we know it today, is a product of scholarly reconstructions based on different existing or assumed chronological layers in later medieval manuscripts. The earliest manuscript of the PVL is dated to 1377 CE. This is called the Laurentian copy, on which most modern editions are based, in contrast to the second most important Hypathian redaction from around 1425 CE (cf. Timberlake 2001). The most noteworthy work on the textual traditions of the PVL is by Shakmatov, a Russian philologist of the early twentieth century in whose shadow chronicle research still lives. The versions deriving from these traditions differ in wording (Ostrowski, Birnbaum, and Lunt 2003), but Shakmatov believed he could reconstruct the earliest layers (mostly based on the Novgorodian versions of the chronicle), which according to him date back as far as the 1030s CE. It is acknowledged that some earlier annalistic traditions must have existed in Kiev before the compilation began, but there are fierce debates on the significance of this, and Shakmatov's views have recently been called into question (Isoaho 2018). The main reason for the debate is the source value of the early entries in the PVL. The chronicle is constructed like an annal, i.e., discussing events year by year, but sometimes contains very little or no information on certain years. From Grand Prince Vladimir's (978/980–1015 CE) years onwards, its history becomes more reliable, but for the ninth and tenth centuries, its information is hard to verify without reference to some Byzantine control sources, making it semi-legendary. Shakmatov's reconstructions raise debate because the earlier compositions (if any existed) would back up the early stories of the PVL, which are credited to even earlier sources in the possession of the Kievan writers; therefore, oral stories about the arrival of the Varangians, the customs of the East Slavic tribes, and the deeds of the early princes of the Kievan Rus' would be closer to the actual events and should not necessarily be dismissed as later fabrications. Some historians, however, doubt the picture of the PVL so much that they omit its use for the early centuries and argue that the history of the Rus' should be written omitting the chronicle entirely (Romenskiy 2017). It is true that its chronology (which adopted Byzantine time reckoning but failed to reconcile it with the different dates for starting a year) is largely unreliable. The chronology of the PVL has been constructed symmetrically to follow known Byzantine–Rus' peace treaties and the ruling years of early Rus' princes (Tolochko 2015, 49–59, 59–68). In spite of these justifiable reservations, I believe the PVL cannot be dismissed as a major narrative source. It is the only source for certain events in the period and cannot be completely disregarded; its information must be handled critically; in what follows, other sources are given preference in chronological matters. For the early events until the reign of Vladimir, the PVL's narratives will be compared to other types of evidence and accepted as reliable if external sources show the same pattern. Archaeological material sometimes contributes to crediting the PVL (or not) and can refine its details. Despite some discrepancies, the chronicle's description matches the reconstructed trends of Scandinavian, Rus' and steppe interplay.

Two other Slavic sources hold information about earlier contacts between the Rus' and steppe peoples. The *Pecerskij Paterik* is a fifteenth-century compilation of eleventh- and twelfth-century records from the Kievan Cave Monastery and a twelfth-century Russian epic poem (*byliny*) called the *Tale of Igor's Campaign* (*Slovo o pŭlku Igorevě*) are deemed authentic.

A collection of Khazar-Hebrew correspondence is unique among the sources. Between 950 and 960 CE, Ḥasdai ibn Shapruṭ, a minister of the Cordovan Caliph 'Abd al-Raḥmān III (912–61 CE), and Khagan Joseph, ruler of the Khazars, exchanged letters discussing the Jewish faith and the Khazars' relations with the Byzantines. In addition, two mid-tenth-century letters were found among the Genizah manuscripts in Cairo. The first, called the Kievan letter, reports on Khazarian Jews living in Kiev. The second, an anonymous letter called the Schechter Letter after its discoverer, was addressed to Shapruṭ and tells about a Khazar–Rus' war in the tenth century. Scholars have debated the authenticity of these letters, but today it is accepted that they are not forgeries, as was believed earlier (Kokovtsov 1932; Golb and Pritsak 1982). There is only one other Hebrew source about trade routes that the Rus' (probably) followed through Hungary. It is quoted in Zedekiah ben Abraham Anav's thirteenth-century work called *Shibbolei haLeket* (Ears of Gleaning) and was copied by an anonymous writer in the mid-eleventh century.

Latin sources that occasionally refer to Scandinavians, nomads or the background of issues here have no shared roots comparable to the categories discussed earlier. These documents were recorded in various times and places, and their genres are equally miscellaneous, ranging from contemporary Western annals, letters and chronicles to retrospective narrative sources. One approach to Scandinavian sources is to look for continuities (or discontinuities) of customs prevalent in the early Germanic world and later in Scandinavia. Histories of the Germanic tribes of the Migration Period were mostly written in Latin and are used extensively for such comparisons in Scandinavian studies. Perhaps the best known is the first-century Roman writer Publius Cornelius Tacitus's ethnographic account of the early Germanic people, known by the short title *Germania* (*De origine et situ Germanorum*). In 551 CE, Jordanes, a sixth-century Eastern Roman bureaucrat possibly of Gothic descent, wrote another work, *Getica*, based on earlier written records and oral history about the history of the Goths (*De origine actibusque Getarum*). Both accounts have some (deliberate) distortions, misunderstandings and imaginative reconstructions, but both describe elements of Germanic cultures that also applied to later histories of the Scandinavians.

Even annals can express prejudice towards foreign people regarded as not or less civilized and confuse or over-generalize their descriptions. They were recorded year by year with the intention of informing their own cultural milieu about significant events. Many of these mention Scandinavians, Rus' and steppe people in relation to either political events or customs. A principal source for the late ninth century, the *Annales Bertiniani* is a late Carolingian Frankish annal written at the abbey of St. Bertin – the first written account to mention the Rus'. Close in time is a *Translatio* written in St. Germain before 851 CE comparing a Viking custom to similar practices in the East among the Scandinavian Rus'. Another source containing sporadic information on the Rus' is the early eleventh-century *Annales Hildesheimenses*, an anonymous Latin prose work written by several Hildesheim authors, some of whom were clerics. A legal document, the *Inquisitio de theloneis Raffelstettensis* dating between 903 and 906 CE, mentions Rus' traders in Central Europe and is the only surviving legal document regulating customs (meaning taxes on trade) in early medieval Europe.

Contemporary (or near contemporary) chronicles produced in diverse places are valuable sources, such as the *Chronicon* of Regino (abbot of Prüm) finished in 908 CE; the *Relatio de Legatione Constantinopolitana* by Liutprand (bishop of Cremona) based on his experience in the Byzantine court, and Adam of Bremen's *Gesta Hammaburgensis ecclesiae pontificum*, written in the 1070s CE. The bishop of Merseburg (1012–18 CE), Thietmar, a German cleric, produced a *Chronicon* that became the chief source for eleventh-century politics and information not found elsewhere on a wide range of Eastern people, including Bulgarians, Hungarians and Slavs. Equally valuable from a source-critical point of view are letters by Theotmar, archbishop of Salzburg, to Pope John IX in 900 CE, by Bruno of Querfurt, a Saxon missionary, to Henry II in 1008 CE, and the shorter redaction of the life of Saint Adalbert, also by Bruno, probably dating between 1005 and 1008 CE.

Later chronicles will be also discussed here, although their arguments have to be verified by comparing them with contemporary information. Some of these chronicles were written at the rise of literacy on the peripheries of Europe and tell the history of a "nation" (in the medieval sense of the term). In Hungary, two thirteenth-century writers each wrote a *gesta* of the Hungarians: P. dictus magister (usually called Anonymous) and Simon of Kéza. Saxo Grammaticus's Danish history, *Gesta Danorum*, is similar, finished at the beginning of the thirteenth century. A Saxon priest, Helmold, wrote a chronicle of the Slavs (*Chronica Slavorum*) in the twelfth century. Although not a chronicle, the *vita* of Bishop Saint Gellért of Hungary was also produced in the fourteenth century, centuries after his death but based on serious written antecedents. The work called *Dormitio Cyrilli* is a similar case, a thirteenth-century re-telling of the life of Saint Cyril based on earlier Pannonian legends and lost records. Between 1136 and 1140 CE the Anglo-Norman chronicler Geffrei Gaimar composed a chronicle of England, *Estoire des Engleis* (written in French), building on previous written sources. It records accounts of Danes travelling between distant parts of Europe, including the East.

In a few cases, later steppe people, such as the Cumans or the Mongols, feature in high medieval sources, such as *Chronica Albrici Monachi Trium Fontium* from 1251 CE (written in Latin) by the Cistercian chronicler Alberic of Trois-Fontaine. The great French chronicler Jean de Joinville's *Life of St. Louis* (*Livre des saintes paroles et des bons faiz de nostre saint roy Looÿs*) was written between 1305 and 1309 CE and also mentions the Cumans. The Flemish Franciscan friar William of Rubruck's itinerary describes his visit to the Mongol court (*Itinerarium fratris Willielmi de Rubruquis*). Afanasy Nikitin, a fifteenth-century Russian traveller from Tver wrote monumental travel notes about his journey to India from 1466 to 1472 CE, during which he crossed parts of the steppes. An earlier work peculiar in its use of comparisons, is Herodotus's widely known description of the Scythians written in Classical Greek in 430 BCE.

Two comparative works relate to the wider Scandinavian background of issues related to communication in the East. One is a later Norwegian didactic work from around 1250 CE, the *Konungs skuggsjá* (The King's Mirror), written in the popular medieval genre of *speculum regale*. The other is a contemporary record by a Norwegian Viking Age traveller, Ohthere of Hålogaland, about his travels to King Alfred of Wessex (c. 871–99 CE), preserved in a compilation in Old English.

These accounts are only relevant in minor issues and figure in short notes relevant to the wider significance and relatedness of Scandinavian, Rus' and nomadic interplay. References to these works here accompany the investigation throughout, and issues related to their historiographical traditions will be addressed there if needed.

Lastly, archaeological material enters the picture discussion. Data from this discipline are increasing; the Scandinavian involvement in Eastern affairs is impossible to understand without it. Coins, found in Scandinavia in abundant numbers, reflect cross-cultural contacts and are of primary importance, although their specific evaluation will be left to specialists. Objects will receive due attention in the following, as they testify directly to contacts between cultures. Weapons, attire, everyday objects, riding equipment and tools of Scandinavian and steppe origin will be discussed. Methodologically speaking, they cannot be linked with ethnic identities, as is clear from the theoretical literature (Härke 1997; Curta 2007; Halsall 2011) or equally, in specific relation to the 'Normanist question', which addresses the identification and role of Scandinavians in European Russia, Belarus and Ukraine (Jansson 1987, 775–79; Brather 2004, 279–83; Hillerdal 2006). Critical theories of ethnic identity will be applied to grave goods, primarily artefacts from the steppe that exhibit signs of Nordic metalwork techniques, traditional Scandinavian artefacts manufactured in steppe styles, or objects of far-away provenance in regions traditionally considered Scandinavian or steppe. This approach extends quite widely in the case of the eastern connections of the Scandinavians. In the past, Scandinavian archaeologists applied the vague term 'oriental' to this material from the East but recognized its patronizing connotations (Said 1978). Now the equally broad term 'Eastern' is used. This dilemma arises because steppe social groups incorporated and transmitted Islamic traits of material culture, which makes it impossible in some cases to assign an artefact to a specific group such as 'Khazarian' (objects of the Saltovo-Mayaki archaeological culture) or 'Volga Bulgharian' or 'Islamic'. The problem is most apparent in the cases of dress and jewellery. It is quite clear, however, that the steppe polities were the middlemen in the transmission and diffusion of these items to the North and their own culture also adopted Eastern traditions, from earlier Sassanian art, for instance. Thus, an 'Eastern' or 'oriental' influence was inescapably involved in the historical contacts of Scandinavians and Turks.

The integration of material culture and written texts will follow the basic methodology of historical archaeology. Archaeology can clarify references that arise from laconic mentions in texts. Archaeological and written evidence can also be useful as empirical control sources for each other. Sometimes the material record directly contradicts the texts, which helps re-evaluate the cultural conformity some of the written records suggest. Rather than filling lacunae, material culture 'expands the text' and advances the discussion with new data.

In such an overview of a large historical problem, usually no specific methodology is presented to answer the basic questions of historical (re)construction: What kind of evidence has been preserved? How reliable is the evidence? How can the evidence be interpreted? The methodology here applies traditional methods of historiography, where the source value of various accounts is measured in the contrasts among them and the (re)constructed picture is widened with as much evidence as possible. Later sources are usually used to shade the argument or accepted when they fit the contemporary records. Some written sources require a closer reading for their terminologies, semantics or authorial intentions and misunderstandings.

One feature of this book needs a short explanation. In cases when evidence is missing or taciturn comments need a wider context in order to interpret their meaning, we must turn to analogies. The burning question is always: How far can an analogy be pushed? As briefly alluded to earlier, comparing texts from the early Germanic period and the Viking Age can illuminate analogies for customs followed in Scandinavia based on centuries-long common Germanic traditions. Determining the continuity or discontinuity of customs is not always straightforward since societies change and become unique in their own ways. Two factors necessitate applying analogies in the study of the steppes. First, most of the steppe people in this period did not have written languages, so most of the information is transmitted to us by outsiders. This leaves a relatively small corpus of evidence about their cultural and social worlds. The other reason for turning to analogies perhaps more often than in other fields of medieval studies is the unique geographic, economic and social circumstances of the steppes. Even though clearly influenced by their neighbours and the sedentary world to varying degrees, nomadic social organization (with scattered communities, few permanent settlements and mobile livestock) was conservative and invited technological innovations mostly concerning the improvement of animal husbandry. Allowing for local variations, nomads in the steppes lived almost the same way throughout the centuries and their successful lifestyle conserved certain social and cultural features.

The cultural stability of tradition is the reason why belief systems, cultural habits and military techniques can be used to demonstrate long-lasting practices and habits. The historic records about nomadic people often allow comparison with other descriptions of earlier and later nomads in historic times (like the medieval period) if there is reason to infer continuity.

# 2 The steppe and the Viking world

According to the sixth-century Gothic writer Jordanes, the Germanic Goths originated in Scandinavia and migrated to the Black Sea steppes, where they lived for a long time until finally being wiped out by the advancing Huns in the fourth century (Mommsen 1882, 57–66, 89–92). Although his narrative is not given much weight today (Goffart 2005), Jordanes's migration (hi)story finds support in the first- to fourth-century archaeological records of the so-called Wielbark culture of northern Poland and its continuation, the Černjachov culture, which spread over the Pontic steppes (Heather 1996, 18–30). Some scholars maintain that the Goths became 'Scythianized' in this region, i.e., adopted some of the customs of the local steppe inhabitants, which seems to be mirrored in the genetic make-up of samples collected from graves of the Černjachov culture (Järve et al. 2019, 2430, 2434). The details of the burial of their chief, Alaric, in 411 CE in a riverbed speaks in this regard. Before completing the ritual and burying their chief and his treasures, the Gothic mourners forced slaves to divert the river temporarily in order to hide the location of the grave. To keep the secret eternal, the Goths then massacred the diggers (Mommsen 1882, 99). This ritual is a widespread *topos*, strongly reminiscent of the cult of Eastern rulers in intention and implementation, most notably those of the steppe, such as the Huns, Khazars, Oghuz' and Mongols, and even further east in China (Roux 1984, 265–66; Ecsedy 1982). Newly acquired "Scythian" habits included the appearance of cavalry, with strings of horses used as alternate mounts, and the use of arrows in Gothic warfare, the custom of hunting with falcons and living in tents. None of these features were usual for contemporary Germanic tribes (Wolfram [1979] 1990, 115; Schäfer 2004). Some of these claims on cultural transfer are similar to those that will be discussed later for the Scandinavians, Rus' and steppe people.

Whether later Scandinavians really followed in the footsteps of the Goths (Golovnov 2009, 192–206) is of less central concern than that Scandinavia's connections with the East trace back to ancient times, probably the Bronze Age. As one theory claims, Mycenaean elite material culture and its related cosmological ideas were transmitted to south Scandinavia through personal visits chiefs made to the Carpathians and the Pontic area before 1500 BCE. Exchange, partly via the Amber Road, also flowed both ways (Kristiansen and Larsson 2005, 200–25; Vandkilde 2007, 126–29).

DOI: 10.4324/9781003037859-2

Migration Period in some scholarly traditions, is the next epoch which witnessed intensive contacts between Scandinavia and the East. A unique fifth-century find complex at the Swedish sites of Sösdala, Fulltofta and Vennebo contained remains of saddle equipment and harnesses in a ritual sacrificial context (Kazanski and Mastykova 2017). The ritual details and accessories were exotic in the Scandinavian landscape of the time and exhibit specific correlations with contemporary nomadic, probably Hunnic, customs witnessed in Central and Eastern Europe. Following up on the Mycenaean example, the find complex seems to be related to migrating warrior elites (maybe the Germanic Heruls), who, during visits to the steppes, adopted material culture and ritual and perhaps mythological notions of horse-cultist nomads (Fabech 1991). Direct trade between the Pontic steppe area, the Germanic world, and Scandinavia is also attested in the sixth century. Migration and commerce were carried on in the regions between Scandinavia and the Black Sea: pelts from the north were exchanged for silk in the south (Mommsen 1882, 59; Procopius 1919, 415; on early trade routes, see also Haussig 1987, 530; Lübke 2001, 181–83). Inventions of the nomads of the steppe, such as the stirrup, also reached Scandinavia long before the Viking Age; the first Scandinavian specimens were found in the Swedish Vendel site (Grave III) dated 720–50 CE (Jonsson 1954; Sundkvist 2001, 236). This period saw the intensification of cavalry warfare based on earlier Persian-'oriental' models (Engström 1997). Scandinavia's eastern connections, therefore, had a long history that developed greater intensity in the following centuries. This chapter introduces this world and its relevance for the study of the Viking Age.

How should the steppe be situated in the Viking world? Who were the main actors there, and how did their relationship with the Scandinavians start? A historical overview will help answer these questions. First, was the East indeed an integral part of the network maintained by Scandinavian groups? Here, Eastern links to Scandinavia and to even more remote areas are stressed; the evidence for contacts is growing steadily. It is also helpful to describe briefly the main steppe polities' political, economic, religious and cultural histories. The nomads were the main partners, or sometimes adversaries, that the newcomers needed to deal with. Finally, I end with the initial contacts between the Scandinavian Rus' and the steppe people in the ninth century, whose details alas still lie in the shadows, although they paved way for the better documented events of the late ninth and tenth centuries.

## Scandinavians and the east

It is increasingly recognized that the artificial scholarly division between a Western and an Eastern Viking Age is no longer tenable. Once this is accepted, the whole region of the East starts to gain importance in scholarly evaluations of the Viking phenomenon (Price 2020, 400–43; Hedenstierna-Jonson 2020b, 189–92). Scandinavian artefacts discovered in the territory of present-day Belarus, the Russian Federation and Ukraine are even more frequent than in Western Europe (Androshchuk 2008).

The story of the Viking Age actually begins in Eastern Europe. A recent archaeological discovery dramatically altered scholarly opinion on the importance of the East in this formative period of Scandinavian history. The remains of a Scandinavian raiding or diplomatic party, buried in two boats, were found on the island of Saaremaa, Estonia, on the coast of the Baltic Sea. A revolutionary discovery, the burials at Salme were dated to 750 CE, predating the first recorded Viking raids on English shores by half a century (Price et al. 2020). Scandinavian settlement in the East followed; contemporaneous with the Salme burial, a Scandinavian merchant community contributed to the emergence of an *emporium* in north-western Russia on the shores of Lake Ladoga, a gateway into the interior of the Russian forest belt as well as a connection point for the Baltics (Mühle 1991, 19–62; Franklin and Shepard 1996, 3–49; Duczko 2004, 60–98). Further south, near the confluence of the Dnieper and other northern rivers, Gnezdovo, another major political-commercial centre, also shows traces of Scandinavian settlement. New radiocarbon dates on tree trunks from the earliest stratigraphic layers at Gnezdovo radically push back the time when the settlement was founded to the eighth century instead of the tenth as previously thought (Murasheva et al. 2020). Remains of Scandinavian clinker-built boats found here suggest that Scandinavian settlement postdated the occupation of Staraya Ladoga by only a few decades.

Scandinavians, finding their way into Eastern Europe via the waterways as early as the eighth century, maintained contacts with a wide variety of local people. The area is divided into three different ecological zones; from Northern Russia to the slopes of the Ural Mountains the region is covered in dense temperate and boreal forests (taiga) threaded with a multitude of rivers and streams. A transitional zone (a wooded steppe) where the forest gradually gives way to grasslands spreads in roughly a crescent shape from the lower forested hills of the Urals and finally disappears in the vast plains of the steppe, a low vegetation area bordering the Black and the Caspian Seas on the north. The different environments presented different economic opportunities and challenges. The northern forests were mostly inhabited by hunter-gatherers of Finnic and Baltic origin. Agriculturalists, mostly Slavic tribes living in dispersed communities, moved into the forest zone from the south, expanding towards thinly populated lands. The wooded steppe and the steppe were the homes of various pastoralist tribes, mostly of Turkic or Iranian descent (Taaffe 1990; Shaw 2006, 19–30; Figure 2.1).

Correlating the Scandinavians' relations to each of these peoples and the geographical situation will not be attempted here in detail (for general works, consult Franklin and Shepard 1996; Duczko 2004; Lebedev 2005, 410–596; Callmer, Gustin, and Roslund 2017; Mägi 2018). In the background to the Scandinavian contacts with (and through) the steppes, modern scholars have made three relevant observations on the contacts that developed in the forest belt among the Scandinavians, Balts, Finno-Ugrians and Slavs. First, Scandinavian groups in the East were not unified, and competition among them triggered the creation of separate communities. Different groups clustered in and around multi-ethnic settlements. The affiliation of individuals living in these places was transferred to local power centres, but despite this ethnic inclusiveness, the Scandinavian links

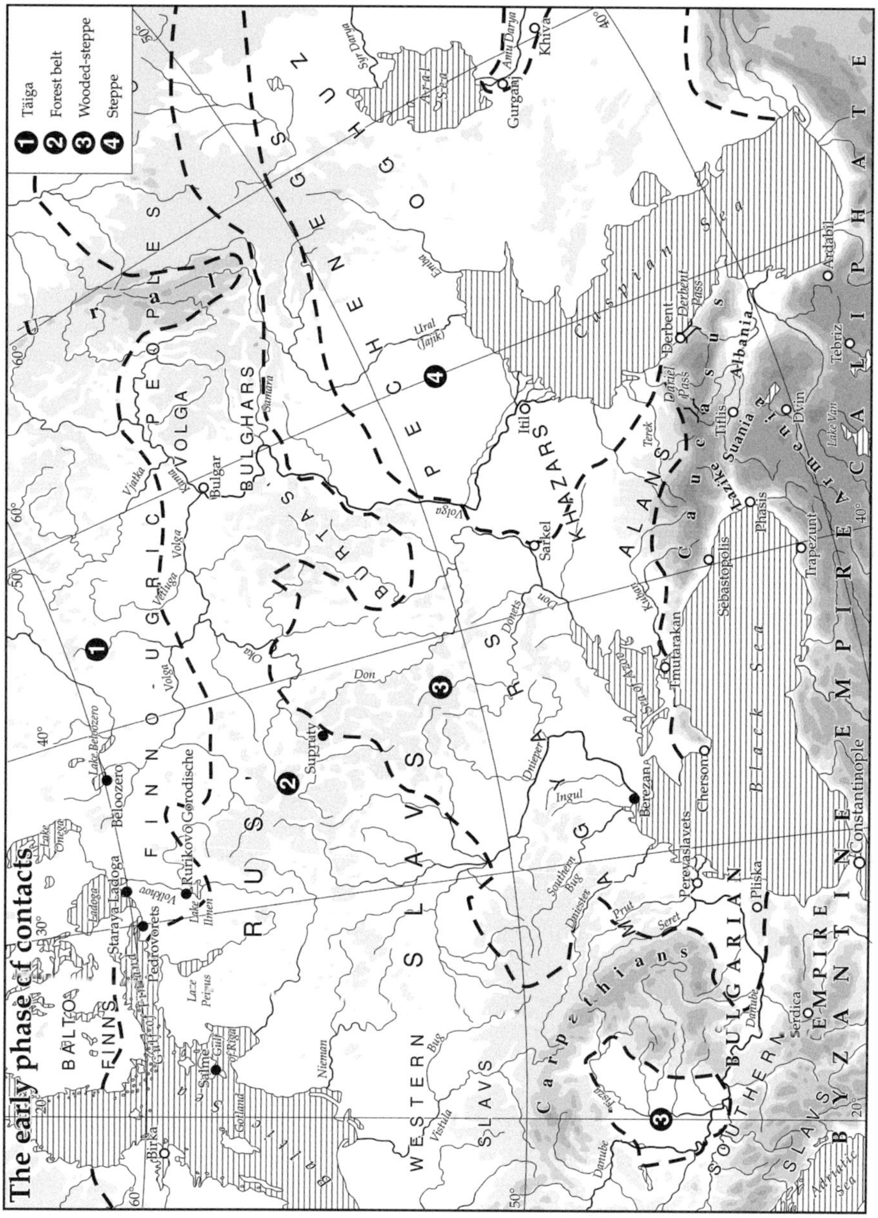


*Figure 2.1* The early phase of contacts

of the military and trading elite did not vanish; they remained integral parts of the Viking diaspora.

There was continuous mass migration from Scandinavia, mainly central Sweden and to a lesser extent from Gotland, to the Baltics and north-western Russia from the mid-eighth and ninth centuries onwards, including pirates, chieftains, mercenaries, traders, craftsmen and even women (Jansson 1997; Stalsberg 1982, 1988). In a famous piece, 'Why the Vikings First Came to Russia', the American numismatist Thomas S. Noonan pointed out that the region was rich in furs and slaves, highly desirable commodities that the Scandinavians could exchange for another sought-after product: Arabic silver dirhams (Noonan 1986). The driving force behind the Scandinavian activities and settlements in the East has recently also been connected to the construction of infrastructural networks needed for complex resource gathering, craft production and trade (Hedenstierna-Jonson 2020b). It is still debated whether settlements in the region developed in the agricultural hinterlands from the needs of the local population (Nosov 1994) or from favourable natural conditions at the confluence of rivers and lakes that were exploited by Scandinavian warrior-merchant elites as ideal locations for developing infrastructure around commercial emporia (Pushkina 2004; Hedenstierna-Jonson 2020b, 202–10). Many of these settlements, such as Rurikovo Gorodische, reachable from Lake Ladoga on the Volkhov River, Gnezdovo on the upper Dnieper, Pskov on the banks of the northern Dvina, or the connected cluster of settlements in the later Jaroslav-Suzdal region (most importantly Timerovo, Mikhailovskoe, Petrovskoe and Sarskoe Gorodsiche) were founded or, alternatively, started to prosper, due to the appearance of the Scandinavians. Settlements served either as station points or strongholds facilitating and supervising long-distance trade conducted towards the south. To the south from there, traces of Scandinavian settlement can only be found in the tenth-century layers of Kiev and the surrounding settlements of Chernigov, Shestovitsa and Vishygorod (for these settlements, see Makarov 2017), and the recently identified Vypozvyv (Jarman 2021, 228–43). The southernmost supposed Rus' headquarters could have been in Tmutarakan on the northern shores of the Black Sea, although its early existence is hypothetical, as no archaeological traces show Scandinavian settlement there and written sources only suggest a late tenth-century Rus' occupation (Bubenok 2016).

Scandinavian Rus' groups remained quite comparable in terms of social and political structures to those of their Scandinavian homeland (Androshchuk 2000; Mel'nikova 2011; Shchavelev 2013; Vukovich 2018). European Russia, Belarus and the Baltics at this time were also a stage for conflicting chieftains and petty kings. Although historical evidence for these early stages is mostly provided by the PVL and thus are semi-legendary, the general outline described by the chronicle is confirmed by Byzantine and some Muslim sources, from which a fragmented territory with competing groups of Rus' emerged (Noonan 1997, 149–50; Jansson 1997, 21–25; Tolochko 2015, 111, 151–55, 175–76). Princes known from the chronicles as *knyaz* only monitored parts of this vast territory, and their 'realms' cannot be defined as states. The term *knyaz* is equivalent to the Scandinavian *konungr*, and thus most of the Rus' warlords would deserve to be called kings

(Raffensperger 2017), a title, however, without omnipotence, easily challenged by ambitious men in Scandinavian societies. Rus' leaders, such as the dynasty founder Rurik, as well as *knyaz* Oleg (c. 882–912 CE) and Igor (c. 914–45 CE) were warlords of Scandinavian origin, as their native names Hræríkr, Helgi and Yngvarr show (Mel'nikova 2014a, 2014b, 2014c). Other competing warlords of the East, such as Askold and Dir, Rogvolod of Polotsk and Tury of Turov, also originated in Scandinavia. The turbulent confrontation between local centres and outside groups is also confirmed by archaeological investigations of the settlement layers of Rus' towns (e.g. Staraya Ladoga, Pskov and Rurikovo Gorodische), which show that they occasionally burned to the ground (Callmer 2000, 75). The Rus' during the Viking Age carried out both major campaigns and small raids in the East, and it is hard to determine exactly which Scandinavian or Rus' community executed these attacks (Konovalova 2000, 231–32; Tolochko 2015, 151–55). The Kievan Rus' polity only crystallized slowly and unconsciously from these various groups and settlements during the tenth century.

Usually the dominant social group, the Scandinavian elite, lived jointly with other ethnic groups in the settlements. Cemeteries, graves, buildings, craft-working techniques and artefacts of various cultural backgrounds mix in these settlements, all suggesting that Scandinavians and the natives formed a single community (Mühle 1991, 44, 58, 208, 250–51; Jansson 1997, 144; cf. Pushkina 2004, 51; Nosov 2017, 179). The multi-ethnic patterns of settlements are visible from the earliest stages of the Scandinavian arrival at Staraya Ladoga and in early Gnezdovo (Murasheva et al. 2020, 81–82). Only one detached, purely Scandinavian cemetery has been identified: the tenth-century Plakun cemetery of Staraya Ladoga (Mikhajlov 2005). The Baltic, Finnic and Slavic tribes of the forest belt shared their world with the Scandinavians, sometimes as victims, but in the long run as actors who were successfully adopted by the Scandinavian elite and finally transformed into their own likeness. Chamber-graves, kurgans and conic mounds called *sopki* (prevalent in northern Russia) are power expressions of an ethnically mixed elite, among which Scandinavian cultural elements not only spread by personal Scandinavian involvement but also as cultural tokens of belonging to the group (Mikhajlov 2001; Callmer 2008, 123; Platonova 2017). That Scandinavian Rus' warrior elites incorporated other ethnic groups should not be surprising, as this was also the norm elsewhere in the Viking world. As shown by isotope analyses, the Great Army ravaging England between 865 and 878 CE happily accepted recruits from various parts of Scandinavia, the North Atlantic, Anglo-Saxon England, the Baltics and Russia (Budd et al. 2004, 137–38; Chenery et al. 2014), and perhaps even from Frankia and the Low Countries (Raffield 2016, 325). Examinations of similar warrior assemblages in other parts of the Viking diaspora, namely, in Trelleborg and Birka, also show ethnic mixing (Lundström, Hedenstierna-Jonson, and Olausson 2009; Price et al. 2011).

In spite of being eclectic in ethnic terms, Rus' groups were just as integral to the Viking diaspora as their Western counterparts. All these proto-towns and trading posts were intricately linked to the Scandinavian homelands, most importantly the Swedish commercial centre of Birka, which emerged around 750 CE at Lake

Mälaren; it participated vigorously in the Eastern trade networks from the end of the ninth century (Ambrosiani 2001). The other central hub of the Eastern connections of Scandinavia was on the island of Gotland in the Baltic Sea, where the largest concentration of eastern coin hoards has been found (Gruszczyński et al. 2021). Based on object typology and ornamentation, other Scandinavian sites were linked with Rus' settlements, as established with the Jelling centres in Denmark (e.g. Avdusin and Puškina 1988; Androshchuk 2000, 263).

This interconnectedness is seen in the visits four Norwegian kings made to the Kievan Rus', a Rus' *knyaz* who was an exile in Scandinavia, and another *knyaz* who won the Kievan throne by recruiting people from there (Birnbaum 1978; Jackson 2019, 115–70). Norwegian and Icelandic travellers, pilgrims, kings, mercenaries and traders venturing to the East are frequent characters in Icelandic sagas and mentioned on Scandinavian runestones (Blöndal 1978, 193–233; Jakobsson 2006; Jackson 2019). Other sources, such as the eleventh-century Thietmar of Merseburg's account about Danes in Kiev (Holtzmann 1935, 531) and seals of the ninth-century Byzantine Emperor Theophilos found in Tissø, Hedeby and Ribe, demonstrate contacts between the West and East on diplomatic and military levels (Lind 2014). The Icelandic *Laxdæla saga* involves a slave woman captured by raiders in Ireland and finally sold to an Icelander in Norway by a Rus' named Gilli (Sveinsson 1934, 23–24). This is an often-quoted and vivid example of how intricate the links were in the trade networks between West and East (Shepard 2015). Scabbard chapes with embellishments of falcons, the emblem of the Rus', reached as far as the famous Viking burial of Île de Groix in France (Renaud 2000, 67; Hedenstierna-Jonson 2009b, 169–75). The number of these scabbard chapes is growing; Cat Jarman has recently identified six new stray finds in England (Jarman 2021, 252–53), further affirming contacts between the remote ends of the Viking diaspora. Jarman traces the far-reaching connections of the ninth-century Viking Great Army, which, based on a carnelian glass bead, could even have extended as far as the Indian ends of the silk roads in Gujarat. An identical carnelian bead was found in the Rus' stronghold of Vypozvyv, illustrating that trade networks brought objects to the north from the silk roads (Jarman 2021, 1–7, 228–30). A Russian brooch pin, a Permian ring and several Arabic dirhams from Repton and Torksey, once in the possession of members of the Great Army, are similar mementoes of far-reaching networks (Jarman 2021, 1–8, 55–67, 105–6, 291–98; Hadley and Richards 2021, 42, 95, 97–99, 115, 214–15). The transfer of people, news, ideas, knowledge and material culture between East and West was probably more common than has hitherto been held.

The steppe played an important part in this network. The political decentralization, ethnic inclusiveness and far-reaching networks of the Scandinavian and Rus' elites in the East are characteristics that make it possible to evaluate the 'steppe experience' that probably affected communities in a variety of ways, likely unevenly. Recent genetic and isotopic studies of Viking Age human remains from the Oseberg ship burial and the Trondheim fjord area of Norway suggest that individuals with haplogroup types prevalent in the Black Sea region were buried there (Holck 2006; Krzewińska et al. 2015). The movement of people between the steppes and remoter parts of the Viking diaspora probably had precedents. Naturally, the steppe contacts and influence were felt most strongly at the Eastern ends of the diaspora. In a political sense, a new scholarly trend sees a difference between the evolving Rus' community around Kiev merging with the Slavs, and another community that operated in looser formations along the Volga and came under more 'oriental' influences (Hraundal 2014, 65–66; Tolochko 2015, 175–76). I agree on a possible political division, but 'oriental' influence was integral to Rus' ways of life in both areas, even if not distributed evenly.

In a world with conflicts among rival and geographically distant groups, loose warrior-merchant organizations, led mainly by Scandinavians primarily occupied with the fur and slave trade, looked for markets with an inexhaustible need for human labour and a taste for northern furs. In the ninth and tenth centuries such markets lay in the Islamic world and Byzantium. The road to these international markets, either from the Dnieper or the Volga, however, was impeded by the Eastern European branch of the Eurasian steppe belt.

## The steppe

The territories settled by Scandinavians were surrounded by the steppe on the south and south-east, flat plains with patches of forest. Scandinavian activities in the east depended on the lake and river systems. The Finnish appellation *Routsi* (rowers) – deriving from the Swedish *rōþer* (rowing) – referring to Scandinavian crews navigating the northern waterways on small portable vessels carried from river to river – aptly describes the main occupation of Rus' groups (Heide 2005). These waterways were the sole passable option in the dense forests of north-western Russia and were also the main transportation routes in the open steppes. The land routes also followed the rivers through the steppes, as without them "desolate and disagreeable roads" had to be taken, as the eleventh-century Persian historian, Gardīzī, succinctly summarized the trade routes crossing the Pontic-Caspian steppe (Martinez 1982, 152). No doubt his warning was also significant even in the earliest periods for the availability of provisions, food and drinking water, as well as safe havens of islands where ships could be repaired and supplies loaded (Cross and Sherbowitz-Wetzor 1953, 76; Likhachev 1966, 161; Constantine Porphyrogenitus 1967, 61–63), also led travellers to prefer the river system over land routes (Różycki 2014).

Rivers played a central role in the life of the 'nomads of the sea', and also in the way of life of the 'nomads of the steppes'. Contacts with the various mobile pastoralist communities that lived along the Dnieper, Don, Dniester, Oka and the Volga were especially significant. These were the main rivers where Rus' merchants appeared with their goods or that their warriors travelled to ravage more distant lands. Seasonal migration along the rivers was a regular undertaking in the life of nomadic or semi-nomadic communities that mostly relied on extensive animal husbandry. The periodic shift from summer to winter headquarters in pastoralist communities was an effective economic way to eliminate problems arising from temperature and weather fluctuation, which endangered adequate pasture and drinking water for the livestock and threatened the basis of a nomadic livelihood. Even at the beginning of the Scandinavian appearance in the east, when missions to the Islamic world or Byzantium were launched from more northern areas, the steppe had to be traversed and its inhabitants dealt with. In contrast to the communities dispersed in the fragmented and hard-to-traverse forest belt, on the vast flat area of the steppe centralized polities of extensive scale sometimes formed. These large groupings (states or tribes) interacted with smaller units (clans and families) of steppe society that were based on kinship, in a dynamically changing arena of political co-operation and struggle. The rapid rise of political units on the steppe and the sheer extent of their territorial control could profoundly affect (limit or bolster) Scandinavian and Rus' relationships with Byzantium and the caliphates.

The documentary sources on steppe people are full of ethnonyms that designate various political levels, such as states, tribes, armies and ruling elites, each with individual agency. The perspective of sources written by outsiders using different names for the same group further hinders conceptualizing them from a modern point of view. Ethnic identity on the steppes, just as in the case of the early Germans and the Rus', cannot be defined by common-blood descent or language alone. My conceptualization of these ethnic labels aligns with Walter Pohl's (2018, 190), who convincingly argues that ethnonyms of steppe people "are entangled with political and social identities indicating affiliation to a polity or social status within it". They served as "a principle of organization of the social world into named groupings which are perceived as naturally constituted" (Pohl 2018, 192). While some migrating groups might have retained ethnic homogeneity, others were evidently mixed. Both patterns are seen in the genetic make-up of Iron Age nomads (Unterländer et al. 2017; Damgaard et al. 2018) and the Magyars in recently concluded DNA studies (Csáky et al. 2020 with further references). With this in mind, we now turn to the steppe 'ethnic' groups (political and partly cultural entities) of the Western Eurasian steppes during the Viking Age.

The major power on the Ponto-Caspian steppe in the period between the seventh and ninth centuries was the Khazar polity, which emerged as a successor state of the Western Türk Khaganate of Central Asia. The early development of this state and the exact origin of the Khazar tribe remain unclear, but in most of their cultural traits (language, religion, political structure) the Khazars resembled other Turkic ethnic groups. In the initial centuries, the Khazars were at war with the Arabs along the Caucasian frontier. They slowly started to extend their influence in the Pontic steppes and to the north-east. Their empire, at its zenith, from the end of the ninth century to the early decades of the tenth, stretched from the Volga Bulghar state in the north to the Slavic-populated lower Dnieper (according to some only the Don) in the west, and to northern Caucasus territories in the south, and as a consequence incorporated various ethnic groups. In their capital, Itil, in the Volga delta, a sizable Muslim population lived together with Turkic, Finno-Ugric and Slavic people. From the ninth century onwards the Khazar state was weakened by continuous onslaughts from other steppe tribes, such as the Pechenegs, Oghuz', Magyars and sedentary Rus'. After the final strikes, delivered by the Rus' and other enemies sometime between 965 and 969 CE, the Khazars dispersed in the region or were amalgamated into neighbouring tribes. Their ruling system is characterized as 'dual kingship', in which a sacred ruler, the *khagan*, held supreme religious power, but the practical government was directed by a king, often referred to in the sources as *beg* or *iša*. This might be a glimpse of the Khazar ruling system, but the khagan was also said to act independently sometimes. In the Khazar Khaganate, all major religions were entitled to their own judges, even though the ruling strata of the society converted to Judaism at around the turn of the ninth century (with a turn to Islam for a short time). The Khazars practised a semi-nomadic way of life based on nomadic pasturage and transit commerce (their main income was various customs duties), coloured with sedentary elements, such as cultivated fields. They established several fortified permanent settlements for trade (for their general history and further literature, see Artamonov 1962; Pletnjeva 1978; Sinor [1990] 2008, 263–70; Golden 1992, 233–44; Vásáry 1993, 152–58; Zhivkov 2015).

The Volga Bulghars were a branch of the Bulghar tribal union, who, after a defeat by the Khazars on the Pontic steppe in the mid-seventh century, migrated to the Middle-Volga-Kama region. Like other (semi-)nomadic groups, the Volga Bulghar tribes were not ethnically homogenous. The territory around the Volga-Kama rivers was already subject to small-scale migrations of people of Turkic and Iranian origin, and the Volga Bulghars included Sabir and Khazar ethnic elements. The Volga Bulghar state, which vanished during the Mongol invasion in the thirteenth century, was the best-organized military power in the area during the tenth century, playing a significant role as a middleman in the transit trade between Asia and Northern Europe by founding marketplaces along the Volga. The most notable was Bulgar, near the confluence of the Kama and Volga, but other settlements, such as Suwar and Biljar, were also important in the period. Other fortified settlements have also been excavated in their territory. Initially subordinates of the Khazars, the Volga Bulghars adopted Islam in the early tenth century in order to attain independence from the Jewish khaganate. Little is known about their political structure. In and around 922 CE, their ruler, named Amish, 'king of the Ṣaqāliba', co-ruled with his sons, who were sub-kings. Hostilities between separate Volga Bulgharian tribes occurred occasionally, and the process of their unification and state organization is unknown. The Volga Bulghar economy was complex, based on agriculture, nomadic cattle-breeding on the steppe with winter and summer headquarters, and forest exploitation at the expense of the neighbouring Finno-Ugric population of the forest belt (Sinor [1990] 2008, 231–42; Golden 1992, 253–58; Vásáry 1993, 146–49; Zimonyi 1989, 1998).

The early history and ethnogenesis of the Proto-Hungarian tribes, who called themselves Magyars, is a topic of continuous debates which will not be elaborated upon here. The view in modern scholarship is that today's Hungarian language belongs to the Finno-Ugric language family, while their early culture was Turkic in character. Leaving the Finno-Ugric tribal communities at some point, the Magyars moved southwards to the forest steppe zone and intermingled with local Oghuric groups in the vicinity of the Volga Bulghars, probably gradually embracing a steppe nomadic lifestyle. The area near the southern Ural Mountains is frequently considered to be the ancient homeland of the Magyars, from where their steppe migration began in the mid-eighth century or earlier, which, according to traditional interpretations, lasted a few hundred years. Based on archaeological remains, a new understanding sees a rapid 70-year migration from the Ural steppe to the south Russian and Ukrainian steppes and finally to the Carpathian Basin, where the Magyars arrived at the end of the ninth century. What prompted the Magyar migration remains unknown, however; during the ninth century they probably lived in the orbit of the Khazar Khaganate at a place called Levedia and then Etelköz (west of the Dnieper), driven away by a Pecheneg attack in the middle of the century. In 895 CE, The Magyars were finally pushed out of the Dnieper region by the Pechenegs and migrated into the Carpathian Basin, where they maintained contact with the steppe for a long time, possibly even keeping their influence up to the Dniester until the mid-tenth century. Their political organization evolved and eventually became centralized; the sources give various titles for aristocratic leaders, such as *k.nd.h* (*kende* or *kündü*) and *j.l.h.* (*gyula*), and later *karcha* (*horka*). The distinctions among them are unclear, and scholars usually ascribe a double leadership system similar to the Khazar ruling structure. Three Khazar groups (tribes) joined the Magyars on the way to their new homeland. During their stay in the Black Sea steppe, the Magyars' economy rested on cattle-breeding, raids and the slave trade (Sinor [1990] 2008, 242–48; Golden 1992, 258–62; Vásáry 1993, 158–66; Róna-Tas 1999; Zimonyi 2016; for the new interpretation, see Türk 2012; Langó 2017, 79–85; Komar 2018).

The Pechenegs first appear in Chinese sources of the seventh century as a tribe inhabiting a territory somewhere between today's Kazakhstan and the north Caucasian steppe. Later, as the Oghuz federation pushed them continuously, they migrated from the Aral Sea–Syr Darya region to the Volga. Under continuous pressure, the Pechenegs were again forced to migrate westwards, ousting the Magyars before them. Some of their defeated remnants stayed behind along the Volga under Oghuz rulership. Most of them, however, remained in the Pontic steppe from the late ninth to the mid-eleventh century, when an Oghuz attack with allied Cumans (another Turkic tribe), forced them to the Danubian frontier of the Byzantine Empire. Finally, they were crushed there by a joint Byzantine–Cuman operation in 1091 CE, after which they ceased to be a decisive military force and dispersed among the nearby Turkic tribes or settled in the empire, Kievan Rus' and Hungary. Eight tribes, each with its own ruler, lived on both sides of the Dnieper in the tenth century and managed trade routes that crossed their territory. The Byzantines called their aristocrat leaders *archones* and their tribal structure in the tenth century seems to have been similar to that of the Magyars. In contrast to the Magyars, the Pechenegs probably formed only a loose federation, with a weak and probably only informal central authority. The Pechenegs were a ferocious people, often hired by the Byzantines as their agents to balance power relations in the steppe. Besides the bribes and gifts they received as mercenaries, the Pechenegs garnered riches through raids launched against almost anyone in the region, most often the Rus', the Bulgars on the Danube, and the Byzantines. Apart from plunder, their economy was nomadic, characterized by extensive animal husbandry and the lack of permanent settlements. Their mercantile relations with the Crimean Greeks and the Rus' involved barter in slaves and livestock, and they also acted as middlemen for the northern products of the forest belt farther to the south (Pritsak 1975; Sinor [1990] 2008, 270–75; Golden 1992, 264–70; Vásáry 1993, 167–70; Paroń 2021).

This series of ethnicities on the steppe was further coloured by other groups, which feature less often in the following here but are nevertheless important. Among these, the Oghuz' and the Bashkirs were two large tribes, both of Turkic origin. The Oghuz' had earlier inhabited the Aral steppes between the Syr Darya River and the eastern bank of the Volga, troubling the Khazars with incursions. During the Viking Age, the Bashkirs occupied a territory stretching from the southern slopes of the Ural down to the Volga and shared linguistic and (perhaps) ethnic elements with the Magyars, although their exact relationship is far from clear. In the sources both the Oghuz' and the Bashkirs appear as warlike cattle breeders, among whose ranks, despite their pagan beliefs, Islam had already started to spread. Oghuz' culture was similar to that of the early Türk Khaganate, themselves dissidents from the realm. Their ruler was called the *yabghū*, a title borrowed from the Türks, who reigned with the help of his deputies, called *kūdharkīn* (Sinor [1990] 2008, 245–47, 275–77; Golden 1992, 205–11, 262–64; Vásáry 1993, 169–70). The Alans were an Iranian-speaking population that lived in the Caucasus, from where some groups moved to the Don-Donets area in the orbit of the Khazars. Despite being regarded as traditional pastoralist horsemen, they had established several settlements (including some forts), converted to Christianity and played a decisive role in the development of the Saltovo-Mayaki horizon, an amalgam of related but not identical smaller archaeological cultures thought to manifest close links with the Khazar state and other ethnic groups (Alemany 2000; Pletnjeva 1978, 2003, 52–81, 98; cf. Afanas'ev 2018). The Burtas lived further north from the Khazar core area, also subjects of the khaganate. The Burtas' territory bordered the Middle Volga and the Oka rivers. They were said to be extensive herders of various species, including camel, but their land stretched into the forest steppe region, which allowed them to supplement their economy with fur trapping and beekeeping. They were probably an amalgam of Turkic pastoralist groups and Finno-Ugrian hunter-gatherers that were both sedentary and mobile, changing from wooden houses to tents seasonally (Sinor [1990] 2008, 248–49; Tortika 2006, 302–46). Apart from the Oghuz, no centralized governmental structure is known for these societies, they were led by local headmen or a council of elders.

The steppe was a colourful place, with groups sharing similarities but also variation, which also characterized the Viking world at the time. All these steppe polities shared a cultural background and an economic base centred on the rivers and characterized by mobile pastoralism, although political and economic structures differed considerably. The steppe was a turbulent political scene where political formations were created or merged; ethnic communities dispersed or amalgamated; and social structures, hierarchy and religion changed over time. It is hard to come up with an umbrella term for all these societies; alternatives catch some of the principal characteristics of these people but are difficult to generalize to all groups; thus, a short note on terminology is desirable here.

One of the variant umbrella terms used frequently here is 'Turkic'. As a linguistic category, it excludes the Iranian-speaking Alans and the Finno-Ugric-speaking Magyars. It is more useful as a cultural marker, alluding to cultural practices from Central Asia that were prevalent in the steppes. 'Steppe people' is also problematic because the Volga Bulghars, Bashkirs and Burtas lived deep in the wooded steppe, which implies a need to recognize a combination of the lifestyles of two different ecological zones. "Nomadic" is usually applied in the sources to people living in tents and yurts who practise large-scale pastoralism and migrate seasonally with their herds. Nomadic, however, is a broad term and, as noted earlier, most of these polities had a more complex economy of which pastoralism and a pastoralist population were only one segment. In addition, many of these people, most notably the Khazars, Volga Bulghars and Alans, maintained permanent settlements. This mixed palette of social, political and economic variation in steppe communities has led to inconsistency in scholarly terminologies.

Furthermore, the term 'nomadism', used to describe the central feature of a steppe lifestyle, is perhaps the most contested of all. The term derives from the Greek word *nomas*, meaning 'feed, pasture'. Nomadism has a wide resonance in Anglophone scholarship, referring not only to pastoralist groups but also hunter-gatherer and horde societies. Central and Eastern European scholarship usually employs a narrower meaning restricted to extensive animal herding communities that migrate seasonally (Kradin 2016). Irrelevant of time and space, some communities have been labelled nomadic from historic times until today. Thus, nomadism cannot be seen as a unified phenomenon similar to agriculturalism or sedentism, lifestyles that are usually contrasted with nomadism. The nomads of Eurasia are relevant here, but even within this category great variations exist among nomadic economies, coloured in part by the combination of animal species the herders specialize in in different ecological zones, such as Tibetan yak and horse breeders, north Eurasian reindeer herders and the camel-sheep-goat trinity of Near Eastern nomadism (Barfield 1993; Khazanov 1994).

Central Asian nomads focused on three animal species: sheep, horses and cattle. This is probably where nomadism originated – possibly as a suitable alternative to agriculture (Markov 1976, 8–48; Golden 2011, 8–11). Horses played indispensable military, economic and spiritual roles in these societies. By domesticating the horse, Central Asian nomads were the first in history to connect Eurasia by a single communication highway as early as the Bronze Age (Anthony 2007; Cunliffe 2015). Historically, the medieval nomads of the Eastern European steppe resembled Central Asian–type nomads culturally.

For a long time earlier (and still in popular circles), nomadism connoted constant migration, sometimes a lifestyle of pointless wanderings and the inability to settle down. Nomads were regarded as inferior and poor, in some contexts purely predatory and parasitic in comparison to the sedentary world (for discussion, see Khazanov 1981, 142–44). These notions were mainly generalized from anthropological research on contemporary nomadic communities (e.g. Gavin 1996), and most of them have been successfully refuted (in short: Khazanov 1981) and will also be addressed in context here.

Motion is the central feature of nomadism. In most cases twice a year, or sometimes more often, the whole community, or at least the majority, embark on a journey together with their livestock – compared to more sedentary communities where usually only a specialized class of people are entrusted with shepherding. The periodic shift between summer and winter headquarters is far from an aimless, disorganized march but is a carefully planned undertaking driven by the practicalities of nature. Resources, weather and geographical and political conditions all affect the route of travel. Nomadic migrations usually follow the seasonal temperature and are based on a thorough knowledge of the locations of suitable pastures, drinking water, and protection for beast and man. In addition, a nomadic economy is supplemented by fishing and hunting and even small-scale agriculture. In this sense, many of the steppe tribes discussed here were rather semi-nomadic, although the boundary between nomad and semi-nomad is somewhat arbitrary (Markov 1976, 8–10; Khazanov 1994, 15–21).

Social and political structures of nomads are complex and vary and change in relation to the ownership of livestock and people, and the right to use pastures. Nomadic empires were assemblages of many levels of nomadic organization, such as clans, tribes, tribal unions and so on (Suleymenov 1989; Kradin, Bondarenko, and Barfield 2003). The system of sequential building blocks of social forms – clans, tribes, chiefdoms and states – is a matter of ongoing debate (Kradin 2015). In steppe societies, large political units called tribes formed by a leading clan allying with others through conquest, military alliance, intermarriage, gift exchange and kinship (Ecsedy 1972; Lindner 1982). The terminologies in medieval sources, however, do not always distinguish clearly between 'clans' and 'tribes'. The term 'tribe' here will be used to designate steppe polities of various sizes and does not imply primitiveness. It has been even argued by David Sneath that steppe state formations were sometimes on a par with sedentary societies, with all the functioning principles of social organization, including social stratification, aspirations to privatize pastures, enforced taxation systems, slavery and military obligations. Some of these units operated without a central ruler in a horizontal power relation arrangement called a 'headless state', in which leaders used fictional genealogies and claims of noble descent to secure their place (Sneath 2007). Although rule by members of the social elite could sometimes outweigh and dominate kinship-based groupings of clans and tribes, kinship was the governing principle of local organization in the steppes (Golden 2009).

The rhythm of life on the steppe, described earlier, was not completely alien to the Scandinavian Rus'. It has been recently remarked that the usual 'sedentary-nomadic' division is inappropriate for early medieval conditions because members of sedentary societies were also highly mobile throughout the year. In addition, certain groups with lifestyles similar to nomads are not termed as such in the sources; a prime example of this are the Rus'. In contrast, nomadic people, the Pechenegs, for instance, were not labelled 'nomadic' by contemporary sedentary observers because, like agriculturalists, they had territorial boundaries and fixed places where they could be found at certain times of the year. During certain activities, such as mercenary service, craft production, trade and resource gathering, nomadic people also spent considerable time in one place and embarked on mobile missions no more frequently than contemporary 'sedentary' merchants, diplomats, rulers and armies (Standen and White 2018, 158–66).

In several regards, the Rus' indeed resembled the nomads more closely than other sedentary populations. Like 'pure nomads', they did not cultivate fields, according to a report from the mid-ninth century by the Persian ibn Rusta (de Goeje 1892, 145; Lunde and Stone 2012, 126). Ibn Rusta, acquiring his information from Jayhānī (perhaps even orally), is trustworthy in this regard, and likely caught a glimpse of Rus' communities in their early stage of development, when permanent settlement and agriculture did not play a part in their way of life (Montgomery 2001, 81–84). In addition, mobility and movement were the central features of the Viking and a nomadic way of life. Movement was mostly driven by inner social dynamics rather than purely economic reasons. Hunger for wealth and prestige increased social competition and triggered great movements in Scandinavia and the steppes (Golovnov 2009, 156–310; Raffield, Price, and Collard 2017). Thus, the Scandinavian Rus' were used to being on the move, just like many of the steppe people, only on ships rather than horseback. Although it might have been a figure of speech referring to their uncivilized manners, a Byzantine eyewitness, Patriarch Photius, remarked in 860 CE that the Rus' were 'nomadic' (*nomadikón*) (Photius 1883, 168; Mango 1985). Rus' communities also practised seasonal migration. In the mid-tenth century, their centre in Kiev, for instance, was a starting point of recurring winter trips into the forest belt (called *poliudia* in Greek). Upon their return to Kiev in the spring, they quickly prepared for commercial trips to Constantinople, only to return home the next winter:

> The severe manner of life of these same Russians in winter-time is as follows. When the month of November begins, their chiefs together with all the Russians, at once leave Kiev and go off on the 'poliudia', which means 'rounds', that is to the Slavonic regions of the Vervians, Drugovichians and Krivichians and Severians and the rest of the Slavs who are tributaries of the Russians. There they are maintained throughout the winter, but then once more, starting from the month of April, when the ice of the Dnieper river melts, they come back to Kiev. They then pick up their 'monoxyla', as has been said above, and fit them out, and come down to Romania.
>
> (Constantine Porphyrogenitus 1967, 62–63)

The Volga Rus' similarly embarked annually on long trading expeditions, and in fact travelled with their women, a sign that a large segment of their community moved rather than only a professional group of entrepreneurs (Montogomery 2014, 240–41). In both the Dnieper and Volga examples, the mainly Scandinavian elite layers of Rus' society embarked on such ventures. This was not drastically different from the usual practices of contemporary steppe migrations in which agriculturalists stayed in place and the ruling strata of a nomadic society moved

(Györffy 1970, 191–96). In light of these reports, which offer snapshots of various Rus' communities from the mid-ninth to the mid-tenth century, the Rus' may rightly be called 'nomads of the rivers', if a certain fluidity is allowed in the term's interpretation (Pritsak 1977; Naimushin 2003; Golovnov 2009, 253–310).[1]

For other reasons than the rhythms of life and movement on the steppe, the steppe inhabitants may have felt familiar to the Rus'. Multi-lingual and multi-ethnic communities of the steppe formed martial societies, allied into polities based on loose connections of blood-related or fictive kinship. Steppe tribes were no more egalitarian than those in the Viking Age societies in Scandinavia. Although the material is quite fragmented among sources pertaining to various steppe communities, many of them believed in sky deities, practised animistic cults headed by ritual specialists, produced culturally distinctive metalwork in animal-art style, sacrificed animals in funerary rites, held horses and weapons in high esteem, used the ritual swearing of oaths, sought plunder and tribute and received gifts from their ruler for faithful service. These were familiar phenomena in Scandinavia and European Russia during the Viking Age, and many of the Scandinavian Rus' must have sensed the steppe as somehow familiar.

## The earliest contacts

My main focus falls on the tenth century, when both written and archaeological sources proliferate, allowing a deeper analysis. Some of the findings based on the main tenth-century materials seem to mirror the ninth-century situation in various ways, but the pieces of the picture are more fragmentary and thus the interpretation more speculative. Although some ninth-century accounts will be referenced in the following chapters, I will place less emphasis on the prelude to Scandinavian interactions with the steppe peoples.

Scandinavian contacts with the steppe left their first explicit mark on posterity only in the early decades of the ninth century (see Figure 2.1). Intriguingly, even the very first mention of the Rus' in written records hints at political (one would almost dare to say 'state-level') connections between them and the steppe polity of the Khazars. The principal source is the Frankish *Annales Bertiniani*, which describe the arrival of Byzantine envoys at the court of the Frankish king Louis the Pious (813–40 CE), in Ingelheim in the year 839 CE. This embassy of Emperor Theophilos (829–42 CE) was accompanied by another delegation of diplomats belonging to a group called *Rhos*. The justification for the *Rhos* following Theophilos's mission to Frankia was based on the challenges they faced if they wished to return home from Constantinople. They argued that the route was blocked by savage tribes. Upon inquiry, Louis determined that the *Rhos* were Swedes, identifying their ruler as *chacanus*, a Latin rendering of the nomadic title 'khagan' (Waitz 1883, 19–20). Thus, the Rus' (who evidently hide behind the word *Rhos*), were subjects of a khagan, a title only known from nomadic history and applicable to a supreme ruler of the steppes solely by inheritance. The Avars and the Central Asian Türks had a khagan previously, but by the time of the Ingelheim delegation only the Khazars on the Western steppes were ruled by a khagan.

This passage of the *Annales Bertiniani* still puzzles researchers; how and why would the Scandinavian Rus' label their ruler a khagan? It has been suggested that this might be a corruption of the text and that instead the Scandinavian name Hákon might lie behind the annal's word for designating the ruler of the Rus' (Garipzanov 2006). This interpretation, however, cannot solve the dilemma with a single thrust, as the title not only appears in another Carolingian correspondence (Caspar 1928, 388), but unrelated sources also mention a Rus' khagan. Ibn Rusta and other Islamic authors copying Jayhānī, speak of a swampy island where the Rus' and their *ẖāqān* dwell (de Goeje 1892, 145; Bosworth 1982, 159; Lunde and Stone 2012, 126). Later Slavic sources, such as Metropolitan Ilarion of Kiev, the Russian *byliny* called *Slovo o pŭlku Igorevě* (The Tale of Igor's Campaign) and a graffito in the Saint Sophia cathedral in Kiev also preserved the memory that Rus' rulers were sometimes called khagans (Vysotskiy 1966, 49–52; Franklin 1973, 3–29; Moldovan 1984, 77–196; Likhachev et al. 2006, 116, 313).

It seems likely that among the Rus' one group designated their ruler as khagan in the ninth century. Two possibilities remain to explain this, neither of which is without controversy. The Rus' either borrowed the title from the Khazars, which, given the rigid rules of transmitting this title and the consequences of raising their ruler to an equal footing with the Khazar khagan, was contested by Peter Golden (1982). The other solution is more appealing, namely, to take the text in the narrowest sense. The Rus' envoys simply stated that their ruler was called *chacanus*, without any further commentary on whether he was one of them. This interpretation, James Montgomery argues, means that the *chacanus* of the *Annales Bertiniani* simply refers to the Khazar khagan (Montgomery 2010, 163–64). This, however, is in conflict with ibn Rusta's report, who locates the Rus' *ẖāqān* on an island in a lake far into the forest belt. The Arabic author can be expected to recognize whether the ruler of the Rus' was the Khazar khagan, about whom he speaks separately (de Goeje 1892, 139–40; Lunde and Stone 2012, 116–17).

The matter is further complicated by the supposition that having a khagan equals having a firm political unit, a khaganate, before 839 CE, when it is first mentioned, to probably well into the tenth century. This can be reinforced by ibn Faḍlān's travelogue from 922 CE, in which he fails to mention the title khagan but famously describes the customs of a Rus' king as strikingly similar to those of the Khazar khagan – a sacred ruler who never leaves his palace, is protected by an elite guard to the extreme, is surrounded by concubines, and leaves the practical government of his polity to a deputy (Montgomery 2014, 253–57, for discussion see Golden 2006).

Speculations about the whereabouts of this khaganate are legion. Every scholar locates the Rus' khaganate according to their own disentanglement of the conflicting texts. Following ibn Rusta and the archaeological record, which preserves ninth-century Scandinavian traces in north-western Russia, the khaganate of the Rus' is described around Staraya Ladoga or Rurikovo Gorodische (Franklin and Shepard 1996, 31–41). Others believe that strong Khazar influence could only be exerted from somewhere closer, either along the Oka or the Volga (Golden 1982) or in Tmutarakan (Font 2007, 37–38), implying Rus' settlement remarkably far south in the ninth century. Some researchers think the title of khagan in this context refers to the ruler of Kiev (Vernadsky 1959, 193–98; Goehrke 1992, 151; Sverdlov 2003, 99; cf. Petrukhin 2007). The most extreme solution suggested the Danube delta as a possible location for the island of the Rus' and their khagan (Rybakov 1982, 342–58). The notion of a khaganate as a firm political unit has recently been questioned by Þórir Jónsson Hraundal, who argues that the memory of such a ruler among the Rus' should be seen as a reflection of Muslim opinions on the similarity of Rus' and Turkic groups (Hraundal 2013, 175–81). The plethora of interpretations illustrates the uncertainty of the situation. Who the Rus' khagan was and where he lived cannot be determined with the current evidence.

More secure evidence, however, exists in this early period for continuous contacts between eastern Scandinavian groups and the steppes. Besides the *Annales Bertiniani*, another written source unequivocally attests that Khazaria was the foremost steppe partner of the Rus' in the ninth century. The Arab ibn Khurradādhbih's information from the mid-ninth century describes Rus' merchants venturing towards Baghdad passing through Khazaria, where they sold beaver pelts, swords and slaves. The Rus' even made the effort to understand the local conditions and learn the tricks of the system, alluded to by the fact that they pretended to be Christians at the Islamic borders in order to pay a lower tax (de Goeje 1889, 154; Lunde and Stone 2012, 112). This account describes a system of regularly used trade routes.

Archaeological evidence also confirms connections. Chronologically, the earliest evidence comes from the so-called Peterhof treasure, a coin hoard found on the Baltic coast near Staraya Ladoga at Petrodvorets. The hoard was dated to the *terminus post quem* of 804 CE and contained around 80 coins, among which 13 specimens showed Scandinavian runes and four others Turkic runes, attributed to a wide range of origins ranging from the Khazar centre, Sarkel on the Don, to the Orkhon-Yenisey valley in Central Asia (Mel'nikova, Nikitin, and Fomin 1984). The transmitters of the Turkic coins in the Peterhof treasure were likely also the Khazars, the only power centre at the time closely connected with Central Asia. The Khazar dominion was centred in the Volga-Don region, from where artefacts of the Saltovo-Mayaki culture reached the northern Rus' settlements at an early date. Ninth-century layers at both Ladoga and Rurikovo Gorodische contained Khazar ('oriental') objects: Caucasian beads, steppe strap-ends and a finger-ring (Davidan 1986; Mühle 1991, 34; Nosov 2017, 117).

A fortified site at Supruty, established early near a minor tributary of the Oka River, evinces even closer relationships between Scandinavians and the Khazars. This hillfort lies on the eastern Oka-Volga trade route in the frontier zone between the Khazar Khaganate and the Rus'-controlled parts of the Russian forest belt. Many artefacts of Scandinavian origin were found in the hillfort, mixed with objects from regions under Khazar overlordship (most notably a small treasure hoard) or showing typical 'oriental' influence that researchers label (post-)Sassanian art, also transmitted by the Khazars (Figure 2.2). The population of the hillfort comprised a Scandinavian elite ruling over the local Slavs and maintaining close ties with the khaganate, attested by riding equipment manufactured in

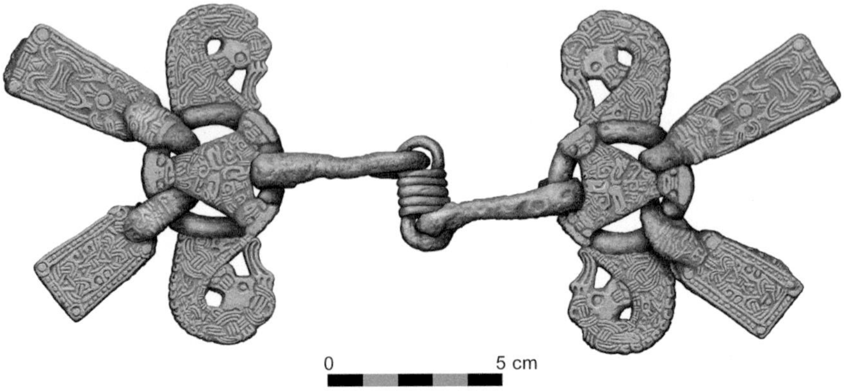


*Figure 2.2* Horse trapping from Supruty

Source: Redrawn after Murasheva 2019, 267

steppe style. The site vanished tragically as the result of a brutal attack in the first half of the tenth century. Who the attackers of this early community formation were is unknown, but it seems to be a uniquely early example of identity building on a Scandinavian-steppe heritage (Murasheva 2019). Perhaps the Scandinavian appearance in European Russia added a twist to earlier Slavic–Khazar relations on the steppe and the forest frontiers and prompted the leaders of an emerging community to imagine themselves on a par with the khagan.

The only certain conclusion is that the Rus', after their first appearance in the East, entered into close contact with the Khazar world and its milieu. The complete lack of information about Rus' connections with other steppe areas is quite revealing. The first appearance of Scandinavians in Staraya Ladoga dates to the 750s, after which there is a long interval between the first recorded steppe contacts of the Rus' in 839 to the 850s. By the time written records reveal increasing Rus'–steppe contacts, Scandinavian groups had already lived in the East for almost 100 years. When information on the first contacts appears, the sources already hint at a relationship on a fairly advanced level. None of the shock usually expressed upon encountering strangers or an alien situation can be detected. The accounts paint a picture of a well-functioning long-distance communication channel between people familiar with each other. Diplomatic, political and commercial ties were already solid between the Rus' and the steppe by this time; thus the earliest contacts must have preceded them by decades. The Rus' not only traded with and through Khazar territory, and probably also maintained political relationships with it – at least one of their groups might have been ruled by a/the khagan. The notion of a Rus' khagan remained firm and lingered on in memories of rulership in the Slavonic sources of a later age. Although further details of early

Scandinavian–Khazar contacts remain blurred, the evidence hints that the steppe had already made its mark on the Rus' in the ninth century.

## Note

1 Designations such as 'nomads of the sea' and 'nomads of the rivers' referring to Vikings and Rus' are not to be confused with the current anthropological label of 'sea nomads', which refers to highly skilled fishing and diving communities in South Asia. They dwell almost exclusively on the water in floating houses.

# 3 Armed conflicts

In 965/969 CE, the Rus' launched an extensive campaign of co-ordinated attacks on various steppe abodes along the Volga. The assault, mainly directed against the Khazars, was of unprecedented cruelty, as recorded by Arabic intelligence of the era: "The Rūs have left nothing to the Bulghār, Burtās and Khazars but a few worthless ruins. They fell upon them and looted everything" (Kramers 1939, 393; Lunde and Stone 2012, 178). In a later passage, ibn Ḥawqal, the same author, laments again: "I asked a man about the vineyards and he said: 'There is not enough left of a vineyard or garden worth giving to a beggar. If a leaf were left on a branch, one of the Rūs would carry it off. Not a grape, not a raisin remains in that country" (Kramers 1939, 393; Lunde and Stone 2012, 178).

A belt of steppe dwellers surrounded the parts of European Russia and Ukraine where Scandinavians had settled and controlled in the ninth and tenth centuries (see Figure 2.1 and Figure 3.1). At intervals this proximity led to conflict. According to the traditional view of Russian scholarship, this was an eternal war of ecological zones, that of *les i step*, "forest and steppe" (Solov'yov 1896, 9–13; Kliutschewskij 1925, 56–59, 158–60; Tolochko 1987, 7, 17; cf. Zhivkov 2015, VIII). The notion mostly derived from the later experience of the Rus' lands, which suffered Oghuz, Cuman and finally Mongol invasions. It was also projected back to the Khazar era, culminating in the previously quoted campaign of *knyaz* Sviatoslav (945–72 CE), son of *knyaz* Igor, who put an end to a long struggle between the nomads and the Rus' societies, which followed different lifestyles that led to clashes. In spite of the harshness of the outcome described in the previous quotes, I take a different view. Although fighting and its severe consequences might have dominated Rus'–Cuman, and certainly did Rus'–Mongol relations at the time of conquest, the earlier phase of connection between "steppe and forest" does not seem to embody endless wrestling (Figure 3.1).

Conflicts between the Rus' and the steppe dwellers in the Viking period varied in intensity, from small-scale raids serving short-term economic needs through a rigorous monitoring of boundaries and finally to expansion and conquest. I find it useful to subdivide these conflicts into further categories to clarify the socio-economic contexts of these encounters. Three main types of belligerence can be distinguished, each with different characteristics and underlying motivations: crossing steppe territories, small-scale raiding and large campaigns. I will

DOI: 10.4324/9781003037859-3

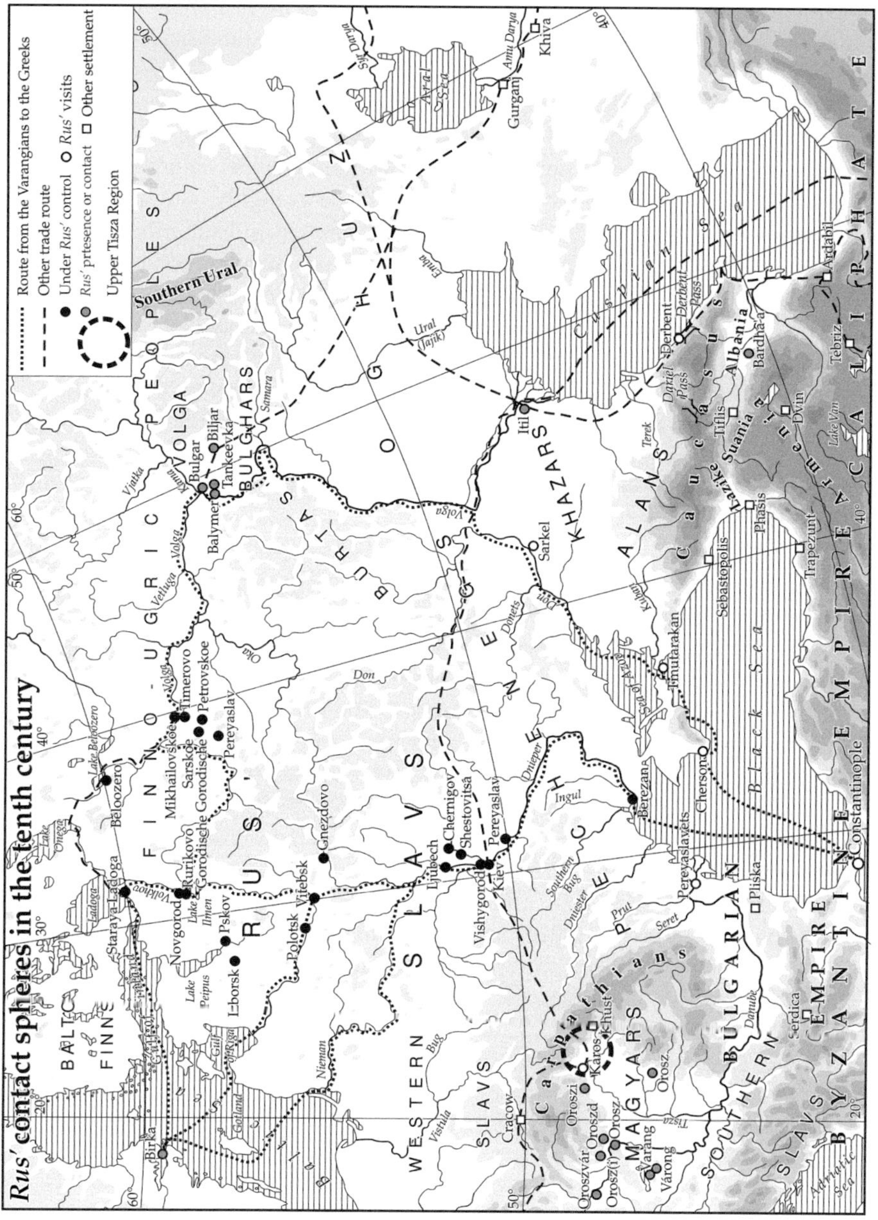


*Figure 3.1* Rus' contact sphe-es in the tenth century

elaborate further on these types of conflict by assessing the frequency of Rus'–nomadic encounters. Looking at events chronologically can help explain certain patterns of frequency in terms of the conflicts and relations the Rus' had with each neighbouring steppe tribe. Although no statistics can be compiled, the evidence suggests that major oppositions were uncommon between the Rus' and the neighbouring nomads.

Recent scholarly theory on Viking warfare colours comparisons of these encounters. Knowledge of Viking military organization has increased in recent decades; the scholarly view now challenges the homogenous nature of Scandinavian warbands and argues that their organization was highly complex. Retinues of various size, called *lið* in Scandinavia, were bound to each other by ties of kinship and sworn to a leader. Enlarging such a unit required adding men from outside groups (Raffield et al. 2016, 38–40; Hedenstierna-Jonson 2020c, 179, 183–84), non-relatives and even people from abroad. An army had to be recruited and organized on a supra-regional level, including forced conscripts, mercenaries and allies from other ethnic milieus. As Benjamin Raffield (2016) argues, in some of the larger armies that went on long campaigns members also engaged in craft production and trade to supply themselves. Viking armies in the west also included women and children, making them more 'mobile societies' or even 'polities'. Small detachments of a large army could manoeuvre independently, which made it easier to gather large contingents in a relatively short time, but also hindered large armies from holding together for a long period.

Many new findings apply to the situation in the east as well. Scandinavian warbands arriving in the east soon mixed with local people, and large campaigns were launched with the help of a multitude of allies of Slavic and Balto-Finn origin. Prince Oleg, for instance, as early as the 880s CE, is described as setting forth towards the south, "taking with him many warriors from among the Varangians, the Chuds, the Slavs, the Merians and all the Krivichians" (Cross and Sherbowitz-Wetzor 1953, 60–61; Likhachev 1996, 14). According to the PVL, similar mustering was also carried out before later campaigns (Cross and Sherbowitz-Wetzor 1953, 64, 72; Likhachev 1996, 16, 23), and, based on similarities with the West, there is no need to discredit the general picture provided by the chronicle. The huge Rus' army of 860 CE that attacked Constantinople, perhaps advancing slowly southwards and living off the land as a mobile society, can usefully be compared with the Great Viking Army that operated in England at roughly the same time (Tolochko 2015, 142–49). Mas'ūdī provides further comparative evidence on a 913 CE Rus' force plundering along the Caspian Sea coast. After entering the sea, the Rus' spread out into several independent raiding parties that attacked Jil, Daylam, Tabaristan, Abaskun and Azerbaijan simultaneously. They stayed in the region for several months in temporary headquarters established in the safety of the Caspian Islands, only to re-group later and finally sail away (Maçoudi 1863, 21–22; Lunde and Stone 2012, 145–46). This Rus' force operated much like Viking armies did in England and on the continent (Raffield 2016, 324–26). Admitting other groups into the Rus' warrior elite added further complexity to the social organization. The military leadership and small retinues were still mainly Scandinavian in character even after the mid-tenth century, but local names appear among them (Struminski 1996, 162–80; Sitzmann 2003, 58–61; Mel'nikova 2004). Thus, comparable socio-military structures existed in both Scandinavia and the Rus' territories, and armed units were ethnically heterogenous.

Similarly, steppe forces were cavalcades of miscellaneous ethnic groups due to the principles of forming nomadic tribes throughout Eurasian history. Tribes formed when blood-related clans merged with non-blood-related ones. Tribes subjugated other tribes and accepted the defeated into their ranks, who then adopted the ethnicity of the victors, although sometimes keeping their original tribal affiliations (especially the language). Clan and tribe leaders could even develop independent "foreign policies" with neighbouring groups. Not all groups formed complex political organizations; some successfully manoeuvred on their own in smaller kinship units. Most of the steppe people mixed with other steppe dwellers and occasionally sedentary people. The Magyars, for instance, were said to have been joined by three other tribes, known together as Kabars (*Kabaroi*), who seceded from the Khazar union in the ninth century (Constantine Porphyrogenitus 1967, 174–75). The Khazars themselves administered an army made up not only of 'ethnic Khazars', but also Persian Muslims, Slavs and Rus' (Ludwig 1982, 286–98). Pecheneg remnants remaining in the Volga area after the rest of the group was pushed westward by the Oghuz', willingly joined the victors but still distinguished themselves within the Oghuz federation by wearing sleeveless garments as a distinctive sign of their Pecheneg identity (Constantine Porphyrogenitus 1967, 168–69).

Thus, Rus' and steppe armies were complex composite entities, especially in ethnic terms. Encounters between them therefore did not take place in an 'ethnic vacuum'. From the Scandinavian perspective, this did not change later, when the Kievan Rus' polity and Rus' identity crystallized further around the millennium. From the eleventh century onwards Scandinavian mercenaries, mostly termed Varangians in the sources, faced nomads who were parts of Rus' or Byzantine armies.[1]

## Traversing nomadic territory

Thanks to their technological advancement and experience in naval warfare and seafaring, the Scandinavian Rus' were able to travel far beyond their immediate territory where water systems allowed. The first type of conflict between them and the steppe people broke out when commercial or pirate fleets tried to reach a destination beyond nomadic habitats, mainly through waterways that traversed the steppes. A target area under Muslim control could be reached via the Don, Volga, Caspian and a Byzantine target area via the Dnieper and the Black Sea. In the Volga area, the Khazars, in the Dnieper area, first the Magyars and later the Pechenegs, hindered passage. Rus' fleets elicited varied reactions from the steppe people.

The Khazars, the most complex of the steppe societies discussed here, established a blockade protected by strongholds (Pletneva 2003, 67–81) at the confluence of the Volga and Don rivers, most notably Sarkel (built with Byzantine help), partly to tax Rus' ships passing through (Constantine Porphyrogenitus 1967, 182–85; Zimonyi 2016, 340–42). The blockade also let pirates slip through claiming a portion of the expected booty, as noted in the mid-tenth century by the Arabic historian Mas'ūdī:

> When the Rūs vessels reached the Khazar checkpoint that guards the entrance to the strait, they sent to ask the king for permission to cross his kingdom and make their way down the river of the Khazars and so enter the Khazar Sea (Caspian Sea). . . . The Rūs contracted to give the king half of anything they managed to pillage from the people along the shores of that sea. The ruler agreed to their request and they entered the strait.
>
> (Lunde and Stone 2012, 144–45; original: Maçoudi 1863, 19–20)

The mission of 913 CE that is referred to in this quotation ended badly, as Muslim subjects of the Khazars turned against the returning Rus' fleet and massacred its members (Maçoudi 1863, 23; Lunde and Stone 2012, 146). The blockade was still in operation later in the tenth century, as Khagan Joseph reported in a letter to Ḥasdai ibn Shapruṭ, a fellow Jew serving in the Ummayad Caliphate of Al-Andalus in 960 CE:

> I protect the mouth of the river (Itil – Volga, V.P.) and prevent the Rus arriving in their ships from setting off by sea against the Ishmaelites (Moslems – V.P.) and (equally) all (their) enemies from setting off by land to Bab ('the Gate', Derbent – V.P.). I wage war with them. If I left them (in peace) for a single hour they would crush the whole land of the Ishmaelites up to Baghdad.
>
> (Petrukhin 2007, 257; original: Kokovtsov 1932, 83–84, 102)

Not all the early Rus' raids in the Caspian, however, involved Khazar-Rus' enmities. According to the later Persian historian ibn Isfandiyār, a Rus' fleet plundered Muslim settlements on the Caspian Sea coast during the reign of Al-Ḥasan ibn Zayd, emir of Tabaristan between 864 and 884 CE. A similar attack took place in 911 CE and was repeated the following year:

> This year [911] 16 ships filled with Russians came to 'Abasgún, as they had already done in the time of Sayyid Ḥasan b. Zayd, who defeated and slew them. This time they wasted and looted 'Abasgún and the adjacent coasts, and carried off or slew many Musulmáns. . . . Next year the Russians returned in greater force, burned Sárí and Panjáh-hazár, and carried off many prisoners. Then they sailed to Chashma-Rúd in Daylamán; but, while some of them were on land, a number of the people of Gílán descended to the sea-shore, burned their ships, and slew those who had landed. Shírwánsháh, King of the Khazars, hearing of this, intercepted such of their ships as had escaped and destroyed them and their crews, and thenceforth the marauding raids of the Russians were stopped.
>
> (Isfandiyar 1905, 199)

Scholars have debated whether ibn Isfandiyār refers to two or three Rus' raids since the last incident seems to be identical with the raid of 913 CE mentioned by Mas'ūdī, and there is even a chance that only Mas'ūdī's account is authentic (Margoliouth 1918; Artamonov 1962, 370; Sakharov 1980, 182–83, 199–202; Gumilyov 1989, 191–92, 215–17). It is clear, nevertheless, that some Rus' fleets could enter the Caspian without hostilities, like the one in 943 CE against Bardha'a, capital of the province of Arran near the estuary of the Kur River (Margoliouth 1921, 67–74). Judging by analogy with the raid of 913 CE, presumably these expeditions also had to pay a tithe to the Khazars in order to pass easily into the Caspian. Pressures probably eased after the fall of the Khazar Khaganate, as it seems that in 987 CE a fleet of 18 Rus' ships passed undisturbed into the Caspian when summoned by the Derbent emir Maymūn ibn Aḥmad (Minorsky 1958, 45). Also, in 1035 CE a Rus' fleet was comfortably rowing the waters of the Caspian, as the Ghaznavid ruler Mas'ud ibn Muḥammad noted during a picnic on the southern shore (Pritsak 1981, 449–50).

The Volga could be reached from the Don, and navigation was easy on both rivers, but the Dnieper presented natural obstacles for the Rus'. Some features aided Rus' expeditions, such as islands where supplies could be loaded, ships repaired and rituals performed in safety. Besides islands, however, the Dnieper also had seven cataracts. In addition to presenting physical difficulties by forcing the crews to unload their cargos and boats and drag them on land around the obstacle, this also offered nomads an opportunity for ambushes (Constantine Porphyrogenitus 1967, 57–63). The offences committed by the Pechenegs are well known from the Byzantine report of Emperor Constantine Porphyrogenitus in the DAI:

> Nor can the Russians come at this imperial city of the Romans, either for war or for trade, unless they are at peace with the Pechenegs, because when the Russians come with their ships to the barrages of the river and cannot pass through unless they lift their ships off the river and carry them past by portaging them on their shoulders, then the men of this nation of the Pechenegs set upon them, and, as they cannot do two things at once, they are easily routed and cut to pieces.
>
> (Constantine Porphyrogenitus 1967, 50–51)

The geographical and political circumstances along the Dnieper in the DAI are confirmed by a later travelogue that notes the existence of the same islands before modern water regulation (flood control) and also notes the permanent danger from nearby mobile groups (the Cossacks at that time) (Różycki 2014). The Pechenegs, who inhabited the area throughout the tenth century, were regarded as extreme foes even by nomadic standards: the Magyars were reported to fear them (Constantine Porphyrogenitus 1967, 50–51). The risk the Pechenegs presented in the Dnieper area should not be underestimated; Sviatoslav fell victim to them when returning from his Byzantine campaign in 972 CE. The Pechenegs, previously supporting Sviatoslav in the campaign, ambushed him and his entourage at one of the river fords, beheaded him and made a drinking cup out of his skull (Diaconus 1828, 157; Cross and Sherbowitz-Wetzor 1953, 90; Thurn 1973, 310; Likhachev 1996, 35).

Thus, Rus' commercial missions or assaults on Constantinople could only be launched if the river was secured. According to the PVL, major campaigns along the rivers were launched in 860, 907, 941, 944 and 1043 CE. All of these assaults are confirmed by independent sources, except the one in 907 CE, but Georg Ostrogorsky demonstrated that there can be little doubt about the historical veracity of this event (Ostrogorsky 1940). I shall review how the Rus' managed to cross the steppe in each case, best approached chronologically backwards.

The last Rus' expedition against Byzantium travelled exclusively by boat and passed the Dnieper undisturbed, possibly due to an earlier depredation of the Pechenegs by the Rus' *knyaz* Yaroslav the Wise (1019–54 CE) in 1036 CE, after which they dispersed (Cross and Sherbowitz-Wetzor 1953, 136–37; Likhachev 1996, 66). The Oghuz', who occupied the Black Sea pastures in place of the Pechenegs, are not mentioned in the sources for this incident.

A former successful strategy of dealing with the Pecheneg danger is described in the PVL. In 944 CE, Igor made a pact with the Pechenegs to support his campaign, insured by Pecheneg hostages (Cross and Sherbowitz-Wetzor 1953, 72; Likhachev 1996, 23). Thus, there is reason to suspect that the Pechenegs were bought off somehow because they were not part of the expedition in 941 CE. They probably also supported Oleg in 907 CE, as the chronicle reports that he led his people towards Constantinople "by horse and by ship", the same way as Igor did in 944 CE when he was allied with them (Cross and Sherbowitz-Wetzor 1953, 64, 72; Likhachev 1996, 16, 23). This mention of horses might also relate to the Danube Bulgars' or Oleg's own horses (Sakharov 1980, 100–1). Another possibility is that the raid in 907 CE passed through a no-man's land; after driving the Magyars out of the Dnieper region in 895 CE, it is not clear whether the Pechenegs immediately occupied the area (Font and Sudár 2019, 45). The first Pecheneg attack on the Rus' that might support this theory was only recorded in 915 CE, or, according to more reliable Byzantine sources, it might have been in 917 CE (Bekker 1838, 386–90; Cross and Sherbowitz-Wetzor 1953, 71; Likhachev 1996, 21). The hypotheses that the Rus' were either allied with the Pechenegs in 907 CE or that they went through a yet-uninhabited landscape both add to the point: the nomadic presence implied authority and influenced crossings of the steppe. These precedents make us contemplate the safety of passage through the Dnieper area in 860 CE, when the Magyars occupied the land.

The Magyars, inhabiting the area from around 850 to 895 CE, also carefully guarded their boundaries, as did the Pechenegs and Khazars. This situation is reflected in the story of Cyril, the Slavic missionary, who was heading to the Khazars in 861 CE but was detained by aggressive Magyars when he entered their territory (Lavrov 1930, 155; Kantor 1983, n. p.). Cyril escaped, but the episode illustrates nomad principles. Under the year 839 CE, the *Annales Bertiniani* also reports "barbarian and savage tribes" (*barbaras et nimiae feritatis gentes*) blocking the way of Rus' envoys returning from Constantinople (Waitz 1883, 19–20). Judging from the geographical proximity of the Dnieper as the closest route leading north from Constantinople, many scholars have expressed the opinion that this passage refers to the Magyars (Kristó 1996, 86, 128; Balogh 2004 with further references). Based on these analogies, the assumption seems fair that negotiations might have been needed to neutralize the Magyar threat. The Rus' attack of 860 CE also had to travel on the Dnieper, controlled by the Magyars at the time. The campaign could only have been managed if the Rus' had secured their passage on the Dnieper by either paying tribute or by being on good terms with the Magyars in general (Fettich 1931, 54; Vernadsky 1959, 213; Boba 1967, 128; Petrukhin 2015, 58–59; Zimonyi 2016, 327). The only other possibility would have been for the Rus' to pass through the Khazar-Alan strongholds along the Don and descend from the Azov Sea towards Byzantium (Shepard 2017).

Lastly, Magyar artefacts dated to the mid-tenth century have been found near the Dniester River at two sites (one a stronghold). A new hypothesis connected to these complexes adds to the history of the Magyars and the southern campaigns of the Rus'. Archaeologists argue that these Magyar find complexes imply authority over the territory, meaning that even after moving to the Carpathians the Magyars continued to rule in the East as far as the Dniester, at least until the mid-tenth century. This would be logical because the centre of the polity lay in the Upper Tisza region of the Carpathian Basin and stretched approximately the same distance to west and east (Türk 2016; Langó 2017, 79–85). Rus' campaigns trying to reach Byzantium by travelling along the Dnieper and the western shore of the Black Sea therefore faced a Magyar power centre along the Dniester. As allies of Sviatoslav, the Magyars (their Dniester branch at least) may sometimes have been the 'horsemen' of the PVL.

Finally, a specific phenomenon of traversing steppe territory is related to terrestrial crossing. Land routes presented even more danger for Scandinavians and Rus' than water routes, as they could not withdraw to the water to prevent attacks. Contemporaries duly noted this. Mas'ūdī relates an illuminating example in his history of the raid of 913 CE. After being defeated in battle by Muslim subjects of the Khazars, the Rus' fled towards the Volga on ships. Some of the survivors left the ships behind and continued on land routes, but they were hunted down by the Muslim Volga Bulghars and the Burtas', who controlled the Volga route north of the Khazar nuclear area (Maçoudi 1863, 23; Lunde and Stone 2012, 146). The Burtas' were not interested in religious retaliation against the Rus' (as were the Muslims of Itil and Bulgar), thus their bloodthirstiness towards the Rus' is better explained by steppe attitudes protective of their territory. Simple greed could also have played a part. Although the fleeing Rus' left behind their ships, presumably some of the cargo and previously plundered riches were taken by the fugitives, as in similar situations in 943 and 972 CE (Margoliouth 1921, 73; Cross and Sherbowitz-Wetzor 1953, 90; Likhachev 1996, 35).

I suggest that the Burtas' shared the attitude that considered any vessel (and its cargo) that drifted ashore on their territory as their property. This mode of thinking was explicitly expressed in the fifteenth century by Afanasy Nikitin, a merchant from Tver. He describes vividly how Tartars and Kaytaks impounded such ships (Wielhorsky 1857, 5–6). Ibn Ḥawqal, describing a similar situation in which a nomadic Oghuz group broke off from the main Oghuz tribal union and settled on an island in the Caspian, warns sailors to avoid a shipwreck on the island because "it is not possible to salvage anything due to the Turks, who seize it; they take everything which is in them" (Kramers 1939, 389; translation by István Lánczky). The behaviour of the Pechenegs escorting the Rus' ship caravan all the way along the Black Sea coast echoes this; that is probably why the Rus' had to disembark and assist the crews of drifting vessels (Constantine Porphyrogenitus 1967, 62–63). Terrestrial routes did not cease to be perilous even later; Adam of Bremen noted in 1070 CE that the Swedes preferred to sail to Greece rather than use land routes hindered by "barbarian nations" (*barbarae gentes*) (Schmeidler 1917, 242).

The problems of traversing steppe territories arose because nomads vigilantly guarded their territories and interests. The continuous references in contemporary and later sources to the perils of such a journey (sometimes appearing only as general references to 'barbarians') derived from the nomads' aggressive attitude, as tribes fiercely defended their livestock and pasture. The steppe people had various means of monitoring their areas. Establishing fortified watchposts, as the Khazars did, was effective on frequently travelled river and land routes. Neighbouring nomads on the Black Sea steppes – the Magyars and Pechenegs – probably had different ways of identifying potential threats. The territory between Kiev and the Black Sea steppes included a few days' march through a no-man's land that served as a frontier zone between the Rus' and the nomads. Bruno of Querfurt, a missionary headed from Kiev to the lands of the Pechenegs, described it in a letter in 1008 CE. He states that after leaving the border of the Rus' ruler (*senior Ruzem*) they met no one for two days in Pecheneg territory, but were confronted on the third day (Karwasińska 1973, 99). Gardīzī also informs his readers that between the country of the Pechenegs and the Saqlābs there is no "cut highway", and the journey takes ten days (Martinez 1982, 163). No hostile force could get through this vast flat landscape unnoticed, and, as the examples of both Cyril and Bruno illustrate, even a small group was easily spotted by patrols. Predictable operations, such as the annual Rus' trade journeys travelling from Kiev to Constantinople, were even more vulnerable. Pecheneg ambushes struck at the most vulnerable phase of the expedition, when cargoes, slaves and boats were all ashore, which prevented the Rus' from withdrawing easily to the river.

Thus, terrestrial and river routes in nomadic areas could only be used if the steppe dwellers were bought off. Unannounced expeditions in their pastures provoked aggression, which resulted in short-term financial gain from looting the Rus' in passage. The only strategy for managing this situation was to promise a later share, either an agreed-upon sum to be paid later or by joining forces with the nomads, who would then acquire their share during a campaign. Immediate payment for safe passage was also possible, as nomadic polities collected fees at border control points (see Chapter 4). The Rus', in the minority compared to the tribes, had to sacrifice profit or else risk their physical well-being in order to cross the steppes.

## Small-scale raids

The first scenario presented earlier was a source of tension between the Scandinavian Rus' and nomads but was not violence deliberately directed against the other's territories. Another level of conflict between them was manifested in small-scale raids aiming to take prisoners and livestock as well as riches. The history of Inner Asian nomadism demonstrates that in times of insecure commerce, nomads took needed goods by force from sedentary neighbours (Khazanov 1994, 222–27). Likewise, the Vikings were well known for raiding and enslaving in Western Europe, and the evidence from eastern lands corroborates that their counterparts to the east were no less eager to exploit local communities, most notably the Slavs and Finno-Ugric people of the forest belt (de Goeje 1889, 154; de Goeje 1892, 145; Cross and Sherbowitz-Wetzor 1953, 59–61, 71, 78, 81, 84; Constantine Porphyrogenitus 1967, 60–63; Likhachev 1996, 12–14, 21, 23, 27–28, 31; Göckenjan and Zimonyi 2011, 81–82, 180, 234; Lunde and Stone 2012, 112, 126; Montgomery 2014, 242–43). The custom of feuding, prevalent in both nomadic and Scandinavian societies, would also have played a part in frequent confrontations.

The intensity and frequency of these raids between the Scandinavian Rus' and neighbouring steppe people is hard to measure. Reports are sparse and taciturn on the scale of the operations. Also, they supply no numbers. Gardīzī, for instance, briefly notes that the Magyars "go [forth] on raids against the Saqlābs and Rus'. They bring back slave[s] (or captive[s] *barde*) thence, take them to the Byzantine [country] and sell them" (Martinez 1982, 161–62). Although this account was written in the eleventh century, when the Magyars had settled in the Carpathian Basin and were no longer nomadic, the locations and lifestyle described in the text suggest that the account refers to events of the ninth century. This interpretation is plausible since Gardīzī was building on the earlier tradition of Jayhānī, whose work (as noted) is lost (Zimonyi 2016, 19–20, 309–15). According to another source describing this same practice, the Magyars led their Slavic slaves to the Byzantine market of Kerch in the Crimea (de Goeje 1892, 142–43; Lunde and Stone 2012, 121). It is noteworthy that Gardīzī's text differentiates the Rus' from the *Ṣaqāliba* (rendered here as *Saqlābs*), although both terms were likely used in the period more inclusively than as pure ethnic markers for Scandinavians and Slavs (cf. Guichard and Meouak 1995; Mishin 1999; Ayalon 1999, 349–52), in this context they must refer to people from both ethnic groups. We can be quite sure that Gardīzī's statement (or Jayhānī's, on whom he built his own account) referred to Scandinavian captives as well.

It is, however, more difficult to confirm the statement's validity. Gardīzī was following earlier accounts, and the control source, ibn Rusta in his *Kitāb al-A'lāk an-Nafīsa*, mentions only Slav captives as victims of the Magyar raids during the ninth century. Although Gardīzī is probably correct in adding the Rus' as potential targets of nomadic raids (cf. Minorsky 1942, 35; Zimonyi 2016, 309–15), it is debatable whether Scandinavians had already appeared in the Middle Dnieper area in the ninth century when these raids are supposed to have taken place (Franklin and Shepard 1996, 98–109).

The anonymous late tenth-century Persian world geography, the *Ḥudūd al-'Ālam*, is similarly generalizing, stating that the Magyars border the Rus' on the west and north and go on raids against their neighbours, from which they always return victorious (Bosworth 1982, 101). Given the complicated mapping and orientation of the source's anonymous author, it has recently been suggested that this passage refers to two Magyar communities of the tenth century, one in the Carpathian Basin and another that had stayed near the Ural Mountains after the Magyar migrations began (Sudár 2019). This suggests that the Rus' were frequently engaged in war on all fronts, but how threatening these incursions might have been is untold. Understanding the results of these encounters is further blurred because the *Ḥudūd* reports the same about the Rus': they wage war on their neighbours and always come out victorious (Bosworth 1982, 159).

The same is true for Pecheneg raids, although these may seem more recurrent because the period is better documented. Constantine notes to his son that the Pechenegs should be used by the Byzantines to police the territories north of the empire, especially to check on the Rus':

> The Pechenegs . . . often, when the two are not at peace with one another, raid Russia, and do her considerable harm and outrage. . . . Moreover, the Russians are quite unable to set out for wars beyond their borders unless they are at peace with the Pechenegs, because while they are away from their homes, these may come upon them and destroy and outrage their property.
> (Constantine Porphyrogenitus 1967, 48–51)

Constantine warned repeatedly of the Pecheneg danger to the Rus' (Constantine Porphyrogenitus 1967, 52–53). No doubt these small-scale forays were irritating, but how serious a threat they posed is hard to determine. The only image conveying the seriousness of such attacks is presented in the PVL for the year 968 CE. While Sviatoslav was away on campaign in Bulgaria, a Pecheneg force allegedly surrounded Kiev with an "innumerable multitude". The Rus' under siege had problems in getting help, but a local commander, whom the Pechenegs took to be the prince himself, routed the nomads. The fact that the news of Sviatoslav's return was enough to deter the Pechenegs suggests that this was not a formidable army. Sviatoslav is also said to have driven them back to the steppe with no difficulty (Cross and Sherbowitz-Wetzor 1953, 85–86; Likhachev 1996, 31–32). This story, however, is unconfirmed by contemporary evidence and clearly means to glorify the image of the prince. The hyperbole in the representation of the event clearly aims to downplay the danger the Pechenegs posed to the Rus' hinterlands. The reality, that the Rus' hinterlands were vulnerable to Pecheneg threats, is supported by both Constantine's warnings and later events (such as Sviatoslav's own death) but was perhaps more mundane than what is reported in this story.

In addition, it is possible that many of these occasional Magyar and Pecheneg raiding parties went unrecorded, thus we might underestimate the frequency of such attacks. The PVL frequently reports that Vladimir, the later grand prince, had conflicts with the Pechenegs in 980, 988, 992, 996, 997 and 1015 CE (Cross and Sherbowitz-Wetzor 1953, 93, 119–24; Likhachev 1996, 37, 54–58). Gaps between raids might be explained by the complete lack of recorded events in the chronicle between the years 998 and 1013 CE, and this might also hold true for earlier events. Nothing is recorded between the two Rus'–Pecheneg conflicts of

915 and 920 CE, and data for the events between 920 and 941 CE cover only two years (929 and 934 CE), both of which were taken from a Byzantine source (Font 2015; see also the introduction in Cross and Sherbowitz-Wetzor 1953, 30–35). Perhaps the peace the Rus' concluded with the Pechenegs in 915 CE and presumably again in 920 CE, lasted for five years and more than two decades respectively. The relationship between the Rus' and the Pechenegs remains hypothetical even if the events are arranged in a logical sequence from hostile (915 and 920 CE) to neutral (941 CE) to, finally, alliance (944 CE). The gaps in the chronicle compilers' knowledge make this a hypothetical argument. The only certainty seems to be that Pecheneg raids occurred frequently.

In contrast, it is striking that only a few dubious records exist of Rus' offensive raids against steppe people. One exception is the entry for the year 920 CE in the PVL, which states that *knyaz* Igor (otherwise known for his expansive politics) "voevashe na pechengi" (Likhachev 1996, 22) "waged war against the Pechenegs" (Cross and Sherbowitz-Wetzor 1953, 71). The verb *voevat'*, meaning "lead a war, fight" (Vasmer 1953, 213) does not indicate who started the conflict, but many times the PVL uses this verb to signify the attackers in campaigns. This taciturn note also illustrates a lack of knowledge on the scale of these conflicts and probably places Igor's actions among the exceptions. The later Kievan Rus' had mainly a defensive policy towards the steppe, best reflected in Vladimir's building of strongholds and the so-called Snake rampart around Kiev (Franklin and Shepard 1996, 169–73). The only other reference I found to the Rus' raiding steppe territories was noted by the thirteenth-century Dimashqī, who built on previous intelligence: "They have islands in the Mānīṭaṣ Sea, which they inhabit; and they have warships (*marākib ḥarbiyya*), on which they wage war against the Khazars" (Mehren 1866, 262; translation by István Lánczky). One may wonder about the scale and effectiveness of these raids on 'warships' from the small islands of the Azov Sea.

Small-scale raids led by nomads against the Rus' seem to have been a recurring feature of encounters between the two groups. The descriptions in the sources, however, are weak, either taciturn and unspecific about numbers, dates or the exact scenarios of the incidents, or dubious due to later editing. Some of the authors, of course, should be excused as the events happened far from their own areas of primary interest.

Only modest conclusions can be drawn from these accounts. The nomads posed an imminent danger of disrupting the Rus' hinterlands but not the occupation of land. The main goal was probably taking slaves from vulnerable parts of the sedentary Rus' population. Most slave-taking raids were launched while the Rus' were away from their headquarters, and there seems to have been no other source of conflict. Another likely inference is that Byzantine politics encouraged the nomads to act against the Rus'; this was the political counsel Constantine offered to his son (Constantine Porphyrogenitus 1967, 50–51, 56–57, 66–67). The losses suffered during these small-scale raids are impossible to estimate apart from Constantine's brief comment on the "considerable outrage" they caused. Destruction, if indeed serious, could work as a political tool to spur the Rus' to withdraw when they were out on campaign. The core of the account of a Pecheneg raid against

Kiev in 968 CE might look sensible in spite of the literary representation of the actual events in the PVL.

Another conclusion concerns the main adversaries in Scandinavian Rus'–nomadic hostilities. The sources do not refer to the Khazars regarding this particular type of conflict. The only reference that fits this pattern of raids somewhat is Khagan Joseph's words in the tenth century (quoted earlier), remarking that he constantly waged war with the Rus' and could not let them rest for a single hour because if they got through the Khazar blockade they would ravage the Muslim lands beyond. This, however, seems to describe border skirmishes that were preventive or defensive and does not seem to refer to Khazar raids on the Rus'. The lack of references to Khazar raids is surprising because their bellicosity was part of their way of life; ibn Rusta states that the custom of the Khazar nomadic elite, led personally by their king, the *īshā*, was to go on annual raids against the neighbouring Pechenegs (de Goeje 1892, 140; Lunde and Stone 2012, 117). Geographical distance does not explain the lack of Khazar raids reported against the Rus' because the Pechenegs also lived a ten-day march away from the Khazars in the ninth century who had to cross unpleasant marches and forests to reach them (de Goeje 1892, 139; Lunde and Stone 2012, 116). Similarly, Khazar small-scale raids against the Rus' are not mentioned in the tenth century.

The main adversaries of the Rus' in the tenth century were eminently the Pechenegs. The dilemma, however, is whether these recurrent raids reflect a historical reality or arise from the nature of source preservation. The tenth century is admittedly better documented than earlier; information on the 'nomadic peril' surpasses the evidence from the ninth century. Nevertheless, similar to Constantine's hint about the constant Pecheneg danger, the Magyar raids of the ninth century also seem to have been frequent, perhaps annual, expeditions. Jayhānī suggests their frequency; he clearly means that this is the Magyar's usual way of living and one of the most important parts of their economy. There is no way to decide conclusively, but the next sub-chapters will raise the issue of periodic halts among these fairly regular nomadic raids. Surprisingly, peace between the Scandinavian Rus' and the Black Sea nomads was as common as minor clashes.

Furthermore, there are relatively few references to Scandinavian Rus' raids on nomadic territory, which cannot be explained by the nature of the sources because various accounts describe Rus' expeditions against other territories (mainly the caliphates and Byzantium). It could be claimed that only the victims of these raids felt the need, and had written culture, to record these attacks while nomads, having little or no written culture, simply did/could not document them. The very same sources that record nomad raids on the Rus', however, do not mention any assaults, or even retaliatory actions, by the latter. I think this difference represents the reality, which will be explored further later.

## Major conflicts

Major campaigns were different than raids because they were large-scale operations aimed at acquiring abundant booty, sometimes even to take the territory occupied by the other party. Nomads often preferred not to conquer other states or territories permanently, as it was more productive to tax sedentary populations from time to time to ensure the flow of prestige items on a regular basis (Khazanov 1994, 222–27). In addition, occupying pastures was advantageous, but the Rus' were largely situated in the forest belt, a territory unsuitable for a herding way of life. This may partly explain why the Rus' undertook major campaigns, in contrast to the small-scale raids the nomads launched against the Rus'.

The expansion of the Scandinavians began immediately after they moved south along the Dnieper. The PVL wants us to believe that Kiev at the time was under Khazar suzerainty and that the tribe of the Polynians inhabiting the area were their subjects. Scandinavians, led by Oleg, started to take authority over the eastern Slavic tribes of the region, many of whom, such as the Severians and the Radmichians, paid taxes to the Khazars (Cross and Sherbowitz-Wetzor 1953, 61; Likhachev 1996, 14). These tribes allegedly surrendered to Oleg in 884 and 885 CE, after which subjugations ceased until 964 CE, when Sviatoslav conquered the Vjatichians, the last of the forest tribes still under Khazar vassals (Cross and Sherbowitz-Wetzor 1953, 84; Likhachev 1996, 31). The Scandinavian subjugation of these tribes would automatically have entailed a political conflict with the Khazars, but there is no way to verify such events, and it is further suspect that Constantine does not mention two of the largest Slavic tribes, the Slovenes and the Polynians (the latter allegedly subjects of the Khazars). Later chroniclers' reconstructions of ninth-century geography assigned ethnic or tribal names largely based on later knowledge of the dialectical and political differences in the Rus'ian lands (Tolochko 2008). In addition to such justified reservations, it is hard to imagine that such expansion would not have provoked (re)action from the Khazar side, but there are no such mentions. This greatly discredits the PVL's narrative and raises the question of the factuality of Rus'–Khazar conflicts flaring up due to the subjugation of East Slavic groups.

Whether the occupation of Kiev might have entailed Magyar–Scandinavian hostilities is similarly dubious. The PVL refers to a place by the name of *Olmin dvor*, the 'castle of Ol'ma', where Prince Oleg buried his rival Askold and where Ol'ma later erected a Christian church (Cross and Sherbowitz-Wetzor 1953, 61; Likhachev 1996, 14). This has generated much scholarly debate. Some identify the Slavic name Ol'ma with the Hungarian Álmos, the leader of the Magyar tribes at the time, suggesting that Kiev was in fact a Magyar centre in the mid-ninth century, having developed from a previous community that the Khazars had established there as tax collectors (Vernadsky 1959, 101; Soloviev 1960; Franklin and Shepard 1996, 96–97; Fodor 2007). Others consider the name completely Slavic (Kristó and H. Tóth 1996) or even Khazarian (Bartha 1988, 364–65). Transliterating the name Álmos into Ol'ma is doubtful, making a Magyar presence in Kiev dubious at that time (Komar 2018, 23–26).

Sviatoslav's reign is more safely reconstructed, and it marks a difference – greater expansion – in Rus' politics (Franklin and Shepard 1996, 139–51). His subjugation of the Vjatichians was probably part of his plan to take over the lucrative Volga trade route. Simultaneously with the weakening of the Khazars from the tenth century, the Rus' gained considerable strength. The qualities of Rus'–steppe war relations changed compared to earlier periods that had been characterized mostly by minor conflicts. One example can illustrate the change in the scale of Rus' endeavours: the prince waged war against his neighbours within an 8,000 kilometre orbit reaching from the Lower Danube to the Upper Volga (Rybakov 1982, 374–77). As quoted previously, in 965/969 CE Sviatoslav attacked both the Volga Bulghar capital (Bulgar) and the main Khazar headquarters (Kramers 1939, 393–94; Cross and Sherbowitz-Wetzor 1953, 84; Likhachev 1996, 31; Lunde and Stone 2012, 175, 178). This campaign cannot be categorized as a series of simple raids, as is attested by Sviatoslav's cruelty to the Khazars. It was not only Sviatoslav's ambitions, however, that finally disrupted the *status quo* and led to the collapse of the Khazar Khaganate. Between 965 and 969 CE, Rus', Turks, Shirwanians and Khorezmians attacked Khazaria, and Khazar diplomacy failed on all fronts across a wide political arena (Konovalova 2000).

Besides Sviatoslav's aggressive entry, there were only two other Rus' campaigns against steppe abodes; both ended with modest results that cannot be compared to the havoc caused by Sviatoslav in either *casus belli* or outcome. The first attack is hard to date precisely. It was preserved in the Hebrew Schechter letter as part of the Jewish-Khazar correspondence of the 950s–960s CE. According to the complaints of the anonymous Khazar-Jewish writer, one night (on an imprecise date) a Rus' fleet made a surprise attack on the Khazar town of Samkarch, presumably Tmutarakan, on the Black Sea coast. Upon hearing of the attack, the Khazars launched a counter-offensive and after four months of hard fighting were victorious due to the leadership of their commander, Petah (Golb and Pritsak 1982, 114–19). What is telling is the motivation behind the attack. According to the correspondence, the Byzantines urged the Rus' to attack the Khazars, who, in the peace agreements, obliged the Rus' to attack the Byzantines. The source tells how the Rus' fleet suffered defeat from Byzantine Greek fire and that their leader, a certain (and still not conclusively identified) *HLGW*, perished later somewhere in Persia (Golb and Pritsak 1982, 118–19). Although the chronology of the event is hard to establish, most scholars (including myself) believe the raid took place in 941 CE (for discussion, see Zuckerman 1995).

The last attack, in 985 CE, was led by Vladimir, from whose reign onwards the PVL is more trustworthy:

> Accompanied by his uncle, Dobrȳnya, Vladimir set out by boat to attack the Bulgars. He also brought Torks overland on horseback, and conquered the Bulgars. Dobrȳnya remarked to Vladimir: 'I have seen the prisoners, who all wear boots. They will not pay us tribute. Let us rather look for foes with bast shoes.' So Vladimir made peace with the Bulgars, and they confirmed it by oath.
>
> (Cross and Sherbowitz-Wetzor 1953, 96; original: Likhachev 1996, 39)[2]

Although victorious, Vladimir had no intention to occupy Volga Bulgharia permanently, which shows again that besides Sviatoslav's campaigns no major politically motivated warfare took place between steppe groups and the Rus'.

The only instance when perhaps a larger campaign was led by steppe people against the Rus' was caused by a mass migration and not driven by the intent of conquest or to acquire large booty. This event was part of the Magyar 'land-taking' (settlement) in the Carpathian Basin. The migrating Magyar tribes on their way to the Carpathian Basin partially touched Rus' territory. Erroneously recorded in the PVL as taking place in 898 CE (Cross and Sherbowitz-Wetzor 1953, 62; Likhachev 1996, 15), this occurred in 895 CE (Kristó and H. Tóth 1996), and the description of the encounter includes many fictional details. It is recorded in the chronicle with the sole comment that Magyars passed Kiev over the hill named after them (*Ugorskoye*) and pitched camp nearby (Cross and Sherbowitz-Wetzor 1953, 62; Likhachev 1996, 15). In contrast, in his *Gesta Hungarorum*, Anonymus (a mysterious scribe writing under the name *P. dictus magister*, the thirteenth-century Hungarian source for the event) reports that in a Hungarian attempt to conquer all of Rus' (*Rutenorum*), serious fighting broke out in Kiev that ended with the ultimate victory of the united Magyar tribes, who then forced the *Ruthenes* to pay tribute and send their sons as hostages (Bak and Rady 2010, 20–27). It is unclear whether the battle was left out of the PVL to spare the reputation of the Rus' or included in the *Gesta Hungarorum* to provide a powerful account of the Hungarian forebears. A later Hungarian scribe, Simon of Kéza, building partly on Anonymus's *Gesta* and other earlier sources, simply notes that the Magyars marched past Kiev, without mentioning any warlike activities (Veszprémy and Schaer 1999, 79). Just as in the case of Gardīzī's account, the report of Scandinavian subjects taken captive by the Magyars can only be accepted as historical truth if the PVL's chronology is accurate for ninth-century events. This would mean that Magyar raids affected Askold and Dir, who lived in Kiev with their troops in the 860s CE, and Oleg in 882 CE (Cross and Sherbowitz-Wetzor 1953, 60–61; Likhachev 1996, 13–14).

Reconstructing major conflicts between the Scandinavian Rus' and their steppe neighbours suffers from the same problems as understanding the small-scale raids. Contemporary sources for larger conflicts are few, and the later records are untrustworthy. Among these, only a handful of operations preserved in contemporary accounts can be viewed as historically accurate. It should be noted, however, that large operations did not escape the notice of contemporaries, and the lack of accounts therefore likely mirrors the frequency of events.

Thus, a picture emerges that, contrary to rare small-scale Rus' raids to the south, steppe people seldom conducted major campaigns towards the northern regions and all such instances were of limited intent. The only steppe campaign (mentioned previously) was the retaliatory attack the Khazars launched for the sack of Tmutarakan, and perhaps also the mass migration of the Magyars, which may have caused tensions.

The Rus' occasionally initiated larger conflicts, however, but played by the rules of limited violence on both sides. This is best illustrated by the 'Tmutarakan conflict' between the Rus' and the Khazars depicted in the Jewish-Khazar correspondence. The modest aim of this mid-tenth-century incident, merely robbing a seaport unexpectedly and returning home with the booty, is intriguing.

The Khazars, despite the account's insistence on a four-month campaigning season, actually concluded peace with the Rus' immediately once all the plundered riches were returned. Vladimir's attack on the Volga Bulghars in 985 CE was similar in scale and intent; realizing that the people he looted were in fact poor, Vladimir immediately concluded peace with them. These conflicts can only be regarded as 'major' since they presumably involved larger forces, more complex preparation, and more expected booty than small-scale raids. Sviatoslav's reign, however, saw a marked contrast. He was a ruler of previously unprecedented ambition, acting like certain nomad chiefs of history who aimed to conquer on horseback much more territory than they could actually control effectively. Had it not ended the Khazar rule on the steppe, it would probably be regarded as an anomaly in the general practices of the era; Vladimir's later modest attack on the Bulghars returned to the norm. All of this implies that fighting on a large scale was of no interest to either the nomads or the Rus'.

## The frequency of wars

Looking at the wider picture of Scandinavian Rus'–nomadic conflicts requires care in sorting armed incidents according to their frequency (for a relative chronology of these events, see Table 3.1). These events can be arranged differently by distinguishing between 'major campaigns' and 'small-scale raids', as the categories may overlap (Halsall 2003, 15–16). I argue that the three main types of conflict between the steppe people and Scandinavian Rus' presented earlier were a sequence that actually mirrors the frequency of these historical events. Traversing steppe territory is likely to have been by far the most widespread source of conflict, as Rus' commercial operations were conducted on a regular basis with steppe settlements and also beyond, starting in June and returning by November (Cross and Sherbowitz-Wetzor 1953, 76; Constantine Porphyrogenitus 1967, 59–63; Likhachev 1996, 25; see also: Table 3.2). How often the nomads raided the Rus' or *vice versa* is difficult to judge due to presumably unrecorded minor skirmishes in frontier zones and hiatuses in the sources. Major campaigns, however, rarely went unnoticed by contemporaries, and the available data suggest that these were the least common form of conflict.

Most of the information on the chronology of conflict episodes comes from the PVL, which is hardly to be trusted except for recording the major attacks against Byzantium, which are aligned with the subsequent peace treaties. Nevertheless, upon examining Rus'–nomadic conflicts numerically, marked differences stand out concerning each steppe tribe's relationship with the Rus' and the commonality of their strife (Table 3.3). In terms of intensity, the Volga Bulghar conflicts stand out clearly as only one major campaign (985 CE), and no raids or hostile traversing are known. The evidence is at best circumstantial even for smaller conflicts. For instance, the Volga Bulghars and Rus' were both interested in obtaining furs from the Ves', the inhabitants of Wisu, a region north of Bulgar (Cross and Sherbowitz-Wetzor 1953, 55; Likhachev 1996, 10; Montgomery 2014, 232–33). There may have been minor clashes for resources sought by both parties, indicated by an

*Table 3.1* Chronology of Rus'–nomad wars

| *Date* | *Event* |
|---|---|
| 839 | Magyars blocking the way of Rus' envoys* |
| 882* | Conquering the Polynians, Rus' taking of Kiev where the Magyars were agents of the Khazars* |
| 882–95* | The Magyars raid the Slavs and the Rus' regularly |
| 884* | Conquering the Severians, who are Khazar tributaries |
| 885* | Conquering the Radmichians, who are Khazar tributaries |
| 895 | Magyar attack on Kiev* |
| 900–* | Uralian Magyar raids against the Rus' |
| 913 | Caspian raid |
| 915 (or 917) | First Pecheneg raid against the Rus' |
| 920 | Igor is at war with the Pechenegs |
| 941* | Attack on Tmutarakan |
| 950–* | Rus' raids from the Azov Sea against the Khazars |
| 950– | Pecheneg ambushes along the Dnieper waterway |
| 964 | Conquering the Vjatichians, who are Khazar tributaries |
| 965/969 | Destroying the Khazar Khaganate |
| 968 | Pecheneg attack on Kiev |
| 972 | Killing of Sviatoslav by the Pechenegs |
| 980 | Pecheneg attack |
| 985 | Vladimir attacks the Volga Bulghars |
| 988 | Vladimir is in constant war with the Pechenegs |
| 992 | Vladimir faces a Pecheneg raiding party upon his return from campaign |
| 996 | The Pechenegs defeat Vladimir's small force at Vasil'evo |
| 997 | The Pechenegs unsuccessfully besiege Belgorod in Vladimir's absence |
| 1015 | Pecheneg attack during Vladimir's illness |

* = questionable

*Table 3.2* Traversing nomad territory

| *Territory* | *Date* |
|---|---|
| Magyar | 839*, 860 |
| Khazar | 864–84, 911*, 912*, 913, 943 |
| Pecheneg | 907*, 941, 944, 968, 972, 1043* |

* = questionable

analogous example of Bulghar honey gatherers being ambushed in the woods by unnamed enemies (Montgomery 2014, 232–33).

The Rus'–Khazar hostilities seem severe, but one gets the impression that the seriousness was judged by the final outcome: increasing Rus' threats in the second half of the tenth century and the destruction of Khazaria. In earlier Russian scholarship, Khazaria was depicted as an eternal enemy of the Kievan Rus', a foe that hindered the growth of the Old Russian state throughout its history (Grekov, Cherepnin, and Pashuto 1953, 86–87; Artamonov 1962, 365–84; Pashuto 1968, 91–95; Rybakov 1982, 257–58; Tolochko 1987, 27–28; Sverdlov 2003, 103).

*Table 3.3* Rus'–nomadic conflicts by tribe

| | *Recorded conflicts with the Rus'* |
|---|---|
| Volga Bulghars | 985 |
| Khazars | 882–85, 913, 941, 964–65 |
| Magyars | 895 |
| Pechenegs | 915/917, 920, 972, 980, 988, 992, 996, 997, 1015 |

Examined in a wider perspective, a different picture emerges in which the exchange of armed blows between the Rus' and Khazars is rarely documented before Sviatoslav's grandiose political plans. Rivalry with the Khazars over the subjugation of some Eastern Slavic tribes might indeed have begun from the beginnings of Rus' settlement in the south (882–85 CE), but the evidence is not secure. Only a single Rus' raid in 913 CE incited hostilities, not directly with the Khazars, but with their Muslim subjects. This raid was actually conducted with the approval of the khagan(!), proving that it was not a deliberate conflict between the two parties. Finally, the Rus' only came to direct blows with the Khazars in 941 CE, and even this incident is better explained by the original Byzantine–Khazar rivalry in which the Greeks, as usual, played potential enemies against each other. All of this does not seem to suggest that the Khazars and Rus' were 'eternal enemies', but quite the contrary; their relations seem calm enough to enable them to conduct mutually beneficial lucrative commercial and piratical operations for a century. Re-evaluation of the numismatic evidence found in Russia even shows a connection between the cessation of Samanid dirhams flowing west in the mid-tenth century and Sviatoslav's aim of taking over Khazar trade. The hunger for silver might have prompted Sviatoslav to correct the trade deficit by plundering. A future hope of reopening the flow of precious metals by taking over the Khazar trade network might have been an element in his final attack (Kuleshov 2021, 165–66; cf. Kovalev n.d., 23–25).

Rus'–Magyar conflicts cannot be evaluated numerically since the two groups did not share a geopolitical space for long. Nevertheless, the more complex Rus' undertakings, such as the raid and occupation of Kiev in 860 CE, did not trigger any Magyar counterstrikes. This implies a well-coordinated relationship that is best seen in contrast to Rus'–Pecheneg affairs. The Magyars had a tribal federation under centralized leadership from the mid-ninth century, when the unity of the tribes was ritually sanctified and sealed by a blood oath (although the ritual itself might have been based on ancient *topoi*) (Bak and Rady 2010, 16–17). Although maintaining some independence even later, such as when launching raids independently towards Western Europe from the Carpathian Basin, the elite leaders submitted to a central rulership; first to the loose voivodeship of Levedi (who was *primus inter pares*) and then to the princes Árpád or Álmos (Constantine Porphyrogenitus 1967, 170–73; Szabados 2019, 19–22). A dual kingship system among the Magyars, deduced from accounts of Muslim informants (de Goeje 1892, 142; Martinez 1982, 159–60; Lunde and Stone 2012, 122), is somewhat controversial but does not impede categorizing the political structure as centralized. Thus, it is possible that making agreements with the Magyar tribes of the Pontic steppe was a relatively safe and trustworthy business compared to concluding agreements with the Pechenegs.

In contrast to the Magyars, the Pecheneg socio-political system was not centralized. Their society in the tenth century seems to have been based on unequal power relations among eight tribes. No centralized ruler or institution is noted within their tribal federation, with the exception of some 'nobles' acting *primus inter pares* during regional assemblies (Paroń 2021, 132–60). Although the PVL labels the Pecheneg chief, *Knyaz*' Kurya, (Cross and Sherbowitz-Wetzor 1953, 90; Likhachev 1996, 35), one of Constantine's comments makes it unequivocal that each Pecheneg tribe had a prince or ruler, an *archon* in Greek (Constantine Porphyrogenitus 1967, 166). Thus, the Pecheneg polity comes close to what has been termed a "headless state" (Sneath 2007), an acephalous tribal conglomeration in which members were capable of both united action and independent manoeuvers. In the sources, the Pechenegs, considered treacherous, were always required to send hostages when making agreements (Cross and Sherbowitz-Wetzor 1953, 72, 123; Constantine Porphyrogenitus 1967, 48–49, 54–57; Likhachev 1996, 23, 57). It seems that the Pecheneg nomads were less predictable or not all of their tribes were willing to share the actual political decision of the others. This is illustrated by Sviatoslav's last campaign (noted previously), where they initially supported him, but later deserted and finally assassinated him. In this light, it is remarkable that peace reigned between the Rus' and the Pechenegs for long periods, perhaps even decades.

## Power relations

Until they began to employ extensive cavalry in Sviatoslav's times, the Rus' were on the defensive and even later suffered heavy blows from nomadic incursions. Armed clashes between the Scandinavian Rus' and the people of the steppe, although they definitely occurred, were not endemic. The main areas of tension were connected to short-term commercial interests that seldom led to large-scale conflicts. Nevertheless, infrequency of wars should be examined further, especially the lack of Scandinavian or Rus' raids on nomads. The reasoning that steppe territories offered no wealth for plunder is not a sufficient explanation; nomads in general, especially the steppe societies, were not necessarily poor. In addition to describing the most prosperous commercial hubs in the region, Itil and Bulgar, individual comments by medieval authors also emphasize the material wealth of the elites of the steppe dwellers. Ibn Faḍlān, for instance, was amazed at the magnificence of the Volga Bulghar court, first by the size of the king's yurt, which could hold a thousand people, and second by the furnishing of the interior, carpeted with Armenian rugs, and the king's throne, bedecked with Byzantine silk (Montgomery 2014, 228–29). He writes about the Oghuz' that they are poor, but nevertheless some of them own 10,000 horses and 100,000 sheep (Montgomery 2014, 212–13), which suggests that the elite was indeed wealthy. Gardīzī straightforwardly says of the Pechenegs: "These Pechenegs are the possessors of great wealth, for they are possessors of abundant horses and sheep. They have many gold and silver vessels. They have many weapons. They have silver belts" (Martinez 1982, 152). He similarly says of the Magyars that: "their clothes are of brocade and their weapons are made of silver and are goldplated" (Martinez 1982, 162), which is confirmed by the *Ḥudūd*: "They are very rich people but base" (Bosworth 1982, 101). Other examples related to the lucrative steppe commerce, such as paid mercenary service for gold and lavish gifts from Byzantine rulers, have been further enumerated (de Goeje 1892, 143; Constantine Porphyrogenitus 1967, 52–57; Lunde and Stone 2012, 123). Thus, the main riches of the steppe were movable property, quite a suitable target for raiders.

The difference, compared to Western Europe, lies in the fact that the wealth of steppe societies lay with the military elite, who, even had they not been surrounded by a multitude of warriors, could muster forces in a hurry and quickly pursue attackers on horseback. If raiders intended to take livestock, their escape, slowed down by animals, would have been problematic. The Pechenegs persistently followed Rus' ship caravans all the way to the Byzantine border in the hope of ambushing them at fords or capturing their drifting vessels. These Rus' expeditions were not hostile towards the Pechenegs but were simple commercial enterprises. The retaliation a direct raid on a tribal chief's household or a steppe state's town would have called forth must be wondered at; the four-month-long retaliatory campaign of the Khazars for the sacking of Tmutarakan is an example. The organizational principles of nomadic societies ensured that a considerable number of the pastoralist population (and probably the majority of men) were trained to become warriors from early childhood, constantly ready for deployment (Sinor 1981; Irons 2003). 'Hit-and-run' actions on steppe territories were hazardous, greatly contrasting with the ease of robbing un- or poorly defended towns and ecclesiastical sites in Western Europe and escaping quickly on the rivers before the local lords could gather their men. The only exception, recorded by Dimashqī (noted earlier), is revealing (if authentic); from the safety of the Azov Sea islands the Rus' could have raided the Khazar periphery successfully and then withdrawn to the open sea, where the Khazars, having no fleet, could not pursue them.

Another point of comparison is the warlike nature of Eastern adversaries compared to those in the West. Westerners describing the Vikings as the 'scourge of God' because of their merciless and savage nature is nothing new to any scholar of the Viking Age, and similar stories are told about the Rus' (Maçoudi 1863, 21; Photius 1883, 162–73; Mango 1985, 74–110; Margoliouth 1921, 69; Lunde and Stone 2012, 145). Whether this picture painted by outsiders is exaggerated or not, nearly the same brutality is reported about the nomads of the East at the same time, implying that in terms of cruelty Scandinavians and Rus' were as fierce as the steppe dwellers. The shock ibn Faḍlān expresses at the Oghuz' custom of punishing adulterers and thieves by tearing them apart with two tree branches and the Volga Bulghars' chopping them up with axes and putting their limbs on display, are vivid mementos of everyday harsh realities (Montgomery 2014, 202–3, 232–33). Facing nomads, Scandinavians and Rus' confronted enemies that were not so different in mentality.

Lastly, the odds in numbers were not in favour of the Scandinavian Rus'. A comparison between army sizes conveys an idea of the relative power relations in the region, even though the trustworthiness of the historical accounts conveying these numbers is hard to verify except for a few cases when control sources are available. Even then, however, as Guy Halsall notes (2003, 121), no medieval authors "ever went and counted an army", which makes the data questionable. In addition, most of the accounts in sources were not even produced by eyewitnesses of the armed clash or by military men. Medieval authors' tendencies to magnify army numbers are well known, and the information that can be inferred relatively safely from the accounts is far from precise. It only makes it possible to estimate an army's size as 'small' or 'large'; it is most useful to examine the socio-political (and economic) context of the encounters (Halsall 2003, 119–24). In the case of the Rus', data on the sizes of western Viking armies provide useful comparisons.

To make my point that the relative power relation scheme favoured the nomads, I first present the data known about steppe armies in the period. According to István Zimonyi, who collected all possible data from Muslim sources pertaining to steppe armies in the period, the generally emerging picture, even if some data are contradictory or might have been corrupted during copying, is that the nomads' fighting forces numbered "ten thousands", for which the Turkic word was *tumen*. Even the Burtas', just a tribute-paying tribe of the Khazars, could provide 10,000 warriors, according to ibn Rusta. The Magyars were said to be able to mount 20,000, or according to Mas'ūdī, 50,000, warriors. The central unit of the Khazar army consisted of 4,000, and later 7,000, bodyguards, supplemented by 10,000–15,000 Khorezmian mercenaries and some Slavic and Rus' slave warriors. The Khazars could also call for reinforcements from their subject groups: the Burtas', the Alans and the Sarirs; in certain periods the Volga Bulghars; and probably also the Magyars. The size of the Volga Bulghar military forces is not precisely known; the data seem to refer to entire tribal groupings rather than to weapon bearers only. Nevertheless, they probably also had an army of no fewer than 10,000 horsemen based on comparison with neighbouring tribes (Zimonyi 2016, 102–16).

Questions regarding these numbers arise because it is uncertain whether they (suspiciously rounded up by Muslim writers) apply only to arms bearers or to whole tribal groupings. This is especially important in the cases of those who were subject to the Khazars, such as the Burtas' and the Magyars. One favourable aspect of the accounts is their relative conformity in counting steppe military forces in the thousands. Furthermore, as noted earlier, nomadic communities were martial societies in which most of the able-bodied males were trained in warfare. What is generally known about nomadic economic and social organization also suggests that the population was denser than in the forest belt and could quickly be mustered. The political history of these tribes, such as the Khazars' repulse of the Arab advance or the early and mid-tenth-century military incursions of the Magyars into Western Europe, also speaks favourably of the military potential of such societies.

For comparison, according to available evidence, Scandinavian Rus' armies in the period varied from raiding parties of a few ships' crews to tens of thousands of men levied from subordinate Slavic, Baltic and Finnic tribes, supplied by nomadic allies. Scandinavian Rus' warbands enslaving the Slavs and taking their provisions for themselves moved around in "bands of a hundred or two hundred", according to Gardīzī (Martinez 1982, 169). Smaller raiding parties or armies are also mentioned occasionally, such as the 16 ships plundering the Caspian coast, as recorded by ibn Isfandiyār (Isfandiyar 1905, 199), or the 38 ships mentioned in the history of Sharvan and Derbent in 1030 CE (Minorsky 1958, 47). The Caspian Rus' army of 913 CE operated in small military detachments or raiding parties called *sarāyā* (sing. *sarīya*), used in Muslim documents to refer to groups never exceeding a few hundred warriors (Lane 1872, 1356). The Rus' force attacking Bardha'a in 943 CE is not likely to have exceeded a few thousand Rus' (Margoliouth 1921, 67–74).[3] These numbers correspond to the standards of smaller western Viking fleets or warbands (see, for instance, Gillmor 1988; Nelson 1997, 39) and support the veracity of at least some of the contemporary (or near contemporary) accounts mentioning Rus' warband or army sizes.

The sizes of larger Scandinavian Rus' armies, however, seem excessively magnified in a first glance at medieval accounts. What to make of Rus' ship numbers in the PVL, for instance? Askold and Dir led 200 ships against the Byzantines in 866 CE (correctly 860 CE), Oleg 2,000 in 907 CE and Igor 10,000 in 941 CE (Cross and Sherbowitz-Wetzor 1953, 60, 64, 72; Likhachev 1996, 13, 16, 22). The number of ships of the attackers in 860 CE is a rare example confirmed by other sources (Vasiliev 1946, 189). Pertaining to Oleg's time, the chronicler even provides the necessary multiplier to estimate the size of the army: a crew of 40 men per ship (Cross and Sherbowitz-Wetzor 1953, 64; Likhachev 1996, 16). According to this calculation, Oleg was advancing towards Constantinople with 80,000 people. Such a number is so unreliably large that it is impossible to take it at face value. Although there is no way to know what kind of a conglomeration of boats really made up this fleet, Viking ship standards of the period hardly exceeded the norm of 30 people per vessel, and the types of watercraft utilized on Russian waterways were probably even smaller (Stalsberg 2001; cf. Larsson 2011).

Compared to the numbers given for smaller raiding parties earlier, however, the conclusion that this was a large force cannot be questioned. The socio-political situation of Rus'–Byzantine conflicts unequivocally accounts for this. First, the Rus' brought a vast alliance of diverse people under one flag. The army of Oleg, for instance, was said to be levied from all the tribes living within the orbit of the emerging Kievan Rus': "Varangians, Slavs, Chuds, Krivichians, Merians, Polyanians, Severians, Derevlians, Radimichians, Croats, Dulebians, and Tivercians" (Cross and Sherbowitz-Wetzor 1953, 64; Likhachev 1996, 16). Likewise, Igor's "inumerable" fleet "covering the sea" in 944 CE was recruited among "the Varangians, the Rus', the Polyanians, the Slavs, the Krivichians, the Tivercians, and the Pechenegs" before marching on Byzantium "by ship and by horse" (Cross and Sherbowitz-Wetzor 1953, 72; Likhachev 1996, 23). Mas'ūdī reports a similar incident that supports the ability of the Rus' to organize a large force. For the Caspian Rus' raid, he reports a comparably large Rus' army that was launched in 913 CE on 500 ships, each carrying a crew of 100 (Maçoudi 1863,

18; Lunde and Stone 2012, 144). Regardless of the possible carrying capacities, hundreds of ships plundering far and wide on the Caspian Sea coast for months suggests a considerable enterprise, something comparable to the massive attacks on the Byzantine coastline and capital. Although the figures and possibly also the multipliers for ships' crews were exaggerated, I have no reservations about accepting that even if not 80,000 men, armies attacking the Byzantine capital and successfully forcing one of the contemporary superpowers to peace treaties, were huge.

A comparative example from the western Viking territories supports the relative sizes of the Rus' armies and helps explain the socio-political background of assembling powerful forces. New research on the Great Viking Army of the mid-ninth century suggests that the size of this exceptional force has been underestimated previously (Hadley and Richards 2021, 69–71). According to recent archaeological fieldwork on winter camps where the Great Army bivouacked, the camps were even larger than Scandinavian towns of the period. The Torksey camp, for instance, stretched over 55 hectares and could house 4,000–5,000 people, if not more (Hadley and Richards 2021, 109–10). Such a vast force, however, included women, children and slaves and was assembled from all areas of the Viking diaspora, even some territories under Viking threat. This pattern looks quite applicable to Rus' armies levying troops and forging alliances over a wide socio-political arena relatively under control.

Along with this, although the numbers were rounded up and magnified by later medieval authors, I see no reason to dismiss the core of this information. Rus' armies were sometimes exceptionally large. The opponents being threatened were far more powerful than Wessex or Frankia. The fact that militarily advanced societies in command of large fighting units joined together, shows that Scandinavian Rus' leaders were able to amass, mobilize and control huge numbers. The seriousness of these assaults is also demonstrated by the fact that they were commemorated in writing at great length: Patriarch Photius dedicated two sermons to commemorating the devastating Rus' raid in 860 CE, whilst Mas'ūdī devoted multiple pages to the Caspian incursions (Maçoudi 1863, 18–25; Photius 1883, 162–73; Mango 1985, 74–110; Lunde and Stone 2012, 144–46). Prince Sviatoslav's campaigns are further examples that strengthen the point that outsized Rus' armies posed an imminent danger to the empire.

As large as they may have been, however, major Rus' campaigns were rare (in fact, they are all enumerated previously) and always needed large-scale recruitment (the case of Oleg and Igor). With the exception of Sviatoslav's campaign in 965/969 CE against the Khazars and Bulghars, none of the large attacks targeted nomadic abodes. To historians favouring low army numbers in the Early Middle Ages, the figures given earlier on nomadic armies, even if some of them are overstatements, provide a satisfying reason in themselves to question whether Scandinavian and Rus' warbands (or even armies) on their own would have stood a chance against the nomads in open battle. This would also partly explain why there is a suspicious silence in the sources about Rus' small-scale raids directed towards the steppe.

More importantly, in many cases it was the nomads who increased the size of Rus' armies; Skylitzés, for instance, makes it clear that during the Balkan campaigns the enormous Rus' army of Sviatoslav – numbering 308,000 people, according to him – was a joint force of Rus', Magyars and Pechenegs (Thurn 1973, 288). The PVL states that Sviatoslav's own troops numbered 10,000 (Cross and Sherbowitz-Wetzor 1953, 88; Likhachev 1996, 33), which is many fewer than in the Byzantine records, which note from 15,000 to 60,000 troops at different stages of the campaign.[4] Although undoubtedly exaggerated, the main message of Skylitzés is probably correct: nomads were the bulk of the Rus'. The wording of the peace treaty between Sviatoslav and the Byzantines in 971 CE backs this up indirectly. Since the Byzantine–Rus' peace treaties are genuine information copied by the chronicler from Greek originals, no doubt the clause forbidding Sviatoslav to attack with his own Rus' warriors or to hire 'foreign mercenaries' against the empire means that this was viewed as a real danger (Cross and Sherbowitz-Wetzor 1953, 89; Likhachev 1996, 34). The Pecheneg presence in Igor's and Oleg's campaigns probably also provided considerable manpower. As will be seen later, there is reason to suppose that Sviatoslav's military might have owed a great deal to nomadic influence.

The size of Scandinavian warbands became more modest from Vladimir's reign onwards, reflecting the phenomenon that Varangians turn up as foreign mercenaries in the sources and not as integral parts of Rus' society. Mercenary forces of this kind number 500, 600, 800, 1,000 and a few thousand in the sources (Bekker 1839, 478–79; Vigfússon and Unger 1862, 122; Beazley 1914, 1; Cross and Sherbowitz-Wetzor 1953, 131, 138; Likhachev 1996, 62, 67; Kekaumenos n. d., 4–7). These figures are not large at all, although doubts have been expressed about the size of the notorious Varangian 6,000-strong contingent dispatched by Vladimir to Basil II, which later allegedly became the nucleus of the Varangian Guard of Byzantium. Since even later Scandinavian kings were unable to amass such a huge force let alone one that could operate independent of the central power, this number is suspiciously large (Scheel 2015, 91–93). These late tenth- and eleventh-century figures do not help sketch a pattern of power relations because these Scandinavian contingents were part of larger forces, followed 'foreign' commands and did not attack any territories independently.

To sum up, Scandinavian and Rus' raiding parties in the ninth and tenth centuries did not look favourably on steppe destinations. Besides the possible reward, which could not be measured beforehand, neither the geographical situation (escaping unpursued) nor power relations (the military strength of the others) would have supported such a choice. Thousands of horsemen probably seemed to be an insuperable obstacle to defeat on the battlefield. Logic dictated that if the risks were high, the reward should equal them in size. Major campaigns directed towards Byzantium were almost always assisted by nomads. The Muslim colonies on the Caspian shore offered a better target for raids, but major operations here failed. Even though Rus' armies, enlarged with local conscripts, probably outnumbered their western Viking counterparts, the enemies in the east still had the upper hand against them in numbers and military tactics or technologies (examples are the river blockades built by the Khazars, Greek fire utilized by the Byzantine navy, and nomadic cavalry in general that would have been hard to defeat in open combat). It was wiser to maintain peace with the closest neighbours, the steppe-nomads, to follow their rules and try to acquire wealth from beyond the spheres of the steppes.

## Notes

1 Varangians could have served in Byzantine armies against the Pechenegs regularly, although their involvement in these campaigns is based on speculation (Blöndal 1978, 63, 105–06, 127–28, 148–53). The most secure evidence is provided by the poet Einar Skúlason referring to a battle in which the Varangians broke through a Pecheneg wagon fort. Unfortunately, it is not clear which battle the episode refers to; opinions range from 1040 to 1091, 1094, 1114 and even to 1122 CE (for discussion, see: Pintescu 2001). Magyars and Pechenegs fought against the Varangians during Bolesław the Brave's siege of Kiev in 1018 CE (Holtzmann 1935, 530). Yaroslav the Wise had Varangian contingents who faced Pecheneg armies multiple times, as in 1016, 1018, 1019 and 1036 CE, and once some Khazar remnants, who aided Mstislav (Cross and Sherbowitz-Wetzor 1953, 131–37; Likhachev 1996, 62–66).

2 It is not said explicitly in the text which Bulgharia was the target of the expedition, but the presence of the Torks makes it more than likely that it was Volga Bulgharia. The designation 'Tork' refers to the Oghuz' in Russian sources, who pastured around Alania and Khazaria at this time (Constantine Porphyrogenitus 1967, 62–63; see also: Vásáry 1993, 170) and could have hardly escorted the Rus' anywhere else than along the River Volga.

3 According to the account, 700 Rus' were killed in the campaign and 300 more waited for their fleeing comrades on their ships anchored at the Kur River. This means that the Rus' force was larger than 1,000 people. That even 30,000 Muslims were unable to retake the town by siege implies that the Rus' were numerous. Previously, however, Salar Marzuban had dared to attack them with only 5,000 soldiers, which suggests that the Rus' hardly numbered more than a few thousand.

4 Leo the Deacon estimated the Rus' army to be 15,500 strong at Preslav and 60,000 strong at Dorostolon (Diaconus 1828, 134–40, 156–57). Skylitzés gives a similar number for Preslav (16,500), but an unusually high number for Dorostolon: 330,000. This contrasts with the numbers he reported previously: 308,000 for the whole alliance (Thurn 1973, 288–300). For various scholarly reconstructions of the army sizes, see: Hanak 1995, 141–45.

# 4 Trade

Apart from occasional hostilities, peaceful relations between the Scandinavian Rus' and steppe people flourished in the sphere of trade, confirmed by several trustworthy accounts. The ninth-century report of ibn Rusta, for instance, describes the main activity of the Rus' as: "The Rūs raid the Saqāliba, sailing in their ships until they come upon them. They take them captive and sell them in Khazarān and Bulkār [Bulghār]" (de Goeje 1892, 145; Lunde and Stone 2012, 126). The mid-ninth-century ibn Khurradādhbih, however, notes that the Rus' were accustomed to bypass Khazaria to trade in the Islamic ports of the Caspian or even further away in Baghdad (de Goeje 1889, 154; Lunde and Stone 2012, 112). A century later, Prague, one of the central nodes of contemporary commercial traffic, had a market with Rus', Slavs, Muslims, Jews and Turks, the latter referring to the Magyars, who brought goods from the Carpathian Basin (Mishin 1994–95, 186). Each of these three accounts highlights a slightly different aspect of what I call broadly 'Viking–nomadic trade', a commercial network in which Scandinavian, Rus' and steppe actors were in a kind of partnership, mainly along the northern branches of the Silk Roads, often called the 'Fur Road' by analogy (Kovalev 2000–01). The network had three dimensions. First, there were transactions conducted with the closest neighbours, established through mutual or unilateral visits of merchants. As the immediate neighbours of the Rus' were the Volga Bulghars, the Khazars, the Magyars and the Pechenegs, it is no surprise that there was commerce among them. Trading parties, however, also aimed to reach other partners. Contacting them was harder if the road crossed the territory of other communities; the Khazars, for instance, levied a ten percent tithe on the cargoes of passing Rus' ships. The scenarios outlined in the previous chapter also affected the sphere of trade; lucrative Byzantine and Muslim markets and traders could only be reached via the steppe dwellers, either by travelling through with their approval or through closely guarded meetings in steppe territory. The third (and last) hubs where Rus' and steppe people could make commercial contact were international markets, such as the market in Prague, outside the zones of influence of both groups.

This description differs from previous approaches to the topic, which never covered Viking–nomadic trade completely. Scholars have mostly viewed the Volga Bulghar– and Khazar–Scandinavian trade through a lens of Scandinavian–Islamic connections (Noonan 1990; Piltz 1998) or saw Rus'–steppe commercial relations

DOI: 10.4324/9781003037859-4

as Slavic–Turkic dealings and minimizing the relevance of Scandinavians (Marquart 1903; Boba 1967; Noonan 1992; Golden 2003). Here I will contrast the Rus' trade along the Volga and Dnieper rivers, the two leading trade routes, to offer a macro perspective and highlight hubs through which cultural borrowings from the steppe entered the Scandinavian and Rus' worlds. I begin with an introduction to the network of waterways.

## Trade routes

As discussed in the introduction, rivers played a central role in transportation and communication in the East. Rivers in the region attracted settlement and had important ecological functions in Scandinavian, Rus' and steppe lives. Besides the centrality of rivers in the economic systems of these cultures, there were social aspects in play as well that made it likely that the two communities would establish contact with each other. Indeed, as Scandinavian ships pushing southward on the rivers in order to explore and build (social and financial) capital, sooner or later they encountered nomad communities on the banks. Initial contacts, probably established on the riverbanks, led to the development of a commercial system that connected Scandinavia and Russia with the northern branches of the Silk Roads. Apart from commercial river routes running north–south across the steppes, a direct trade route also connected the steppe dwellers with Kiev in the tenth century. It started from the eastern-steppe power centres of Bulgar and Itil, then crossed the Carpathians and extended towards the western markets of Cracow, Prague and Regensburg (Nazarenko 2001, 71–112).

An important feature of this trade network was that it consisted of alternative routes. Due to the geography of the area and the ship-building and navigational skills of the Scandinavian Rus', a desired destination could be reached by way of various rivers. Based on anticipated or actual political and financial reasons, one could choose between alternatives to reach a market. The development of these alternate routes must have been connected to the geographical proximity of one market to another and also affected by the shifting political and economic relationships of the Rus' and the steppe neighbours, in which the main goals were to avoid conflict and customs' duties.

The waterway system used by the Rus' is not described fully in any historical source, but has been reconstructed from contemporary and later sources and sometimes also general geographical knowledge (Brim 2002; Jackson 2019, 19–114). Another approach was to follow the traces of archaeological evidence along the rivers to discover a route (Dubov 1989).

By combining data from different sources, we can reconstruct the river system. Scandinavians settling in north-western Russia around Lake Ladoga and Ilmen entered the region either through the Gulf of Finland and the Neva River or through the Gulf of Riga and the western Dvina. These, connected by the Volkhov and Lovat rivers through smaller tributaries and overland portages, provided a connection to the Dnieper or through Lake Beloozero to the Volga (Boba 1967, 19–23; Callmer 2013). The two rivers formed the backbone of a system connecting the Baltic Sea with the Mediterranean and the Caspian that the PVL calls the "way from the Varangians to the Greeks" (Cross and Sherbowitz-Wetzor 1953, 53–54; Likhachev 1996, 8–9). Although the main route led along Russian rivers, the PVL highlights that from the "Varangian Sea" one could reach Rome by ship, from where one could continue on the sea to "Tsargard", the Slavic name for Constantinople. The description also confirms this route for the Volga, with the difference in destination now lying in the lands of "Ham", the Arabs (Cross and Sherbowitz-Wetzor 1953, 54; Likhachev 1996, 9). Thus, by analogy with the "way from the Varangians to the Greeks", some have labelled this route the "way from the Varangians to the Arabs" (Dubov 1989, 57, 163). The Scandinavians created a cross-cultural transport network that connected their homelands with the Muslim sphere and Byzantium (and the rest of the Mediterranean) through two alternate routes: either south on the Russian rivers or passing English and Frankish lands and sailing via the Gibraltar to the Mediterranean Sea (Shepard 2010).

Practicalities stood behind the development of alternate routes. Although the Russian rivers might seem to offer shorter routes, records from later voyages indicate that the water-route option was less time consuming from other parts of the Viking world. Military companies sailing to Constantinople from the British Isles, as in the *Orkneyinga saga* and *Játvarðar saga*, probably chose this route deliberately (Vigfússon and Unger 1868b, 470; Guðmundsson 1965, 218–33). Unlike the Russian rivers, which froze in the winter, the Mediterranean was mild, which greatly extended the possible time frame of a voyage (McCormick 2001, 450–68). Even though longer, it might have also been more convenient to travel all the way to the East on seagoing ships when (in the view of most researchers) it was not possible to follow the rivers. Small, light ships with shallow drafts had to be manufactured to make it possible to drag the boats from one river to the next, to lighten the boats' weights, and to prevent them from running aground in shallow water (Stalsberg 2001; Edberg 2009; cf. Larsson 2011). This was surely the case from the Middle Dnieper southward, as confirmed by the DAI, which describes the huge preparations before Rus' expeditions of crafting small dug-out canoes (*monoxyla*) specifically designed to travel to Constantinople on the Dnieper (Constantine Porphyrogenitus 1967, 56–63). Further north, larger ships navigated the rivers, as attested in clinker-built boat planks and Scandinavian types of rivets found around Rostov and Gnezdovo (Shepard 2015, 281–82). There is also a chance that Scandinavians departed from Scandinavia on ship types suitable for the rivers in Russia (Edberg 1996), and some evidence supports the opposite scenario: travelling east in seagoing vessels, anchoring them in the northern Rus' ports (e.g. Novgorod, Staraya Ladoga) and changing to smaller vessels (Braun 1924, 164–65; Stalsberg 2001, 368–77; Sorokin 2006), maybe draft animals and carts (Müller-Boysen 1990, 55) or sledges in the winter (Sindbæk 2003).

Besides the practicalities, when travelling south, the Rus' had other reasons for choosing among alternate routes, all of which were directly connected to their attitude to the steppe dwellers and *vice versa*. One of their primary concerns was to avoid central toll stations, where cargoes were checked and heavily taxed. Sources report that all the main trading partners – steppe powers, including the

Khazars and Volga Bulghars – imposed customs' duties on Rus' merchants at some point (de Goeje 1889, 154; Lunde and Stone 2012, 112; Montgomery 2014, 238–39). The Magyars (after their settlement in the Carpathian Basin) were probably no exception. Avoiding checkpoints was essential to return higher profit and to hide smuggled goods and counterfeit items that might be confiscated. Viking warrior-merchants were well known for smuggling in the Western areas, exemplified by several Carolingian *capitularia* trying to prevent them from selling arms to the Scandinavians (Boretius and Krause 1897, 167, 321). These embargoes were largely unsuccessful, as witnessed by numerous artefacts, most notably authentic and counterfeit double-edged swords of Frankish origin found in Scandinavia (Kalmring 2010). That the Rus' might have also engaged in such illegal activities can be seen in a description of Rus' merchants along the Volga carrying "Frankish swords" (Montgomery 2014, 240–41), although this designation was vague enough to include weapons manufactured in Scandinavia that conformed to original Frankish blades. In addition, ibn Khurradādhbih reports a ruse in which Rus' merchants pretended to be Christians in order to pay the Muslim *jizya* ('poll-tax') and trade freely in Baghdad (de Goeje 1889, 154; Lunde and Stone 2012, 112). Thorough searches were probably best avoided if possible. In the tenth century, Byzantine agents conducted searches of Rus' traders – requiring them to enter the gates of Constantinople unaccompanied and unarmed while their cargo was inspected in a designated place outside the city walls (Cross and Sherbowitz-Wetzor 1953, 74–75; Likhachev 1996, 24).

The variety of routes leading to and beyond steppe lands were probably also used for smuggling. The Dnieper, for instance, was not a good choice if a trader only wanted to reach the Khazars because, according to ibn Khurradādhbih, both the Byzantines and the Khazars levied a ten percent tax on through trade (de Goeje 1889, 154; Lunde and Stone 2012, 112). It would have been impractical to reach Tmutarakan or Itil through the Black Sea; it is not even sure whether Itil could be reached directly from there. Mas'ūdī questioned several captains sailing the rivers and seas in the area and found that none of them confirmed that waterways connected directly to the Caspian and the Black Seas (Maçoudi 1861, 273–74), although he later contradicts himself on this point (Maçoudi 1863, 15). Whether such a waterway existed or not, ibn Khurradādhbih states that the Rus' also sailed on the Tanīs River, the Arabic name for the Don (de Goeje 1889, 154; Lunde and Stone 2012, 112). Independent Muslim informants confirmed this route, labelling the Don as the "Rus' River" (Bosworth 1982, 75, 181). Avoiding the Byzantine-controlled Black Sea by following the Don was a sensible choice if one wanted to be spared double taxing. The Khazars, however, must have realized this, and building the Khazar fortress of Sarkel on the Don with Byzantine aid in the mid-tenth century was connected to taxing Rus' and other merchants (Zimonyi 2016, 340–42). Scandinavian artefacts – two Viking swords and a boat rivet – found along the Donets indicate that the Rus' used this river, too (Androshchuk 2016, 97), which would have been logical as sailors could bypass Sarkel, which was further upstream on the Don, and enter the Sea of Azov to trade in Tmutarakan (see Figure 3.1). The Khazars, however, evidently built other riverbank fortresses, which have been discovered by archaeologists in the Don-Oskol-Tikhaiai Sosna river area. Approximately 25 fortified sites have been dated to between the eighth and tenth centuries (Pletneva 2003, 67–81; Kovalev 2005a, 81–86; Shepard 2017, 120–28).

The Khazar capital, Itil, could also be reached from the north through Bulghar (Noonan 1990), by following the Oka (Dubov 1989, 173–74) or by cutting across the steppe (Zhivkov 2015, 152–54). Itil itself, on the Caspian Sea, could be avoided through the rivers of Azerbaijan and Georgia, although this probably only developed in the early eleventh century (Larsson 2011, 123–24). Rivers like the Dniester and Bug were sailable and probably also used (Edberg 1996, 40–41), which, if the Magyar material remains in the Dniester area indeed signal control over these routes, would mean that there was another contact zone between Scandinavian and steppe groups.

The great variety of routes, besides avoiding customs' duties, must also have been linked to changing political relations between the Scandinavian Rus' and the steppe people. Rivalries between Scandinavian Rus' groups were often caused by conflicting commercial interests and a general fear of crossing the others' lands since they could impound cargoes and threaten the lives of the travellers. Sources related to these problems have been discussed in the previous chapter.

## Trade in the Volga area

The main trading partners of the Rus' along the Volga River were Turkic groups and probably also Muslim merchants who had to conduct business at markets under Khazar and Bulghar control (see later). The dynamics and chronology of this trade system have been established by great numismatists based on the most sought-after item: Islamic silver dirhams. Scandinavia's trade with the Orient went back to sixth- and seventh-century antecedents, but only intensified from the ninth century, as witnessed by an influx of dirhams, mostly imported from the Abbasid caliphate (Noonan 1990). Abbasid coins dominate Viking Age silver hoards found in Russia, the Baltics and Scandinavia for the period around 800–80 CE, but from the tenth century onwards the main components of Scandinavian silver hoards are Samanid Persian coins minted in Central Asia. Interrupted by a period of 'silver crisis' between c. 880 and 900 CE, the large flow of dirhams continued from c. 900 CE and totally ceased after the 1030s CE. There is a marked difference in the route by which dirhams reached the Rus' and Scandinavia. In the initial period, silver arrived through the Caucasus and the Khazar-controlled Caspian, while in the tenth century Samanid dirhams were brought from Khorasan across the steppe directly to the market of Bulgar on the Middle Volga. Scandinavian-Islamic trade was conducted solely through Turkic intermediaries: the Khazars and the Volga Bulghars (Noonan 2000–01; Kovalev 2011).

The change in coins from different Islamic polities is associated with a shift in trade routes, which had vital consequences from the point of view of Viking–nomad trade. Ibn Khurradādhbih's work suggests that in the ninth century Rus' traders ventured on boats to the Caspian, from where they continued to the Abbasid capital, Baghdad, on camelback. This long journey across Khazar territory could be shortened somewhat if traders stopped in the Khazar capital. Although still not verified archaeologically, Itil, somewhere in the Volga delta lay at the crossroads of river and land routes. It was a contemporary melting pot of different cultures, attracting merchants from all over the steppe and Islamic world. In the first half of the tenth century, however, Khazar international trade declined in Itil and was gradually taken over by Bulgar, a town to the north near the confluence of the Middle Volga and Kama rivers, which became a meeting point of Islamic, steppe and Rus' merchants. Routes crossing Bashkir, Pecheneg and Oghuz tribal territories followed the Volga and made it unnecessary for Rus' merchants to travel far into Islamic lands for silver; Muslim merchants could also reach the town on a caravan route from Transoxania, leading across the steppe on the left bank of the Volga. Ibn Faḍlān followed this route, starting from Baghdad. His journey exemplifies the intention to keep off Khazar lands on journeys to the north for both political and commercial reasons. The turbulent migrations and increasing activity of the Rus', Magyars and Pechenegs in the Pontic-Caspian steppe no doubt contributed to the decline of the Khazars in at least two ways, first by disturbing the peaceful travel of merchants and, more directly, by occupying Khazar zones of influence. Based on the chronology and spatial spread of Eastern and Northern European dirham deposits, some estimates suggest that these political and economic transitions led the value of Khazar trade to decline so considerably that the Volga Bulghar income from trade eventually surpassed it by four or five times (Noonan 2007, 235–36).

What products were brought and exchanged in these markets and how this trade was managed are the basic questions relevant to Scandinavian– and Rus'–steppe connections. Ninth-century Rus' merchants heading to Baghdad via the Black Sea and the Caspian were carrying "beaver and black fox pelts, as well as swords" (de Goeje 1889, 154; Lunde and Stone 2012, 112). The question is whether any of these products was offered for sale in Itil before reaching the final destination of Baghdad. The Khazars indeed imported furs from the lands of the Rus' and the Volga Bulghars (de Goeje 1927, 221; Lunde and Stone 2012, 155), so there was surely a market for Rus'-supplied skins in Itil. The case of double-edged swords wielded and distributed by Scandinavians and Rus' is more complicated. In a dubious episode of the PVL, the Khazars are said to refuse tribute paid by Slavic households in double-edged swords, saying that they were only accustomed to fight with the lightly curved sabre (Cross and Sherbowitz-Wetzor 1953, 58; Likhachev 1996, 11–12). Although the story is anachronistic for the ninth century, when not every Slavic household could have owned a double-edged sword, it reflects a distinctive difference in sedentary and steppe warfare. The Khazars, nomadic riders fighting with the lighter sabres that were more suitable for mounted warfare, were probably not interested in acquiring double-edged swords for themselves. This might be confirmed indirectly (albeit only on the *argumentum ex silentio*) by the absence of relevant archaeological evidence: so far only a single Scandinavian bronze sword chape, found in Danilovka, is known from the whole Lower Volga region (Androshchuk 2008, 523). Nevertheless, many Muslim mercenaries in Khazar employment, like their fellow countrymen, were fond of Scandinavian blades (Validi 1936). Ibn Miskawayh illustrates this fascination, noting the fate of fallen Rus' warriors buried after the battle of Bardha'a in 943 CE: "after they [the Rus'] left, the Muslims dug up the graves and found a number of swords, which are in great demand to this day for their sharpness and excellence" (Margoliouth 1921, 73).

Khazar interest in other products that the Rus' widely traded in the East is similarly obscure, such as honey and wax, slaves and tin from the mysterious Rus' town of Arta (de Goeje 1927, 226; Lunde and Stone 2012, 159). Nothing is known of the tin, but according to Gardīzī, the Khazars were well supplied with honey and wax (Martinez 1982, 155), probably due to customs levied on the Volga Bulghars and the Burtas', who were expert beekeepers (de Goeje 1927, 141; Lunde and Stone 2012, 118; Montgomery 2014, 218–19, 228–29). The often-quoted statement of Iṣṭakhrī is somewhat contradictory: "Nothing is produced in the land of the Khazars for export to other regions except for isinglass [gharā]. As for the mercury and honey and wax and beaver pelts and other skins, they are imported to the Khazars" (de Goeje 1927, 223–24; Lunde and Stone 2012, 156). The idea that the Khazar Khaganate was unable to export products, however, has been severely criticized (Noonan 2007), and it cannot be ruled out that the Rus' were interested in the vast numbers of sheep and cattle coming from these lands (Bosworth 1982, 161).

Besides slaves, contemporary documents do not specify a direct exchange of commodities between the Rus' and the Khazars, although there are some archaeological indications that the Khazars joined in the processes of exchange and were not mere intermediaries between the Rus' and Muslim merchants. As early as the ninth-century layers of Rurikogo Gorodische and Ladoga, belt fittings and finger rings from the Saltovo-Mayaki culture speak of direct Khazar–Rus' exchange. These appear together with Caucasian and Central Asian beads, silk fragments and shells from the Indian Ocean, typical 'oriental' items transmitted through the Khazars (Mühle 1991, 34; Nosov 2017, 117). In exchange for Rus' products, the Khazars, just like the Muslims, probably also offered dirham coins. Khazar coins imitating Muslim dirhams even reached the Swedish island of Gotland, testifying that Khazars were involved in the Scandinavian–Islamic trade (Kovalev 2005b).

Ibn Rusta's words quoted at the beginning of this chapter list the traditional Rus' commodities brought to Itil and traded simultaneously in Bulgar. Besides slaves, the Rus' earned their living by selling various furs; sable and grey squirrel were prime commodities. The high value of such furs was balanced almost exclusively with silver coins, which the Rus' tucked into their belts to boast publicly of their wealth (de Goeje 1892, 145; Lunde and Stone 2012, 126).

Middlemen conducted most of the trade in Volga Bulgharia. Products brought there from Slavic and Nordic territories were transported further towards Khazaria or Khorezm by Muslim merchants. Arriving in Bulgar, Rus' traders prayed to their gods to bring them a trading partner with "many dinars and dirhams", suggesting that he was probably a Muslim (Montgomery 2014, 242–43). Items traditionally traded by the Rus' and carried to Volga Bulgharia, such as sable, grey squirrel, ermine, mink, fox, marten, beaver, spotted hare, wax, walrus or narwhal tusks, honey, amber and swords, appear on the tenth-century list of export goods of Muqaddasī, and are said to have been delivered directly from Bulgar to Khorezm (de Goeje 1877, 324–25; Lunde and Stone 2012, 169–70).

Slaves, carried by the Rus' to Bulgar in great numbers according to ibn Faḍlān (Montgomery 2014, 242–43), according to Iṣṭakhrī and Muqaddasī, were also traded forward to Central Asia, (de Goeje 1877, 325; de Goeje 1927, 305; Lunde and Stone 2012, 170) together with furs, which became the fashion in Islamic lands (Howard-Johnston 1998). In exchange, besides dirhams, the Rus' also accepted valuable beads and precious stones of glass, amber, ceramic, coral, amethyst and jasper (Kovalev 2000–01, 30–34). The Rus' also bought 'Oriental' silk, clothing and related decorative fittings to bring back to Scandinavia (see Chapter 6).

The summary thus far of the Scandinavian and Rus' trade along the Volga is the well-known and established view of modern researchers. There are, however, a few other aspects of this network which have not been addressed or emphasized by others. One of these was the purchase of live animals. As discussed next, trade in livestock was of primary importance in the Dnieper Rus' community and one of the motors driving Rus'–nomadic trade there.

In the Volga region, the trade in animals served only immediate needs. Rus' traders in Bulgar are described with many different animals used for religious rituals, not solely as provisions. Although Viking ships in general could transport even large animals, it seems unlikely that a wide variety of animals would have been transported to Bulgar for ritual purposes alone, even from the closest Rus' settlements in the Suzdal region, especially if the ships were also laden with slaves, weapons, honey, wax and furs. When making sacrifices to their gods and later when burying one of their chieftains on the Volga shores in Bulgar, the Rus' are described as slaughtering multiple sheep, cattle and horses, as well as a dog, a rooster and a hen. Although only a single creature was killed from the last three, it is quite sure that they were present here in large numbers; dogs (in the plural *kilāb*) are said to have been fed with meat left from the initial trading sacrifices that were made upon arrival (Montgomery 2014, 244–45). Rus' voyagers may have carried animals on board for rituals along the way, as might have been the case of a rooster sacrifice on Saint Gregory island in the Dnieper in the mid-tenth century (Constantine Porphyrogenitus 1967, 60–61). This interpretation is unsure, however, given that the Rus' were stationed on this island and roosters could have been used to feed the garrison and arriving sailors. Even if assumed to be brought there on ships, carrying a few roosters cannot be compared with the vast array of animals the Rus' were associated with in Bulgar. These animals, or at least most of them, must have been purchased onsite along the Volga, as can also be inferred from the wording of the text: "he [a Rus' merchant] acquires sheep or cows" (Montgomery 2014, 244–45) for a ritual in front of wooden idols. For longer voyages down towards Itil, provisions were surely required. All the steppe tribes bordering the Volga were extensive herders; the Volga Bulghars, Oghuz', Burtas' and Baskhirs owned huge flocks of sheep and cattle, as well as herds of horses and camels, and offered them for sale (de Goeje 1877, 324–25, 1885, 329, 1892, 140,

1927, 288, 305; Minorsky 1942, 33; Bosworth 1982, 100; Martinez 1982, 156–57; Lunde and Stone 2012, 118, 169–70; Montgomery 2014, 212–15, 232–33). Rus' crews sailing on the Volga most likely availed themselves of the opportunity to upload supplies from local sources or to purchase individual animals for occasional ritual purposes from the steppe people that lived along the rivers.

Another important aspect of the Volga trade was the high level of organization. First, it encompassed a huge area of interest; commodities flowed into it from Russia and the Baltic on one end and from the Near East and Central Asia on the other. It is thus noteworthy that almost all products the Rus' exchanged there were acquired outside Scandinavia. Wax, honey and furs were traditional products of the forest belt; slaves were levied from the local Slavic communities; and even many double-edged swords were manufactured in Russia. No doubt maintaining this system required a high level of co-ordination. Considerable preparations were also taken for the journey, as indicated by the analogy of the Dnieper trade. Stockpiling resources began in the winter; trees suitable for making boats were felled and after the ice melted in the spring were floated down to nearby lakes. Oars, rowlocks and other tackle had to be added to the tree trunks before the expedition could set out in June. Even this was problematic because the boats had to regroup for two to three days downstream in the river near another Rus' settlement (Constantine Porphyrogenitus 1967, 56–59).

The steppe peoples were as complex as the Rus' in organization. On the side of protective measures (guided by self-interest), many steppe polities built well-functioning tax systems. Ships and terrestrial caravans were intercepted at Khazar fortresses along the way, as was noted earlier. The Khazars levied a ten percent tax on passing Rus' ships or let their pirate fleets through only in exchange for certain returns from the final profit. The Volga Bulghars had a similar policy. Rus' traders sailing from Itil to Bulgar were again subjected to the tithe:

> When the boat from Khazar territory reaches Ṣaqālibah territory, the king goes on board and counts its contents, taking a tenth of its cargo. When the Rūs or any other people come with slaves, the king of the Ṣaqālibah has the right to choose one in every ten.
>
> (Montgomery 2014, 239)

Apart from seeking profit, steppe polities also had to provide services visitors needed because if visits had only entailed rigorous inspection and customs' duties, the allure of steppe fairs would have faded quickly. Services for visitors probably included insuring food supplies (the large numbers of live animals discussed earlier) and living space. Archaeological evidence from Sarkel suggests that there was a caravanserai there (Kovalev 2005a, 81–84). Traces of a pelt warehouse and a caravanserai in Biljar have also been identified, and judging from the camel bones found in Bulgar, a caravanserai must also have operated there, at the latest from the mid-tenth century (Kovalev 2000–01, 61–62). In Itil, Muslim artisans and traders had a designated quarter in the town (Maçoudi 1863, 12; Lunde and Stone 2012, 133–34; Montgomery 2014, 256–59), and Rus' traders in Bulgar were probably granted an empty site and the necessary resources to construct temporary quarters on the banks of the Volga to "build large wooden houses on its banks" (Montgomery 2014, 242–43).

The friendly attitude and hospitality of nomadic hosts is reflected in one of ibn Faḍlān's observations on the Oghuz'. The nomads welcomed Muslim traders, lent them horses and camels, and offered them lodgings in their own homes for the duration of their stay in exchange for gifts and the hope of future co-operation. Nevertheless, practicalities loom large in the background. Covetousness immediately outweighed hospitality; treating visiting Muslim traders as respected friends in Oghuz tents ended quickly if payment was not forthcoming (Montgomery 2014, 204–5).

The well-organized steppe polities along the Volga were militarily strong enough to secure a safe environment for trade to flourish while still maintaining a balance between welcoming gestures and their own financial benefit. The complexity of this trade system is best contrasted with the situation in the Dnieper area.

## Trade in the Dnieper area

If the Rus' did not travel down the Don on commercial missions aiming to reach the Caspian from the Black Sea or for the raid against Constantinople in 860 CE (cf. Shepard 2017), then they must have been following the Dnieper. The river's real significance in Rus' history increased in the next century, when Scandinavian Rus' groups moved down from northern Russia and settled in Kiev. This move to the south and settlement in Kiev probably rested on the town's strategic location; it lay at the convergence of the forest and the steppe and was much closer to the lucrative Byzantine markets than northern Rus' settlements. Kiev was the southernmost option for sedentary life, lying just a few days' journey from the harsh open steppe environment, where no settlement is known from this period.

The Rus' trade with Byzantium has attracted attention from researchers (Hellmann 1987; Androshchuk 2016), but the tenth-century nomadic mercantile relations of Kiev are discussed less often. All the available data on the latter come from the tenth century, with only circumstantial evidence for earlier connections. The main two trading partners of Kiev at the time were the Pechenegs on the bordering steppe and the Magyars in the Carpathian Basin.

The main concern of Rus' traders in the region was the security of the Dnieper waterway. Compared to hosting markets on the shores of the Volga for different ethnic groups to meet, the Pecheneg tribes exerted predatory control over a section of the passing-trade route itself. Since the Pechenegs only set upon Rus' trading companies violently near the cataracts of the river and had no settlements of their own, the pros and cons of becoming potential trading partners were not balanced. The closest market town to the steppe region was Cherson on the Crimea, which, similarly to Itil and Bulgar, owed its long-lasting prosperity to its geographic location (Shepard 2009). Although the town lay within the reach of steppe tribes inhabiting the Pontic steppe, neither the Magyars nor the Pechenegs attacked the town apart from some short-term profit-seeking raids (Constantine

Porphyrogenitus 1967, 49), but both traded there – mostly slaves (Zimonyi 2016, 336–37). Lacking the cultural infrastructure to found or maintain market towns, the Pechenegs had few opportunities to attract traders to their region. This did not mean that the Pechenegs had no products of interest to offer, but probably only that they brought them to the others' markets rather than the reverse. The Magyars had a more complex trade relationship with Rus' groups in and around Kiev, but it was similar in the sense that, after settling in the Carpathian Basin, they only bordered on the trade route that Rus' merchants took towards more prosperous markets, notably Cracow and Prague. In contrast to the Pechenegs, however, as will be argued here, the Magyars hosted a local fair in the Upper Tisza region and probably supplied provisions to Rus' merchants stopping to rest on their way west.

This context differs fundamentally from the Volga trade, as steppe agents only exerted authority over Rus' traders for a limited time (as they passed by) and, apart from collecting fees on the cargoes of Rus' caravans, they had no chance for serious gain from the advantage of international transactions and the flow of a large variety of goods and ideas. It is also striking in this regard that although it was probably not in their long-term interest to disrupt trade in the region (Golden 2003, 94–95), the Pechenegs did not try to maintain systematic control over the Dnieper trade route. Compared to the Khazars, who tried to impose order on the river routes by establishing strongholds, the Pechenegs only and (as the DAI indicates) immediately resorted to violence against Rus' traders once they stepped ashore to portage their cargo and finally return to the river. Judging by their ambushes at the seventh cataract of the Dnieper, called the "Little Barrage" (Constantine Porphyrogenitus 1967, 59–60), the Pechenegs were perfectly aware of which cataracts and fords made the Rus' most vulnerable. Thus, they could have established and maintained a permanent presence there for a more peaceful and perhaps more profitable relationship. At present, the best way to explain this difference is by referring to the internal organization of the Pecheneg tribes, where the economic organization, with shifting alliances and enmities among themselves, was closest to a purely nomadic economy', and included an aggressive attitude towards acquiring wealth.

In spite of these disadvantages, the emerging Kievan Rus' polity had great need of something the steppe bred in great numbers: live animals, especially horses (Froianov 1986). Constantine succinctly summarized the situation:

> The Russians also are much concerned to keep the peace with the Pechenegs. For they buy of them horned cattle and horses and sheep, whereby they live more easily and comfortably, since none of the aforesaid animals is found in Russia.
>
> (Constantine Porphyrogenitus 1967, 48–51)

Although the text implies that it was in the interest of the Rus' to conduct trade with the Pechenegs, in reality, as the first sentence indicates, they must have been driven more by the necessity of avoiding conflict. Commerce was an alternative way to acquire goods. The party strong enough to force its terms on the other by violence was actually the one more bound by the need for mutual exchange, which was usually less of a necessity for the other. This was surely the case in Rus'–Byzantine trade relations, where all commercial treaties granting privileges to Rus' tradesmen were confirmed after a Rus' attack on Byzantium. Similarly, the Pechenegs probably used the force of arms to try to persuade the Rus' to trade, and their relationship is best be understood in this light.

A scholarly model called 'dependency' or 'need theory' holds that it is usually nomads whose existence depends on the sedentary neighbours and not the reverse, as the steppe does not provide certain resources vital for the survival of any community such as metals, grain or textiles (for the discussion, see Di Cosmo 1994, 1092–94). Nicola Di Cosmo has criticized this view, pointing out specific contexts in which most medieval nomads were evidently able to manufacture good quality formidable weapons, tools and objects of precious metal, as well as to supplement their diet with agricultural products from the steppes (Di Cosmo 1994). It is difficult to say whether or not the Pechenegs were in severe need of grain and metal tools that were harder or (in the absence of resources) impossible to manufacture on the steppe (Noonan 1992, 318). They definitely appear well-to-do; according to Gardīzī, the Pontic Pechenegs were rich in gold and silver vessels, weapons and strap mounts decorated with silver (Martinez 1982, 151–52). This contrasts with the Pecheneg remnants left behind wandering on the western banks of the Volga, described by ibn Faḍlān as living in "miserable poverty" (Montgomery 2014, 212–13), indicating how much different contexts could affect conditions for Pecheneg groups. Their apparent ignorance of the potential for exploiting trade routes across their pastures in an economically more favourable way than robbery, the lack of signs of permanent settlements and the frequency of reports of Pecheneg violence in the written sources suggest that the Pechenegs' wealth in the Pontic steppe likely derived from their neighbours; the Rus' and the Byzantines, both of whom they raided and forced to trade.

From the Byzantines, the Pechenegs acquired "purple cloth, ribbons, loosely woven cloths, gold brocade, pepper, scarlet or 'Parthian' leather and other commodities" (Constantine Porphyrogenitus 1967, 52–53). In the case of the Rus', exchange and co-operation resulting from coercion might be indicated by objects associated with the Pecheneg archaeological culture. Belt-buckles, sabretache-locks, boot mounts and harness equipment discovered in the Don-Dnieper area and the Crimea (Gayovka, Kamenka, Kotovka, Staro-Shvedskoye, Gorozheno) exhibit influence of Nordic metalwork, suggesting the spread of common techniques (Pálóczi 1989, 31–32, 264) or the existence of nomadic purchasing power for desired objects produced by craftsmen in Kievan workshops.

Another characteristic of the Pecheneg–Rus' trade was the exchange of products for resale. This seemingly fairly common practice in the region was also part of the nature of steppe trade, but within quite a different framework than letting foreign merchants exchange their goods with one another in a steppe fair, as at the Volga markets. The distribution of goods in the Dnieper area was not driven by sheer profit, but sometimes by simple vital need. It is reported, for instance, that if the Chersonites did not "journey to Romania and [sell] the hides and wax that they [got] by trade from the Pechenegs, they [could not] live" (Constantine Porphyrogenitus 1967, 286–87). The hides, if referring to oxhides, could indeed have been brought from the Pechenegs to Cherson, but wax is more problematic. Wax was one of the most important products of the forest region, given by the Rus' to the Byzantines as a gift and also as a commodity (Cross and Sherbowitz-Wetzor 1953, 77, 83, 86; Likhachev 1996, 26, 30, 32). Whether wax was produced at this time on the Eastern European steppe can be debated. As noted earlier, in this region only the Khazars are said to have had abundant wax; however, Gardīzī's statement taken to confirm this refers to the lands of the Burtas' and the Volga Bulghars, allies of Khazar tribes, both lying in the more northern, forested parts of the steppe. Bees probably did not inhabit the open steppe where the Pechenegs lived. It seems more reasonable that the Pechenegs – similarly to the Chersonites, who, according to the previous quote, exchanged it in the Byzantine Empire – transferred wax from the Rus' to the Chersonites. Thus, the suggestion that the hides mentioned in the DAI are actually furs rather than oxhides (Polgár 2000, 197) makes the most sense in this context: the Pechenegs, blackmailing the Rus' with raids, extorted furs and wax, which they, as intermediaries, passed on to the Chersonites.

It is also possible that the Rus' acted likewise and drove excess horses westward to the market in Regensburg. The famous customs' regulations of Raffelstetten, from the very beginning of the tenth century (c. 903–06 CE), list traders called *rugi*, usually identified with the Rus' (Franklin and Shepard 1996, 89–90; Nazarenko 2001, 48, 81–82), bringing wax, slaves and horses to the German markets (Boretius and Krause 1897, 251). Besides the Pechenegs, the Magyars may have been an alternative source of horses for the Rus'.

## The Carpathian Basin

Trade between the Magyars, the Rus' and Scandinavia left traces in both the written and archaeological record, mostly for the tenth century. Connections might go back to the previous century, as was advocated in the pioneering work of the Hungarian archaeologist Nándor Fettich, who noted that the tenth-century Magyar material from the Carpathian Basin displays elements such as niello embellishment and red copper inlay that were borrowed from Nordic metalworkers as early as the ninth century, when the Magyars lived back in Levedia or Etelköz and bordered the Scandinavians (Fettich 1937, 36–54). Evidence, however, only supports this interpretation in later artefacts of Nordic origin that exhibit typical Magyar-style embellishments or steppe-nomad objects decorated with Nordic metalwork techniques. Exclusively tenth-century, these objects mostly cluster in Kiev and the surrounding settlements and could well be signs of co-operation between the two ethnic groups (Arne 1914, 123–39). The famous Chernigov drinking horns and the Viking sword from Grave 108 of the Kievan Golden Gate, both decorated with palmette motifs, are good examples (Bálint 1989, 113–17; Melnikova 1996, 71; Androshchuk and Zotsenko 2012, 97; Figure 4.1; Figure 5.2). Steppe-nomad

*Figure 4.1* Magyar-style objects from Grave 108, Golden Gate, Kiev

Source: By the kind permission of Oleksiy Komar

weapons, such as the Khoinovsky and the so-called Charlamagne sabres, with Nordic inlays are prominent examples of Nordic metalwork (Figure 4.2; Figure 4.3). A stone mould found in the Podol district of Kiev, inscribed with the epigraph *Yazid* (meaning 'Turk') has been interpreted as a sign of Turkic–Rus' manufacture (Mesterházy 1989–90, 236–37), although it might also be related to Muslim craftsmen living with the Rus' (Duczko 1998, 113).

*Figure 4.2* The so-called Khoinovsky sabre from Kiev

Source: Redrawn from Zhuravlev and Murasheva 2012, 97, fig. 248

Goods, techniques and ideas flowed both ways, as indicated by the wide distribution of sabretaches. Besides the Carpathian Basin, these objects and their accessories are found in Kievan Rus' territory (Gnezdovo, Shestovitsa, Chernigov, Kiev, Staraya Ladoga) (Fodor 1986), among the Swedish Birka and Rösta (farther north) (Arbman 1940, 222–24, 295, Taf. 129/1a – 1b; Petrukhin 2016, 129–33) and in the Volga-Kama area (Krylaszova, Belavin, and Türk 2014). They reflect the spread of manufacturing techniques, and a taste for a common fashion may have originated in multi-ethnic workshops in the Kiev area (Fodor 2017a; Figure 4.4). Similar arguments have been advanced for a distinctive decorative technique called the 'spica pattern', in which criss-crossed silver wires are hammered into the base material to create a motif reminiscent of heads of grain. This ornament was known in Scandinavia and also appears on Magyar objects; for instance, on a now-lost stirrup from the Karos cemeteries and on the grip of Conquest-period sabres from Berehove/Beregszász (now in Ukraine) and Tiszavasvári (Dienes 1996; Fodor 2017b). Thus, although the evidence is fragmentary, most Hungarian archaeologists accept the idea that lively commercial contacts existed between the Scandinavian Rus' and the Magyars during the ninth and tenth centuries, culminating in the development of merged styles and mutual borrowings of techniques and craftsmen (Fettich 1931; Mesterházy 1989–90, 236–37; Fodor 1994, 47–65; Kovács 2003).

Objects found in the Carpathian Basin also indicate trade; they arrived through perhaps two distinct trade routes: one from the Kievan Rus' and the other straight from Scandinavia (Katona 2017a). Artefacts indicating trade are all portable, different types of jewellery, bracelets and rings that have counterparts in Gotland and the Kievan Rus' territories (Márkiné 1934; Mesterházy 1993); a type of stirrup thought to be a Carolingian–Northmen blend (Mesterházy 1981; Kovács 1986); a conical hat from Berehove/Beregszász ornamented with braids in a Scandinavian style (Kovács 2003) and weapons such as straight double-edged swords (Paulsen 1933; Fettich 1933, 61, 394–97; Fodor 1986; cf. Bíró 2012), axes (Petkes 2006) and a spear (Kovács 1970a). It seems unlikely that these artefacts would have come directly from Scandinavia. Based on both typology and ornamentation, however, in a few instances a Scandinavian provenance cannot be questioned. This is the case with a spear embellished in the Ringerike

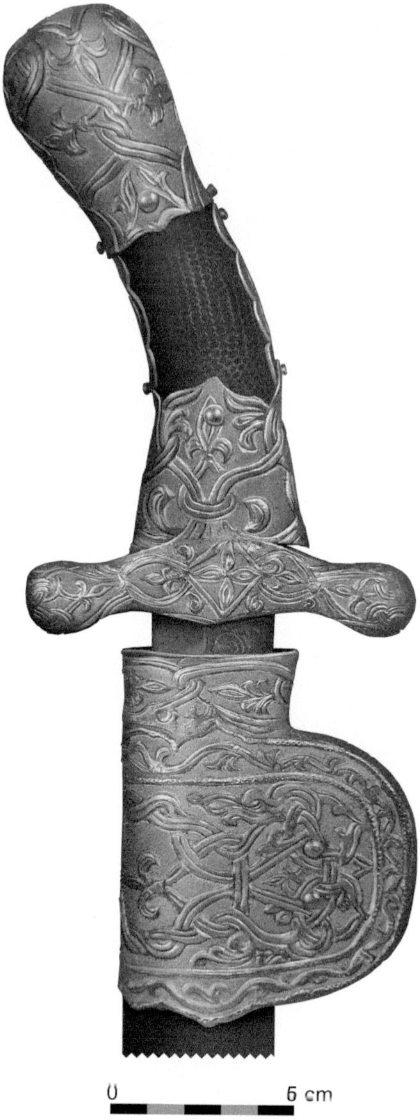


*Figure 4.3* The Charlemagne sabre

Source: Redrawn from Fodor et al. 1996, 67, fig. 1

style found in Budapest in the bed of the Danube, the famous tenth-century 'Saint Stephen sword', decorated in the Mammen style (now kept in Prague) and other swords (Katona 2017a, 37–38). There is every chance that, similarly to the axes and related items, such as miniature axe pendants that only have parallels

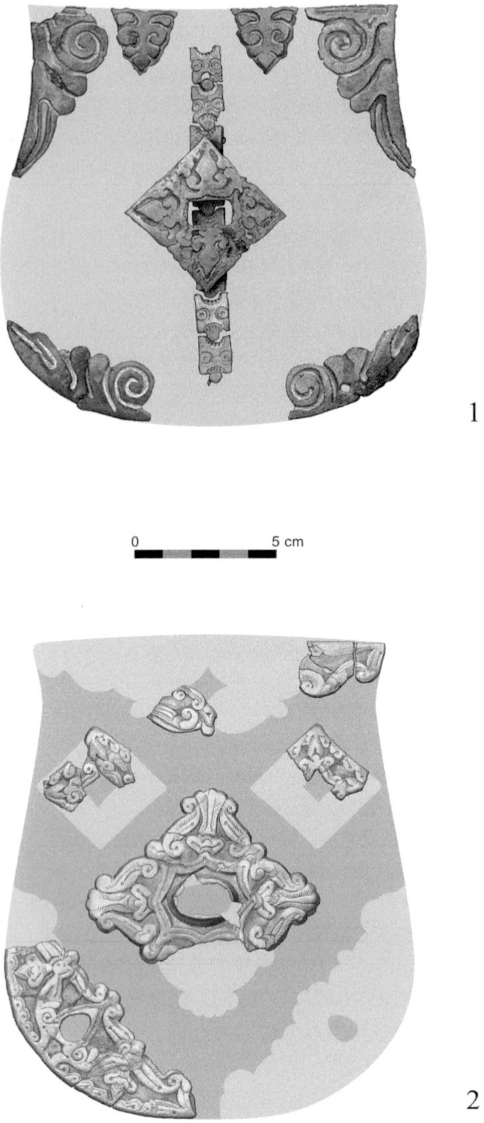


*Figure 4.4* Sabretaches from Shestovitsa and Budapest-Farkasrét

Source: Redrawn from Zhuravlev and Murasheva 2012, 100, fig. 256, and Fodor et al. 1996, 360.

in Russia (Petkes 2006; Füredi et al. 2017), these Scandinavian artefacts also reached Hungary through the Rus'. Objects in Magyar style from Birka's garrison are likely to be connected with military co-operation and will be discussed in the next chapter. They definitely indicate the close connection of these worlds.

Coins of King Saint Stephen (1000–38 CE), widely spread in Scandinavia in the early eleventh century, however, could easily have been payment to people of Scandinavian origin for goods and services for Magyars or, later, Hungarians (Huszár 1967; Gedai 1980).

The written evidence corroborates this picture painted by archaeologists to some extent. In the tenth century, Rus'–Magyar trade seems to have been indirect, through markets foreign to both the Rus' and the Magyars. It can also be argued, however, that direct commerce between Kiev and Hungary also took place, especially in the first half of the century.

Starting with the undoubted evidence, after the middle of the tenth century Magyar–Rus' commercial meetings definitely took place in two markets associated with the Magyars which Rus' merchants also visited. The market of Pereyaslavets near the mouth of the Danube was where Sviatoslav intended to transfer his seat, saying, "that is the center of my realm, where all riches are concentrated: gold, silks, wine and various fruits from Greece, silver and horses from Hungary and Bohemia, and from Rus' furs, wax, honey and slaves" (Cross and Sherbowitz-Wetzor 1953, 86; Likhachev 1996, 32). Although not much weight should be given to PVL's dating of this event to 969 CE, it seems to coincide with the time when the Pechenegs were a serious threat to the Dnieper waterway. They later murdered Sviatoslav himself at a river ford, and, given the prince's hostility towards them, it is likely that with the 'Pereyaslavets plan' he partly planned to look for supplies of horses from the Magyars rather than the Pechenegs, who did not have a unified rule and were less trustworthy. That this trade in Magyar horses might have had earlier precedents is suggested by the *rugi* merchants noted earlier, who ventured as far as the Carolingian border at the very beginning of the tenth century with herds, possibly for resale.

The other major market in the period emerged in Prague in Bohemia. Besides Pereyaslavets, Rus' merchants as well as Magyars also visited the market of Prague. In 965 CE, al-Ṭurṭūshī, a Jewish traveller, noted:

> Russians [Rus'] and Slavs come there from Karakwa [Cracow] with goods. Moslems, Jews and Turks [Magyars] come there from the country of the Turks [Hungary] and bring goods and trade balances. Flour, tin and various kinds of furs are exported from there.
>
> (Mishin 1994–95, 186)

The nature of these meetings between Rus' and Magyar merchants differed from the Scandinavian and Rus'–Turkic encounters in the Volga region. In the fairs of both Pereyaslavets and Prague, the Rus' and Magyars were guests, and thus profit from regulations did not go into the pockets of Turkic people. In addition, these markets provided the opportunity for Rus' traders to engage with the Magyars, who had commodities valued by the Rus', namely, silver and horses, for which they paid with the same products as they did with Muslim merchants along the Volga: furs and slaves. The Turks here were not mere intermediaries but were probably sought after by Rus' merchants.

The scope of their activities suggests that the Rus' operated in every possible direction from Kiev. Before Prague and Pereyaslavets became important, the Rus' were certainly also active on the Middle Danube, as confirmed by the Raffelstetten regulations. Rus' activities here had ninth-century antecedents, attested by a settlement in the vicinity named Ruzamarcha after them (Nazarenko 2001, 14–17; Franklin and Shepard 1996, 88–90). Rus' traders also travelled in the region between the Carpathians and the Dnieper. According to a Gotland runestone (G 134), *blakumen*, identified as inhabitants of the Dniester, killed a Scandinavian named Hróðfúss on an expedition (Jesch 2001, 257–58) in the first half of the eleventh century, when the runestone was erected. There are suggestions that a trade route was in operation even earlier through today's Romania (Spinei 2009, 53–54), which is supported by tenth-century archaeological artefacts of Scandinavian origin found there – a miniature axe pendant, strap-ends, fibulae and bracelets (Yotov 2015; Kolev 2015). In present-day Moldova, along the Dniester and the Raut, mercantile activity was protected by small ring-shaped forts established to guard trade routes. These structures were accompanied by buildings the excavators termed 'long-houses' and interpreted these complexes as stations on the Rus'/Scandinavian trade network (Teuntiuc 2018–19). If this is accepted, Rus' traders surrounded the tenth-century Magyar Carpathian core area on all sides. Is it so unlikely that they also visited the Magyars at the time (Haussig 1987, 530–31; Katona 2017b; Figure 4.5)?

No source explicitly mentions Rus' traders in the Carpathian Basin during the tenth century. To set up a hypothesis that the Rus' visited the Carpathian Basin we have to examine the possibility of such an undertaking from multiple angles. The 'system of alternative routes', rivalries among the various Rus' groups, local conditions and the possible intentions behind a visit to Magyar-controlled territory all need to be taken into consideration.

The Rus' were most willing and talented in discovering new routes towards a destination if the consequences were greater profit or a safer passage. A question arises as to why no alternative routes were sought towards Constantinople after the Pechenegs started to endanger the Dnieper waterway. Such a route would have been possible along the Danube, which could have been reached from the Tisza River in Hungary. Judging by archaeological evidence along the riverbanks, a Hungarian trade route led south along these rivers in the period (Mesterházy 1993, 455). In 1985, Swedish experimental archaeologists carried out an ambitious and imaginative undertaking by sailing a replicated Viking ship on Eastern European rivers, among them the Hungarian Bodrog, Tisza and Danube, all the way to Istanbul. Their goal was to demonstrate that Vikings were able to travel in their own boats all the way from the Baltics to the Black Sea (Nylén 1983, 1987). Although the route seemed navigable, this was not necessarily the case in the Viking Age, as the Hungarian rivers were seriously regulated in the modern era for flood control. It took 107 days for the Krampmacken expedition (as the Swedes called the project) to reach the Black Sea from the Bodrog River (Nylén 1987, 255), which is much longer than the Dnieper alternative. Calculating from the DAI, it took from 17 to 28 days to reach the mouth of the Dnieper from Kiev

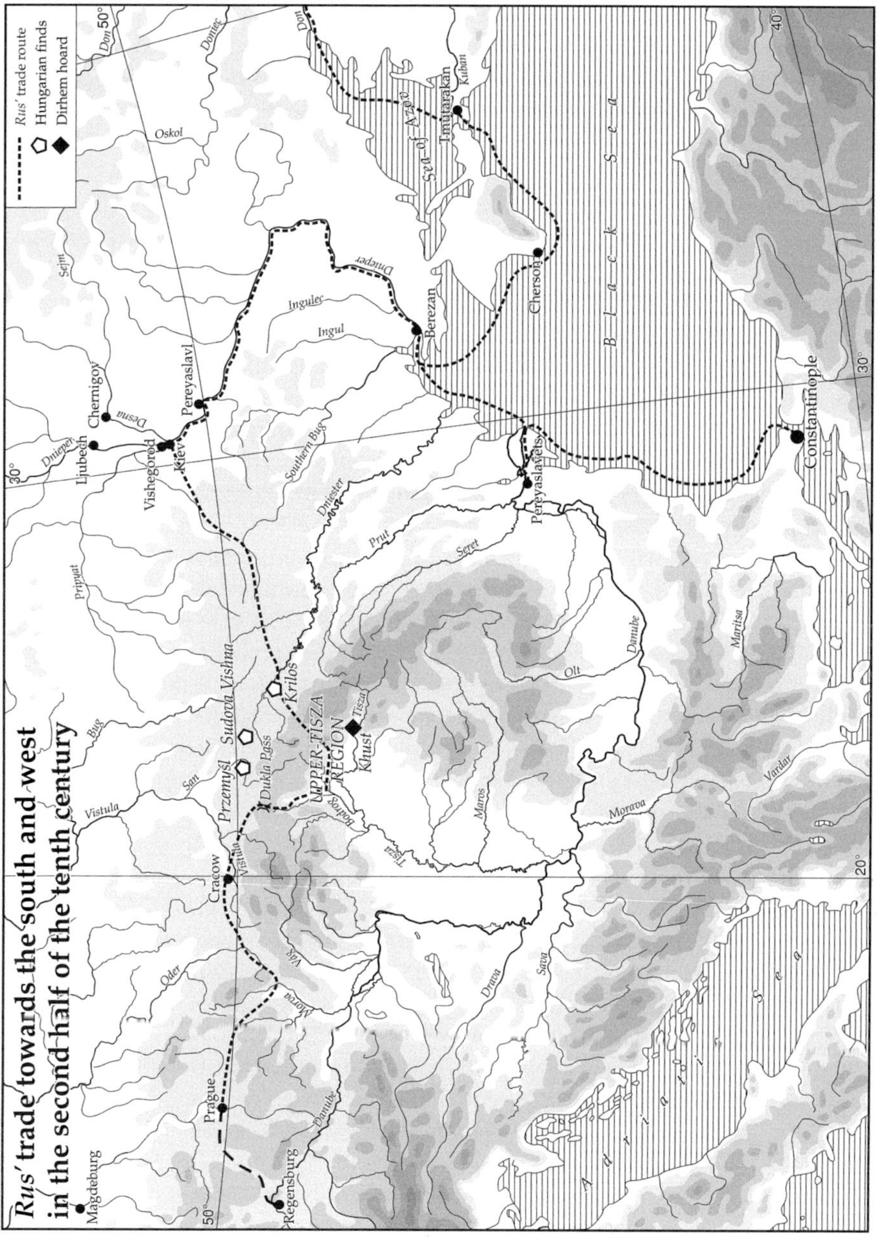


*Figure 4.5* Rus' trade towards the south and west in the second half of the tenth century

(Petrukhin 2006). Even adding the remaining distance to Constantinople along the Black Sea coast and taking into account the difference between the navigational skills and physical tolerance of tenth-century sailors and twentieth-century modern men, the trip is considerably shorter on the Dnieper. In addition, the Krampmacken entered Eastern Europe via the Vistula and portaging the boats over the Carpathians to continue on the Hungarian waterways was no easy task; something comparable would have been needed if a Rus' expedition were to start from Kiev. In the Viking Age another ten days was required from there to the Magyar area (Polgár 2002, 223).

Nevertheless, Viking Age Scandinavians were famed travellers, willing to cover huge distances between markets if it was in their interest (Sindbæk 2008). The length of the route in itself would probably not have deterred them from the trip. Its hardships would have been more important. Portaging the boats through the Carpathians would have been a logistical nightmare. Although the Rus' are reported to have used wheels on which they could drag the boats for huge distances on land (Cross and Sherbowitz-Wetzor 1953, 64; Likhachev 1996, 17), their return would have been in the winter, when this would have been impossible. Rus' trading expeditions from Kiev set sail in June, according to Constantine (Constantine Porphyrogenitus 1967, 58–59), and had to return before the winter, as is stated in the proviso to the 944 CE treaty: "The Russes shall, moreover, not have the right to winter at the mouth of Dnieper, either at Belobereg or by St. Eleutherius, but when autumn comes, they shall return home to Rus" (Cross and Sherbowitz-Wetzor 1953, 76; Likhachev 1996, 25). This also pertained to the Rus' staying in Constantinople, who did not have "the privilege to wintering in the St. Mamas quarter" (Cross and Sherbowitz-Wetzor 1953, 75; Likhachev 1996, 24). This tallies with the statement in the treaty of 907 CE that Rus' merchants in Constantinople received provisions for six months (Cross and Sherbowitz-Wetzor 1953, 65; Likhachev 1996, 17).

The Bodrog route would not have been favourable from a financial point of view. At the crossroads in the Carpathians, the Magyars were firmly in control of the commercial route leading from Volga Bulgharia through Kiev and further west. Archaeological finds related to the Magyars found on the north-eastern side of the Carpathians are interpreted by experts as station points securing the passes (see Figure 4.5; Fodor 1994, 55–56; Révész 1999, 155) and levying tithe (Györffy [1977] 2003, 108–9, 332–36). As previously noted, the Byzantines levied taxes on the Rus' in the ninth century; there is a chance that further toll stations would have awaited them down the rivers in Hungary. This is illustrated by an anecdote in the fourteenth-century hagiographical account of Saint Gellért of Hungary. Although the *vita* is a later source, it builds on earlier official records. It tells of the actions of the Magyar chief, Ajtony, who, after the death of Grand Prince Géza (972–97 CE), expropriated the rights to the salt tariffs on sections of the Maros River and "placed toll-keepers and guards along the river's ferry points up to the Tisza and declared a tax on everything" (Szentpétery [1938] 1999, 489–90, translation by the author). Contrary to the Magyar tolls, which seem to have applied as early as the reign of Géza, Rus' traders enjoyed exemptions from taxes in Byzantium during the tenth century, and, as stated in the treaty from 907 CE, obtained free provisions as well as "anchors, cordage and sails" for the return journey, also confirmed in the treaty of 944 CE (Cross and Sherbowitz-Wetzor 1953, 65, 75; Likhachev 1996, 17, 24).

The only element favouring the Bodrog route was safety. It has been argued that around the end of the 980s CE Rus' mercenaries joined Grand Prince Géza's service on their way to and from Kiev and Constantinople as the safest route between these places led through the Carpathian Basin because of the threat of Pecheneg attacks on the Rus' along the Dnieper (Györffy 1959, 92). This theory, seemingly sound, is not supported by contemporary evidence, and the circumstances might suggest otherwise. The controversial events of 988 CE place the political conditions of the era in quite a different light. This was the year when Vladimir besieged the Byzantine city of Cherson but in the same year offered to help Basil II against the revolt of Bardas Phokas by sending a (presumably Scandinavian) contingent – labelled 'Varangian' by the later chronicler – to aid the *basileus* (Cross and Sherbowitz-Wetzor 1953, 93, 111–12, 243, 247–48; Likhachev 1996, 37, 49–50). The chronological sequence of the events is not clear, but it seems sure that Vladimir did not command the second of these military actions and that, on the contrary, the Scandinavians abandoned him and changed sides. This is how the PVL depicts the event: the 'Varangians', not paid by Vladimir, departed for Byzantium (Cross and Sherbowitz-Wetzor 1953, 93; Likhachev 1996, 37). Some Scandinavians were already in Byzantine employ at this time, as the peace treaties between the parties attest (Cross and Sherbowitz-Wetzor 1953, 68; Likhachev 1996, 19), and thus, viewed against the background of the general discontent between Scandinavian and Rus' groups in general, this period actually shows strife between Scandinavian groups in the service of the Byzantine and Rus'. This makes it unlikely that any groups of Scandinavians/Rus' would have regarded the route through Hungary as 'safe' since nothing more is known about this relationship, let alone about the relations of the Magyars to each of the various Scandinavian/Rus' groups.

The lack of unity among the Magyar territories in the tenth century blurs the picture further. Although the seven Magyar tribes sealed their political unity with a blood oath as early as the ninth century (Bak and Rady 2010, 16–17), it seems apparent from later events that the Carpathian Basin was a place of rivalry before Saint Stephen's reign, who himself had to overcome a great deal of opposition. Attempts at centralization began as early as Géza's rule and were likely finished by the end of his reign, at least temporarily, which is suggested by the note of the German missionary, Querfurt of Bruno, that an unnamed ruler of the Magyars became the sole sovereign by the end of his reign (Bruno of Querfurt 1973, 61). Based on chronology, this ruler could have been no one but Géza, although there is no further information about these events and what political circumstances prevailed along the Tisza, especially if Ajtony's entry on the political scene after Géza's death had earlier precedents. Byzantine-backed claims of autonomy were revived by Ajtony in the Tisza-Maros region (Szentpétery [1938] 1999, 489–90), again highlighting that political relations with Byzantium and Kiev were significant for safe travel in Magyar territory. The appearance of the Magyars in the area probably led to the end of the Rus' route by foot to Ruzamarcha and made the Danube waterway unsafe (Franklin and Shepard 1996, 89; Nazarenko 2001, 108–9; Gieysztor 2008, 501).

Summing up, going south through Hungary would have been more time consuming, more expensive and probably more dangerous for the Rus' than travelling along the Dnieper. Because the Rus' could also obtain valuables from the south directly from the Byzantines and could acquire Magyar wares in Pereyaslavets, there was no point in taking the route through Hungary. All these factors explain well why Scandinavian and Rus' warrior-merchant groups preferred the danger from the Pechenegs on the Dnieper.

Given that a southern river route through Hungary can be excluded from the alternatives of Rus' merchants, only two hitherto undiscussed options remain for Magyar–Rus' commercial dealings after the Magyars occupied the Carpathian Basin. The first is that trade was restricted to moving goods between Kiev and the Carpathian passes, i.e., direct commerce between the Rus' and Magyars. Such a trade system must have depended on peaceful periods based on the analogy of Rus'–Pecheneg trade, in which the former bought cattle, horses and sheep from the latter in times of truce. The second scenario is related to reaching the Polish and Bohemian markets, Cracow and Prague, which the Rus' probably reached by travelling through Hungary. The Magyars, controlling a section of the trade route Rus' merchants followed towards the west, had a position similar to that of the Pechenegs in the Dnieper area, only they handled the situation in a more peaceful manner.

If the assumption of direct tenth-century trade between Kiev and Hungary is correct, it left little trace in the archaeological record. Only indirect evidence can be adduced, such as the clusters of Hungarian dirham finds in the Upper Tisza area, the region closest to the passes where incomers from the East arrived in Hungary and where the richest tenth-century Magyar graves are found. Based on the richness of the area in terms of archaeological findings, most scholars argue that the Upper Tisza region served as the princely headquarters of the era. The number of dirhams found in the local graves confirms that the elite resided in the area closest to the known trade routes and, as would be expected, actively took part in commerce (Kovács 1994; Révész 1999, 155–57; Polgár 2002, 224–25). The expert on Hungarian dirham finds, László Kovács, attributes the appearance of dirhams to visiting Volga Bulghar, Khazar, Muslim and Jewish traders, but omits the Rus' from his enumeration (Kovács 2008). The numismatic evidence is more than just dirham hoards; it also suggests internal monetary circulation in the territories of the emerging Kievan Rus'. Thus, some form of correlation with Scandinavian and Rus' warrior-merchants can be expected (Kuleshov 2021), especially since some Rus'-related artefacts (e.g. spiral-head rings, weapons) also cluster in the Upper Tisza region (Mesterházy 1993, 457–58; Istvánovits 2003, 338–39; Kovács 2003; Fodor 2017b; Figure 4.6). These artefacts of Rus' provenance hint that even though the form and circumstances remain faint, goods were exchanged in the Upper Tisza region.

Besides live animals (horses and possibly also cattle and sheep), the Rus' might have been interested in another product of the Carpathian Basin – salt. Recently,

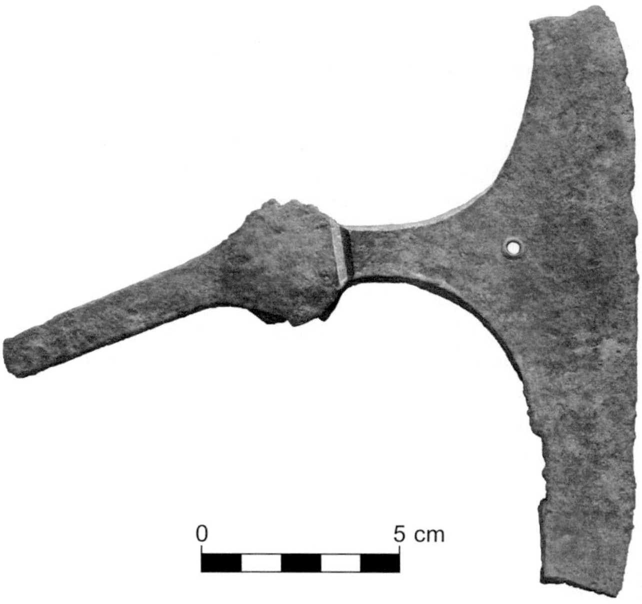


*Figure 4.6* Axe from Streda nad Bodrogom (Slovakia) characteristic of the blended 'druzhina culture' found in the grave of a Magyar horseman. The weapon has two parts: a broad blade typical for Slavic territories and a *chekan*-type tip common in nomadic areas

Source: Redrawn from Nevizánsky and Košta 2009, 340, Fig. X/3

several scholars have suggested that the Scandinavians responded to a decisive demand for European salt in Frankia, Poland, Bulgaria and even al-Andalus (Lübke 2001, 194; Duczko 2004, 77–78; Lewis 2006; Pires 2011, 128; Gardeła 2015, 218). It can be suggested that salt from Transylvanian salt mines also interested the Scandinavian Rus'. The salt mines in the Carpathian Basin were of great value from the ninth century on; the Avars and Bulgars who occupied the territory at that point both traded in it. Many surmise that the Bulgars occupied Transylvania for the salt and that the Byzantines were also involved in the salt trade with this region (Stephenson 2004, 42–45; Fiedler 2004, 162; cf. Spinei 2009, 58–60). When the Magyars took over the Carpathian Basin, salt production continued under their control (Madgearu 2005; Vékony 2004). As noted, it even resulted in internal conflicts between the first king, Saint Stephen, and the local chieftain, Ajtony, who tried to monopolize the tolls of the salt trade on the Maros River for himself near the turn of the millennium.

Later sources suggest that salt as an exchange commodity might have been more important for the Rus' of Kiev than previously assumed. William of Rubruck, the Franciscan friar, reports that the Rus'ians were still in need of salt in the thirteenth century, and at that time they had to venture to the Caspian Sea to get it (Michel and Wright 1839, 219). Earlier, at the end of the reign of

Sviatopolk II of Kiev (1093–113 CE), uprisings broke out in Kiev as the Halichian salt import ceased and the city remained without salt in stock, resulting in various merchant groups and the grand prince speculating in salt (Heppell 1989, 171–74). The Kievan prince, Mstislav Iziaslavich, was also disturbed by the fact that the Cumans blocked the so-called salt route of the Rus' in 1168 CE (Franklin and Shepard 1996, 325–27). These incidents show that a continuous salt supply was a necessity in the Kievan Rus', and even in later centuries ensuring it from local resources was not without difficulties. Apart from the salt collected by the Chersonians on the Crimea (Constantine Porphyrogenitus 1967, 186–87), the mines in Transylvania would have been one of the closest options for the Kievans to import salt in the tenth century. Since Rus' merchants travelled all the way up to Regensburg for salt in the ninth century, the Tisza region would have been an easy reach for salt that could be transported on carts or muleback if Pecheneg groups disrupted the Crimean salt supplies.

Besides allowing for the possibility of direct trade between Kiev and the Magyar territory, there are clear hints in the written record that communication between the Kievan Rus' territories and the West took place via Hungary in this period. Two sources record a diplomatic and commercial mission through Hungary. The first merchants who managed to cross the territory in safety were two Jews, who, according to a Hebrew source by an anonymous writer in the mid-eleventh century quoted in Zedekiah ben Abraham Anav's thirteenth-century work *Shibbolei haLeket* (Ears of Gleaning), travelled from "Russiyah" (*rvsy'h*) to Regensburg with their non-Jewish servants (Slavs? Rus'?) in the mid-eleventh century (Spitzer and Komoróczy 2003, 116–19). Although commerce was revitalized when the situation was secured by kingly control after the millennium, another account implies that such a route had also operated in the tenth century. The Khazar–Jewish correspondence uses even more specific terms to highlight that in 955 CE Jewish envoys tried to pass along a letter written by the Cordovan Ummayads from Prague to Kiev via Hungary (Kokovtsov 1932, 65). It is striking that in the mid-tenth century communication between Kiev and Prague seems to have run through Hungary. Therefore, Rus' merchants visiting the fairs in Cracow and Prague probably followed the same paths; the Upper Tisza region would have been the most logical choice.

So far only a single dirham hoard (371 specimens) is known from the Carpathian Basin, which does not unequivocally confirm the existence of a trade network. Nevertheless, the find was discovered at Khust/Huszt (now in Ukraine) at the confluence of the northern branch of the Tisza and the Rika rivers (Kovács 1989, 80–81), an area where communication has been predicted. Since hoards were hidden in troubled times, some archaeologists argue that the lack of numerous deposits might actually reinforce the idea of a well-functioning, peaceful commercial network (Bálint 1981; Kovács 2008). The around 70, mostly Samanid and Volga Bulghar, dirham finds of the tenth century (dating from 903 to 942 CE) come from graves in Hungary, and, as noted, cluster in the Upper Tisza region (Kovács 1989, 78–81, 120–34; Kovács 2008).

Long-distance trade usually emerged around nodal points when nature presented obstacles and where the likelihood of meeting other long-distance traders was high (Sindbæk 2007, 2008). Prague and Pereyaslavets both met these requirements, as they were located at the junctions of land and water and were visited by a variety of foreign traders. Rus', Slavs, Jews, Muslims and Magyars all visited Prague, while Rus', Slavs, Greeks and Magyars were present in Pereyaslavets. It is still possible, however, that the Upper Tisza region also served as a temporary nodal point for Rus' traders, who could rest, replenish their provisions and sell some of their wares before journeying on to Cracow and Prague in the north. Even if not marking the region as their final destination, Rus' merchants were warranted to stop near the Carpathians. The province, however, started to lose importance from the second half of the tenth century (no more burials are recorded thereafter), which is usually explained by Prince Géza's Western-oriented foreign policy and the moving of the princely headquarters to Transdanubia (Szabados 2011, 232–35 with further references). This shift surely affected Rus'–Magyar dealings.

Understanding Scandinavian– and Rus'–Magyar exchange and communication in the tenth century requires a broad spectrum of evidence. Scandinavian and Rus' traders, when selecting a destination, were less stressed about the length of the voyage than attending fairs with the greatest promise of profit. Markets at the intersections of land and water routes were usually favoured targets, especially if the traders' security was ensured by a central power. The greatest takings could be made at these fairs, as other long-distance traders were also in attendance from neighbouring regions. Another critical point for Rus' merchants, undeterred by the physical dangers and hardships of the trip, was to avoid taxation, which led to developing alternate routes, some of them crossing through Hungary. Following a river system to the south from the Carpathian Basin would not have attracted Rus' merchants for geographical, financial and security reasons. Such considerations affected Scandinavian groups in Byzantium and other rival Scandinavian groups in the Kievan Rus' territories, always in the light of Magyar foreign relations. Judging from the tenth-century campaigns led by the Kievan Rus' with Magyar assistance, they were on amicable terms (Sakharov 1986). In this context, Rus' merchants could express interest in Hungarian salt and livestock, for which they may have paid in furs, weapons and goldsmith products or perhaps Islamic dirhams. Such products changed owners in the Upper Tisza area; the Rus' arrived by chance, deliberately from Kiev or en route towards the lucrative markets in the north, which the Magyars also visited. Developments over time suggest that after the second half of the tenth century the Upper Tisza region declined as a trading location, which allowed Scandinavian Rus'–related artefacts to reach the Carpathian Basin as a result of dealings between the Rus' and Magyars conducted at important international fairs at crossroads such as Prague and Pereyaslavets.

## Conclusion

Scandinavian traders had already encountered steppe people in the early stages of their eastern settlement, at the latest in the ninth century, when evidence of interaction seems to increase in the sources. Major rivers crossing the dense forests of northern Russia and flowing southward across the steppe became communication routes between Scandinavian and Turkic cultures. Through their traditional activities of riverine commerce as well as seasonal pastoralist migrations following waterways, the paths of the Scandinavians, Rus' and steppe nomads were interwoven. Long-distance trade routes reaching north and towards the great civilizations of the south crossed the main grazing grounds of steppe pastoralists, some of whom successfully joined this cross-cultural trade network by establishing market towns at points along the Volga, or by blocking the way on the Dnieper. The nature of this network, complemented with land routes through the steppes, was marked by negotiations, resale transactions, shifting trade routes and interests and a high level of organization that included fixed customs and tolls, the use of interpreters, caravanserais and informal rules of hospitality. Such an enterprise also entailed considerable organization on the part of the Scandinavian Rus'. Serious preparations were carried out before setting sail; suitable vessels had to be constructed, defensive and supply outposts had to be set up on river islands, alternate routes had to be scouted and tested and divine assistance had to be constantly assured through rituals connected to travel and commerce.

In this network, the Khazars were the main middlemen between the north and south during the ninth century; over the next hundred years their role was gradually taken over by the more northerly Volga Bulghars. Both created powerful polities with flourishing international markets with secure transactions, sophisticated regulations and comfortable conditions for visiting merchants.

After securing a firm foothold in Kiev, the Scandinavian Rus' became neighbours with other steppe tribes, the Magyars and later the Pechenegs. Rus' commerce with these tribes was not a necessity for profit, but to prevent raids and guarantee safe crossings of the steppe to the lucrative markets beyond. Business along the Dnieper was not conducted at fairs like those along the Volga, but probably took place in the frontier zone between the sphere of Rus' influence and that of the steppe. Frontier markets were probably considered safer than letting nomads into a town. The products exchanged at these frontiers satisfied basic needs in the usual patterns of trade between nomadic and sedentary societies elsewhere in Eurasia. In the second half of the tenth century, international fairs began, approachable from Kiev on land and offering a wide spectrum of commodities for exchange between the Rus' and nomads (then in the process of becoming sedentary).

The Rus' presence among merchants looms large in the sources and bolsters the view that it was they who visited the steppe to trade, although there is also evidence for the opposite scenario. Terrestrial routes from Itil and Bulgar, with a possible branch to the Carpathian Basin, led towards Regensburg with several stops along the way in Rus'-controlled territories. Here, merchants could rest in caravanserais and replenish their goods. Archaeological research has identified trading places along the tracks (Motsya 2009).

After that, the road turned north all the way up to the Danish town of Hedeby, where an 'Eastern horizon' of objects clearly points towards the East – mostly Birka and the Kievan Rus' – and even to more remote steppes. Two items have been considered direct evidence for serious contacts, but their identification has changed recently. A conical bronze boss was thought to come either from an 'Oriental' brooch or a Khazarian helmet (Kalmring 2014). Another notable find was a trader's grave containing a characteristic triangular-shaped bronze bowl on which previous research identified engravings of Turkic runes (for discussion, see Steuer 1975). It has been argued that personal mementoes like this were rarely exchanged and that they are possible traces of Turkic visitors (Khazar or Volga Bulgharian) to the far north (Lübke 2001, 96, 185). It turned out, however, that the conical boss was a better match for hexagonal copper-alloy bells known from Ireland, Scotland, the Isle of Man, northern Wales and England (Lebsak 2021, 50), while the triangular bronze bowl was of possible Irish origin. The reading of Turkic runes on its surface has been seriously questioned (Steuer 1975). Nevertheless, more mundane items of 'oriental' provenance are found in Hedeby that favour the existence of a trade connection with the steppes. Such artefacts include 'oriental' belt fittings and textiles as well as garments or accessories of Eastern styles, such as buttons used on caftans and pendant belt pouches (Steuer 1975; Kalmring 2014; cf. Lebsak 2021). Two Khazar belt mounts and a gilded bronze plaque depicting a horse drinking from a waterhole also reached the Scandinavian-populated Janów Pomorski (Truso) on the northern coast of Poland, possibly remnants of ninth-century visits from the east (Bogucki 2007). Although the paucity of evidence does not seem to support an optimistic view of a regular trade route of Khazar or Bulghar traders all the way to Hedeby (cf. Haussig 1987, 530–31), it is possible for individual cases.

The largely one-directional movement of merchants foreshadowed regular cultural exchange through trade, which mostly affected the regular visitors: the Scandinavian Rus'. As Christian Lübke (2001) has demonstrated, the major contribution of East European trade relations should be sought in the development of 'cultural acceptance' among the various ethnicities in the region. Trade was a first step in acquainting communities with each other, which laid foundations for deeper contacts. During commercial transactions, the two communities temporarily had to share a living space. A safe environment and the peaceful exchange of goods created a context in which cultural commodities and values could flow undisturbed and the 'other', foreigners, became 'friends'. Commercial exchange was the primary vehicle behind cultural contacts and in itself a trigger for cultural innovation and diffusion of objects and ideas. This background was essential for facilitating the Scandinavian Rus' adoption and absorption of steppe customs. Another contact sphere where these group came in contact was joint service in retinues.

# 5 Retinues

At some time between c. 960 and 970 CE, a powerful Rus' ruler, probably of princely status, died, was cremated and buried in the Rus' town of Chernigov (now in Ukraine), widely known today as the 'Black Grave' (Mel'nikova 1996, 70–71; Duczko 2004, 239–41), first excavated in the early 1870s. The body rested under a monumental ten-metre-high kurgan together with other bodies, maybe his son and accompanying slaves, although there are debates on the exact number, sex and age of the buried individuals (Vasyuta 2016). The burial became famous for its size and for the opulent grave goods from a variety of cultural backgrounds. Two Byzantine gold coins, of Constantine Porphyrogenitus and Romanos II (959–63 CE), were thought to date the burial safely to the second part of the tenth century, but new investigations based on artefact typology do not exclude a later date at the turn of the tenth century (Lushin 2019). The burial was discovered in the early twentieth century, and its contents were gifted to various collections. Re-examining some of the objects in the grave has led to new interpretations.

The Chernigov burial likely included a boat (indicated by surviving rivet mounts only discovered in 1996), which was characteristic for Scandinavian burials (Price 2008, 264–66). Bones of horses and rams were also recovered, probably sacrificed during the funeral feast. The weapons' complex found in the grave, however, is the most intriguing (Figure 5.1). Remnants of chainmail and two typical Viking swords in a contemporary Nordic style amply testify that either the deceased or those burying him were well acquainted with close combat. Many spearheads and arrowheads were found, too, weapons that were part of traditional Scandinavian weaponry in the period, although some of them were also standard elements of other cultures' arms. The steppe environment is clearly referenced among the Rus' mourners by a nomad-type sabre best suited for mounted warfare. A conical helmet found in the grave was described as being of Khazar type. In addition, the steppe motifs on the silver plates on two Nordic drinking horns in the grave show the fusion of Scandinavian and steppe ideas and were probably crafted in Russia (see Figure 5.2). A statuette of the Norse god Þórr, another product of Rus' workshops, was also found in the Black Grave; invisible details of the figure discovered during restoration cleaning indicated that it was manufactured by a Scandinavian craftsman on Iranian and steppe models (Murasheva, Orfinskaya, and Loboda 2019). The grave reflected the material culture of a warrior elite

DOI: 10.4324/9781003037859-5

*Figure 5.1* Cremated pile of weapons from the Black Grave in Chernigov

Source: Samokvasov 1916, 20, fig. 23

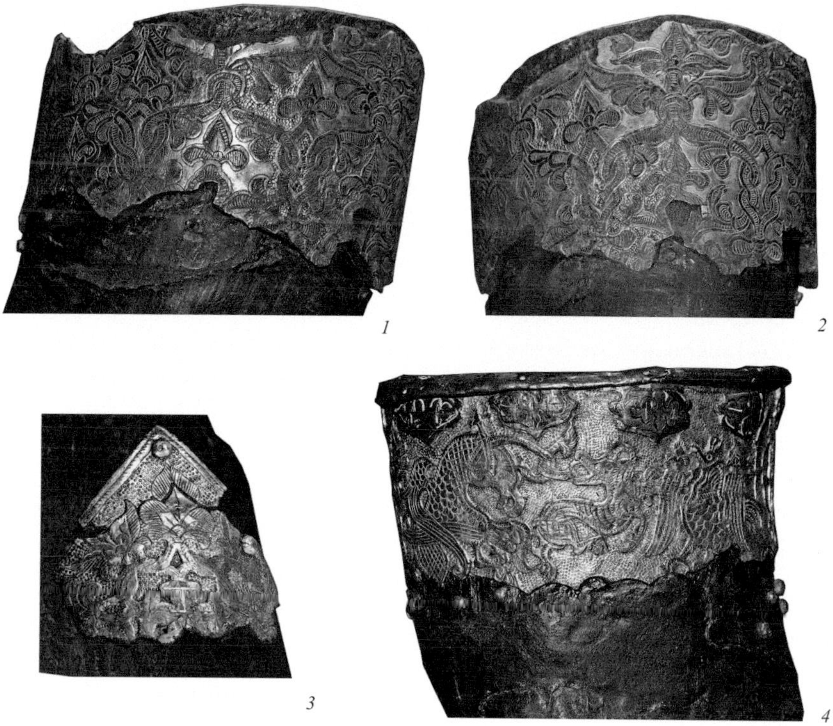


*Figure 5.2* The Chernigov drinking horns from the Black Grave (Ukraine)

Source: By courtesy of Oleksiy Komar

closely connected to both distant and neighbouring networks of trade and culture, including the steppes.

Besides trade relations, this influence came through military channels. Alliances in which nomads and Scandinavians and Rus' fought together were discussed in Chapter 3. They were sometimes also allied under the leadership of various powers other than Kiev as members of a ruler's retinue or as his mercenaries. From the ninth to mid-eleventh centuries, Scandinavian warrior groups were sought after as retainers in several areas along the *austrvegr*. Called Rus' or Varangians, they were present in various courts of the region, such as Kiev and other Rus' courts, Constantinople, and Itil, the capital of the Khazar Khaganate. The possibility of Scandinavian and Rus' retainers entering local service has also been raised for three other areas – Volga Bulgharia, Hungary and Poland – and this seems possible (see Figure 3.1).[1] According to written accounts, the courts mentioned earlier also employed steppe warriors, mostly of Turkic origin, during the Viking Age. In this chapter, I discuss their joint participation in the service of several courts, together with the effects this common service had on them in a military-cultural sense. Scandinavians and Rus' taking service in these areas adopted local cultural and military habits, and I propose that the additional presence of steppe retainers might have had similar impacts.

## The Kievan Rus'

The Scandinavians arrived in the Middle Dnieper area after occupying Kiev; according to the semi-legendary tradition preserved in the PVL, this occurred in the middle of the ninth century (Cross and Sherbowitz-Wetzor 1953, 60–61; Likhachev 1996, 14). Archaeological evidence in the Rus' 'capital', however, suggests that the Scandinavian presence only became decisive there during the late tenth century (Franklin and Shepard 1996, 98–109; Duczko 2004, 220, 257; Androshchuk 2013, 31–32, 216–17). Regardless of the precise date, in Kiev the Scandinavians probably made up a large part of the retinue called a *druzhina*, taking possession of the town as an aggressive military unit. The term *druzhina*, which derived from the Russian word *drug* ('friend'), was used to denote the armed retinue of princes living in the territories of the Kievan Rus' and other Slavic polities of Eastern Europe (Halbach 1985, 94–110; Mel'nikova 1996; Stefanovich 2012). The *druzhina*s contributed decisively to the emergence and operation of the Kievan Rus' state itself.

Even though local warriors were employed, Rus' warbands in the period included (if they were not mostly composed of) Scandinavians who arrived in Eastern Europe with their own ships, crews and weapons in search of plunder and glory. This is inferred from later copyists of the Jayhānī tradition, who clearly distinguish the Rus' from the Slavs, whom they ruled over and raided (de Goeje 1892, 145–47; Martinez 1982, 166–68; Göckenjan and Zimonyi 2011, 234; Lunde and Stone 2012, 126–27). Later evidence, such as runestone inscriptions and sagas such as *Eymundar þáttr Hringssonar* and *Haralds saga Sigurðarsonar*, also support this (Vigfússon and Unger 1862, 120; Braun 1924, 164–65; Sturluson 2002b, 69–70).

For later Rus' princes such as Vladimir and Yaroslav, the logic of hiring ethnically distinct retinue members rested on two basic principles. Mercenaries coming from abroad to tribal societies were not linked to any kin group, thus rulers did not have to be afraid that their own men would betray them or refrain from taking action due to ties of blood with a local family (Font 2010). Foreign retainers enhanced the court's prestige by displaying their traditional warrior gear, often together with a distinctive body-build and special martial skills. Such general features of retinues were noted in earlier centuries by the Roman historian Tacitus (Tacitus 1914, 282).

During the ninth and tenth centuries, settling Scandinavians merged with the Slavs, which is usually evidenced by the appearance of Slavic names among the Rus' elite contracting treaties with the Byzantines (Sitzmann 2003, 58–69; Mel'nikova 2004). Ethnicities merged greatly during the tenth century. Vladimir supposedly set up pagan idols of different kinds on the Kievan castle hill to create a common identity among his ethnically mixed retinue (Vernadsky 1959, 123; Font 2007, 44).

Later, *druzhinas* incorporated not only Scandinavians and Slavs but also men from the steppe. This phenomenon probably started with the Rus' and nomads conducting joint campaigns. The army of the Polish prince Bolesław the Brave (992–1025 CE) launched at Kiev was accompanied by Magyar and Pecheneg auxiliaries (Holtzmann 1935, 530). Long periods of service are surmised from the information that Bolesław interfered in a dispute between his Polish and Pecheneg troops and put the latter to the sword, which indicates that they were his own warriors rather than mercenaries under their own command (Holtzmann 1935, 382). According to the PVL, after the Kievan campaign in 1018 CE, Bolesław returned home with elite prisoners of war (Cross and Sherbowitz-Wetzor 1953, 132; Likhachev 1996, 63), who were probably enrolled in his retinue together with other Scandinavians arriving from the north voluntarily (Shepard 2005, 269–70). Thus, during Bolesław's reign, retainers of Scandinavian and steppe (culturally Turkic) origin both came into contact with the Polish *druzhina*.

Magyar and Pecheneg warriors, similarly to the Polish example, also took part in Rus' campaigns led by Kiev during the tenth century. In 944 CE Prince Igor advanced against the Greeks after assembling warriors from a wide array of tribes, including, according to the text, "'Varangians', Rus' and Pechenegs" (Cross and Sherbowitz-Wetzor 1953, 72; Likhachev 1996, 23). Similarly, the battle of Arcadiopolis (970 CE) was fought between the Byzantines and an alliance of Rus', Magyars, Pechenegs and Bulgars (Diaconus 1828, 108; Bekker 1839, 288–91). Scandinavians and steppe-nomads learned tactics from each other during common campaigns; the result may have been the introduction of horses into Scandinavian Rus' warfare techniques (Androshchuk 2013, 222–23), commonly exemplified in the words of the Byzantine chronicler Leo the Deacon, who highlighted that the Rus' cavalry that advanced against the Byzantines in 971 CE at the battle of Dorostolon was inexperienced because they were not trained for mounted warfare (Diaconus 1828, 134).

Some of Prince Sviatoslav's retinue members, however, were already experienced horsemen, according to the descriptions in the PVL and Leo the Deacon's work (Diaconus 1828, 156–57; Cross and Sherbowitz-Wetzor 1953, 84; Likhachev 1996, 31). At the same time, however, some warriors of the prince still carried arms more typical of Scandinavian Vikings than nomads, namely, the chainmail, shield and double-edged sword. The Rus' commander, Pretich, gifted these weapons to the Pechenegs during a peace treaty negotiation, and they offered him their own distinctive weapons: spear, sabre and arrows (Cross and Sherbowitz-Wetzor 1953, 86; Likhachev 1996, 32). The participation of Rus' merchants in contemporary arms dealing also shows that the Rus' wielded straight double-edged swords (Polgár 2004), and Leo the Deacon describes their tactics as analogous to the Viking shield wall (Diaconus 1828, 133). He also reports that during the battle in front of the city of Dorostolon certain Rus' warriors behaved like mad animals and gave out savage roars (Diaconus 1828, 133). Combat ecstasy like this is mostly known from the Scandinavian pagan tradition of the berserks, who allegedly acted like mad bears and wolves during battles (Blaney 1993). Although this passage might be a Byzantine *topos* to illustrate the barbarity of their enemies (Ivanov 1981), the description is quite specific. Scandinavians still held high-status offices in the Rus' military at the time, such as Sveinald, the deputy commander of the prince, and Asmund, Sviatoslav's personal preceptor (Cross and Sherbowitz-Wetzor 1953, 78–80, 89–90; Likhachev 1996, Talbot and Sullivan 2005, 181, n. 38).

According to the PVL, not only did Sviatoslav hire nomadic mercenaries from the steppe, but he himself lived his life in the saddle and was always prepared for war like a typical nomad:

> Stepping light as a leopard, he undertook many campaigns. Upon his expeditions he carried with him neither wagons nor kettles, and boiled no meat, but cut off small strips of horseflesh, game, or beef, and ate it after roasting it on the coals. Nor did he have a tent, but he spread out a horse-blanket under him, and set his saddle under his head.
>
> (Cross and Sherbowitz-Wetzor 1953, 84; original: Likhachev 1996, 31)

As will be seen in the next chapter, Sviatoslav's (nomadic) appearance in the PVL is backed up by Leo the Deacon's description of the Rus' *knyaz*. The retinues of Sviatoslav and the later Rus' princes were unique, culturally distinct fighting corps that amalgamated steppe and traditionally Scandinavian warfare tactics and weaponry.

That steppe people also occasionally benefited from Scandinavian warfare tactics might be supported with the individual case of a retainer in the service of the Rus' prince Yaropolk I (972–78 CE). This retainer, apparently also the prince's counsellor, was called Varayazhko, that is, 'Varangian'. After Yaropolk's death and defeat by Vladimir, Varayazhko defected to the Pechenegs "in whose company he fought long against Vladimir till the latter won him over only with difficulty by means of a sworn pledge" (Cross and Sherbowitz-Wetzor 1953, 93; Likhachev 1996, 37). The Arabic writer ibn Ḥawqal also noted in his work of the 970s CE that the Rus' were allied with the nomadic Pechenegs and harried Al-Andalus (Kramers 1939, 14; Birkeland 1954, 48), although such an extreme case should be taken with a grain of salt. Although accounts are taciturn on how such campaigns were conducted, other common joint operations of Rus' and steppe people are known. Such examples include Sviatoslav's alliance with the Oghuz' in 965 CE (Golden 1972, 80; Franklin and Shepard 1996, 145), Vladimir's in 985 CE (Kramers 1939, 282; Cross and Sherbowitz-Wetzor 1953, 96; Likhachev 1996, 39) and the joint Rus' and Alan attack on Sharvan and Derbent in 1033 CE (Minorsky 1958, 47).

## The Byzantine Empire

The *austrvegr* led to Constantinople, the region's largest centre, although it was located far south of Scandinavia. Although also recruited from Anglo-Saxons, Franks and Normans, the notorious Varangian Guard, which was responsible for the personal defence of the *basileus* himself, was made up of Scandinavians from the eleventh century onwards (Shepard 1973; Cigaar 1974; cf. Scheel 2015). Although the term Varangian is not mentioned in texts before the eleventh century, it seems safe to assume that Scandinavian mercenaries had already arrived in Byzantium.

Evidence supporting this comes from documents that mention Scandinavians from the Kievan Rus' taking up service in Byzantium. References to Rus' troops in Byzantine pay starts as early as the beginning of the tenth century. In *De ceremoniis aulae Byzantinae*, Constantine mentions 700 Rus' sailors participating in the Cretan campaign of 911 CE (Constantinus Porphyrogenitus 1830, 651). A provision in the Rus'–Byzantine peace treaty of 912 CE clearly states that the Rus' could enter Byzantine service whenever they desired (Cross and Sherbowitz-Wetzor 1953, 68; Likhachev 1996, 19). The flow of troops to Byzantium increased after 988 CE (for dating and discussion, see Blöndal 1978, 43–44). An old view that all Rus' retainers in Byzantine employ were actually Slavs (Vasilievskii 1908) is now untenable in light of new knowledge on early Rus' identity.

Serving for years doubtlessly influenced Scandinavians living in Byzantium, who became accustomed to the environment. Many of them were later baptized, and it seems likely that they had their own church in Constantinople, consecrated to Saint Olaf or the Virgin Mary (Ciggaar 1996, 126). They also started to adopt Byzantine fashions; for instance, wearing the well-known Byzantine tunic, the *skaramangion* (Androshchuk 2008, 535). That they indeed availed themselves of the cultural amenities in Constantinople is illustrated by their demand for unlimited access to the city's bathhouses in a Rus'–Byzantine peace treaty from 907 CE (Cross and Sherbowitz-Wetzor 1953, 65; Likhachev 1996, 17).

The Byzantine Empire's art of warfare also left an impact on the Scandinavians. The *Laxdæla saga* reports that a 'Varangian' named Bolli Bollason, returning from Byzantine service to Iceland, wielded a *glaðel* (short sword) according to foreign customs (Sveinsson 1934, 225). Even though the description of Bolli's attire in the saga is not completely authentic (a knight painted on his shield could not have been a Viking Age custom), it is still probable that warriors active abroad acquired distinctive new weapons (Zanchi 2008, 32–33). Weapons from abroad, especially gifts from rulers, were highly esteemed in the north (Ashley 2013, 217–20). For instance, the armour, *Emma*, of the most famous Varangian guard, Harald Hardruler, was manufactured in Byzantium, if one of the short stories about Harald's life is to be believed (Vigfússon and Unger 1868a, 418). Although finds of Byzantine weapons in Kievan Rus' territory and Scandinavia are rare, some are known and confirm this picture. These include a piece of lamellae armour from Birka's garrison and several Byzantine-type scabbards from Kiev, Turaida (Latvia), Gotland and Ocksarve (Sweden) (Androshchuk 2016, 104–5).

Scandinavians adapting to Byzantine courtly and military fashions took service alongside Turkic retainers. Parallel to the Byzantine employment of Scandinavian and Rus' troops, Byzantine sources attest to the presence of Khazars and the so-called *Tourkoi* (Turks) among the personnel of the Byzantine bodyguard as early as the late ninth century. Called *Tourkoi*, Byzantine historiography usually meant Magyars in this period (Moravcsik 1970, 37, 1983, 320–27; Zimonyi 2001). During the Bulgarian–Byzantine battles in 894 CE, the Byzantine bodyguard troops defeated by the Bulgarian Tsar Symeon the Great (893–927 CE) included Khazar warriors, whose noses Symeon cut off and sent to the Byzantine court (Bekker 1838, 853–55). At the turn of the ninth century, Hārūn ibn Yaḥyā, a Muslim prisoner of war in Constantinople, described Khazars and Turks among the guards at the city gates and among the emperor's bodyguard (de Goeje 1892, 120–24; Zimonyi 2016, 86–87). In his list of Byzantine offices and court precedence in 899 CE, the Byzantine official Philotheos confirms that the imperial bodyguard's officers included Magyars (*Tourkoi*) and Khazars, among others (Oikonomidés 1972, 208–9; see also: Zimonyi 2016, 87–89). Constantine also mentions steppe warriors in Byzantine service, with 84 Magyars (*Tourkoi*) taking part in Romanos Lekapenos' (920–44 CE) Italian campaign (Constantinus Porphyrogenitus 1830, 466).

Besides the continuous flow of Scandinavian and Rus' warriors, Turks continued to serve in Byzantium. During the tenth century, continuous and parallel mentions of Rus', Pharganian, Khazar, Magyar and probably Pecheneg warriors (*Toulmatzoi*) among the palace guard are mentioned in Constantine's *De ceremoniis* (Constantinus Porphyrogenitus 1830, 579, 661–68). Liutprand of Cremona (in 986 CE) also reports that Emperor Nikephoros Phokas II (963–69 CE) captured 40 Magyar warriors in 966 CE, all of whom were accepted into the emperor's bodyguard (Becker 1915, 199).

The influence of Byzantine fashion also reached the steppe retainers; Emperor Nikephoros, for instance, made the captured Magyar warriors dress according to Byzantine fashion in "valuable garments" (*vestibus ornatos*) (Becker 1915, 199). Turkic retainers who carried out duties during ceremonial events at the court wore the finest Byzantine clothing (Constantinus Porphyrogenitus 1830, 576–79). Guards at the city gates encountered by Hārūn ibn Yaḥyā bore gilded spears, shields and lances (de Goeje 1892, 120–24). Thus, various foreign groups living in the empire adopted local cultural styles.

Besides bodyguard duties in the capital, common campaigns were another possible contact sphere for Turkic, Scandinavian and Rus' retainers. Rus', Pharganian, Khazar and Magyar warriors all took part in the Langobard campaign of 935 CE (Constantinus Porphyrogenitus 1830, 660–61). The note in the *Annales Barenses* for the year 1027 CE (probably referring to events of 1025 CE) records Magyars, Rus' and *Guandali*, sometimes identified as Varangians, among the Byzantine auxiliary forces that participated in the Italian campaign (Olajos 1998, 220–21).

Conflict could have arisen at the court between the Scandinavian and some Turkic retainers during the reign of Emperor Michael V (1041–42 CE), who changed his bodyguards to 'Scythians' (possibly nomads) (Psellos 1967, 95). After his death, however, Scandinavians were again installed in their former positions.

Thus, in tenth- and eleventh-century Byzantium, the presence of Turkic, Scandinavian and Rus' bodyguards and retainers is almost continuously verifiable, which raises the possibility that these groups were in close contact with each other. Written accounts about steppe impact on Scandinavian retainers in Byzantium is not available, but archaeological material (which will be discussed later) might be linked to the common Turkic–Scandinavian duties in Constantinople.

## The Khazar Khaganate

It was a well-established custom among the Eurasian nomads to employ foreign bodyguards (Györffy 1994a, 87; Golden 2001, 2006, 79). A Khazarian version of the Varangian Guard is usually accepted among scholars by referring to Mas'ūdī's description of the Khazar's armed forces (Györffy 1959, 60; Blöndal 1978, 7; Montgomery 2010, 161–64). Mas'ūdī recounts that "the Rūs and the Saqāliba . . . served as mercenaries and slaves (*'abīd*) of the [Khazar] king" (Maçoudi 1863, 12; Lunde and Stone 2012, 133). The term *Ṣaqāliba*, as already discussed, referred to people of Slavic origin in this period (Golden et al. 1995; Mishin 1999; Ayalon 1999, 349–52). It is also known from Mas'ūdī that in Itil, the Khazar capital, Rus' were in the ruler's service together with Jews, Muslims and steppe nomadic people (Maçoudi 1863, 10–12; Lunde and Stone 2012, 133). The Khazars themselves were of Turkic origin, although Mas'ūdī's wording seems to indicate the presence of other steppe people in contemporary Itil: "The pagans who live in this country belong to many different races, among which are the Saqāliba and the Rūs" (Maçoudi 1863, 9; Lunde and Stone 2012, 132). Since according to this account, the Rus' and the *Ṣaqāliba* were only part of the country's pagan population, it can be asserted that other heathen – probably Turkic/steppe – people also lived there, as the context of the source notes Jews and Muslims separately (Maçoudi 1863, 8; Lunde and Stone 2012, 131).

It has also been posited that the ruler called *chacanus* (khagan) of the Rus' envoys who arrived at the court of the Frankish king Louis the Pious in Ingelheim in 839 CE did not mean the ruler of a separate Rus' khaganate, but referred to the Khazar khagan himself (Montgomery 2010, 163–64). Objections against this assertion were put forward in previous chapters, but if this is accepted then the appearance of the Rus' in Khazar service should be dated to the 830s CE.

The Khazars definitely maintained close ties with the Rus' in the ninth and tenth centuries. Prince Sviatoslav's campaign against the Khazars took place in 965/969 CE, which is close in time to Mas'ūdī's report about Rus' warriors in Itil. Thus, a theory may be advanced that Rus' and steppe warriors fought on both sides in the Rus'–Khazar war, although I find it unlikely that even the Rus', who appear in ibn Faḍlān's famous description of 922 CE, would have been the Khazars' mercenaries or 'slave soldiers', as James E. Montgomery suggests (Montgomery 2010, 163). The group ibn Faḍlān describes came to conduct commercial business in Bulgar and actually traded in slaves. In addition, according to the testimony of the Muslim emissary, the Volga Bulghars were trying to become independent from the khaganate at just that time (Montgomery 2014, 190–91, 238–41), so linking or mentioning Khazar–Rus' (slave) warriors to the current situation would be expected from the report.

Although not affecting the argument about the potential Turkic impact on Rus' warriors in Khazaria, the view of their involvement in the local retinue has to be slightly modified. First, Mas'ūdī explicitly states that Muslims formed the main component of the Khazar army and that the bodyguard (or retinue) of the khagan was recruited from Khazar-born Jewish warriors who lived with him in his palace. Second, although the Rus' definitely had roles in the Khazar army, inferences from several Muslim writers suggest that they lived in a part of the town across the Volga River, while the retinue resided with the Khazar ruler in the other part (Maçoudi 1863, 9; de Goeje 1927, 221–22; Lunde and Stone 2012, 132, 153–54; Montgomery 2014, 256–57). This makes it apparent that the Rus' were not among the troops of the Khazar retinue.

Understanding the role the Rus' played in the military life of the khaganate must take into account that the Muslims also serving in Itil were not under the full control of the Khazar rulers. This can be seen through the Rus' raid in the Caspian in 913 CE, which ended with the massacre of the Rus' force by Muslims living under Khazar rule. Despite an earlier pact with the Rus', the Khazar ruler could not stop the Muslims from taking revenge on them (Maçoudi 1863, 18–23; Lunde and Stone 2012, 144–46). In addition, Mas'ūdī also claims that Muslims were not willing to take up arms against their own kind and that if the Christians and the Muslims of the town united the Khazar ruler would have no authority over them (Maçoudi 1863, 12; Lunde and Stone 2012, 133–34). The Rus' and Slavs in Itil might have served as a counterbalance against the disobedient and sometimes unreliable Muslim contingent (numbering some 7,000– 12,000) (cf. Maçoudi 1863, 11 with de Goeje 1927, 221), which can be inferred from the reference to them as *'abīd*, slaves. In the Islamic world, the Arabic word *'abd* (pl. *'abīd*) was used as a general term for slaves (Brunschvig 1986), and the original Arabic text does not differentiate between the Rus' and the *Ṣaqāliba* as one being warriors and the other slaves.

Despite these objections, Khazar cultural influence on the Rus' is beyond controversy. The retinue of the so-called Rus' king described in ibn Faḍlān's account, for instance, strikingly resembles the bodyguards of the Khazar khagan (see Chapter 6).

## Hungary

The possibility of hiring Scandinavian and Rus' bodyguards has also been proposed in the case of Hungary, a theory less well known in Western historiography. As early as the 1950s, noted Hungarian medievalist György Györffy asserted that "Varangian-Rus' mercenaries" were in the service of Grand Prince Géza and the first king, Saint Stephen I, from the end of the tenth century onwards (Györffy

1959, 86–92, 1984, 831–32; [1977] 2013, 313–14). Even though his hypothesis was questioned by Gyula Kristó (another famous Hungarian medievalist and contemporary of Györffy) on chronological and linguistic grounds (Kristó 1983), the thesis is still popular in scholarly circles (for references, see Katona 2017a).

According to this theory, 'Varangian-Rus'' bodyguards were present in Hungary in the 980s CE, near the end of Géza's reign, when the Pechenegs were becoming a serious threat on the Dnieper waterways. This prompted the Rus' to march from Kiev to Constantinople (and back) through the Magyar territories, which were believed to be more friendly, and some of them entered Géza's service (Györffy 1959, 92). Migrating Rus' bodyguards could have come to Hungary in larger numbers with time since, according to the PVL, Stephen (who followed Géza on the throne) maintained good relations with Grand Prince Vladimir of Kiev (Cross and Sherbowitz-Wetzor 1953, 122; Likhachev 1996, 56). The presence of Magyar warriors in Vladimir's court is supported by archaeological material from the so-called druzhina-graves (Tagán 1941; Borosy 1981, 34; Fodor 2007, 193–99). Besides the bodyguard exchange between the Kievan and the Hungarian courts, a wave of 'Varangians' arrived in Hungary with the Byzantine fiancée proposed for Stephen's son, Emeric (Moravcsik 1938; Györffy 1959, 92; Makk 1999, 37). Since Emeric is labelled as *dux Ruizorum*, that is, "Prince of the Rus'", in the contemporary *Annales Hildesheimenses* in the year 1031 CE (Waitz 1878, 36), Györffy claimed that he was the leader of the royal bodyguard, as traditionally the heir to the throne commanded the foreign auxiliaries. The 'Varangians' escorting Emeric's fiancée from Byzantium could have been settled near the central territories of the kingdom, in Tolna and Somogy counties, where the name of two settlements, Várong and Varang, seem to have an Old Norse root – *væring* (meaning 'a companion who takes an oath'). In contrast, retinue members arriving from Kiev might have come to reside not far from the contemporary frontiers, as is suggested by settlement names with the Hungarian stem *orosz*, originating from the word *Rus'*. The secondary meaning of *orosz*, 'bodyguard' or 'doorkeeper', strengthens this point (Györffy 1959, 83–92, 1966–98: I, 126, 464–65, III, 365–66, IV, 169–71), although Kristó argued that this meaning did not appear before the sixteenth century (Kristó 1983, 199–201). The Varangian-Rus' bodyguard in Hungary was paralleled with analogous institutions in Kiev, Poland and Byzantium (Györffy 1959, 87–92, [1977] 2013, 108, 313, 417).

Although the evidence for this theory accumulated incoherently (Katona 2017a), we should still entertain the possibility that some Scandinavians and Rus' indeed took service in Hungary. The evidence can be best synthesized by assuming that the Rus' bodyguards only stayed in the country for a short time and left after Emeric's death in 1031 CE. Their settlements in the countryside can perhaps be explained as supply stations on the kingly itinerary where Rus' bodyguards assured the king's safety.

Individual cases of Scandinavians taking Hungarian service surely also occurred in the joint campaigns of Sviatoslav. The meeting in Quedlingburg in 973 CE where both Prince Géza's and Harald Bluetooth's representatives were present, would have been an opportunity for similar exchanges. A French source composed between 1136 and 1140 CE by the Anglo-Norman chronicler Geffrei Gaimar, for instance, mentions a Danish lord named Walgard who accompanied fugitive Anglo-Saxon princes, the sons of Edmund Ironside, to Hungary as they were fleeing their homeland from the wrath of Cnut the Great (Gaimar 2009, 251–53). If any Scandinavian warriors appeared in Hungary during this period they would have had close contact with nomadic military culture since the Hungarian army still consisted mostly of steppe nomadic light cavalry (Györffy 1984, 750).

The case of the Kylfings is another topic related to the question of Scandinavian retinue members in Hungary. The Scandinavian name, *Kylfingar*, occurs in various forms in medieval sources as the Slavic *kolbiagi* and the Greek *koulpingoi*, always differentiated from the Rus' and Varangians. The Kylfings remain largely unknown; there is not even agreement on the nature of their organization, whether they should be considered a tribe or some kind of association. Various attempts to trace their original ancestry illustrate the ambiguities; theories about the Kylfings see them as Finnish, Danish, Norwegian, Swedish or Slavic in origin (Andersson 2001).

Hungarian historiography often associates the Kylfings with the Kölpénys, a nomadic tribe, possibly of Pecheneg origin. According to the Hungarian chronicle *Gesta Hungarorum*, they arrived in Hungary during the reign of Grand Prince Taksony (955–c. 972 CE), judging by the personal name Kölpény in the chronicle (Székely 1975, 11; Tóth 1988; Benkő 1999). According to Györffy, Saint Stephen's new royal army, which included heavy cavalry, was partly recruited from among the Kylfings (Györffy [1977] 2013, 313).

Modern Western research expresses doubts on the connection between the two names (Scheel 2015, 143–44), but I am less sceptical, mostly due to the obscurities in the history of the Kylfings. The Kylfings appeared in various areas of the Nordic and Eastern regions, and thus their organization might have been similar to that described for the Rus': a merchant-warrior group that was active in Northern Europe, the Baltics, European Russia and Byzantium (Golden 1995; Arbman 1961, 90–91). Different sources in which they appear, including *Russkaya Pravda*, place names along the Baltic coast, Swedish runestones, Icelandic works and Byzantine chrysobulls (Scheel 2015, 142–51) corroborate this. Their absence from the Arabic sources, which were mostly concerned with the affairs in the Volga area, is remarkable and either indicates that they were absent or less active there, or perhaps that they were known by a different name.

With an organization similar to that of the Rus', the Kylfings would also have been adaptable, taking up local customs and norms, and could easily have become acclimatized to Slavic, Scandinavian and Turkic cultures. The Kylfings, who plundered the Sámi in the Icelandic *Egils saga Skallagrímssonar* during the tenth century (Nordal 1979, 27–28), were perhaps more closely related to the Scandinavian cultural milieu than the Kylfings, who somehow joined Pecheneg tribes in the Dnieper area and arrived in the Carpathian Basin in the time of Prince Taksony. Evidence from his reign mentions the immigration of Volga Bulgharian and Pecheneg groups.[2] The Pecheneg Suru Kül Bey tribe, perhaps the origin of the name Kölpény, lived near the Khazar Empire. Their territory lay west of the Dnieper River, next to the route that Rus' and probably also Kylfing warrior-merchants took on their way to Constantinople. Lack of further concrete evidence leaves the identification of the Kylfings with the Hungarian Kölpénys as speculation.

## Archaeological traces

The picture from written sources about Turkic–Scandinavian Rus' co-operation in warfare is tinctured by archaeological evidence. Some Scandinavian weapons, mostly straight double-edged swords found in Hungary, have also been ascribed to the retinue formed by Géza and Stephen (Györffy [1977] 2013, 108), despite the fact that they were stray finds or came from graves furnished with typical Magyar-style objects. Stephen's personal sword, kept now in the Saint Vitus cathedral in Prague, is decorated in the Mammen style and probably signals diplomatic contacts with the Jelling dynasty (Figure 5.3). Finding Viking weapons in Hungary would strengthen the theory of a Rus' bodyguard, but only a single burial seems to be relevant to the possibility of a Scandinavian warrior being buried in Hungary. This has been interpreted as containing a "high status Rus' warrior" buried partially according to Magyar customs (Kovács 1995). The burial, dated to the tenth century, was discovered in the Székesfehérvár-Rádiótelep site (Grave 'A'), but the grave was disturbed and poorly documented. Its interpretation is problematic, and no parallels are known.

Several swords, and a spear decorated in the Ringerike style, have been found in Hungary, showing clear connections to Scandinavia based on typology and ornamentation (Paulsen 1933; Kovács 1970a; Fodor 1986; Figure 5.4; Figure 5.5; Figure 5.6). These weapons, however, are mainly stray finds; interpreting them as signs of a 'Varangian-Rus'' retinue's armament is questionable. It seems more likely that the Hungarian army adopted these weapons for its own use. Attempts to adapt weapons to local use (e.g. Figure 5.6) can also be discerned in some examples usually labelled 'hybrid sabre-swords' in which a straight double-edged blade was inserted in a curved sabre grip (Kirpichnikov 1966a, 34, 61; Bíró 2012, 202–03). They are found in the Baltic region and Russia as well as in Hungary.

In Poland, it was long held that the elite hostages Bolesław brought from Kiev were actually Scandinavians, who were interred in the graves at Lutomiersk. This has been challenged recently, and instead the cemetery is argued to hold Slavic military elite (Gardeła 2018). It is undeniable, however, that both nomadic and Scandinavian military cultures were present in Poland. The cemetery of Bodzia on the Vistula in Central Poland is one of the biggest twenty-first-century discoveries of Polish archaeology. The forms and contents of the graves differ from normal Polish cemeteries of the period in several ways, most notably in Scandinavian, Rus' and nomadic Khazar elements, suggesting that the population of the nearby settlement was multi-ethnic. Weapons among the grave goods and injuries on the bones make it evident that some of the inhabitants were warriors. The Scandinavian element at Bodzia was clear in chamber-like burials closely analogous to those widespread in Denmark and Sweden. Weapons, a *langsax* and a sword decorated in the Mammen style, were recovered, and precious-metal objects, such as a pendant with a dragon-head end, also signal Nordic contacts. Multiple burial

*Figure 5.3* Sword of Saint Stephen, decorated in the Mammen style. Petersen type S

Source: Redrawn after the Digital Archive of the National Museum. Online: https://mandadb.hu/dokumentum/823721/000039.jpg [Accessed 03.02.2021]

pits with annexes, the stylistic features of two silver pendants, a nomadic battle axe and the custom of 'sprinkling' the deceased with beads and coins, as in one of the women's graves, are all features supporting the interpretation that Bodzia's population included Khazar elements. Rus' were also found, indicated by the symbol of Sviatopolk I of Kiev (1015–19 CE) on a belt fitting. As the only Rus' ruler using the sign of the Rus' bident with a cross on the right prong, it has

*Figure 5.4* Double-edged swords from Hungary: Danube bed, Erzsébet bridge. Stray finds
Source: Redrawn after Buzinkay and Havassy 1995, 47, fig. 43; Fodor et al. 1996, 367, fig. 2

been suggested that the owner of the belt was close kin of Sviatopolk (or maybe even the prince himself). The Bodzia cemetery is an outstanding example of how foreign connections and cultural mergers shape a community and how far such cultural packages might travel (for Bodzia, see the collection of essays in Buko 2015).

Based on the presence of Viking weapons, mostly double-edged swords and a shield boss, found in the territory between the Volga and Kama rivers, and in Biljar and Bulgar, archaeologists believe that a similar Scandinavian Rus' retinue operated in the Muslim-convert court in Volga Bulgharia (Izmailov 2000, 2003; Kirpichnikov and Izmailov 2000). Besides the swords, the archaeologist developing this idea, Iskander L. Ismailov, built his argument on parallel institutions, among which he enumerated the Hungarian Rus' retinue. The possibility that some Rus' warriors entered Volga Bulghar service cannot be ruled out and might be connected to Turkic cultural borrowings in the Volga area that demonstrate the

*Figure 5.5* Double-edged swords from Hungary: Szob-Kiserdő and Vác-Csörög. Stray finds

Source: Fodor et al. 1996, 410, fig. 1; a courtesy picture from Tragor Ignác Museum

close link between Scandinavians and the local population in the region. It has also been suggested that particular indigenous Volga Bulghar coins struck in the 950s and 970s CE might also be signs of Swedish mercenary activity in Volga Bulgharia. These specific dirhams are abundant in Sweden but rare in the Kievan Rus' and have been interpreted as military pay brought back to the Scandinavian homelands directly from Bulgharia (Kovalev 2013, 89). Fifteen kurgans dated

*Figure 5.6* Tenth-century double-edged swords from Székesfehérvár (Hungary)

Source: Photos by Bertalan Zágorhidi-Czigány

to the mid-tenth century were found in Balymer, interpreted as a remnant of a Scandinavian armed elite force. The burial rite of cremation in all cases and two swords of Scandinavian provenance, one intact and the other deliberately bent, indeed allow the identification of a Scandinavian mercenary force on Volga Bulgharian territory, even if only short lived (Izmailov 2000, 2003).

If a Volga Bulghar–Scandinavian retinue indeed existed, it is probable that the warriors were not wielding only their traditional Viking weapons but also using local weaponry and fighting techniques. Volga Bulghar military and cultural influence – in the form of weapons, steppe ornaments and treasure – is attested in adjacent areas of the Ural region, where Finno-Ugrian people lived (Belavin 2000, 111–20). The merging of Scandinavian and steppe cultures can be detected on a nomadic-style axe found in the Kazan region that is decorated with a scene of the Germanic Siegfried legend clearly based on Scandinavian models (Abrams 2016, 41–50; Figure 5.7). Kurgan number 13 of the Balymer complex also shows this fusion; besides the clearly Scandinavian style of the burial rite, objects of steppe origin were also found in the grave. These include pottery from the Saltovo-Mayaki culture, copper plates from a bridle, harness covers and belt bag fittings, all analogous with Magyar material from the Carpathian Basin (Izmailov 2000, 74–80).

Archaeological data connected to Rus' *druzhinas* is abundant. In the cemeteries of Rus' settlements, assemblages often labelled 'druzhina-graves' have been discovered that frequently contain grave goods of steppe origin, such as belts, mount fittings, sabres, axes, bows, plumed helmets and bone carvings (Kirpichnikov 1970, 73–76; Fodor 1986, 219–20; Bálint 1989, 113–16; Franklin and Shepard 1996, 123–24; Androshchuk 2000, 263, 2013, 64; Duczko 2004, 248; Murasheva 2006; Movchan 2007; Pushkina 2007). These objects not only reached the regions adjacent to the steppe, such as Chernigov, Shestovitsa and Kiev (Komar 2017a, 2017b, 2018, 160–63, 203–11, 393–94, 410), but also more northerly areas, such as Izborsk and Timerovo (Lopatin 2017, 141). Changes in weapons and military style that occurred in the second part of the tenth century are seen in these graves and affirm the picture in the written evidence from Sviatoslav onwards. Numerous graves and kurgans with military equipment have been discovered in the core areas linked to Kiev through the river tributary to the Dnieper. An examination of 220 burials showed that half of them contained lances, arrows and bow quivers, far more than the number of double-edged swords and even axes, of which 60 were found. Riding gear was also found in 60 of these graves, and a few sabres, a close-combat slashing weapon associated with horsemen, however, only once

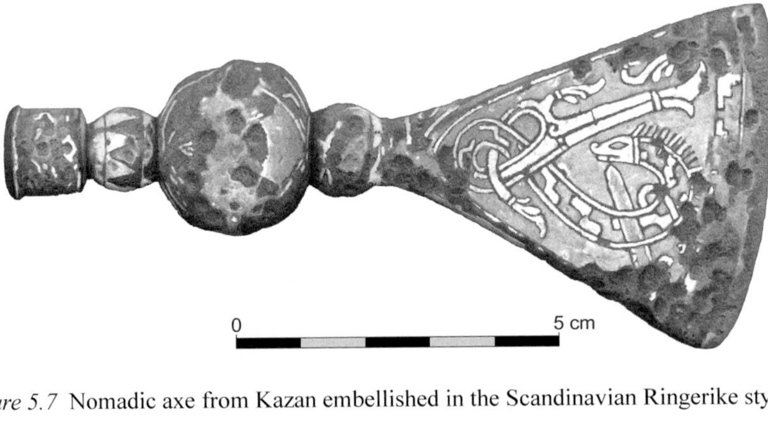


*Figure 5.7* Nomadic axe from Kazan embellished in the Scandinavian Ringerike style

Source: Redrawn after Olausson and Petrovski 2007, 233, fig. 6

was a sabre paired with a sword (Mocja 2000, 269–71). Hundreds of steppe belt mounts and horse harness fittings found in Gnezdovo also illustrate the spread of cavalry among the Rus' military elites. Most of the harness fittings were manufactured by the lost wax method, known to be practiced by the Volga Bulghars (Eniosova and Murashova 1999).

The question is, how was this material connected to the ethnic make-up of retinue culture? That traditional steppe armament in Rus' territories should be regarded as the equipment of Khazar, Pecheneg, Volga Bulghar, Magyar or other steppe warriors in Rus' princely service is the first option. No find complexes are known in which these are the only dominant elements, which either suggests that steppe military influence spread due to individual choices rather than whole fighting units or that steppe warriors soon became acclimated to Rus' communities. Another interpretation of this material is that it was the remnants of a warrior culture where retinue members could acquire distinctive weapons of other cultures regardless of their own 'original' ethnic ancestry. For instance, the deceased man in the Black Grave of Chernigov and the related mourning community were likely subject to influences similar to those of Prince Sviatoslav. There is no doubt that Rus' *druzhinas* were ethnically mixed, making it hard to determine the place(s) of origin of the men in the Black Grave of Chernigov. Weapons cannot help, even though some objects, such as double-edged swords, shield bosses and *scramasaxes*, seem to indicate Scandinavia as a point of diffusion, as sabres, arrows and quivers point towards the steppe. Details of similar graves, however, strongly suggest that the original homeland of many of these military men lay in Scandinavia, even though they followed the fashions of a widespread retinue culture.

Most indicative, of course, are the large barrows; boat burials; Scandinavian cult objects (such as the Þórr statuette in the Black Grave and pendants of the same god); ritual details, such as placing weapons in a pile during cremation, and the presence of cauldrons and animal skins and bones (Petrukhin 1998). The chamber graves in Russia and Ukraine that closely parallel those in Birka are notable examples (Gräslund 1981, 44–45); the grave goods of some of these reveal steppe influence. For instance, a chamber grave from the urban area of Vladimir in Kiev (near the Alexander Nevsky Church) contained grave goods clearly reminiscent of the Magyar material culture of the Carpathian Basin. Besides a Magyar-type quiver and arrows and the Magyar-style fittings of its sabretache, the grave held a Viking sword of Petersen type X and a scabbard chape depicting the characteristic falcon motif of the Rus'. This, together with the chamber-grave ritual and the clothing accessories, such as buckles, link the grave to examples in Birka (Kleingärtner and Müller-Wille 2008). Another notable example is a tenth-century chamber-grave in the Shestovitsa VI cemetery. The deceased was buried with a number of Scandinavian weapons – axe, lance, sword and *scaramasax* – and other characteristic artefacts, among them a drinking horn. The chamber also held a horse sacrifice and typical steppe accessories, horse trappings, a conical helmet and sabretaches (Kovalenko, Motsya, and Syty 2012). Other burials in the Shestovitsa cemetery and Chernigov's barrows are clearly similar to this pattern (e.g. Arne 1931; Melnikova, Nikitin, and Fomin [1984] 2011, 289).

Fragments of composite bows associated with the *druzhina* culture have been discovered in major Rus' settlements and are growing in number; many of these weapons and other accessories (quivers, bow cases) have been found in graves furnished in Scandinavian style (Mikhailov and Kainov 2011). Characteristic axes of originally nomadic provenance, called *chekan*, spread extensively in the Kievan Rus' and reached as far as Birka (Arbman 1940, Tafeln 14/9–10; Kirpichnikov 1966b, 29–31; Jansson 1988, 617; Ambrosiani and Androshchuk 2006, 6, 15–16; Mikhajlov 2011, 213). One of the largest clusters of this axe type (narrow bladed at one end and pointed at the other), was found in Gnezdovo, the most militarized Rus' location along the Dnieper. Here, in the second half of the tenth century, there was a massive distribution of nomadic armament: helmets, sabres, axes, lances, clubs and whole complexes of equestrian and archer's equipment (Kainov 2018, 238). These are usually found with Scandinavian weapons and accessories (also chainmail fragments) and Eastern objects, such as the caftan found in Grave Dn4 (Avdusin 1969; Avdusin and Puškina 1988, 25–28).

Further, co-operation between steppe (Turkic) and Scandinavian Rus' craftsmen is discernible on certain weapon finds. Viking weapons with steppe-style decoration and typical nomadic weapons with Nordic embellishments (or in Scandinavian graves) are known from settlements in and around Kiev. As noted, these are usually interpreted as proof of vivid cultural transfer between the Rus' and Magyars in the Dnieper area that culminated in the development of merged styles and mutual borrowings of techniques and craftsmen (Katona 2017a, 26).

At the other end of the spectrum lay Birka. The town has yielded rich grave goods of Eastern origin; three clusters can be differentiated that point towards Volga Bulgharia (the cemetery of Tankeevka offers the closest parallels), Hungary and Byzantium (Ambrosiani and Androshchuk 2006). Lamellae from an armour of 'Old Turkic type', dated between 900 and 950 CE is most closely paralleled in Kurgan 11 from Balyk-Sook in the Altai mountains (Stjerna 2004). Multiple finds of steppe origin found in the garrison of Birka probably belonged to Scandinavian warriors who had spent a long time in contact with steppe groups, acquired their fighting habits and adopted their weaponry (Lundström, Hedenstierna-Jonson, and Olausson 2009). This could have happened in the Byzantine border zones, but equally could have resulted from the presence of both Scandinavians and Turks in Byzantine imperial bodyguards (Hedenstierna-Jonson 2015). The Scandinavians could have learned how to shoot with nomadic bows from the Magyar bodyguards during guard duties or common campaigns. Certain finds from Birka can be associated explicitly with Magyar material culture of the tenth century – sabretaches, finger rings, remains of bows and quivers – and might be evidence of Magyar–Scandinavian contacts in Constantinople (Hedenstierna-Jonson 2009a, 2012). Other examples of steppe culture related to military groups, most notably 'oriental' belt mounts and fittings, are found in other places in the Baltic area and Scandinavia (Jansson 1987, 1988; Jansson and Nosov 1992). Thus, the Magyar features discernible at Birka are only one example among a number of indications of the circulation of artefacts and motifs among the Baltic, Rus', Byzantine and Magyar milieus. A Saint Stephen coin found in the Sandur hoard in the Faeroes shows that connections, even if through intermediaries, could be far-reaching (Huszár 1967; Gedai 1980).

## Conclusion

Scandinavian and Rus' mercenaries serving as bodyguards or retainers in Eastern courts often adopted local customs. This is partly attributed to the ethnically mixed nature of contemporary retinues, the flexibility of the social environment, and the adaptability of the retainers themselves. Scandinavians in Constantinople developed a taste for Byzantine fashions and lifestyles; those in Kiev readily accepted Slavic notions, and in Itil they became accustomed to Muslim and Turkic forms of service. The steppe Turkic impact stands out among the foreign impulses that affected the Scandinavians in the East. If the retainers' opportunity to change courts is taken as a serious possibility, the options for creating one's own style in a military-cultural sense were almost infinite when we consider various combintations of fighting habits (infantry, navy, cavalry, archers) and hardware (clothing, weaponry). It is noteworthy that Scandinavian groups were affected by diverse cultural habits and thus could also become different from each other.

The interaction between nomadic horsemen and Scandinavians started in two ways and had slightly different, although certainly overlapping, effects in relation to cultural and military borrowings. First, Scandinavian and Rus' warriors participated in campaigns as hired mercenaries and auxiliary troops in the service of most of the courts in the region, even in Georgia, for instance (Shepard 1984–85; Larsson 1986–89). In all the places where the Scandinavians' presence as hired warriors is assumed (Byzantium, Kievan Rus', Khazaria, Volga Bulgharia, Hungary and Poland) – as auxiliaries, retinue members or forced conscripts – written sources attest that people of steppe origin also took service at the same time. Many of these power centres or their enemies controlled armies trained for steppe nomadic warfare. While on campaign, the Scandinavians would probably have witnessed the overpowering superiority of cavalry in clashes fought in the open. This also occurred when nomads were hired as auxiliaries in an army consisting mostly of Scandinavian and Rus' infantry, which similarly accustomed them to fighting alongside cavalry and at the same time acquiring related tactics and strategies. Although Scandinavians were well aware of the use of horses in military contexts as early as the Vendel period (c. 540–790 CE) (Engström 1997), open battles in Viking Age Scandinavia were mostly fought on foot in close formation (Williams 2019, 42–50). Several independent accounts about the Rus' emphasize that they fought on foot (de Goeje 1892, 146; Margoliouth 1921, 67; Minorsky 1942, 36; Göckenjan and Zimonyi 2011, 254; Lunde and Stone 2012, 127). From the tenth century onwards the growing influence of horsemen in Rus' fighting units, seen in both textual descriptions and archaeological material, suggests that they became accustomed to the nomadic fighting habits of mounted warfare.

Scandinavian and Rus' warriors were also employed more permanently in the regional courts as bodyguards or parts of larger retinues. These services were probably built on a greater level of trust than occasional military alliances and resulted in longer service. During common bodyguard duties with other nomads, Turkic cultural borrowings were perhaps more easily transmitted to Scandinavian retainers. These could have been manifested in a universal retinue culture or fashion in which retinue members adopted and disseminated culturally diverse elements of attire, clothing and weapons from the fringes of the Muslim world to Scandinavia. Joint campaigns in retinue service were still significant, however, providing space and time for various groups to adapt to each other and new fighting techniques and weapons.

It is also evident that the military contingents of both Scandinavians and Turks in the period did not all function the same way. Military retinues and armies in the East operated differently, which probably had consequences for the relationships within ethnically and culturally diverse warrior groups. In the same way as a certain environment affected the retainers themselves, to some extent diverse warrior components also shaped the local military system. Scandinavians or Rus' and steppe nomads were, or could be, used as substitutes for each other or to balance power relationships among military units serving within a polity (e.g. Byzantium and Khazaria).

A last question remains to be addressed, namely, how mixed fighting units were created and held together so as to be effective, especially in the Rus' territories and Birka. Anthropological theories – in-group formation and identity fusion – have recently been applied to the operation of Viking Age warbands. Viking Age retinues and larger armies were heterogenous in both social and ethnic terms and heterogeneity weakened their cohesiveness. Therefore, smaller units of an army, like the retinues often called *lið*, were held together by creating solidarity and shared identities through sets of common traits that did not characterize outsiders. Their primary means of doing this was to be selective about how men were accepted into the in-group. Members were expected to live up to a warrior ideal that advocated reckless behaviour on the battlefield, and their acceptance into the in-group was sealed by ritual oaths. Material markers were also meant to create a distinctive cultural image shared by the whole group. The ideals of the in-group were advocated to young members in poetry recited at communal feasts, where bonds between members were also re-affirmed. A common sense of belonging was further strengthened by traumatic experiences while on campaign, creating lasting bonds sometimes stronger than kinship ties. A shared world view or ideology was the final binding bond in a warrior community (Raffield et al. 2016; Hedenstierna-Jonson 2020c).

Many of these strategies can be envisaged for the ethnically mixed fighting units described earlier. Rus' warriors are said to have worn gold bracelets on which oaths of allegiance were sworn in Viking Age Scandinavia (de Goeje 1892, 145; Martinez 1982, 168; Lunde and Stone 2012, 126). Sanctioning oaths taken on bracelets and weapons during the Byzantine–Rus' peace negotiations also implies that the practice of binding rituals was also widely practised in the East (Cross and Sherbowitz-Wetzor 1953, 65–66, 74, 77; Likhachev 1996, 17, 24, 26). The Viking Age warrior ideal expressed in contemporary runic inscriptions and skaldic poems expected a warrior 'not to flee' from battle and to distance himself from battlefield horrors (Jesch 2009). Both ibn Rusta and Miskawayh report a similar form of ideal conduct among the Rus', stressing the courage of Rus' warriors as they never fled from battle (de Goeje 1892, 146; Margoliouth 1921, 67; Lunde and Stone 2012, 127). Others who could live up to these ideals were readily admitted to the in-group, illustrated by the appearance of Slavic names among the members of the Rus' warrior elite in later Rus'–Byzantine treaties and by the evidence for Rus'–Turkic co-operation in warfare described earlier. One can similarly imagine how a conglomeration of Scandinavian and Turkic warriors gathered in a leader's hall could facilitate the later development of literary genres like the Russian *byliny*, songs reminiscent of both Icelandic sagas and steppe ballads.

Distinctive material markers of mixed Scandinavian–Turkic warrior groups can also be detected in the archaeological record. Burials of mixed style, incorporating both originally Scandinavian and Turkic grave goods, attest an 'international' warrior elite culture that included not only Scandinavians, steppe nomads and other ethnicities but also people with mixed or even multiple identities. The Scandinavian retinue buried in the Balymer kurgan, the interred in the Dn4 grave of Gnezdovo, the chamber grave of Kiev in Vladimir's town, the horse burials in Shestovitsa and the Black Grave of Chernigov all came from communities that lived combined steppe and Scandinavian lifestyles.

A brief return to the enigmatic Black Grave illustrates the wide-ranging networks of this warrior elite. After restoration, it turned out that one of the swords can be categorized as a special development of type-Z swords (in the terminology of Jan Petersen), which were manufactured in Anglo-Saxon England during the early eleventh century (Kainov 2019). The Þórr figure of the grave, according to recent interpretations, was a *hnefatafl* piece used for a popular board game in Scandinavia (Murasheva, Orfinskaya, and Loboda 2019, 76–77, 81). What was thought to be a Scandinavian *scramasax* in the grave may now be considered a (magical?) rod instead, parallels of which are known from Gnezdovo and the Swedish island of Öland (Lushin 2019, 21). Although a typical pagan grave, the interred (or the mourners) were probably acquainted with Christianity, as indicated by what is probably a cross on the tip of one of the spears found in the grave (Kainov and Shchavelev 2005). A bold hypothesis recently suggested that the name of the mound has historic roots in Old Russian chronicles and reflects the tradition of naming burial places after their interred. A ruler who bore the Slavic name Chern' might have rested in the *Chorna Mohyla* (Shchavelev 2007).

This warrior elite rode horses equipped with steppe horse gear, shot with nomadic bows, wore caftans, conical hats and helmets, as well as nomadic belt fittings and sabretaches and at the same time wielded straight double-edged Viking swords, practised cremation rites, rowed boats, played Scandinavian board games and drank from horns. Although they venerated Scandinavian gods, and probably practised Old Norse magic, monotheistic religions may have already started to penetrate their ranks. Some of them bore Slavic names. That these were communities in formation rather than distinct ethnic groups living together and keeping their own traditional habits might be envisaged through objects where the Scandinavian and the Turkic worlds met in fusion. The Chernigov drinking horns with

Khazar and Magyar mythological motifs and the nomadic *chekan* from Kazan illustrated with the Völsung legend are the most prominent examples. Owners and transmitters of this blended material culture merged their cultural traditions and likely developed a new (cultural) identity. Their networks extended from Anglo-Saxon England to the Arabic world and Byzantium, a strong reason for making them part of the Viking diaspora. This idea is conveyed in the term: 'Vikings of the steppe'. The next question to be explored is whether shared sets of beliefs or world views can be detected among these mixed communities, which could have worked as effective ideological tools for creating a new identity.

## Notes

1 Throughout the chapter the centres of these territories are referred to as 'courts', although great differences must have existed among them. Thus, 'court' as a general term denotes the residence (whether itinerant or not) of a given ruler and his entourage.
2 Taksony himself took a wife from the land of the Cumans (*de terra Cumanorum*); however, during his reign, the Cumans were not present in Eastern Europe, and thus the chronicler probably employed an ethnic designation of his own time for the inhabitants of the Pontic steppe. Thus, Taksony's wife may have come from the Pechenegs or the Volga Bulghars. In addition, the *gesta* also notes three Muslim immigrants with the name Billa, Baks and Hetény from Bular, referring to Volga Bulgharia. Tonuzoba, a Pecheneg prince, also arrived in Hungary during Taksony's reign and received lands along the Tisza River (Bak and Rady 2010, 127).

# 6 Customs and religion(s)[1]

Like the Black Grave of Chernigov, in 922 CE a Rus' ruler was cremated in a boat lavishly furnished with prestige goods on the shores of the Middle Volga near Bulgar. Animals and a slave girl were sacrificed during the funeral. After the cremation, his boat was dragged to the shore and a huge mound was built on top of it. In contrast to the Black Grave, known only through archaeology, this information comes from the eyewitness description of the Arab traveller ibn Faḍlān (Montgomery 2014, 244–53). His account offers unique ethnographic insight into the ethno-religious world of a community comparable to the one that created the burial in Chernigov. The Rus' emerge from the report as a militarized and hierarchical society that engaged in long-distance commerce and, similarly to the Kievan Rus', maintained far-reaching networks and connections with various cultures, including Byzantium, the Arabic world and the steppes. Even a cursory glance at the material culture of the group confirms this; the *Rūsiyyah* (as the Rus' are called) are described with axes, Frankish swords and daggers, the last item probably identical to the Scandinavian *scramasax*. Their 'cloak' (also discussed later) left their arms bare; ibn Faḍlān describes it as a *kisā'* (Montgomery 2014, 240–41), a general term for Islamic garments wrapped around the body like a toga, an attire that may have been adopted during their annual visits to the Volga Bulghar Muslim converts. They also had silk brocade, which, contrary to expectations, was Byzantine (*alrūmiyy*) (Montgomery 2014, 246–47). Silks from Byzantium reached the Bulghar markets and could have been acquired there. These Rus' seem to have been part of the same networks as the deceased of the Black Grave of Chernigov. The account complements the archaeological interpretation of culturally mixed graves with several details about customs and beliefs, stories which objects cannot tell. Objects in the Black Grave show undoubted steppe features (or were made on the steppe itself) and attest such links among the Rus' elite. Ibn Faḍlān's travelogue reflects the same influences.

Interactions between the Scandinavian Rus' and the inhabitants of the steppe had cultural consequences in the spheres of war and trade. I alluded to some of these earlier, and now I present them more systematically. Customs, ritual practices and beliefs were subject to change and adaptation, which gave rise to an eclectic Rus' culture and identity that raises many questions. What kinds of change can be detected in either the external or internal features of Rus' society? How unified

DOI: 10.4324/9781003037859-6

was this impact on Rus' customs and religious perceptions in general? Were there differences among the different communities spread along the Dnieper and Volga, and if so, what were they? How much can we still regard these communities as 'Scandinavian' in terms of identity? To address these questions, I will examine everyday customs and ritual practices separately. Then I will compare elements of Rus' ritual traditions with those of the neighbouring pre-Christian religions in the East to assess how much influence from the steppe can be detected in Rus' religious life and what kinds of variations existed therein. Finally, I will explore how the nature of contemporary pagan religions facilitated this merging of customs.

## The merging of everyday customs

Steppe influence on the Scandinavian Rus' had an everyday dimension that may have contributed indirectly to more abstract shifts in belief. These mainly concern externalities, such as military equipment, dress, jewellery, hairstyles and decorative motifs. One characteristic of the steppe cultural influence on Rus' or Scandinavian culture is that these 'foreign' elements were not simply borrowed but were sometimes combined with traditional Scandinavian features or modified to suit local tastes. This was not assimilation but a combination of indigenous and borrowed elements that gave rise to eclectic (or perhaps new) expressions of identity.

The *druzhina* warrior graves with mixed Scandinavian, Slavic and steppe weapons and accessories were discussed in the previous chapter. Eastern fashion, in the form of kaftans, loose baggy trousers and hats, spread among the Scandinavians and Rus'. The written evidence includes the buttons and silk garment of the dead Rus' chieftain described in ibn Faḍlān's travelogue (Montgomery 2014, 246–47), and ibn Rusta's description of the same cloth: "They use up to a hundred cubits of cloth to make their trousers. The man must wrap himself in the cloth and fasten it between his knees" (de Goeje 1892, 146; Lunde and Stone 2012, 127). Such baggy trousers are known from picture stones on Gotland (Tängelgårda and Smiss) and the Oseberg tapestry. The same Rus' fashion is described in the *Ḥudūd* but amended with "woolen bonnets" that are "let down behind their necks" (Bosworth 1982, 159). A conical hat, probably originating in the Kievan workshops or on the steppes (specimens are also found in Hungary, Khazaria and Kievan Rus') was similar to that of the Scandinavians, as indicated by surviving cap ends in Birka (Fodor 2017c; Jarman 2021, 158–59; Figure 6.1). Textile remnants from 'oriental' clothing were also found in the town (Hägg 1984). All this evidence indicates that some Scandinavian traders, possibly somewhere along the Volga, adopted dress styles that were a Muslim–Turkic blend (Jansson 1988, 579–84; Mikkelsen 2008, 41; Steuer 2014).

Hacksilver, frequently used in mercantile exchange in Scandinavia, was sometimes also decorated with steppe motifs (Jansson 1988, 626–27). Belts from the steppe are notable, too, and were treated in a number of distinguished publications by Ingmar Jansson (referenced in previous chapters), which can be expanded with other specimens from Sweden and one from Bornholm (Hårdh 2010, 277–78).

Steppe and Scandinavian styles were also combined occasionally in women's accessories. Such an example comes from the Vårby hoard found in Sweden, in

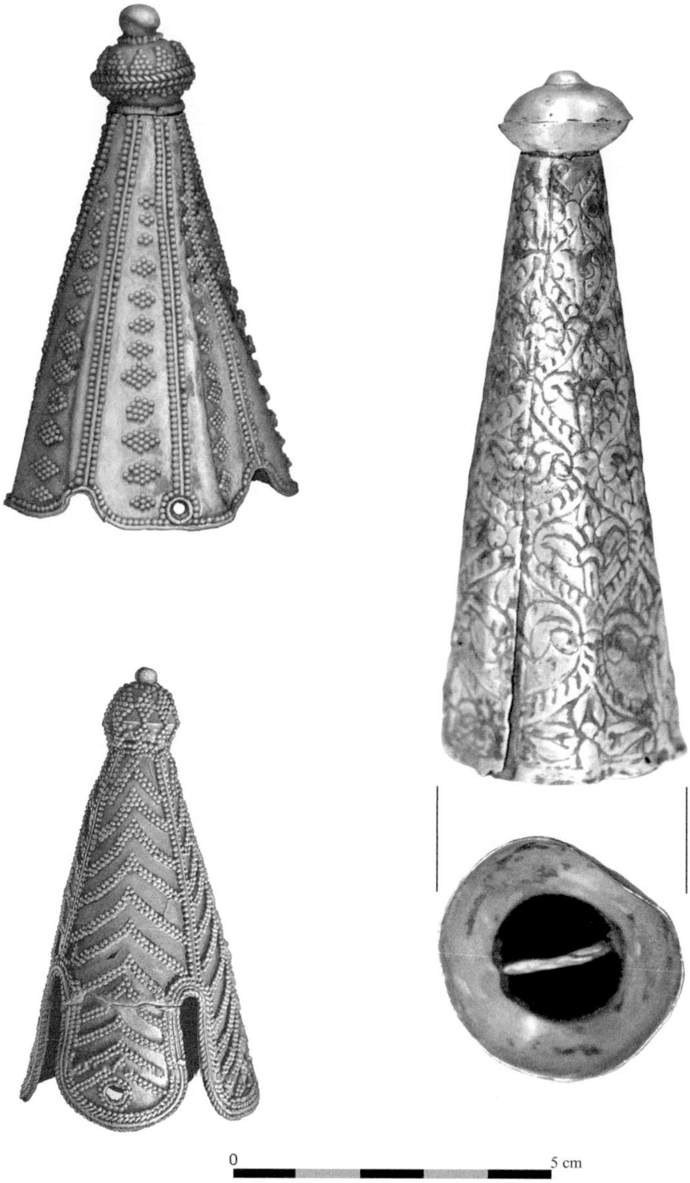


*Figure 6.1* Conical hats and hat tops from Birka, Shestovitsa and Jászberény (Hungary)

Source: Redrawn after Fodor 2017, 250, fig. 13, 251, fig. 16; and by courtesy of Jancsik et al. 2019, 70, fig. 2.

which suspension loops were added to 'oriental' belt fittings so as to hang, probably from necklaces (Jansson and Nosov 1992, 79, 234). Additional examples are a belt end from Birka (Grave 838), converted into a brass, and a locket (even suggested to hold Eastern aromatics) ornamented with an 'oriental' 'tree of life' motif (Jansson and Nosov 1992, 78; Roesdahl and Wilson 1992, 257). In the chamber grave of a wealthy person in Kiev (No. 49, Izyaslav's town), female jewellery of a blended style was found: some pendants of a necklace were decorated with Magyar palmette motifs, and others from the same necklace were of Scandinavian manufacture and had Nordic decorations (Kleingärtner and Müller-Wille 2008, 371–75). Some jewellery of Volga Bulghar provenance was also recovered in Gnezdovo (Pushkina, Murasheva, and Eniosova 2017). Carnelian amulets with analogies in the Khazarian Saltovo-Mayaki culture also spread in Rus' and Swedish territories (Pushkina 2020, 234).

Physical evidence of everyday Rus' culture suggesting Eastern contacts is apparent in ibn Faḍlān's description as well. Tattoos on the Rus', for instance, covered their bodies from top to toe and would probably be better explained as a borrowing from the East rather than Scandinavia. Even though remote in time, the famous burials preserved in the frozen mounds of the Siberian Pazyrik are other examples where the traces of this body embellishment were found, suggesting that the custom was prevalent in Inner Eurasia (Hraundal 2014, 85–88).

Sviatoslav's character confirms the idea that Turkic habits may have been influential (Tarras 1965, 401–05; Shepard 2008, 503; Downham 2012, 6). His description in the PVL is more akin to that of Inner Asian nomads of the steppe, who lived by raiding sedentary societies, took good care of and honoured their horses, and endured harsh circumstances by consuming simple food and sleeping in the open during campaigns. From Leo the Deacon's account it is apparent that Sviatoslav wore his hair in a ponytail and shaved the rest of his head (Diaconus 1828, 166–67). Various sources from the period report that such a hairstyle was unique to the Magyars (Kurze 1890, 133; Becker 1915, 185; Marsina 1971, 34–35). Sviatoslav also wore earrings, a fashion historically associated with the East (nomads and Arabs) rather than with the Scandinavians or Slavs (Tarras 1965, 404–05). Sviatoslav is one of the best examples of the complexity of early medieval ethnic identity: as a descendant of the Rurikid dynasty, he was biologically of Scandinavian origin, just like many of his commanders and warriors; however, he was also the first Rus' prince known to have a Slavic name and, moreover, to lead a nomadic life. Assimilation, however, took time, and the prince was brought up following Scandinavian customs, indirectly confirmed by the presence of his preceptor Asmund, a man clearly of Scandinavian origin.

It should also be noted that steppe influence did not affect all groups evenly and that borrowed material elements (and connected ideas) could be modified to signal a distinctive identity. This tendency echoes behind the words of Iṣṭakhrī, who clearly differentiated the short *qurtaq*, a coat or tunic worn by the Rus' from the long version of the same garment worn by the Khazars, Bulghars and Pechenegs (de Goeje 1927, 226; Lunde and Stone 2012, 159). This contrasts with ibn Faḍlān's description of the Rūsiyyah: "they wear neither tunics nor caftans. Every man wears a cloak (*kisā'*) with which he covers half of his body, so that one arm is uncovered" (Montgomery 2014, 240–41). The *kisā'* was a garment made of wool, usually wrapped around the body (Dozy 1845, 383–86); leaving one arm open was one possible way of wrapping the mantle around the shoulders (Stillman 51, 88–90, 2003, see especially plate 37). This costume probably originated in the Arab Maghreb and was worn by desert Berbers. Ibn Faḍlān might have used his own terminology to describe foreign attire, but nevertheless the peculiarity of the dress among the Rus' is interesting. It is also curious that ibn Faḍlān, despite his denial that the Rus' wear caftans, mentions later that their chieftain was buried in a tunic and silk caftan (Montgomery 2014, 246–47). So far, the evidence is ambivalent; the archaeological material clearly confirms that Scandinavians and Rus' wore Eastern-type tunics and caftans in the tenth century. The written sources suggest that some groups preferred a short version of this style but that among others it was restricted to high-ranking individuals or else they did not wear it at all.

The inconsistencies in the descriptions should be attributed (in my opinion) to the differences among the various Scandinavian and Rus' communities. An example from the Pechenegs, who (according to Iṣṭakhrī) were said to wear long tunics generally, can help to resolve the contradiction:

> At the time when the Pechenegs were expelled from their country, some of them of their own will and personal decision stayed behind there and united with the so-called Uzes [the Oghuz'], and even to this day live among them, and wear such distinguishing marks as separate them off and betray their origin and how it came about that they were split off from their own folk: for their tunics are short, reaching to the knee, and their sleeves are cut off at the shoulder, whereby, you see, they indicate that they have been cut off from their own folk and those of their race.
>
> (Constantine Porphyrogenitus 1967, 168–69)

Costume can work as a powerful marker of identity, and there is no reason not to believe that Scandinavian and Rus' groups in various situations consciously chose distinctive attire to express such ideas. Both the Pecheneg group described in the DAI and the Rus' in ibn Faḍlān wore different garments than most of the others in their ethnic groups. It also might not be a coincidence that one arm was left uncovered by clothing in the dress styles of both 'atypical' groups. Members of the Pecheneg diaspora cut off their sleeves to show their bare arms, while the Rus' of the Volga turned their cloaks aside to expose theirs. Their naked arms were quite visible, indicated by reports of tattoos seen to cover them (Montgomery 2014, 240–41). A body embellishment like this would indeed be worth putting on public display. There is no certainty about the function of the 'bare-arm garment', but it seems fitting to suggest that distinguishing attire did convey a departure from the norm, even if the precise message conveyed by the custom could vary.

The norms in external style for Scandinavians venturing to the East, and which group should be identified as the most 'typical', however, risks blurring the intricate complexities of contemporary identities. Besides group identities, individual decisions should also be taken into account. Iṣṭakhrī states about Rus' facial hair that some of the Rus' shaved and others braided their beards, suggesting that there were individual choices in style in Rus' communities (de Goeje 1927, 226; Lunde and Stone 2012, 159). Although being clean shaven was not without precedent in the Viking Age north (notably, the Normans on the Bayeux tapestry are beardless), it is hard to believe it was common (Jakobsson 2007; Phelpstead 2013). Beards in steppe societies at the time were restricted to high-ranking individuals (Bogachev and Frantsuzov 2011, 556–57), and ordinary members shaved regularly, as ibn Faḍlān reports for the Oghuz', the Pechenegs and the Baskhirs (Montgomery 2014, 208–15), and several independent observers for the Magyars (see earlier on Magyar coiffure). Iṣṭakhrī's words about Rus' dress and facial hair styles may have captured a Rus' community in a phase of collective, and at the same time individual, transition between habits brought from the homelands and adopted in the East.

## Rituals: sources and problems

External appearances were subject to alteration in Rus' culture, and there are indications that steppe influence did not stop there but also entered Rus' ritual traditions and beliefs. Sources describing tenth-century Rus' ritual practices at length, however, are problematic in several regards. Three of these accounts are relevant here. They include ritual sacrifices and a funeral along the Volga River recorded by ibn Faḍlān; the cremation of hostages and dead warriors carried out by the army of Prince Sviatoslav at the Battle of Dorostolon described by Leo the Deacon; and rituals performed by Rus' merchants on the island of Saint Gregory on their way to Constantinople as depicted in the DAI. All these rituals took place within a period of roughly 50 years (922–71 CE).[2]

Whether these rituals depict a tradition more akin to Slavic or Scandinavian culture is debated (Simpson 1967, 180; Obolensky 1982, 158; Montgomery 2000; Duczko 2004, 138; Petrukhin 2006, 189; Schjødt 2007; Luján 2008). This stems from two facts: first, inconsistencies and a lack of scholarly consensus about the ethnic connotations of the term Rus', and second, that none of these rituals were recorded by the Rus' themselves but by outsiders. Ibn Faḍlān was an Arab emissary of the Abbasid Caliphate in Baghdad, and the other two authors were Byzantines: the chronicler Leo the Deacon and someone possibly from the court of Emperor Constantine Porphyrogenitus.

This naturally presents obstacles in trying to reconstruct beliefs or practices, since the authors, not belonging to the cultures they describe, could have misunderstood and misinterpreted certain elements or perhaps simply adjusted the information to fit the terminology of their own religious world (Bartlett 2007, 47–54). Ibn Faḍlān, for instance, communicated with the Rus' through an interpreter, and Constantine also gathered his information on them through a translator. Leo's source had not even spoken to the Rus', as he had only observed the ritual from a distance.

Analogies from different sources, however, hint at the cultural backgrounds of the different rites, strengthening the relative authenticity of the three sources.

A diverse range of other sources, including contemporary Latin, Muslim and Slavic sources and later Old Norse literary works, will be compared in the contexts of the Scandinavian, Slavic and Turkic religious cultures. The ritual practices or customs examined here also have implications for understanding the belief systems behind particular (presumably religious) behaviours.

It seems possible that among the *austrvegr*, religious and cultural practices traditionally associated with Scandinavian, Slavic and Turkic ethnic groups manifested as fusion. As the Rus' began to merge with the local populations of Eastern Europe, new ritual traditions arose that could not be classified as distinctively Scandinavian or Slavic, especially allowing for regional variations in the ritual practices and belief systems of these groups (DuBois 1999; Brink 2007; Nordberg 2012; Słupecki 2013).

A broad definition of 'Eastern' influence should be applied. 'Turkic', equally, is a dangerously broad term in a religious sense, as steppe tribes could have been just as different from each other as they were from the peoples of the north or the various Rus' groups operating in the area. Jean-Paul Roux compiled the only comprehensive treatment of Turkic (Altaic) religions by collecting sources from a vast area across a long time span (Roux 1963, 1984). Unity over such a vast territory can only be accepted in general terms, even more because Turkic-speaking groups were in contact with a diverse range of other or similar religions and thus subject to change. In some cases, this might have made them more familiar with neighbouring cultures than with their linguistic relatives on the other edge of Eurasia. In addition, Turkic cultures in Eastern Europe were exposed to Muslim (the Volga Bulghars, Bashkirs, Oghuz') and, in certain cases, Jewish (the Khazars) or Orthodox-Byzantine (the Danube Bulghars, Pechenegs) influences that might have resulted in religious syncretism.

Also, Turkic societies were often divided into lower and upper strata that were usually linked to different religious beliefs. In the Khazar Khaganate, for instance, most of the original population practised a Turkic religion akin to that of the Oghuz', even after the Khazar elite converted to Judaism. Additionally, Muslim ethno-religious components were present in the khaganate. Traditional Turkic cultures practised a form of shamanism; shamans, a designated religious elite in tribal communities, conducted religious rites (Hultkrantz 1973). This differed from the sky-god religious system called Tengrism, the prevalent belief system in the steppe, which characterized more stratified societies with a developed hierarchy of a sole ruler, usually the khagan (Róna-Tas 1987; Roux 2005a, 2005b). Besides the Oghuz' and Khazars, some form of shamanism and/or Tengrism was practised by the Magyars, Pechenegs and Bashkirs (Golden 1992, 263, 268–69; Mason 1995; Hoppál 2007; Montgomery 2014, 202–03, 214–15). Religion was also a political factor in steppe societies, sometimes unaffected by the beliefs in the larger social unit. Eastern Europe at this time was a cultural melting pot, thus clear analogies to the practices of specific tribes are hard to discern. The following discussion, however, will discuss tendencies of cultural transfer that may have resulted from Scandinavian Rus'–steppe contacts.

## Changing beliefs?

Eastern Turkic influence on the ritual traditions of the Rus' is discernible on a practical and probably a spiritual level. This can be illustrated by descriptions of Rus' sacrifices in ibn Faḍlān's *Risāla* and Leo the Deacon's *Historia*. Additional details can be added to ibn Faḍlān's eyewitness description (summarized previously) of the funeral ritual of an eminent Rus' chieftain. According to his report, after the chieftain died, his body was kept in a tent for ten days while fitting funerary garments were prepared and the mourners engaged in heavy drinking and sexual orgies. Then the Rus' mourners fill a boat with valuables – treasure, weapons, jewellery, food and drink – and sacrifice animals (horses, cows, a dog, a rooster and a hen) together with a slave girl who volunteered to follow her master to a place known as *al-jannah*, that is, 'Paradise' or 'Garden'. The girl is raped by the followers or relatives of the chieftain and, after being lifted up in a doorframe multiple times, she recites a text about the reunion of family members in the afterlife. Finally, she is stabbed by a woman called the 'Angel of Death' (*malak al-mawt*). After loading the ship with possessions, gifts, sacrificial animals and the girl's body, the Rus' burn the boat, drag its remains to the shore and construct a tumulus on top of it (Montgomery 2014, 240–53).

Although most researchers regard this as Nordic in essence (Warmind 1995; Taylor 2002, 170–92; Duczko 2004, 138; Schjødt 2007), it has long been acknowledged that some of the details of the ritual do not correspond with any known Scandinavian examples or are not fully compatible with them and that parallels should be sought in a Volga Turk cultural milieu (Foote and Wilson 1970, 408; Montgomery 2000, 23, 2010, 163; Hraundal 2014, 79–91). These include accessories and materials used and customs observed during the ritual. Most recently, Thorir Jonsson Hraundal (2014) called attention to these features, including the balsamic leaves used to embalm the corpse of the Rus' chief, his funerary garments embellished with buttons and his silk shirt, as none of these materials were available in Scandinavia at the time. In addition, other actions during the rituals, such as forcing (sacrificial) horses to run to total exhaustion, are also analogous to Turkic practices. The long funerals of early Türk khagans were identical in their treatment of horses, and the custom survived at least up until the time of the later Mongols (Roux 1963, 151, 159–60, 166). The spiritual role of ritual specialists in Rus' culture also supports Hraundal's thesis. Ibn Rusta noted that the Rus' had their own special 'healing men' called *aṭibbā'* (sing. *ṭabīb*), who served a function comparable to that of the shamans of the steppe, ordering sacrifices of men and women as well as horses to the gods (Lunde and Stone 2012, 127; de Goeje 1892, 129). The Rus' group ibn Faḍlān depicts was an ethnic group in formation, developing through interaction among Scandinavian (and Slavic) warrior-merchants and local Turkic tribes along the Volga.

Besides these practicalities, religious ideas attesting Eastern influence are also discernible in the account. Correlating the Rus' eschatological notions described by ibn Faḍlān with Scandinavian beliefs is quite problematic, and it must be stressed that Scandinavian afterlife beliefs were in no way uniform. The dead could reach various afterlife destinations – such as Fólkvangr, Valhöll, Hel, the abode of the goddess Rán or a simple mound – in a variety of ways (Davidson 1968, 65–98; Simek 2006; Schjødt 2011, 276–87). Nevertheless, *al-jannah*, "a beautiful and darkgreen" (Montgomery 2014, 248–49) place where the slave girl follows her master, cannot be associated with any known Scandinavian examples. That women were not even permitted to enter Valhöll, the hall of dead warriors of Scandinavian mythology, is just one instance of incompatible beliefs.

Ibn Faḍlān's 'Garden', of course, could be regarded as just another example of the multitude of flexible beliefs in Scandinavian thought or a reflection of his own understanding of the afterlife, but there were parallels in the steppe world. Leaving the earthly world for 'Paradise' was an expression in medieval Turkic languages, and some of the descriptions of a heavenly place mention flocks that multiply and are herded in endless pastures (Roux 1984, 257–58). The expectations of the slave girl, mentioned earlier, of re-uniting with her family and household in the afterlife ("I see my father and mother . . . all my dead kindred . . . [and] my master seated in the Garden") (Montgomery 2014, 248–49), also match beliefs of the Turkic-speaking Altaic world (Roux 1984, 239, 273–74; Ecsedy 1984, 275; Hraundal 2014, 86) rather than Scandinavia. *Al-jannah*, in addition, features in ibn Faḍlān's work prior to his depiction of the Rus', where he paints a similar picture of the Oghuz Turk views. If Oghuz chiefs' souls are hindered on their journey to the otherworld after their burial, a post-mortem sacrifice of horses might be made. This aids the deceased in catching up with his companions who passed before, relieving him from feeling alone. The similarity of the Oghuz customs to those of the Rus' is further attested in the same passage. The Oghuz' place sick people in tents and leave them there, strikingly akin to the story of the Rus' chieftain who is left to rot in his tent for ten days (Montgomery 2014, 208–09).

There are other similarities between the eschatological views of the Rus' and the steppe people. The slave girl's visionary testimony tells that the Rus' master, similarly to the Oghuz chiefs, rested in the 'Garden' among his male servants or retainers (*ghilmān*) (Montgomery 2014, 248–49). This is important for understanding another passage in ibn Faḍlān, where he describes the court of an unnamed Rus' king (*malik*) as being quite similar to that of the Khazar khagans: the Rus' king never leaves his palace but sits on his throne with his slave girls and selected retinue:

> One of the customs of the king of the Rūs' is to have 400 men in his palace, who are the bravest of his companions, men upon whom he can count. These are the men who die when he dies and allow themselves to be killed for him. Each of them has a slave girl who serves him, washes his head and prepares everything that he eats or drinks, and then there is another slave girl with whom he sleeps. These 400 men sit below the king's throne, which is immense and encrusted with the finest gems.
>
> (Lunde and Stone 2012, 54–55; original: Montgomery 2014, 252)[3]

It is noteworthy that ibn Faḍlān himself did not visit the Rus' court described here, thus his account has to be viewed circumspectly. He may have been misled or confused the information with the Khazar court discussed in the passage that follows immediately (Montgomery 2014, 254–57). Such scepticism, however, may be eased by the fact that ibn Faḍlān was clearly aware of the different titles of rulers, and he clearly distinguishes the Rus' *malik* from the *malik* of the Khazars who held the title khagan. The historical existence of the Rus' *malik* is confirmed by a separate piece of information in a different layer of the text. Ibn Faḍlān himself witnessed that the *malik*'s name (unfortunately unrecorded by him), together with the name of the dead Rus' chieftain, were carved on a post erected on top of the deceased's mound. This note immediately precedes the introduction of the Rus' court in the narrative. It is not hard to imagine the actual situation which inspired the depiction: the Arabic diplomat, inspecting the carvings on the tomb post, likely asked who this king was and what was known about his rule. This, of course, does not automatically confirm the authenticity of the information, but ensures a counterargument against the straight dismissal of the passage as fantasy. More importantly, details of ibn Faḍlān's depiction of the Rus' customs and beliefs here are supported in analogies from various ethnic milieus, some of which contributed indirectly to the development of an eclectic Rus' culture.

A traditional reading would put it that it is the Germanic *comitatus* of the Rus' king that is described here, the members of which serve their lord in the framework of a patron–client relationship in exchange for gifts and die loyally for him in battle. In such an honour-bound warrior ideology, outliving one's lord was considered a disgrace (cf. Smyser 1965, 102–03). The interpretation of the passage can be taken a step further based on the crucial sentence: "These are the men who die when he dies and allow themselves to be killed for him." The expression "yuqtalūna dūnahu" (Montgomery 2014, 252) literally translates as "they get killed without him". This is indeed how other translations render and also interpret the passage: [they] "are killed for his sake" (Frye 2005, 70–71), "take a leave because of him" (Kovalevskiy 1956, 146), "subject themselves to death for him" (Kovalevskiy 1956, 264, n. 880), "make themselves killed for him" (Fadlân 1988, 84; Fadlán 2007, 99) or literally "die upon his death (together with him)" (Togan 1939, 97). The semantics are in accord with the first part of the sentence, that is, with the retainers' death upon their master's. The statement that they "die when he dies", is explicit and alludes to the retinue's (self-)sacrifice upon the master's passing. Although a literal reading of this passage may raise doubts, the historical circumstances give weight to the interpretation of this custom as not so extraordinary in that ethno-cultural milieu.

First of all, human sacrifice is not unknown in Scandinavian sources, but usually of female servants and widows (*suttee*) as well as men on account of shame or another reason (Edholm 2020, 214–22), never a group of retainers with the intention of following their lord to the afterlife. The custom of the *suttee* is well-documented among the Rus'. Besides the slave girl's voluntary sacrifice in ibn Faḍlān's description, other Muslim writers, ibn Rusta, Mas'ūdī, ibn Ḥawqal and Miskawayh, also note the same custom (Maçoudi 1863, 9; de Goeje 1892, 146–47; Margoliouth 1921, 73; Kramers 1939, 397; Birkeland 1954, 51; Lunde and Stone 2012, 127, 132, 151).

Among the Scandinavians and the Rus', it seems that human sacrifice was not confined to the female sphere (Upham 2019, 22–23). Miskawayh notes that when a Rus' dies, his wife or womenfolk or perhaps his male slave, are buried with him (Margoliouth 1921, 73). Ibn Faḍlān is also explicit in gendered terms, as he notes that male servants are also asked whether they are willing to die with a lord, and sometimes volunteer even if less frequently than women (Montgomery 2014, 246–47). It is also remarkable that he employs the Arabic word *ghilmān* (sing. *ghulām*) to describe these slaves and also those who surround the chieftain in the 'Garden'. The term most frequently denotes soldiers of slave origin in Islamic documents across the centuries but had multiple semantic resonances and could incorporate other related meanings, such as 'apprentice', 'youth/boy' and 'personal servant' (Pipes 1981, 195; Sourdel, Hardy, and Inalcik 1991, 1079; Forand 1971, esp. 62). Ibn Faḍlān employs the word in several meanings in his text (Montgomery 2014, 262, n. 8), and it cannot be determined whether the afterlife *ghilmān* of the Rus' chieftain are actually household servants or truly armed retainers.

Among his varied semantic usages of the term, however, there are indications that allow seeing the *ghilmān* as warriors. Once, he remarks, somewhat astonished that the Volga Bulghar ruler was riding through a market unaccompanied, "without (a) *ghulām*" (Montgomery 2014, 228), a surprise probably arising from seeing the ruler unprotected by his bodyguard. In another passage that is even more telling, he explicitly calls warriors killed by an Oghuz chief *ghilmān* who (in addition) serve the chief in the afterlife (Montgomery 2014, 208–9). This is a straightforward expression of his concept that *ghilmān* protecting a lord in the afterlife denoted armed retainers. Also, Rus' warriors are explicitly called *ghilmān* in the eleventh-century Persian *Ta'rīkh Bāb al-abwāb* describing their service under the emir of Derbent, Maymūn ibn Aḥmad, between 987 and 989 CE (Minorsky 1958, 45–46). A further indication supporting the interpretation of *ghilmān* as armed retainers in the afterlife comes from general knowledge of the Viking Age organization of warbands. In a Viking Age retinue, and in similar social structures across Eastern Europe and the steppes, retainers were regarded as the extended family of a chieftain. Recruitment stretched outside kinship or family ties, but retainers were adopted into the household by sacred oaths and shared the same space under the chieftain's roof (Hedenstierna-Jonson 2020c, 179, 183–86). In the case of ibn Faḍlān's *ghilmān*, it is striking that they are described in the 'Garden' with the whole dead kindred of the Rus' chieftain and are specifically listed alongside the other men (possibly relatives) who surround him (Montgomery 2014, 248–49). The mention in an enumeration of kin members might show a symbolic integration into the extended kin group. Thus, while Ibn Faḍlān adjusted his experience to his knowledge of Islamic socio-political concepts, he might actually have described the same phenomenon here as in the case of the *malik*'s retainers. That is, that male armed followers were on occasion sacrificed and follow their lords to the afterlife.

It is still hard to verify ibn Faḍlān's statement on the sacrifice of as many as 400 elite warriors, however. The main problem is not only the unusually large number of warriors but that ibn Faḍlān's passage is the only one on similar customs in the documentary evidence about the Rus' or Scandinavians in general. Evidence of this custom comes from Eastern Eurasia, where mass sacrifice of one's (own) retainers was also practised. One account suffices to make it clear that these texts do not suggest mere symbolic disgrace after the master's death, but literally the sacrifice of retainers. A Latin account, Alberic of Trois-Fontaines, probably building on well-informed intelligence, describes such an instance in the thirteenth century. Prince Jonah, a Cuman chief who died in Constantinople in 1241 CE, was buried outside the city walls in a tumulus (following pagan custom), and he was accompanied by 26 horses and 8 armour-bearers who volunteered to die with him ("*octo armigeri appensi sunt vivi a dextris et a sinistris et ita voluntarie mortui*") (Albericus Trium Fontium 1925, 950). Although Alberic might have exaggerated in his account, the specificity of the description suggests that the core information came from an eyewitness. This can be supported by an analogous passage in the thirteenth-century chronicle of the French writer Jean de Joinville, who relied on the eyewitness report of a certain Philippe de Toucy when recording a Cuman funeral quite similar to Alberic's. According to this, at the funeral of a high-ranking Cuman official, his best sergeant followed him into the grave alive, seemingly voluntarily (Corbett 1977, 186–87).

The timespan of these accounts from the Viking Age is not as problematic as it might seem at first glance. The custom, in fact, had a long history in Eurasia and continuity in the steppe and neighbouring cultures along the Silk Roads. Self-sacrificial retinues are recorded in analogous situations among the Scythians, Hephtalites, Xiongnu, Tibetans, Türks and later even some Indians, covering a time span from antiquity to the thirteenth century (Yule 1871, 276, 283–84, n. 5.; Ecsedy 1988; Beckwith 2009, 13–24; Cunliffe 2015, 225–56, 272). The most enigmatic of these anthropological descriptions is that of Herodotus about Scythian royal funerals, where five retainers of specific tasks are killed during the first phase, and later 50 other young males are strangled and put on stuffed horses to guard the king's mound (Wilson 2015, 370–71). Herodotus's anthropological descriptions can of course be accused of distortion and the application of classical *topoi* that characterized ancient literature. A comparison of his passage with archaeological evidence of the Scythians, however, yielded shocking results. As demonstrated by Askold Ivantchik, almost all the details of Herodotus's description are supported in various kinds of Scythian aristocratic and royal funeral evidence (Ivantchik 2011). This also entailed the sacrifice of retainers to accompany high-ranking leaders to the grave. The most emblematic mound containing such male retainers comes from Arzhan in the Tuva region of Siberia, where 15 retainers and 160 horses were freshly killed for the ritual. Other similar kurgans are found in Solokha, Chertomlÿk, Tolstaya mogila at Ordžonikidze, Aleksandropol and Ogyz (Rolle 1979, 91–96).

Such a comparison works to reinforce some trust in ancient descriptions of customs which seem extravagant from a modern critical point of view. Ibn Faḍlān was concerned with a conscious construction of the 'other' in his description of the steppe people and Rus', picking out details from their customs that were farthest from his own cultural background. Nevertheless, the agreement of unrelated sources on a custom that was preserved for a long time deserves serious historical consideration. Most of these accounts even agree that the closest and most distinguished retainers of a ruler were sacrificed or committed suicide, just as in the case of the Rus' king's bravest companions ("ṣanādīd aṣḥābihi") and most trusted men ("ahl al-thiqa ʿindahu") (Montgomery 2014, 252–53).

The least reconcilable part of ibn Faḍlān's report with knowledge of historical realities is the unusually high number of (sacrificial) retinue members. The comparative examples usually give much lower numbers of retainers, individuals or a few dozen men, who followed their leader to the afterlife, with the exception of Herodotus's 55. A statement of the second-century BCE Chinese 'Grand Historian', Sima Qian, on "hundreds or even thousands" of favoured ministers and concubines following Xiongnu rulers to their graves (Watson 1993, 137), is quite extreme in light of the lack of comparative evidence, written or archaeological. Hundreds of Rus' retinue members following their master to the grave *en masse* should be dismissed as inaccurate, not only for the lack of analogies and other contemporary witnesses. Such a mass sacrifice would probably have shaken a contemporary military structure like that of the Rus'. There is a chance that the information, conveyed to ibn Faḍlān by an outsider and through an interpreter, was partly misunderstood. Most logically, it means that some retainers had to volunteer for death when the king died, similar to the Rus' chieftain's *ghilmān*, where it is made explicit in the text. The situation can be compared with what was reported about Türk generals in Chinese service, who, upon the death of T'ai-zong, the second emperor of the T'ang Dynasty (626–49 CE), requested permission to commit suicide and be buried with their dead leader. Although they were denied permission, one committed suicide anyway (Beckwith 2009, 21). The sacrifice of retainers probably could have occurred by individual selection.

An exceptional Rus' ruler and his retinue, heard about in a steppe cultural milieu along the Volga, would fit a picture of the spread of a wider custom that had originated in Central Asia. The most likely transmitters of such customs would have been those who descended from the Türk Khaganate, the Oghuz' and the Khazars, for instance, although influence could come from further as well. As briefly noted, the Rus' custom of running horses until total exhaustion during funerals matches Chinese records of the burial of early Türk rulers, a reminder of the persistent survival of similar customs even in the post-Türk world. Taken together with the other details of Rus' external appearance and ritual practices reminiscent of the steppes, it is attractive to suggest that aspects of Rus' afterlife beliefs as described by ibn Faḍlān, such as the afterlife reunion of families and service of retainers bound to a human lord in the afterlife, resulted from steppe contacts.

Further evidence supports this hypothesis; steppe influences were by no means confined to the Volga area. The Dnieper region was home to other steppe tribes, such as the Pechenegs and the Magyars, both of whom seem to have had considerable contact with the Rus' in the ninth and tenth centuries. A second account, that of the Byzantine Leo the Deacon, strengthens the previous argument on the afterlife beliefs of the Rus'. He based his own account of the ritual on a report by an eyewitness (Kaldellis 2013a). The ritual took place during the Byzantine siege of the Bulgarian city of Dorostolon, where Sviatoslav retreated with his remaining army of Slavs and Scandinavians in 971 CE after being abandoned by their steppe nomadic allies, the Magyars and Pechenegs. After clearing the ethnographic and classical *topoi* of Byzantine literature from the text, the description of Rus' customs is distinct enough to be regarded as authentic (Kaldellis 2013b, 102–5). According to Leo the Deacon, the Rus', whom Leo calls "Tauroscythians" according to Byzantine historical traditions, made sacrifices during the siege:

> When night fell, since the moon was nearly full, they [the Tauroscythians] came out on the plain and searched for their dead; and they collected them in front of the city and kindled numerous fires and burned them, after slaughtering on top of them many captives, both men and women, in accordance with their ancestral custom. And they made sacrificial offerings by drowning suckling infants and chickens in the Istros, plunging them into rushing waters of the river.
>
> (Talbot and Sullivan 2005, 193; original: Diaconus 1828, 151–52)

One specific detail can help to locate another cultural trait in this ritual besides the Slavic and/or Scandinavian features of these sacrifices, such as the riverbank location, and the cremation of humans and animals. The account goes against the usual Rus' custom whereby the victims are not said to be forced into participating. Although how 'willingly' servants and widows went to death is questionable in a psychological sense (Taylor 2002, 96–108, 128–34), the underlying cultural norms governing this practice clearly expected these victims to *appear* to be volunteers. The sacrifice of prisoners, on the other hand, suggests a spiritually different purpose. It was rare for the victims of Scandinavian human sacrifices to be captives (for examples of human sacrifices, see Simpson 1967, 185–86; Davidson 1968, 50–59; Hultgård 2001; Bray 2004; Edholm 2016). The best-known exception and only contemporary record is the sacrifice of 111 Frankish prisoners on the banks of the Seine (Smedt, van Hooff, and de Backer 1883, 78). The few other known examples are always connected with votive offerings to the gods, most notably Óðinn, or come from histories of the early Germanic tribes of the Migration Period. The events along the Seine must have had some spiritual purpose (the number 111 is hardly accidental) with the intention of frightening the enemies on the other bank of the river (Edholm 2020, 222–26). This could have played a part at Dorostolon as well, although there the sacrifices occurred as grave offerings to dead comrades.

The parallels of connected beliefs and practices of sacrificing enemy captives during funerals are documented among steppe people through centuries and clearly represent a continuum of tradition. The Byzantine Theophanes, for instance, recorded about the Khazars in 710/711 CE that after the death of one of their eminent magistrates, the *tudun*, the Khazars sacrificed 300 enemy prisoners to serve the *tudun* as retainers in the afterlife (Theophanes 1883, 378–79). A peculiar variation of this custom is known to have been practised by another contemporary of the Rus', namely the Oghuz', and was briefly alluded to earlier. When their chiefs died, the Oghuz' symbolically replaced the dead lord's afterlife retainers. Ibn Faḍlān says: "If he has shown great bravery and killed someone, they carve wooden images, as many as the men he has killed, place them on top of his grave and say: "His retainers ('ghilmānahu') who serve him in the Garden" (Montgomery 2014, 208–9). These memorial stones or carvings called *balbal* were erected on graves, mainly in the territory of the early Türks (Roux 1984, 260–61). In addition, besides the Türks, Khazars and Oghuz', a belief that defeated enemies served them in the afterlife was also recorded among other steppe tribes, such as the Magyars, the Mongols and the Tatars (Moravcsik 1955; Ecsedy 1984). I suggest that the sacrifices during the siege of Dorostolon should be interpreted in this way, namely, that the Rus' sacrificed hostages to avenge their fallen warriors and force the enemies to serve them in the afterlife. Leo the Deacon himself supports this in a later passage:

> This also is said about the Tauroscythians, that never up until now had they surrendered to the enemy when defeated; but when they lose hope of safety, they drive their swords into their vital parts, and thus kill themselves. And they do this because of the following belief: they say that if they are killed in battle by the enemy, then after their death and the separation of their souls from their bodies they will serve their slayers in Hades. And the Tauroscythians dread such servitude, and, hating to wait upon those who have killed them, inflict death upon themselves with their own hands. Such is the belief that prevails among them.
>
> (Talbot and Sullivan 2005, 195; original: Diaconus 1828, 151–52)

Leo himself admits that what he reports is conjecture (it is only "said about the Tauroscythians"), and it has been argued that he is in fact mistaken in attributing this habit to the Rus' instead of to Sviatoslav's nomadic allies (Tarras 1965, 401). These allies, however, had already deserted Sviatoslav by this stage of the campaign, and the situation is more plausibly connected to a nomadic influence on the Rus'. If Leo's report was groundless hearsay, it must have been persistent and widespread since unrelated commentators note similar behaviour among the Rus' in an identical situation. The Persian historian Miskawayh reports this incident for the Muslim siege of Bardha'a (943 CE), formerly occupied by the Rus':

> Thus there was a story current in the region which I heard from many persons how five Russians were assembled in a garden in Bardha'ah, one of them a beardless lad of fair countenance, the son of one of their chieftains with some captive women. When the Moslems knew of their presence, they surrounded the garden, and a large number of Dailemite and other troops came together to fight these five. They tried hard to get a single prisoner out of the number, but it was not possible, for none of them would capitulate, and they could not be killed before they had slain many times their number of the Moslems. The beardless lad was the last survivor. When he perceived that he was going to

> be captured, he mounted a tree that was near him, and kept slashing away at his vital parts with his scimitar till he fell dead.
>
> (Margoliouth 1921, 73–74)

Even though Miskawayh does not give an explanation of the underlying beliefs of such behaviour, the incident is strikingly compatible with both Leo's and ibn Faḍlān's learned experience of Rus' beliefs in the afterlife. This passage has been also interpreted in a Scandinavian cultural framework as the motif of the 'last survivor', mostly known from sources dealing with the early Germanic tribes of the Migration Period (Edholm 2020, 219). All five Rus' warriors, however, were said to behave according to the same belief: avoiding captivity at all cost. In addition, all three sources, Miskawayh, Leo and ibn Faḍlān, are near contemporary to each other, describe the very same people (the Rus'), and it feels more natural to draw a connection between them rather than with sources related more distantly. Leo and Miskawayh also show that suicide was not completely alien from warrior life among the Rus'. This also aligns with ibn Faḍlān's information on allowing Rus' retainers and *ghilmān* to be killed for their *malik* and chieftain. Theoretical approaches to such fighting units introduced earlier further strengthen this point. Identity fusion creating strong visceral and emotional bonds among group members who shared a similar world view and traumatic experiences could facilitate extreme devotion to the group even at the expense of self (Raffield et al. 2016, 37–38).

To sum up, aspects connected to eschatology in Rus' beliefs are not always paralleled in Scandinavian sources. Two of these aspects should be highlighted. First, it seems especially important at whose hands a warrior was to die, as this influenced his afterlife service bound to a ruler who could also be the enemy. This might occasionally have prompted Rus' warriors to commit suicide in order to avoid serving an enemy or to follow their own master to the otherworld. Second, the belief in the afterlife reuniting of households (families, servants, retainers), are known in the related belief systems of the steppe people. The history of the steppe world provides a clear continuum of customs and beliefs characteristic for people of a similar lifestyle and a shared cultural background across Central Asia and the steppes for centuries. Taken together with the evidence for changes in external expression in the Rus' communities described by ibn Faḍlān and Leo the Deacon, it is likely that eschatological views from the steppe blended into Rus' culture. Although the exact paths and times of cultural transfers remain unidentifiable, Rus' concept(s) of the afterlife seem to have undergone a change, becoming similar to that shared by other inhabitants of the East, most notably the Turks.

## Ritual variations

It is difficult to measure how widespread the previously described Turkic practices and beliefs were among the pagan Scandinavian Rus' in general and how this deep impact came about at all. The nature of ritual performances surely contributed to the reception of new ideas. Even rituals with the very same purpose could be conducted in many ways, and certain practices carried multiple meanings. Thus, the flexible nature of ritual practice probably facilitated adaptation. For instance, certain practices of pagan Rus' rituals could have originally stemmed from Scandinavian or Slavic traditions. These could have been modified, merged or distorted over time, giving rise to eclectic performances. Such an instance is portrayed in the PVL when the Rus' entered into a contract and took oaths upon their weapons, also a well-known Scandinavian tradition (Stein-Wilkeshuis 2002), although at the same time they apparently pledged allegiance to Slavic gods – Perun and Volos (Cross and Sherbowitz-Wetzor 1953, 65, 77; Likhachev 1996, 17, 26).[4]

Due to the cultural mix, variations of ritual practices might have developed in Eastern Europe independently of the original ethnicity of the performers. In most cases, it is impossible to identify how a certain ritual absorbed elements and from which cultural backgrounds it developed. Possible reasons for ritual change could have been foreign impacts and the circumstances and/or available resources. This is discernible by comparing the Saint Gregory Island rituals with those of ibn Faḍlān's account. The comparison can serve as an analogical backdrop to better comprehend the spread of steppe customs in the region.

Rus' merchants made sacrifices during their dangerous passage along the Dnieper to Constantinople in the mid-tenth century. The ritual depicted in the DAI marks gratitude for safe passage, as it was carried out on Saint Gregory Island, after which the Rus' were safe from Pecheneg attacks near the Dnieper cataracts ("From this island onwards the Russians do not fear the Pechenegs until they reach the river Salinas.") (Constantine Porphyrogenitus 1967, 61). The ritual is depicted as follows:

> They reach the island called St. Gregory, on which island they perform their sacrifices because a gigantic oak-tree stands there; and they sacrifice live cocks. Arrows, too, they peg (*pēgnúousi*) in round about, and others bread and meat, or something whatever each may have, as is their custom. They also throw lots regarding the cocks, whether to slaughter them or to eat them as well, or to leave them alive.
>
> (Constantine Porphyrogenitus 1967, 61)

This may have been a Scandinavian ritual, although in the pertinent words of Obolensky, the ritual also "[tallies] with our admittedly meagre knowledge of Slavonic pagan ritual" (Obolensky 1982, 158).

It is also worth comparing the similarities and slight differences between the rituals of Saint Gregory Island and that recorded by ibn Faḍlān. According to him, when they arrive at the Volga, the Rus' sacrifice bread, meat, milk, onions and alcohol to wooden idols, with one idol set up on a pole and representing a main deity and others personifying lesser deities. The reason for the sacrifice is to assure trading with future merchants. When commercial business is concluded, the Rus' honour the idols with another offering of sheep or cows and tie the heads of the slaughtered animals to wooden stakes behind the small figurines of lesser deities (Montgomery 2014, 242–43). In addition to the specific correspondence of erecting poles around unnamed idols, it is notable that both the rituals on Saint

Gregory Island and the Volga were performed by merchants for a successful business trip and that, besides arranging poles (and arrows), in both cases animals and food were also offered. The purpose and performance of the rituals seem to be identical.

In Scandinavia a circular ritual space was defined, with objects thrust vertically into the ground during the *tjosnublót* rituals performed prior to a duel, as recorded in *Kormáks saga* (Sveinsson 1939, 237). The so-called *stafgarþar*, probably 'fenced cult places', are also known from Gotlandic contexts and are mentioned in the *Guta saga* (Peel 1999, 4–5, 27–29). Pegging a single pole in the ground, however, served as an object of pagan worship, according to *Ragnars saga* (Rafn 1829a, 298–99). When a horse's head was piked on a single pole it could symbolize a protector spirit to frighten away malign spirits, as *Egils saga* relates (Nordal 1979, 171). A more contemporary source confirms the custom of erecting ritual poles in the Viking Age as well. The tenth-century Arab emissary, ibn Ya'qūb al-Ṭurṭūshī, writes that the inhabitants of the Scandinavian commercial town of Hedeby celebrate a feast by sacrificing an ox, a ram, a goat or a pig, which they then hang outside in front of their houses on a pole to make it visible to everyone (Georg 1927, 29; Birkeland 1954, 103–4). This closely resembles ibn Faḍlān's description, in which the Rus' tie "the heads of the cows or the sheep to that piece of wood set up in the ground" (Montgomery 2014, 244–45).

These analogies prompt some preliminary conclusions. First, ibn Faḍlān and the DAI likely provide authentic descriptions. The former source is based on an eyewitness description, and given the specificity of the details in the latter account, its informant was certainly one as well, likely a native. Based on the matching analogies, these two observers can hardly be accused of inattentiveness or distortion in relation to these specific rituals.

Second, the way the Rus' rituals correspond with those of the Scandinavian religious milieus strongly suggests that both accounts describe an originally Scandinavian tradition. I find it less likely that the Rus' on the Volga would have erected idols according to indigenous Slavic habits (Słupecki 2013, 344–45), although the custom might have been present in both traditions. Comparative evidence is only available for the Western Slavs, so no definite conclusions can be reached. The Western Slavs seem to have used spears in their sacrifices, but rarely did they stick them in the ground. In Thietmar's chronicle two spears are laid crosswise on the ground (Holtzmann 1935, 302),[5] in Herbord's biography of Otto of Bamberg nine spears are laid a cubit's distance from each other (Köpke 1868, 91) and in Saxo Grammaticus's *Gesta Danorum* the spears are used to point towards lands of interest that the Slavs planned to conquer (Sielicki 2015, 9). In the case of the sacrifice on Saint Gregory Island, the Greek word *pḗgnūmi* unequivocally implies a strong 'thrust' (mainly) downward 'into' something (LSJ 1399; Pape 1914, 608–09). Nevertheless, care is warranted before entirely dismissing any Slavic connections in this case, as the Rus' crews stopping on the island were already mixed ethnically. This is aptly illustrated by the bilingual Slavic-Norse designation for the Dnieper rapids that the Rus' informants told the Byzantines. Arrows, representing lightning bolts, were characteristics of the Slavic thunder god Perun, and as in the instance of oath taking, a compatibility or influence of Slavic traditions cannot be fully ruled out.

The last point here is that ritual performances and connected beliefs were highly flexible and could be replaced or combined, as illustrated by the following list:

1 Poles as markers of ritual space: Kormáks saga, Guta saga, ibn Faḍlān, DAI
2 Poles as objects of worship: Ragnars saga, ibn Faḍlān, DAI (the tree)
3 Poles as protector spirits: Egils saga
4 Poles with animal heads: Egils saga, ibn Ya'qūb, ibn Faḍlān

What is striking at first glance is that certain elements of a ritual could be omitted occasionally or combined in other rituals, and identical elements could serve various purposes. Animal heads mounted on poles during a celebratory ritual in Hedeby served as protector spirits in Iceland and were mutually useful for marking out ritual space and as offerings to deities along the Volga. Furthermore, a combination of several intentions playing some kind of role in each case cannot be ruled out.

Material culture in rituals could change or convey various meanings suited to the circumstances. From the previous examples, only the rituals recorded by ibn Faḍlān and the DAI had the same purpose, ensuring the success of a business mission in foreign lands. Despite the same intent, however, they were expressed variously; animals heads on poles are absent from the DAI, the Rus' on the Dnieper island worshipped a tree instead of the hand-made idols of the Volga Rus' and they marked the space with arrows instead of larger chunks of logs. These must have been variants of the same ritual, and the changes may have arisen in the circumstances of the rituals themselves. While the Rus' merchants on the Volga presumably had a safe passage, the Rus' on the Dnieper were constantly under attack by the Pechenegs. This may explain why the Rus' of the DAI used arrows for the ritual; because arrows were the most optimal weapon for warfare on the river, they probably carried them in large numbers. While not excluding the possibility that the use of arrows was related to the dangers of the trip, it is also likely that the Rus' merchants simply used the objects they had to hand for the ritual. This might have prevented them from effectively mounting animal heads on the poles (if the omission was not deliberately connected to a specific belief or worship of a deity that went unrecorded in the DAI), or they just made a practical decision of not wasting the more substantial food supplies (other than roosters) of the crews and the garrison. The oak tree also served as a convenient place for worship, making it unnecessary to carve wooden idols.

Practical decisions could have outweighed ritual requirements. Sviatoslav, for instance, did not sacrifice weapons and food to his cremated comrades, even though the Rus' on the Volga did. That weapons and food were not mentioned for the Dorostolon sacrifices can perhaps be attributed to the inattentiveness of the Byzantine spectator. But perhaps a safer interpretation is that Sviatoslav, a practical military commander, deliberately chose not to waste valuable tools and supplies while under siege.

The practice of erecting poles is also an example where material culture could easily be replaced or even omitted if necessary. Setting up a temporary tent for the dead man and embalming the body with balsam leaves in ibn Faḍlān's description also shows that alternative materials characteristic of the region could be used.

Thus, Rus' rituals were flexible and manifested variety for several reasons. The reasons for these changes could have been: 1) the inclusion of new groups of people into the ranks of Rus' society, 2) mimicking the customs of another culturally distinctive group, 3) using multifunctional ritual elements and 4) practical reasons. Thus, Turkic ritual elements also surface in Rus' rituals, and such adaptations could happen in a variety of ways. The similar principles of contemporary pagan religions facilitated combinations of ritual elements.

## Adaptation

Flexibility in adapting to local circumstances and customs may have been the result of similar elements among these pre-Christian religions. A polytheistic array of gods, the veneration of natural features and the sacrifice of animals or humans are not ethno-specific features. They characterized pagan practices and beliefs in Scandinavian, Slavic and Turkic cultures.

Strikingly, all three main rituals were performed near water. In Scandinavian cosmology, water has always held a sacred place as a gateway between different worlds. Viking objects found in wetlands, rivers and lakes are well-known examples of putative ritual sacrifices from the Scandinavian and Western European archaeological record (Lund 2010), and archaeologists attribute the same meaning to Viking Age swords found near the Dnieper cataracts (Androshchuk 2002; Komar 2014). Adam of Bremen noted that the Swedes made sacrifices at springs (Schmeidler 1917, 257–58) and the *Life of St. George of Amastris* (a ninth-century Byzantine source of otherwise disputable authenticity) mentions that the Rus' venerated springs (Jenkins et al. 2001, 18). Venerating natural spots was characteristic of most pre-Christian religions, including the old religion of the Slavs (e.g. Álvarez-Pedrosa 2021, 68–69, 71–72; see also Bartlett 2007, 60–61).

Smaller details of the rituals' locations blur the distinctive ethnic patterns of either Scandinavian or Slavic customs. The ritual on Saint Gregory Island is unique in that it is performed at an oak tree. In Scandinavian mythology, the world tree, Yggdrasil, an *axis mundi*, holds together the different layers of the world. The tree on Saint Gregory Island likely symbolized Yggdrasil (Simpson 1967, 176), although it has to be noted that the oak tree was also a place of worship in Slavic mythology as a sacred place of the thunder god Perun (Álvarez-Pedrosa 2021, 40. n. 49). Trees played a spiritual role in Baltic and Slavic beliefs (Vernadsky 1959, 123; Jones and Pennick 1995, 174) and also in the religions of other eastern Turkic tribes, where they functioned in ways comparable to those in Old Norse cosmology (Vernadsky 1959, 32–43; Eliade [1964] 1972, 269–74; Mason 1995, 400–3; Hoppál 2007, 78).

The same goes for the sacrifices. The vague description of cremation and human and rooster sacrifices at Dorostolon could well have been "the ancestral custom" – as Leo the Deacon puts it – of both the Scandinavians and the Slavs. For instance, on the subject of Slavic practices, ibn Rusta notes that they hanged one of the wives of the deceased man by the neck and, after she had suffocated, they cremated her (de Goeje 1892, 143–44; Lunde and Stone 2012, 124).

Thietmar of Merseburg writes that the sacrifice of roosters is a Scandinavian custom (Holtzmann 1935, 23–24), but based on ethnographic analogies, it may also have been a Slavic custom (Wenska 2015). The DAI reports that lots were cast about whether to sacrifice roosters (in an unspecified way), to eat them or to keep them alive. The practice of casting lots is familiar from Scandinavian tradition (*hlutkesti, blótspán*) (Sawyer 1982, 54; DuBois 1999, 48–49; Bray 2004, 126; Gunnell 2009, 108–14). The work *Chronica Slavorum* – written around 1172 CE and describing some of the sacrificial habits of the Slavs – reports that a Slavic pagan 'priest' also casts lots to organize the festivities dedicated to the gods (Lappenberg 1868, 52). Despite the long time span between the DAI and the *Chronica*, Thietmar also records the Slavic habit of casting lots in 1005 CE (Holtzmann 1935, 302–03). Thus, it is difficult to decide whether to ascribe the sacrifice of Saint Gregory Island to Nordic culture or local Slavic habits.[6]

That the Rus' on the island of Saint Gregory allowed for the possibility of eating the sacrificial animals is not unique. It is also reported for Scandinavians in *Hákonar saga góða* (Sturluson 2002a, 167–68) and *Guta saga* (Peel 1999, 4–5) and often in relation to Turkic people as well, such as the instance in ibn Faḍlān's work where he says that the Oghuz' used to eat the sacrificial horse (Montgomery 2014, 208–9). Based on burial customs and ethnographic parallels, this habit also was practised by the Magyars and other Eastern people (Bálint 1970).

Burial customs between the Rus' and the Turkic people show some similarities. Ibn Faḍlān's account provides a description of the burial of the Rus' chieftain on a ship after the cremation. The burying community "built a structure like a round hillock over the beached boat, and placed a large piece of *khadhank* in the middle. They wrote the man's name and the name of the King of the Rūsiyyah on it" (Montgomery 2014, 252–53). Neil Price (2008, 261) suggests, on the analogy of this passage, that it is likely that Scandinavian burials also included carved wooden posts. These would leave little trace in the archaeological record but might account for some post holes found in barrows. Individual standing stones (*bautastenar*) were also erected on single graves in Scandinavia (Price 2008, 261). In the Turkic world, a specific form of erecting memorial stones on mounds involved the *balbal* (mentioned earlier), representing enemies killed (Roux 1963, 186–88, 1984, 260–61; Ecsedy 1984, 280). A connected funerary custom of sticking weapons (mostly spears) vertically into the grave also occurred in both milieus. In Scandinavia, this might have conveyed something different than commemorating the name of the deceased; it was a post-mortem ritual killing that secured an afterlife place suitable for a warrior (Nordberg 2002). Stabbing spears into a tomb, presumably with a flag on them, was also common among the Bulghars of the Volga and, judging by the archaeological evidence and ethnographical parallels, it is likely that the Magyars also followed the same custom at funerals (Kovács 1970b). Thus, wooden and stone commemorative structures, even weapons, on top of grave mounds showed concern for the posthumous legacy of the deceased in both cultural contexts.

The same could be said about the Scandinavian and Rus' mounting animal heads on ritual poles. Ibn Faḍlān mentions an analogue when describing the habits of the Oghuz', who during a funeral sacrifice (sometimes hundreds of) horses and suspend their heads, legs, skins and tails on wooden pales (Montgomery 2014, 208–9). This ritual was well-known in the steppe world; even better documented forms of it were observed among the Türks, Khazars, Cumans, Mongols and later inhabitants along the Volga (Boyle 1965; Roux 1984, 244–45; Ecsedy 1984, 280).

Thus, there were striking similarities among these tenth-century pagan religions and ritual practices, including similarities among the gods (Cross 1946, 79; Pritsak 1981, 73–86; Vernadsky 1959, 40–41). Features of contemporary supernatural beliefs may have made it easier to adapt the practicalities of the different rites. Certain practices seem to have been more or less identical in the East, which have facilitated the development of mixed customs.

The Rus's relatively quick adaptation to foreign, especially Turkic, customs can also be explained by another inference. Scandinavians coming to Eastern Europe had already encountered nomadic people in Scandinavia, the Sámi, who performed rituals similar to those of the nomadic tribes in the East (Eliade [1964] 1972, 379–87; Hultkrantz 1992; Pálsson 1999; for an example: Ekrem and Mortensen 2006, 92–93). Sámi shamanistic rituals and magic seem to have had considerable impact on Old Norse religion, and knowledge of Sámi culture among the Scandinavians must have been widespread (Mundal 2000; Price 2002, 233–329). The Sámi originally occupied the northern parts of present-day Finland, Sweden and the northern and southern parts of Norway. Scandinavians operating in the East also came mostly from these areas, which raises the likelihood that they had personally met Sámi people earlier. Moreover, the Sámi were frequent characters in late medieval Icelandic sagas, which means that besides those with direct experience others could also have been familiar with shamanistic customs, making it less strange for the Scandinavians to meet people with similar practices (Davidson 1976, 283–300).

Perhaps this was why other religions of the Volga region, such as Islam, which was also followed by some Turkic people such as the Volga Bulghars, did not make a stronger impression on the Rus'. Vladimir, for instance, received Muslim envoys at his court in order to get acquainted with Islam but finally refused to embrace the faith due to its restrictions on consuming alcohol (Cross and Sherbowitz-Wetzor 1953, 97; Likhachev 1996, 39). Abandoning the consumption of pork was also impossible for the Rus', as reported by a version of ibn Faḍlān's *Risāla* preserved by Amīn Rāzī, who claims that even those Rus' who converted to Islam could not refrain from eating it (Wikander 1978, 73). As Egil Mikkelsen (2008) notes, Islam's rules were incompatible with Old Norse religious views and practices. The Rus' custom of depicting idols for religious ceremonies would definitely go against Islam's prohibitions on drawing faces. Similarly, the lack of hygiene and the libertine sexual customs of the Rus' (e.g. sexual intercourse with slave girls in public) would have been unacceptable for Muslims, for whom regular bathing was a daily practice with religious overtones and sexuality was a private matter. Old Norse funerary rites went against the Islamic notions as well. The Rus' told ibn Faḍlān during the funeral he described that the Arabs are fools to leave the body for the worms in the ground rather than burning it as the Rus' do (Montgomery 2014, 252–53).

## Conclusion

Turkic cultural impacts on the Rus' were significant and triggered changes in the latter's identity. In the mid-tenth century, Scandinavian analogues of certain features of pagan Rus' rituals could still be discerned. Choosing lake shores or riverbanks for rituals, holy trees, human and animal sacrifices (especially roosters), using weapons among other grave goods all suggest that the Scandinavians had not yet been fully assimilated into the Eastern environment in the tenth century. Although these elements were similar to Slav practices, contextual evidence hints that a decisive number of the participants in these rituals came from Scandinavian ethno-religious backgrounds. Ritual practices evidently changed, giving rise to parallel variations of rites and concepts practised (perhaps universally) in the steppe and the forest-steppe belts by other ethnic groups.

The shared features and striking similarities among contemporary pagan religions helped the Rus' adapt mentally to specific rites and beliefs. In the case of the Slavs, long co-habitation facilitated the merging of cultures on a religious level, although the continuing interaction between the Rus' and steppe tribes also seems to have influenced Rus' rituals. Scandinavians operating in Eastern Europe were not unfamiliar with these customs due to the interconnectedness of religions in the Viking Age North, among which Sámi and Finno-Ugric shamanic traditions resembled the practices of the Turkic tribes further east. The Rus' were pragmatic people who not only embraced new perspectives but also adopted local fashions and replaced their own objects with local material culture, especially when necessitated by circumstances. Such flexibility in managing objects in a ritual context definitely supported the development of varied practices.

As illustrated, syncretism among Old Norse, Slavic and Turkic religions seems to have worked well due to some shared beliefs and common customs present in all three cultures. Since regional variations existed in all three belief systems, it is impossible to assert with certainty which variations affected the others; however, it seems likely that it was mostly Old Norse religious views that were influenced by Turkic beliefs. I am not aware of any evidence to the contrary so far. Although the Scandinavians were the ones who had to adapt to the local environments, the lack of Scandinavian impact on steppe people (clearly to a lesser extent) might be attributable to the dearth of sources about the period. It is equally hard to measure how widespread Turkic practices and beliefs were among the pagan Rus' and in the steppe in general. In terms of steppe cultural features, evidence suggests that Rus' groups active along the Dnieper and Volga adapted certain practices connected to beliefs and borrowed everyday cultural behaviours. The impacts on the Scandinavians can partly be ascribed to the natural environment, which required flexibility in external appearance and in using alternative resources in ritual contexts.

This practical side of the Scandinavian/Rus'–Turkic relationship went hand in hand with changes in belief, as illustrated by the Rus' afterlife beliefs. In a society pervaded with violence, arms-bearing members of the community were expected to live up to ideals centred on self-sacrifice on the battlefield and the ability to disregard the horrors of violent encounters. This warrior ideal was surely not alien in the Turkic world and the steppes. The Rus' groups described by ibn Faḍlān – the kingly court and chieftaincy respectively – expressed similar shared world views perhaps adopted from the Turkic world though with varying degrees of commitment demanded from followers. Selected retainers of an elite professional fighting unit like those surrounding the *malik* perhaps had stricter obligations ("they die when" the king "dies") than others who offered less extreme though nevertheless serious devotion (for instance, the *ghilmān* having a choice whether to follow their lord or, more frequently, be replaced by female slaves). Commemorating their rulers' names on posts on the burial mounds emphasizes that creating bonds among non-kin group members was effective in these communities (for this, see Hedenstierna-Jonson 2020c, 182). A reproach by a Rus' observer during the burial of his Rus' chieftain, addressed to ibn Faḍlān and the Arabs for not burning their 'loved ones' ("those whom you hold in the highest esteem") as the Rus' do (Montgomery 2014, 252–53), also suggests the lasting effects of bonds between rulers and followers. I suggest that the development of fused customs and beliefs enhanced group cohesion in an ethnically, linguistically and culturally mixed warrior-merchant community known as Rus'. Group-specific ideologies evolved along with a distinct material culture and symbolic integration of outsiders into the kin group either on earth or in the afterlife. This facilitated the integration of new members who wished to live up to the ideals of (extreme) devotion to the group. Different activities pursued by Rus' groups in various geographic and cultural environments in the east and competition among them most likely resulted in great variety in the composition of each group. Slavs, Finno-Ugric people and Turks joined and/or made an impact on Rus' groups in different ways, allowing slight variations of cultural markers and practices to evolve. Followers of a mysterious early tenth-century Rus' king along the Volga signalled their distinctive identity with tattoos and half-sleeve tunics undocumented among other groups and seemingly lived up to warrior ideals reminiscent of Turkic elites. This might be seen as a version of ingroup identification and identity that arose from cultural fusion among Scandinavians, Slavs and Turks.

## Notes

1 I would like to thank Brepols Publishers for granting me the rights to reproduce here parts of the following article: Csete Katona, "Otherness along the Austrvegr: Cultural Interaction between the Rus' and the Turkic Nomads of the Steppe," in *Margins, Monsters, Deviants: Alterities in Old Norse Literature and Culture*, edited by Rebecca Merkelbach and Gwendolyne Knight, 189–213. NAW no. 3 (Turnhout, Belgium: Brepols, 2020).

2 I omit the *Gothikon* here, seemingly a foreign ritual in the Byzantine court of Constantine VII that was argued to involve Scandinavians. This ritual, however, does not seem to connect to Scandinavians' borrowing of Turkic cultural practices. On the *Gothikon*, see Gunnell 1995, 71–76.

3 Montgomery (2014, 253) gives a slightly different translation of one of the crucial sentences of the passage: "They die when he dies and sacrifice themselves to protect him." I feel that the translation implies a protective function the retainers had while their lord was still *alive*, which, in my opinion, is *not* in the original Arabic text and would not support my later argument. Therefore, in exception, I follow Lunde and Stone's translation here.

4 Cf. Cross (1946, 81) claims that the Scandinavian retainers swore on Perun and the Slavs on Volos. It is also possible that the later chronicler replaced the names of the Scandinavian gods Óðinn and Þórr with the pagan Slavic deities of Perun and Volos, which were known to him. In light of the previous discussion, however, I do not think that this sentence should be interpreted differently than what it says explicitly: pledging oaths to Slavic gods according to Scandinavian customs.

5 The description of the ritual is elusive. The Latin term used for placing the spears is *fixas*, which can mean 'stuck' downwards into the earth. The horses, however, are gently led over a pit covered with grass, which suggests that the horses crossed the hole through the spears.

6 As far as I am aware, early medieval sources on Slavic beliefs only record that sacrifices during the Dorostolon siege and the island of Saint Gregory included roosters (if ibn Faḍlān's information on the Rus' as Slavs is rejected). The purely Slavic nature of these rituals is contested here, however, and thus it is also possible that rooster sacrifices came into the Rus' tradition through Scandinavian influence.

# 7 Communication

After tracing possible contact spheres among the Scandinavian, Rus' and Turkic people, I will address the practical side of these relations in everyday encounters. This returns to a basic, albeit puzzling, question: How did early medieval Scandinavians and Rus' communicate with the Turks of the steppe? It is time to return to Tyrkir, who featured in the opening scene of this book. Is it possible that the saga preserved reliable information on a steppe Turk who learned Old Norse in the Viking Age? As remarked in the beginning, it is hard to verify Tyrkir's existence. News about the Turks, nevertheless, reached Iceland, probably as early as the Viking Age. Later records confuse the term with the Ottomans, ancient Troy and Asia Minor, but there are instances when genuine information comes through. In this regard, the most notable occurrence of the Turks is in the Icelandic *Eymunds saga*, which describes a Scandinavian mercenary force fighting in the civil wars of eleventh-century Rus'. In one episode, the Rus' chief Burizleifr was said to recruit "Turks, Black men and many other evil folk" ("Tyrkir og Blökumenn, ok mörg önnur ill þjóð") against his brother, Jarizleifr (Vigfússon and Unger 1862, 126; translation mine). Based on events of the eleventh century, the identity of the characters can be reconstructed with relative safety. Jarizleifr has been identified with Yaroslav and Burizleifr as Sviatopolk, who, according to the PVL, "prepared an innumerable army of Russes and Pechenegs" to march against his brother (Cross and Sherbowitz-Wetzor 1953, 131; Likhachev 1996, 62). This identifies the Turks in *Eymunds saga* with the nomadic Pechenegs. By the time the saga was recorded in the fourteenth century in Iceland the proper tribal name of the Pechenegs had faded. Nevertheless, it is remarkable that even the vague memory of a Turkic tribe lingered in the documents of such a faraway place as Iceland. Tyrkir's case is also assisted by the 1015 CE story of the first Rus' martyr, Gleb, who was stabbed to death by his cook, called Torchin, meaning a Turk (Cross and Sherbowitz-Wetzor 1953, 128; Likhachev 1996, 60). The term appears again as a personal name in the PVL referring to a servant of the Kievan Rus' (Cross and Sherbowitz-Wetzor 1953, 198; Likhachev 1996, 116).

Do these references reinforce belief in the narrative of *Grænlendinga saga*? Perhaps. To me, Tyrkir's case seems too specific to be a mere fabrication. His native tongue, if truly German, hardly fits the narrative. Another Scandinavian group in the saga, led by Karlsefni, could not communicate with the native

DOI: 10.4324/9781003037859-7

Americans, as they did not understand their language (Sveinsson and Þórðarson 1935a, 260–61). This episode implies that the late medieval saga composers were aware of the difficulties the Vikings might have faced when confronted by a truly alien language. Also, Tyrkir's tongue does not seem to be closer to Old Norse. Tyrkir's case, therefore, if his identification as a Turkic nomad is accepted, would serve as a good example of highly developed communication between Old Norse and Turkic speakers if his identity and historical existence could be validated. That acquiring distant languages was thought to be a reality (at least in the age of saga writings) is illustrated by an episode in *Eiríks saga rauða* in which the Scandinavians take two Vinland children and teach them Old Norse (Sveinsson and Þórðarson 1935b, 432).

Clearly not all Turks would have learned Old Norse nor Scandinavians Turkic languages. There must have been additional communication channels since conducting trade, negotiating, understanding local customs, adopting fashion, forming alliances and acting together on the battlefield all required the ability to understand each other. How were everyday encounters managed between ethnicities so distant from each other in terms of language? This is the fundamental question I explore in this chapter, discussing the occasional references to linguistic evidence in Muslim, Byzantine, Slavic and Old Norse written sources that describe direct communication among various groups of people in Eastern Europe. These accounts show the multiple means of communication that Scandinavian, Rus' and Turkic groups must have used in the Viking Age.

The following scenarios are possible ways communication could have taken place among or between the Scandinavians, Rus' and the people of the steppes: 1) communication without speech, 2) communication through interpreters employed by one or both parties, 3) both groups learning an intermediary language and 4) some individuals from both groups learning the other's native languages. While not denying that the first possibility could occur occasionally, there is firm evidence for the second and third categories. Even though the attestation is weaker, careful suggestions will be put forward concerning the fourth scenario as well.

## Languages in the east

What languages or language groups were in use in the East that could have played a part in Scandinavian–Turkic interactions? The Scandinavian language group was probably divided into West Norse (Icelandic, Norwegian) and East-Norse (Swedish, Danish) dialects as early as the Viking Age (Barnes 2008, 276). Both groups were present in Eastern Europe, probably with a much higher proportion of the latter. Despite regional variations, it is generally believed that Old Norse speakers understood each other easily throughout the Viking world.

The closest partners of the Scandinavians in Eastern Europe were the Eastern Slavs, who could also understand each other in spite of dialectic variations. From these we are only aware of the Novgorodian dialect, as everyday speech was recorded on birch bark letters (Zaliznyak 2004); all other sources were written in the language of the church. Slavic groups in even smaller territories (like the

West or South Slavic areas) became divided into sub-groups (e.g. Sorbian, Polabian, Polish-Pomeranian, Bulgaro-Macedonian). The Eastern Slavs, however, preserved the mutual intelligibility of their languages over a much larger area, which may have been partly due to the Scandinavian political authority that united diverse tribes (Struminski 1996, 11–23). Considerable dialectic differences do not appear until the twelfth century in the Old Eastern Slavonic language, and the more notable separation of the Ukrainian and Russian languages only started in the fourteenth and fifteenth centuries.

The tribes of Turkic origin, however, were not united and spoke rather different tongues and dialects even in the same empires or tribal federations due to their heterogenic make-up. In these multi-ethnic steppe societies, the functional role of languages dominated, manifested in multilingualism or in the parallel existence of 'official' languages used in cultural or economic interactions. The language of the ruling strata in a given nomadic entity was flexible and subject to rapid change.

What language the Khazars spoke was seriously debated for a long time. Although it was posited that they might have spoken a unique branch of the Turkic linguistic family called Oghuric, most scholars maintain that they spoke in common Turkic (for an elaborate discussion, see Erdal 2007). Various Muslim authors likened their language to that of the Volga Bulghar's, the remnants of which are preserved in the Chuvash language of today (Zimonyi 1989, 8–9).

The Pechenegs' language cannot be identified with certainty either. Their organization was not unified and never developed to an extent that would allow the development of a common 'tribal' language used by all of their existing subgroups. According to some scholars, their confederation included Iranian, Tokharian and Bulgaric (Turkic) speakers, while others surmise that they generally spoke common Turkic (Pritsak 1975, 22–24; Golden 1992, 265).

The language spoken by the Magyar tribes belongs to the Ugrian branch of the Finno-Ugric languages. Thus, despite the fact that their language was distinct, the Magyars followed a nomadic way of life and culturally resembled the Turkic tribes of the steppe. This might be a methodological problem when discussing Scandinavian–Turkic communication since the Magyars should be addressed separately. Turkic elements, however, are present in Magyar culture, as they had considerable contact with the various Turkic tribes of the Volga region, including the Volga Bulghars, the Bashkirs and the Khazars. The large number of early Turkic loanwords – more than 300 – that are part of the Hungarian language are the vestiges of this extensive co-habitation of the seventh to ninth centuries. There is no scholarly agreement on how and when these loanwords entered the Hungarian language; the Bashkirs and Volga Bulghars from the seventh century and/or later the Khazars are the major candidates for the transmission (Zimonyi 2016, 346–48). The Magyar tribal elite – many of them bearing Turkic names – was likely bilingual and fluent in common Turkic (Fehértói 1997; Róna-Tas 1999, 350–51, 389).

All these communities were mixed ethnically, and speakers in the various Turkic-language groups must have understood each other in everyday matters despite occasional dialectical differences. In addition, the functional use of a language is different from the full acquisition of the same language as in most cases it is enough to be able to communicate at a basic level to make oneself understood by foreigners. How much Scandinavians might have needed foreign languages in the East is hard to measure; thus, I will outline certain patterns that may reflect only individual experience.

## Communication without speech

Communication is a prerequisite for any kind of interaction except warfare. The only exception to this rule in traditional societies seems to have been the so-called silent trade, a method of exchanging goods without speaking. Silent trade resulted from the unintelligible or incomprehensible communication between two parties and was secured by mutual trust (Grierson 1903, 41–54). The custom goes back to a long tradition in the northern areas of the Baltics and Russia. Around 1030 CE the Persian scholar, Bīrūnī, confirms that the inhabitants of these northern regions practised this form of barter (al-Tanjī 1962, 108; Lunde and Stone 2012, 179). The fourteenth-century Moroccan traveller ibn Baṭṭūṭah, recorded silent trade conducted between inhabitants of the 'Land of Darkness' (north of Bulghar) and visiting traders:

> Each one of them leaves the goods he has brought there and they return to their usual camping-ground. Next day they go back to seek their goods, and find opposite them skins of sable, minever, and ermine. If the merchant is satisfied with the exchange he takes them, but if not he leaves them. The inhabitants then add more skins, but sometimes they take away their goods and leave the merchant's. This is their method of commerce. Those who go there do not know whom they are trading with or whether they be jinn or men, for they never see anyone.
>
> (Battúta 1953, 151)

Trade without proper communication often failed. That is what later medieval sagas suggest in analogous situations involving Scandinavians on both the western and eastern edges of the Viking world. In *Grœnlendinga saga*, Scandinavians encounter native Americans, with whom they trade peacefully until misunderstandings arise and fighting breaks out (Sveinsson and Þórðarson 1935a, 260–64). The same patterns are visible in *Yngvars saga víðförla*, a legendary saga about a Viking expedition to the East. Here, Sveinn, Yngvarr's son, and his company trade peacefully with some unnamed local inhabitants of the Volga region on the first day, apparently with hand signs and tokens, but engage in battle with them the next day due to confusion over a transaction. Later in the saga, an identical incident is repeated when a fight breaks out at a feast (Olson 1912, 35–36, 39–40). Ultimately, difficulties arose in both cases due to a lack of adequate knowledge of the others' language.

## Interpreters

To avoid situations like these, participants had to establish fluent communication. Employing interpreters for Scandinavian–Turkic communication likely bridged the language gap initially. Here it should be briefly mentioned that translator and interpreter are not synonyms; the former concerns him/herself with the translation of a written text, whilst the latter 'translates' oral communication. The differentiation is important because interpreters could be (and often were) illiterate and probably bilingual by education or from a young age. These two professions are somewhat blurred in the sources, but presumably interpreters were more widespread and they are the subject of discussion here (Sinor 1997, 305–06).

Interpreters appear throughout the sources and were widely employed in the period both in the ranks of Scandinavian, Turkic and other societies. Ibn Khurradādhbih reports as early as the ninth century that the Rus' used their Slavic slaves as interpreters in dealings with the Muslims of Baghdad (de Goeje 1889, 154; Lunde and Stone 2012, 112). The word *tólkr*, meaning interpreter, came into the Old Norse language from Old East Slavonic, suggesting that the interpreters the Scandinavians employed were of Slavic origin (McDougall 1986–89, 218; Struminski 1996, 252).

It was indeed common to find Slavs as interpreters in the East. The ethnonym of the South Slavic tribe, the Tivercians, for instance, derives from the Turkic word **ti-vär*, meaning an 'interpreter' (Ivanov and Toporov 2000, 432), which explains the specific reference of the PVL to the Tivercians as *tolkoviny*, that is, interpreters (Cross and Sherbowitz-Wetzor 1953, 64; Likhachev 1996, 16). The Tivercians, who fought alongside the Rus', are sometimes considered to be originally of Turkic origin, melded with the Slavic population of the Dniester-Dnieper area during the ninth century. This suggests that they were bilingual (Spinei 2009, 83–86). Judging by Slavic words (*zakana*, *voevoda*) used in conversation between Constantine Porphyrogenitus and his Pecheneg and Magyar informants, the negotiations between the Byzantines and these nomads were also likely conducted in Old East Slavonic (Györffy 1990, 16–18). It is also possible that during the Magyar campaigns in Iberia in 942 CE a Slavic servant, many of whom resided in Islamic Spain in the period, mediated between the Magyars and local Muslims (Györffy 1994b, 130).

Ibn Faḍlān, from the caliphate, also had to employ interpreters to understand the words and cultures of the Volga inhabitants and the Rus'. The identity of his middlemen is still a topic of discussion, as it is hard to discern from the Arabic text whether they were Arabs or perhaps Slavs (Schjødt 2007, 133). The number of interpreters accompanying the embassy is also unclear from his text; nevertheless, one of his chief guides was a Turk named Takīn al-Turkī, a local expert (Montgomery 2014, 169–70).

The importance of the nomadic office of *tulmač*, literally meaning 'translator', also merits mention. The Hungarian form of the word, *tolmács*, is of Pecheneg and not Slavic origin (Németh 1958). Since the Slavic word was adopted from the Altaic languages, it seems reasonable to think that the profession/institution developed first in the Turkic world and was adopted by the Slavs when the two groups established contact (Sinor 1997, 294–95; Golden 1998–99, 75).

These examples imply that communication between the Scandinavian Rus' and the Turks, especially during the ninth century, must have included translators, which might have changed somewhat during the tenth century when Scandinavian groups gradually learned the language of Slavic groups. This might not have completely excluded intermediaries, however, from roles in commercial transactions. Such is the impression arising from a fourteenth-century manuscript of *Óláfs saga hins Helga* (the Saga of Saint Óláfr), in which the Old Norse word *brakki* (in the plural form *brakkarnir*), meaning an 'intermediary, broker', is equated to *túlkr* (Johnsen and Helgason 1941, 776). This implies that an interpreter's job was (and is) not merely a formal translation but a sensitive task also involving negotiations on behalf of one's employer. Interpreters were useful, offered clear advantages in business relations and probably recruited preferably from one's own trusted neighbourhood rather than from the local people at the site where the transactions occurred. The high status of interpreters is also attested by the nomadic *tulmač* office from which the word's 'translator' meaning developed. The *tulmač*, an official, was originally linked to the aristocratic princes in the Pecheneg tribal federation. The work of interpreters was likely valued in Scandinavian/Rus' societies as well. The delegation the Rus' Princess Olga led to Byzantium in 945/947 CE, for instance, included three interpreters, one of whom was in the personal service of the princess herself (Constantinus Porphyrogenitus 1830, 597–98).

## The use of an intermediary language

Rus' society was multi-ethnic, and the question of which languages were used in their own communities is complicated. Some scholars think Scandinavians assimilated quickly in the Slavic communities. This is usually illustrated by the appearance and dominance of Slavic names in the Rus' princely family and Rus' elite from the mid-tenth century (Struminski 1996, 162–80; Sitzmann 2003, 58–61; Mel'nikova 2004).

Other evidence, however, suggests that Old Norse was still a spoken language among the Rus' during the tenth century. The DAI corroborates this in the famous descriptions of the Dnieper rapids, which give the names in both Slavic and Old Norse of the river cataracts that Rus' merchants crossed on their way from Kiev to Constantinople (Constantine Porphyrogenitus 1967, 57–63). A rare piece of evidence, a tenth-century Old Norse runic inscription carved on a stone on the island of Berezan (Ukraine), also shows that a considerable number of the travellers following the Dnieper route came from a Scandinavian community (Braun and Arne 1914). Old Norse runic inscriptions on wooden sticks were also found in the northwestern Rus' town, Novgorod (Mel'nikova 2004, 457).

In the Byzantine Empire, Scandinavians also preserved the *dönsk tunga* ('Danish tongue'), as their language was referred to in their own words. The Byzantines employed their own Greek interpreters to communicate with their Varangian bodyguards, which is confirmed by a Byzantine seal bearing the inscription 'Michael, the great translator of the Varangians', probably dateable to the mid-thirteenth century (Shandrovskaia 2016). The Danish chronicler Saxo Grammaticus also describes an event that strengthens the theory that Old Norse was used in the Byzantine court. According to the story, the Danish king Eric the Good (1095–103

CE), during his pilgrimage to the Holy Land, arrived at the walls of Constantinople but was refused entry to the city owing to the emperor's anxiety that the Varangian palace guards might join their fellow Scandinavians. Finally, the *basileus* let his Varangians visit Eric in small groups, sending spies with them who understood both Greek and Old Norse (Friis-Jensen 2015, 888–89). The Byzantine custom of foreign soldiers saluting the emperor in their own native tongue during ceremonies might also mean that preserving their native language in Constantinople was a reality even before the eleventh century (Davidson 1976, 200).

Not all Scandinavians assimilated to the same extent or at the same speed. Rus' who settled among the Slavs in European Russia may have adapted more, but this took time, especially in the rural areas (Mel'nikova 2003, 464; Androshchuk 2008, 534). The tenth century was a time of transition for the Scandinavians in Eastern Europe rather than the end of cultural-linguistic assimilation, evidenced in that the *dönsk tunga* was still used there.

Evidence for Scandinavians learning Old East Slavic certainly exists. Scandinavian loanwords are found in Old Slavonic and Old Slavonic terms in the Old Norse language (Thörnqvist 1948; Svane 1989). Scandinavian loanwords in the Old Slavonic language are ethnic, place and personal names and terms connected mostly to commercial or political activities (e.g. *væringr* 'Varangian', *griði* 'retinue', *akkeri* 'anchor', *pund* 'pound'). Nearly the same can be said about Old Norse lexical borrowings from Old Slavonic (e.g. *safali* 'sable', *torg* 'market', *polota* 'palace', *Girkir* 'Greeks'), which shows the socio-economic activities that tied together Old Norse speakers and the inhabitants of Eastern Europe (Struminski 1996, 229–54).

In addition to mutual borrowings, Scandinavians not only acquired the local language but adopted the Slavic script as well. In the Saint Sophia Cathedral of Kiev, built in the early eleventh century, the Norse name Yakun (Hákon) is written in Cyrillic letters (Androshchuk 2008, 535), and two graffiti on the walls of the Saint Sophia Cathedral of Novgorod date from the second half of the eleventh century and 1137 CE. Birch-bark letters from the Ladoga region dated to the same period also contain Old Norse names in Cyrillic letters. The first Slavic language relic – an amphora with the inscription *gorouhsha* – was discovered in the famous tenth-century boat grave of a high-status Rus' warrior in Gnezdovo (Mel'nikova 2003, 456). Thus, besides preserving Old Norse, it may be assumed that many Scandinavians living among the Slavs were bilingual by the tenth century.

Most scholars think that Slavic was the *lingua franca* of the region at this time (Obolensky 1982, 161; Golden 1995, 621; Gieysztor 2008, 482). This assumption is probably valid since Slavic was a spoken (native) language stretching from Poland through the vast areas of the Kievan Rus' and the Balkans as far as the caliphate's territory, where there were a considerable number of Slavic slaves (Nazmi 1998, 185–86). Ibn Ya'qub reports that "many Northern tribes speak the Slavic language, for they are mixed with the Slavs. Among them are the Germans, the Magyars, the Pechenegs, the Russians and the Khazars" (Mishin 1994–95, 190). This quote also confirms that nomadic people – the Magyars, Pechenegs and Khazars – also learned (some) Slavic (Paroń 2012, 130), which is additionally supported by a bilingual Turkic–Slavic graffito in the Saint Sophia Cathedral of Kiev (Pritsak 1982). Thus, East Slavic could have become an intermediary language between Turkic groups and the Scandinavian Rus' from the tenth century onwards.

## Learning each other's tongues

More complicated issues such as religious customs and concepts, which the Scandinavian Rus' seem to have adopted from the Turks, had to be transmitted to some extent in the vernaculars. This must have taken place after spending considerable time together, and thus, even though not leaving clear traces in the written records, I find it probable that Turkic languages were involved in the transmission of ideas, although suggested Turkic loanwords in the Scandinavian languages, such as the unit of weight called *bisman* (ON.), stand on shaky ground (Hraundal 2013, 170–73). The outstanding adaptability of both the Scandinavian Vikings and Turkic nomads to learning foreign languages is attested in various sources.

No sources refer explicitly to Scandinavians learning a Turkic language. *Konungs skuggsjá*, the late medieval Norwegian King's Mirror, advises merchants to learn the languages of the places where they do business, and (especially) Latin and French (Keyser, Munch, and Unger 1848, 6). These languages must have been useful for merchants in the thirteenth century – when the source originates – but other languages could have been suggested for ninth-to-eleventh-century Scandinavian merchants who ventured east. The Dane Viðgautr, whose trip is recorded in *Knýtlinga saga*, a compilation of stories about the Danish kings, is said to have conducted business in Novgorod smoothly due to his knowledge of foreign languages never needing an interpreter (Guðnason 1982, 246–47). Travelling merchants were usually fluent in the languages of the territories they visited, as reported about the corporation of Jewish merchants called the Radhanites – going from Western Europe to China – who spoke Arabic, Persian, Greek, Latin, Frankish, Andalusian and Slavic. Their activities are interpolated into the section about the route of Rus' merchants in the ninth-century work of ibn Khurradādhbih (Pritsak 1970). According to an eleventh-century Gotlandic runestone inscription (G 134), a Scandinavian merchant, Hróðfúss, who was betrayed by unidentifiable trading partners (*blakumen*), must also have possessed the necessary language skills for such a partnership (Jesch 2001, 257–58).

Under the year 968 CE, the PVL records an account of a Rus' learning a Turkic language. A Kievan young retainer (*otrok*) who spoke the language of the nomadic Pechenegs was able to infiltrate the Pecheneg lines and call reinforcements from a nearby Rus' army (Cross and Sherbowitz-Wetzor 1953, 85; Likhachev 1996, 31), although the chronicle is silent about the ethnic origin of the boy and the storyline might be biased (see Chapter 3).

The Scandinavian Vikings were famous travellers, and Icelandic sagas, transmitted a few centuries later, all praise travellers with language skills (Kalinke 1983). The sagas are not contemporary accounts, however, and only vaguely reflect the situation in Eastern Europe in the ninth to eleventh centuries. The status of Turkic languages is unclear but might be reflected in the semi-historical saga of

Yngvarr, in which a local princess, Silkisif, besides being able to speak Roman, German, Norse and Russian/Greek, was said to know "many other [languages] spoken along the East road" ("margar adrar, er gengu um austurueg"), without specifying any of them (Olson 1912, 15; translation mine). Even though the saga is unlikely to hold historical truth about Silkisif's existence, it can be assumed that after Latin, Norse, Slavonic and Greek, Turkic languages were important in Eastern Europe, and thus a local princess being fluent in the language of the Turks is a potentially believable story in general.

Historical sources also support the idea that the contemporary elite did not look down on learning foreign languages. According to the testimony of Vladimir Monomakh, his father, Vsevolod I of Kiev (1078–93 CE), son of Yaroslav the Wise and the Swedish princess Ingigerðr, was fluent in five languages even though he never left the kingdom (Cross and Sherbowitz-Wetzor 1953, 211). This statement seems to indicate that one of the five languages he spoke must have been a Norse language, as he was half-Swedish on his mother's side and thus probably bilingual from a young age. Close ties with Scandinavia might have also prompted Vladimir and Yaroslav to learn Old Norse. It has even been suggested that a Slavic–Norse hybrid language could have developed in their courts (Birnbaum 1978, 7).

It is also known that Scandinavians communicated easily with Old English speakers (Townend 2000). The ninth-century account of Ohthere, a Norwegian traveller, says that he communicated with a Finno-Ugric tribe in Bjarmaland, somewhere in the Baltics, by speaking the language of the Lapps (Cross 1981, 19–21). It can also be postulated that some Scandinavians learned Finno-Ugric languages. The Bjarmians' language that Ohthere did not understand, which was compared to the "twittering of birds" (*fuglaklið*), is usually believed to be a Finno-Ugric language (Rafn 1829b, 175; Davidson 1976, 35). According to the saga of Örvar Oddr, a Norwegian was able to communicate with the Bjarmians, as he had lived among them for years (Rafn 1829b, 175–76).

Bilingualism is also reported among nomadic people. Constantine reports that the Magyars had been taught the language of the Khazars by the neighbouring tribes of the *Kabaroi* (Constantine Porphyrogenitus 1967, 174–75). Nomads' adaptability to absorb multiple languages stemmed from the nature of their social organization, that they incorporated (often defeated) tribes who had a similar lifestyle into their federations. Iṣṭakhrī notes that the tongues of the Bulghars and the Khazars were the same (de Goeje 1927, 225; Lunde and Stone 2012, 158). If Iṣṭakhrī is to be believed, this would mean that Scandinavians and Rus' coming to trade in the region could manage with a single language (if they did not wish to use intermediaries), as both of their main trading partners spoke nearly the same tongue.

Based on the provided evidence, it seems that Turkic nomads as well as Scandinavians and Rus' were all mobile societies well accustomed to learning foreign languages. Such groups amalgamated various (ethnic and linguistic) communities and established contact with many cultural groups. Dimashqī's brief and dubious statement that the Northern barbarian Waranks (Varangians) were ignorant of any languages (Mehren 1866, 133; Birkeland 1954, 115) hardly challenges this evidence.

We should consider that certain groups of Turks and Scandinavians spending time together would learn each other's language to a certain degree. Apart from Tyrkir and his namesakes living in the Kievan Rus', other evidence also confirms the possibility of Easterners living among Scandinavians. In an eleventh-century birchbark letter from Novgorod, the Hungarian personal name Ugrin has been deciphered (Gyóni 2016), illustrating that Hungarians could indeed have lived in distant lands where Scandinavians were active. In the Kievan Rus', Vladimir's son, Boris, also had a Hungarian *otrok* by the name György (George) (Cross and Sherbowitz-Wetzor 1953, 127; Likhachev 1996, 59), whose two brothers also seem to have been living in the Kievan Rus' territories during the early eleventh century, according to various traditions (Lepahin 2009). Common guard duties and retinue services that Scandinavians and nomads performed in western and south-eastern European courts (e.g. Kievan Rus', Volga Bulgharia, Khazaria, Byzantium, Hungary) could also have resulted in similar situations. The case of the Varangian Varayazhko (mentioned in Chapter 5) is a specific example. Situations like these presented ample opportunities for Scandinavians to acquire Turkic words, languages and ideas in general.

## Conclusion

Despite the linguistic distances between the Old Norse and Turkic speakers, communication among them might have been smoother during the ninth and tenth centuries than previously assumed. Away from hostility and warfare, even the most primitive ways of exchanging goods required a general understanding or awareness of the transactions by both parties. Even though loanwords are not firmly discernible between Old Norse and any of the Turkic languages, it has to be noted that several of these Turkic languages are largely unknown. The historical situation demanded that Old Norse and many Turkic or Finno-Ugric speakers should understand each other. Communication channels among the ethnic groups developed gradually through extensive military and commercial contacts as well as occasional joint residence along various parts of the 'Eastern Way' that Scandinavians travelled from the eighth century onwards.

In the ninth century, interpreters were the primary channels of communication, probably Slavs who understood the Scandinavians and also the other inhabitants of the region. By the next century, however, the majority of the Scandinavian community in the east became bilingual, which must have resulted in easier communication with the Turks along the Volga and the Dnieper. Turkic groups living along the major rivers also used the Slavic language, which became the intermediary between the Scandinavian Rus' and the various steppe peoples. In time, Scandinavian groups spending considerable time in the vicinity or company of various groups with Turkic cultural backgrounds possibly felt the need to transmit or acknowledge some ideas in the vernacular(s). According to the written sources, highly mobile groups of Scandinavian and Turkic origin showed outstanding skills in acquiring foreign languages. Thus, it seems probable that Scandinavians also learned local languages other than Slavic in Eastern Europe or that a few Turks in turn were able to assimilate those of the Scandinavians.

Scandinavian and Turkic retainers were both hired to serve within courts in the east, which provided opportunities for them to learn each other's language. Furthermore, hybrid *lingua franca*s may have evolved in multi-ethnic warrior groups, as was argued on the basis of dialectical differences between separate Viking contingents in the west (Price 2014, 62). Scandinavian–Turkic communications also developed through mercantile relations in the border zones of the steppe and forest regions or at international markets, where temporary dwellings were established. These fairs, supervised mostly by Turkic people, acted as vigorous melting pots of different cultures where a multitude of contemporary languages were used. Multi-ethnic interactions and regional variations within the same unit contributed to variations within the same language group or tribal association.

The use of interpreters, mediatory languages, bilingualism and learning foreign languages to varying degrees marked the international character of these markets. Despite the gradual developments outlined earlier, it is reasonable that all these factors (interpreters, mediatory languages, bilingualism) were at work simultaneously, depending on the level of acculturation or assimilation of each group. In addition, in business relations it was advantageous in certain situations to hide one's own knowledge of the local language during negotiations, for instance, or to use a basic knowledge of the other's speech to understand transactions and the other's intentions; the case of Hróðfúss illustrates the problem of unreliable trading partners. Thus, there would have been reasons to use interpreters even after the linguistic assimilation of the Scandinavians. These possibilities could have created endless combinations to allow Turkic and Scandinavian or Rus' groups at the same location to communicate effectively.

# Conclusions

Who the Vikings were is a haunting question. The uses and abuses of the term throughout the last decades (Christiansen 2006, 1–4) have triggered a remarkable shift towards stressing the inclusiveness of the designation in terms of ethnicity. Everywhere the Vikings went they shaped local societies and were also greatly affected by them. Foreign impulses seem to have somewhat loosened the 'Scandinavianness' of the Viking phenomenon from the Baltics, through the British Isles to the North Atlantic. In the most restricted meaning of the term, Frisians, Balts and even Anglo-Saxons went 'Viking' and joined the ranks of sea pirate communities. Cultural interactions between Scandinavian settlers and other ethnic groups gave rise to fused forms of material cultures, identities and ways of life in environments outside mainland Scandinavia. The Viking diaspora incorporated both unity and differences. As the late Thomas Noonan put it, one of the tasks of future research is to reveal how one 'Viking' differed from another (Noonan 1991, 205). The dichotomy of unity and difference is best deciphered through specific examples that illustrate both the interconnectedness and variations within this regional network. The Eastern impact, however, has not been in the foreground of these scholarly endeavours. This study aimed to illuminate the role of the vast region of the Western Eurasian steppes as a neglected but nevertheless key geopolitical arena during the period. In all spheres of social life, mobile Turkic pastoralists in the east were no less important partners of Viking Age Scandinavians than Frankish, Celtic, Anglo-Saxon or Inuit peoples in the west.

Scandinavian interactions with the local inhabitants of the eastern regions included complicated and changing trade relations, various aspects of warfare and varying degrees of coexistence. Although the Slavic, Balto-Finnic and Byzantine relations may occasionally be better attested in some of the preserved source material, the steppe dwellers from (or dominated by) Turkic cultures were just as frequently partners of Scandinavian merchants, mercenaries, plunderers and settlers from the ninth through the eleventh centuries.

The steppe was the immediate frontier of the geographical area traditionally considered subject to the Scandinavian warrior elites called the Rus'. The steppe, however, was not a strict border. Scandinavians and Rus' not only traversed it but also deliberately visited certain parts. It was home to communities of diverse ethnic backgrounds. Tribes of the Khazar Khaganate, those dwelling along the Volga, Oka,

DOI: 10.4324/9781003037859-8

Dniester and Don, such as the Alans, Bashkirs, Burtas', Oghuz' and most importantly the Volga Bulghars developed close ties with the Scandinavian incomers. From the late ninth or early tenth century in the steppe zone south of Kiev, migrating Magyar and Pecheneg tribes maintained contact with the newly established Rus' strongholds in the Middle Dnieper area. These relations continued even throughout the next century, when the Magyars settled in the Carpathian Basin.

Armed conflicts among the Scandinavians, Rus' and various steppe peoples naturally occurred. There is even an attractive suggestion that some of the 'oriental' artefacts brought back by Scandinavians and Rus' were souvenirs from successful campaigns directed toward or passing through steppe abodes, especially Khazaria (Pushkina 2020, 236–38). Rather than to the traditional contrast between 'forest and steppe' (*les i step*), however, the Rus' only clashed with the steppe communities in a limited framework of warfare during the Viking Age. The Rus' mostly tried to secure trade routes leading through the steppe, whilst the steppe people attempted to hinder free passage. Steppe people attempted, usually by force of arms, to make the Dnieper Rus' trade with them. These disturbances do not seem to have triggered equal retaliation by the Rus'. Rus' polities did not have political ambitions directed towards the steppe; despite a brief change in the second part of the tenth century, no long-lasting conquest was achieved. The focus of this study, however, is on the more positive aspects of these relations, namely, co-operation.

Longer joint residence affected spheres of warfare, extensive trade connections, and certain cultural transfers (often interconnected); the prerequisite was probably to develop well-functioning and effective communication with partners. This work adopts a thematic approach rather than a chronological or politically oriented one because of the nature of the fragmentary and sometimes quite taciturn source material, which are sometimes problematic from a critical point of view. Many findings either cannot be clearly linked to precise historical events or they are more suggestive than firm evidence. Nevertheless, certain tendencies can be identified. Decisive interactions between the Scandinavian Rus' and the steppe communities can be touched upon in features of religious and everyday customs, trade, warfare and communication.

First and foremost, it was the lucrative mercantile potential of the Volga area that drew Scandinavian traders to Eastern Europe. Islamic dirhams and 'oriental' fashions were communicated here to Scandinavian merchants explicitly through intermediaries of Turkic ethnicity in exchange for furs, slaves and weapons. Scandinavian entrepreneurs acquired all these products in the East. Even in the case of so-called Viking swords, good-quality iron ingots to forge into blades were imported from Central Asia, probably from Samanid Persia (Williams 2012, 120–21). Byzantine and Muslim markets, lying beyond the steppe, could only be reached by adroit manoeuvring among toll stations, river portages and the territory of political rivals. The Turks supervised transmitter markets along the Volga that operated as sophisticated and well-organized systems characterized by the establishment of temporary dwellings, secure food supplies, regulations and customs duties. In contrast to the peacefulness of the Volga trade route, the Dnieper area was less secure due to the changing political relations of the Rus' with the nomads of the Pontic steppes. Political enmities resulted in raids aiming to take prisoners and products from each other. In peaceful times, traditional nomadic merchandise, mostly animals, was supplied to the Rus' in exchange for metal tools, jewellery and weapons or products of the forest belt. The Carpathian Basin might have provided another sought-after resource: salt, which could have been traded with the Magyars through a land route between Kiev and the Upper Tisza region. In the tenth century, other commodities were exchanged in foreign markets which were visited by both Rus' and Magyar traders. Peaceful trade negotiations and reciprocal visits to each other's markets facilitated the construction of mutual trust among strangers. The initial 'stranger', first triggering cultural shock, ceased to be the 'other' as soon as encounters became regular. Steppe fairs with their temporary abodes and multi-ethnic environments secured the conditions for slowly unfolding cultural transfers.

I have also argued that Scandinavian and Rus' warriors showed high rates of assimilation in Eastern Europe as they adapted quickly to local circumstances. Documentary evidence and archaeological remains show that retainers took service in Byzantium, Kievan Rus', Khazaria, Volga Bulgharia, Poland, Hungary, Georgia and even in Derbent on the Caspian Sea. Except for the last two, professional warriors from the steppe were there at the same time. Retainers migrated among courts elsewhere in the Viking world and transmitted knowledge, fashions and material culture (Abrams 2012, 24). Courts in Eastern and South-eastern Europe could also have become first-hand cultural transfer zones for Scandinavian and Rus' retainers. Here, steppe warriors had an effect on these retainers in a military-cultural sense. During common guard duties and joint military campaigns, steppe warfare techniques were introduced to the Scandinavians and Rus'. The 'Eastern Vikings' combined their traditional fighting methods with those of mobile horsemen archers, either directly adopting combat skills and equipment or co-ordinating their campaigns and strategic moves on the battlefield with nomad cavalry. The most usual and successful strategy combined Scandinavian expertise on water and nomadic superiority on open ground. Rus' ship convoys and pirate fleets were accompanied on campaign by horsemen following along the river banks (Cross and Sherbowitz-Wetzor 1953, 64, 72, 96; Likhachev 1996, 16, 23, 39). A useful snapshot of the advantages of having two different mobile forces in a single army comes from the Dorostolon campaign of Sviatoslav. The Rus' *knyaz* held the upper hand in the open field until his nomad allies abandoned him, but he was still able to deliver supplies to his besieged troops along the rivers by evading a Byzantine river blockade (Thurn 1973, 302–03). Whether nomadic people ever boarded Viking ships in joint operations is disputed. A unique note by ibn Ḥawqal on the Rus' carrying Pecheneg hordes on an Al-Andalusian raid might be a confusion with the joint campaign of Sviatoslav and the Oghuz'. It is missing from Iṣṭakhrī's work, which he copied, but ibn Ḥawqal is quite specific in his identification of various Turkic tribes (Montgomery 2008, 558–59). Co-operation can also be seen to some extent in material culture. A few Viking weapons with typical Eastern embellishments and nomadic weapons with Nordic decorations found in Eastern Europe suggest that ties between the groups might have been quite close.

The extent of this blended culture is not well represented in the archaeological record, but the material cultures of the North and the steppe diffused widely and are both represented in notable warrior graves of the period.

Economic and military co-operation paved the way for cultural borrowings, not only external features of dress, military and everyday accessories but also customs of behaviour. The nomadic habit of impounding drifting vessels, for instance, was probably practised by the Rus' as early as the beginning of the tenth century. In clauses in two Byzantine–Rus' peace treaties, of 907 and 911 CE, the Greeks attempted to prohibit this Rus' custom and made it a condition that they aid shipwrecked Byzantine crews. The Byzantine authorities required the Rus' on their next visit to Constantinople, to compensate the owners for cargo they had seized (Cross and Sherbowitz-Wetzor 1953, 67, 76; Likhachev 1996, 19, 25; cf. Malingoudi 1998, 59–64). Similarly, an Eastern form of torture documented among the Slavic Drevljans and Turkic Oghuz' was tearing bodies apart with two tree branches (Diaconus 1828, 106; Ditten 1984; Montgomery 2014, 202–03), and the Rus' also practised it. It is illustrated in Saxo Grammaticus's story of the Rus' pirate Røtho, who, when returning to Scandinavia, habitually tortured people in the same way: he ripped their bodies down the middle by tying each leg to a bent tree branch (Friis-Jensen 2015: I, 500–03).

Some behaviours learned in the east were even brought back to Scandinavia, as is suggested by a burial from the Swedish Rösta; a Viking sword in a grave pointed towards the head of the deceased and a horse was buried beside the corpse. These features are quite uncharacteristic for Scandinavian burials, where swords usually point towards the feet, and horses were buried at the feet of the interred. These customs were practised extensively on the steppe, however, and the horse was also placed next to the body in steppe-affiliated Rus' graves in Gnezdovo, Kiev, Shestovitsa, Chernigov and Staraya Ladoga. The Magyar pouch found within the grave at in Rösta also speaks of steppe influence (Petrukhin 2016, 129–33).

The Turks made a deep impression on the Rus' and eventually affected their identity, even religious identity. Old Norse religion was definitely brought to the East, as attested by details of rituals: waterside locations, holy trees, ship burnings, sacrifices of animals and humans and even weapons. These practices, however, did not exist in a vacuum but were among a huge variety of similar practices among most of the pagan religions in the East. Old Norse religion had to be adapted to the new environment at the expense of dropping some elements. Traces of cult objects relating to fertility rites, cultic sickles, for instance, known from Scandinavia, are missing in European Russia, Belarus and Ukraine, which may be explained by the Rus' not practising agriculture, making a need for such rituals unnecessary there (Musin 2012, 586). Another important change was the merging of new ritual elements into Rus' tradition.

Shared concepts gave rise to parallel variations of rites and rituals even within the same community. A further twist could be added if some of the participants had a home in Scandinavia, where, upon return, the original customs and practices might have been reinforced. It would also have been possible for individuals to perform the same ritual differently in two distinct milieus. Suggesting multiple identities in the tenth century is an option; the pragmatism and adaptability of the Scandinavians and the Rus' allowed a flexible handling of ritual traditions. Exactly what supplies to use for a ritual became varied and religious concepts also changed. One of the documented instances concerns the afterlife service of defeated warriors, which likely gained a foothold among the Rus' through Turkic influence. Embracing these Turkic customs and ritual behaviour on the level of practicalities and beliefs was facilitated by previous Scandinavian experience with the nomadic Sámi, who shared the shamanistic traditions of Central Asian nomads to some extent. Shamanistic elements were even present in Old Norse mythology. The character of Óðinn and the *seiðkonur*, the eight-legged horse Sleipnir – whose exact analogy is found among the Siberian Buryat beliefs – and journeys to the underworld all have parallels in Eastern shamanistic traditions (Eliade [1964] 1972, 375, 379–87; Price 2002, 320–23). Conceptualizing these cultural transfers is not necessarily straightforward, as observed by Neil Price in the case of Sámi–Norse interaction:

> if two broadly similar complexes of beliefs co-exist in the same geographical area, maintained by two cultures living in relative harmony, then there will inevitably be some kind of exchange of concepts. Rather than looking at the influence of one culture by the other, we can instead focus on conceptual similarities and separate development within a common tradition.
>
> (Price 2002, 235)

With some reservations warranted by the lack of evidence of Scandinavian influence on steppe cultures, I find Price's conceptualization applicable to the Scandinavian/Rus'–Turkic interactions. Scandinavians and Rus', spending time in the Eastern forest belt where Slavs, Finno-Ugrians and Balts also lived, became part of a milieu between the Scandinavian and Turkic worlds. There is nothing surprising in the development of shared concepts and similar customs in the broad area of European Russia, Belarus and Ukraine, and perhaps the eastern parts of Scandinavia.

Discussing Turkic influence on the Rus' presupposes the existence of fluent communication between the two groups. Besides hostile aggression, even the most primitive ways of exchanging goods required both parties to have a general understanding or awareness of the transaction. Due to the extensive military and commercial contacts, as well as the occasional joint residence along various parts of the 'Eastern Way' where Scandinavians travelled from the eighth century onwards, communication channels between the two ethnic groups developed gradually and co-existed depending on each group's level of assimilation to the other.

Without doubt, Old Norse was used for a long time in the East, and Turkic languages of various kinds were spoken at the fairs the Scandinavians visited. The initial contacts between Scandinavian and Turkic speakers probably had to be mediated through interpreters. The importance of this profession in negotiations did not fade with time, and even after the Scandinavians and some Turks gradually adopted the Eastern Slavic language, interpreters had respectable roles in these societies. The Eastern Slavic language was the *lingua franca* in the East that both the Scandinavian and Turkic speakers embraced, raising the likelihood that it gradually became the intermediary communication channel between the two groups. With the deepening of Scandinavian–Turkic cultural contacts, it seems likely that a few Scandinavian individuals who spent considerable time in the company of Turkic speakers were able to learn at least a basic vocabulary of the other's language. Turkic people, who settled with the Scandinavian Rus' for various reasons, might also have been able to communicate in Norse. Besides the extensive archaeological evidence for common mercenary service in Eastern courts, only individual cases document such opportunities, characters whose names were preserved in writing, for instance, Varayazhko, Turchin, Ugrin and Tyrkir. Some Turkic individuals who lived among the Scandinavians might have joined them under duress, as indicated by their near-slave status. This is implied, for example, by cooks called 'Turks' in Kievan Rus' or Tyrkir being used as foster-father. This also applied to the Rus' since Scandinavian and Rus' captives were held in many places in the East; the Khazarian Rus' slave warriors are a prime example (Katona 2021a). Voluntarily or not, joint residence made regular conversation between Scandinavians and Turks inescapable.

The legacy of the contacts between steppe people and Viking Age Scandinavians lingered on in later connections. The Magyars certainly met Scandinavians even after they settled in the Carpathian Basin, confirmed by Géza's and Harald Bluetooth's envoys meeting in Quedlinburg. Magyar raids in Western Europe might also have affected Scandinavia. According to Bertil Almgren, the late Viking armies of Svein Forkebeard and Cnut the Great owed their success in invading England partly to the spread of Magyar cavalry equipment (mainly stirrups), which reached Denmark during the tenth century (Almgren 1963, 235–46). Later details remain dim but Saint Stephen, despite turning to Western Europe in high politics, continued to maintain Scandinavian connections on a personal level. Medieval Hungary, transformed into a Christian state in the first millennium, remained in contact with the Scandinavians even later. The Hungarian king, Andrew I (1046–60 CE), residing as an outcast with Grand Prince Yaroslav in Kiev, returned home to regain control of the country with Varangian support. Two Germanic names of possible Old Norse origin appear in the fourteenth-century *Chronicon pictum* among the names of his retainers (Katona 2019a). The crusade led by Sigurd the Jerusalemfarer (1103–30 CE) passed through Hungary on its way back from the Holy Land (Sturluson 2002c, 254), and it is hard to imagine that this might have occurred without interaction with Coloman the Learned (1095–116 CE), the ruler of the Hungarian kingdom at the time. The heritage of the 'Vikings of the steppe' is still unconsciously maintained today by Hungarian re-enactment groups, who blend their attire and re-enacted lifestyle with elements borrowed from the medieval steppe as well as from Scandinavia (Katona 2019b).

All in all, the *austrvegr* united five different worlds from Scandinavia through the Slavic lands to the edge of the Turkic, Byzantine and Muslim spheres. As an intermediary stage of Scandinavian, Slavic and Turkic interaction, Eastern Europe – most importantly the territories of the later Kievan Rus' – brought the Scandinavian and Turkic regions into closer connection with each other than has previously been articulated.

I believe that in order to understand Viking Age Scandinavian history it is useful to know about the other inhabitants of the world they entered. If this were a more popularizing book it could be filled with pictures of 'Vikings' rowing between cliffs with pelicans (Constantine Porphyrogenitus 1967, 58–59), sitting by a desolate vineyard in a looted steppe settlement (Kramers 1939, 393; Lunde and Stone 2012, 178), stopping with their camels at a caravanserai (de Goeje 1889, 154; Lunde and Stone 2012, 112) or purchasing mares and stallions from ponytailed nomads at a market along the Danube (Cross and Sherbowitz-Wetzor 1953, 86; Likhachev 1996, 32). None of these settings are conventionally connected to 'Vikings' even though they are all derived from historical documents describing the Rus', many of whom originated in Scandinavia. The main contribution of studying the steppe contacts of Viking Age Scandinavians will be to further refine the multifaceted identities within the Viking diaspora. The Rus' mercenaries who demanded and received unlimited access to the bathhouses of Constantinople according to the Rus'–Byzantine peace treaty of 907 CE (Cross and Sherbowitz-Wetzor 1953, 65; Likhachev 1996, 17) evidently followed different daily hygiene practices than their fellow Rus' along the Middle Volga, who ibn Faḍlān described as "the filthiest of all God's creatures" in 922 CE (Montgomery 2014, 242–43). The cultural bias of this Arabic observer towards the barbaric 'other' might not project the true nature of this community; they definitely showed inclinations to hygiene. I do not want to fall into geographic or cultural determinism. Many of these people widely travelled and made individual choices when adopting new habits. Scandinavian and Rus' groups differed in cultural diversity, weaponry, religion, diet, and dress and had varied experiences with local languages, mentality, fauna, and flora (e.g. Katona 2021b). Since the Scandinavians came to the East from the North Atlantic, Denmark, Sweden and Norway, Eastern influences further deepened the already existing cultural differences. Thus, 'wandering' back and forth between these places resulted in 'Vikings' becoming carriers of cultural packages, which made courts more alike ('globalized' if one likes the term), and at the same time they themselves started to differ from other members of the diaspora.

The notion of 'Viking' becomes increasingly blurred in an Eastern context, but it should not be ignored. For instance, can Sviatoslav, Chern or the *malik* of the Volga Rus' or his chieftain be considered 'Vikings'? What about Varayazhko and Tyrkir? I would say they all were to some extent. Biology, language, customs and personal history all intertwined in these characters. Born a Scandinavian by ancestry but leading a nomadic way of life or born on the steppe and acting like a 'Viking', Sviatoslav and Tyrkir are two sides of the same coin. Varayazhko and the others are somewhere in between. Perhaps they represented the norm and the others were the exceptions, perhaps the opposite. They were all, however, important actors in the Viking diaspora who also shared in the culture of the Turkic world. Their identities, and those of others unnamed in the sources, featured a fusion of two (or more) cultural spheres. I call them 'Vikings of the steppe'.

# Bibliography


Abrams, Lesley. 2012. "Diaspora and Identity in the Viking Age." *Early Medieval Europe* 20, no. 1: 17–38.

———. 2016. "Connections and Exchange in the Viking Worlds." In *Byzantium and the Viking World*, edited by Fedor Androshchuk, Jonathan Shephard, and Monica White, 37–52. Uppsala: Uppsala University.

Afanas'ev, Gennady E. 2018. "Where is the Archeological Evidence of the Existence of a Khazar State?" *Anthropology & Archeology of Eurasia* 57, no. 3: 166–89.

Al-Azmeh, Aziz. 1992. "Barbarians in Arab Eyes." *Past and Present* 134: 3–18.

Albericus Trium Fontium. 1925. *Chronicon,* edited by Paulus Scheffer-Boichorst. MGH Scriptorum, no. 23. Leipzig: Karl W. Hiersemann.

Alemany, Agustí. 2000. *Sources on the Alans. A Critical Compilation.* Handbook of 'Oriental' Studies. Central Asia, no. 5. Leiden: Brill.

Almgren, Bertil. 1963. "Vikingatågens höjdpunkt och slut. Skepp, hästar och befästningar." *Tor* 9: 215–50.

al-Tanjī, Muhammad B. Tāwīt, ed. 1962. *Kitāb Taḥdīd Nihāyāt Al-amākin Li-taṣḥīḥ Masāfāt Al-masākin.* Ankara: Doğus Ltd.

Álvarez-Pedrosa, Juan Antonio, ed. 2021. *Sources of Slavic Pre-Christian Religion.* Numen Book Series, no. 169. Leiden: Brill.

Ambrosiani, Björn. 2001. "Eastern connections at Birka." *Viking Heritage Magazine* (third yearly issue): 3–7.

Ambrosiani, Björn, and Fedir Androshchuk. 2006. "Vooruzheniye i vostochnyye kontakty Birki [The Armaments and Eastern Contacts of Birka]." In *Rus' na perekhresti svitiv (mizhnarodni vplyvy na formuvannya Davn'o-rus'koyi derzhavy) IX – XI st. (Chernihiv – Shestovytsya, 20–23 lypnya 2006 r.)*, edited by P. P. Tolochko, A. A. Horskyy, M. Dimnik, V. O. Dyatlov, V. P. Kovalenko, O. B. Kovalenko, and O. P. Motsya, 3–16. Chernihiv: Siveryans'ka dumka.

Andersson, Theodore. 2001. "Kylfingar." In *Reallexikon der Germanischen Altertumskunde.* Vol. 17, edited by Heinrich Beck, 520–22. Berlin: De Gruyter.

Androshchuk, Fedir. 2000. "Černigov et Šestovica, Birka et Hovgården: le modèle urbain scandinavie vu de l'est." In *Les centres proto-urbain russes entre Scandinavie, Byzance et Orient*, edited by Michel Kazanski, Anne Nercessian, and Constantin Zuckerman, 257–66. Paris: Éditions P. Lethielleux.

———. 2002. "Har götlandska vikingar offrat vapen i Dnepr-forsarna?" *Fornvännen* 97, no. 1: 9–14.

———. 2004–05. "Vikingarna – ruserna – varjagerna." *Historiska Nyheter. Olga & Ingegerd – Vikingafurstinnor i öst*: 36–39.

———. 2008. "The Vikings in the East." In *The Viking World*, edited by Stefan Brink and Neil Price, 517–42. London: Routledge.

———. 2013. *Vikings in the East. Essays on Contacts along the Road to Byzantium (800–1100)*. Studia Byzantina Upsalensia, no. 14. Uppsala: Uppsala University.

———. 2016. "What Does Material Evidence Tell us About Contacts between Byzantium and the Viking World c. 800–1000?" In *Byzantium and the Viking World*, edited by Fedor Androshchuk, Jonathan Shephard, and Monica White, 97–116. Uppsala: Uppsala University.

Androshchuk, Fedir, and Volodymyr Zotsenko. 2012. *Scandinavian Antiquities of Southern Rus'. A Catalogue*. Paris: The Ukrainian National Committee for Byzantine Studies.

Anthony, David W. 2007. *The Horse, the Wheel and Language. How Bronze-Age Riders from the Eurasian Steppes Shaped the Modern World*. Princeton: Princeton University Press.

Arbman, Holger. 1940. *Birka I. Die Gräber*. Uppsala: Almqvist & Wiksells.

———. 1942. "Einige orientalische Gegenstände in den Birka-Funden." *Acta Archaeologica* 13: 303–15.

———. 1961. *The Vikings*. London: Thames and Hudson.

Arkoun, Mohammed. 1993. "Miskawayh." In *The Encyclopaedia of Islam*, edited by Bosworth et al., Vol. 7, 143–44. Leiden: Brill.

Arne, Ture Algot Johnsson. 1914. *La Suède et l'orient, études archéologiques sur les relations de la Suéde et de l'orient pendant l'âge des Vikings*. Archives d'études orientales 8. Uppsala: K. W. Appelbergs Boktrygkeri.

———. 1931. "Skandinavische Holzkammergräber aus der Wikingerzeit in der Ukraine." *Acta Archaeologica* 2, no. 3: 285–302.

Artamonov, M. I. 1962. *Istoriya Khazar [Khazar History]*. Leningrad: Gosudarstvennyy Ermitazh.

Ashley, Scott. 2013. "How Icelanders Experienced Byzantium, Real and Imagined." In *Experiencing Byzantium. Papers from the 44th Spring Symposium of Byzantine Studies. Newcastle – Durham, April 2011*, edited by Claire Nesbitt and Mark Jackson, 213–32. London: Routledge.

Avdusin, D. A. 1969. "Smolensk and the Varangians According to Archaeological Data." *Norwegian Archaeological Review* 2: 52–62.

Avdusin, D. A., and T. A. Puškina. 1988. "Three Chamber Graves at Gniozdovo." *Fornvännen* 83: 20–33.

Ayalon, David. 1999. *Eunuchs, Caliphs and Sultans: A Study in Power Relationships*. Jerusalem: Magnes Press.

Bak, János M., and Martyn Rady, eds. and trans. 2010. *Anonymus and Master Roger*. Central European Medieval Texts Series, no. 5. Budapest: CEU Press.

Bálint, Csanád. 1970. "A ló a magyar pogány hitvilágban [The Horse in Pagan Hungarian Beliefs]." *A Móra Ferenc Múzeum Évkönyve* no. 1: 31–43.

———. 1981. "Einige Fragen des Dirhem-Verkehrs in Europa." *Acta Archaeologica Academiae Scientiarum Hungaricae* 33: 105–31.

———. 1989. *Archäeologie der Steppe. Steppenvölker zwischen Volga und Donau vom 6. bis zum 10. Jahrhundert*. Vienna: Böhlau Verlag.

Balogh, László. 2004. "Az Annales Bertiniani 839. évi bejegyzése és a magyarok [The Entry of the Year 839 in the Annales Bertiniani and the Magyars]." In *Fegyveres nomádok, nomád fegyverek*, edited by László Balogh and László Keller, 112–23. Magyar Őstörténeti Könyvtár, no. 21. Budapest: Balassi Kiadó.

Barfield, Thomas J. 1993. *The Nomadic Alternative*. Englewood Cliffs, NJ: Prentice Hall.

Barnes, Michael P. 2008. "The Scandinavian Languages in the Viking Age." In *The Viking World*, edited by Stefan Brink and Neil Price, 274–80. London: Routledge.

Bartha, Antal. 1988. *A magyar nép őstörténete [The Prehistory of the Hungarian Nation]*. Budapest: Akadémiai Kiadó.

Bartlett, Robert. 2007. "From Paganism to Christianity in Medieval Europe." In *Christianization and the Rise of Christian Monarchy. Scandinavia, Central Europe and Rus' c. 900–1200*, edited by Nora Berend, 47–72. Cambridge: Cambridge University Press.

Battúta, Ibn. 1953. *Travels in Asia and Africa. 1325–1354*, translated by Hamilton Alexander Rosskeen Gibb. London: Routledge & Kegan Paul.

Beazley, C. Raymond, intr., trans. by Robert Mitchell, and Nevill Forbes, compr. A. A. Shakmatov. 1914. *The Chronicle of Novgorod 1016–1471*. Camden Third Series, no. 25. London: Offices of the Society.

Beck, Heinrich. 1994. "Yngvi Tyrkja konungr." In *Sagnaþing helgað Jónasi Kristjánssyni sjötugum 10. Apríl 1994*, edited by Gísli Sigurðsson, Guðrún Kvaran, and Sigurgeir Steingrímsson, 55–68. Reykjavík: Hið íslenzka bókmentafélag.

Becker, Joseph, ed. 1915. *Liutprandus Cremonensis Relatio de legatione Constantinopolitana*. MGH Scriptores rerum Germanicarum in usum scholarum, no. 41. Hannover: Hahn.

Beckwith, Christopher I. 2009. *Empires of the Silk Road: A History of Central Eurasia from the Bronze Age to the Present*. Princeton: Princeton University Press.

Bekker, Immanuel, ed. 1838. *Theophanes Continuatus, Ioannes Cameniata, Symeon Magister, Georgius monachus*. CSHB, no. 33. Bonn: Weber.

———, ed. 1839. *Georgius Cedrenus*. CSBH, no. 2, Vol. 2. Bonn: Weber.

Belavin, A. M. 2000. *Kamskiy torgovyy put'. Severnoye Predural'ye v yego ekonomicheskikh i etnokul'turnykh svyazyakh [The Kama Trade Route. The Northern West Urals in its Economic and Ethnocultural Connectedness]*. Perm: Permskiy gosudarstvennyy pedagogicheskiy universitet.

Bell-Fialkoff, Andrew. 2000. "The Vikings." In *The Role of Migration in the History of the Eurasian Steppe. Sedentary civilization vs. "Barbarian" and Nomad*, edited by Andrew Bell-Fialkoff, 151–79. Basingstoke: MacMillan.

Benkő, Loránd. 1999. "Barangolások egy ómagyar tulajdonnév körül [Roamings Around an Ancient Hungarian Property Name]." *Magyar Nyelv* 95: 25–40.

Bentley, G. Carter. 1987. "Ethnicity and Practice." *Comparative Studies in Society and History* 29: 24–55.

Bibire, Paul. 2007. "On Reading the Icelandic Sagas: Approaches to Old Icelandic Texts." In *West Over Sea: Studies in Scandinavian Sea-Borne Expansion and Settlement before 1300; A Festschrift in Honour of Dr Barbara E. Crawford*, edited by Beverley Ballin Smith, Simon Taylor, and Gareth Williams, 3–18. Leiden: Brill.

Birkeland, Harris. 1954. *Nordens historie i middelalderen etter arabiske kilder*. Oslo: Jacob Dybwad.

Birnbaum, Henrik. 1978. "Yaroslav's Varangian Connection." *Scando-Slavica* 24, no. 1: 5–25.

Bíró, Ádám. 2012. "Dating (With) Weapon Burials and the"Waffenwechsel. A Preliminary Report on New Investigations of the so-called Viking-Age Swords in the Carpathian Basin from a Chronological Point of View." In *Die Archäologie der frühen Ungarn. Chronologie, Technologie und Methodik. Internationaler Workshop des Archäologischen Instituts der Ungarischen Akademie der Wissenschaften und des Römisch-Germanischen Zentralmuseums Mainz in Budapest am 4. und 5. Dezember 2009*, edited by Tobias Bendeguz, 191–218. Mainz: Schnell & Steiner.

Blaney, Benjamin. 1993. "Berserkr." In *Medieval Scandinavia. An Encyclopedia*, edited by Phillip Pulsiano and Kirsten Wolf, 37–38. London: Routledge.

Blöndal, Sigfús. 1978. *The Varangians of Byzantium*. Cambridge: Cambridge University Press.

Boba, Imre. 1967. *Nomads, Northmen and Slavs. Eastern Europe in the Ninth Century*. The Hauge: Mouton.

Bogachev, A. V., and D. A. Frantsuzov. 2011. "Ibn Fadlan o kostyume tyurkoyazychnykh narodov, vstrechennykh im v 922 godu [Ibn Fadlan about the Costume of the Turkic Peoples He Met in 922]." *Izvestiya Samarskogo nauchnogo tsentra Rossiyskoy akademii nauk* 3, no. 2: 554–57.

Bogucki, Mateusz. 2007. "Some 'Oriental' Finds from Janów Pomorski (Truso), Poland." In *Cultural Interaction between East and West. Archaeology, Artefacts and Human Contacts in Northern Europe*, edited by Ulf Fransson, Marie Svedin, Sophie Bergerbrant, and Fedir Androshchuk, 128–34. Stockholm: Stockholm University.

Boretius, Alfred, and Victor Krause, eds. 1897. *Capitularia Regum Francorum*, Vol. 2., MGH Leges II. Hannover: Hahniani.

Borosy, András. 1981. "Vélemények a kora-feudális fejedelmi kíséretről [Opinions on the Early Feudal Princely Retinue]." *Acta Historica* 70: 19–39.

Bosworth, Clifford Edmund, ed. 1982. *Ḥudūd al-ʿĀlam. 'the Region of the World'. A Persian Geography 372 A. H. – 982 A.D*, translated by Vladimir Minorsky, 2nd ed. E. J. W. Gibb Memorial Series, New Series, no. 11. Cambridge: E. J. W. Gibb.

Boyle, John Andrew. 1965. "A form of Horse Sacrifice Amongst the 13th – 14th Century Mongols." *Central Asiatic Journal* 10, no. 3/4: 145–50.

Brather, Sebastian. 2004. *Ethnische Interpretationen in der frühgeschichtlichen Archäologie. Geschichte, Grundlagen und Alternativen*. Berlin: Walter de Gruyter.

Braun, Fedor, and Ture Johnsson Arne. 1914. "Den svenska runstenen från ön Berezanj utanför Dneprmynningen." *Fornvännen* 9: 44–48.

Braun, Friedrich. 1924. "Das historische Russland im nordischen Schrifttum des 10. bis 14. Jahrhunderts." In *Festschrift für Eugen Mogk zum 70. Geburtstag 19 Juli 1924*, 150–97. Halle and der Saale: Verlag von Max Niemeyer.

Bray, Daniel. 2004. "Sacrifice and Sacrificial Ideology in Old Norse Religion." In *The Dark Side. Proceedings of the Seventh Australian and International Religion, Literature and the Arts Conference*, edited by Christopher Hartney and Andrew McGarrity, 123–35. Sydney: RLA Press.

Brim, V. A. 2002. "Put' iz varjag v greki [The Way from the Varangians to the Greeks]." In *Iz istorii russkoj kul'tury. Vol. II/1. (Kievskaa i moskovskaa Rus')*, edited by A. F. Litvina and F. B. Uspenskij, 227–60. Moscow: Yazyki Slavyanskoy Kul'tury.

Brink, Stefan. 2007. "How Uniform Was the Old Norse Religion?" In *Learning and Understanding in the Old Norse World: Essays in Honour of Margaret Clunies Ross*, edited by Judy Quinn, Kate Heslop, and Tarrin Wills, 105–36. Turnhout: Brepols.

Bruno of Querfurt. 1973. *S. Adalberti Pragensis Episcopi et Martyris vita Altera. Redactio Brevior*. Monumenta Poloniae Historica. Series Nova, Vol. 4/3, 43–69. Warsaw: Panstowowe Wydawnictwo Naukowe.

Brunschvig, Robert. 1986. "'Abd." In *The Encyclopaedia of Islam*, edited by H. A. R. Gibb, J. H. Kramers, E. Lévi-Provençal, and J. Schacht, Vol. 1, 24–40. Leiden: Brill.

Bubenok, O. B. 2016. "Koly Tmutarakan' stala volodinnyam Rusi? [When Did Tmutarakan Became a Rus'ian Property?]." *Knyazha doba: istoriya i kul'tura* 10: 69–76.

Budd, Paul, Andrew Millard, Carolyn Chenery, Sam Lucy, and Charlotte Roberts. 2004. "Investigating Population Movement by Stable Isotope Analysis: A Report from Britain." *Antiquity* 78, no. 299: 127–41.

Buko, Andrzej, ed. 2015. *Bodzia. A Late Viking-Age Elite Cemetery in Central Poland*. Leiden: Brill.

Buzinkay, Géza, and Péter Havassy, eds. 1995. *Budapesti Történeti Múzeum [Budapest History Museum]*. Budapest: Corvina.

Callmer, Johan. 2000. "From West to East. The Penetration of Scandinavians into Eastern Europe ca. 500–900." In *Les centres proto-urbains russes entre Scandinavie, Byzance et Orient*, edited by Michel Kazanski, Anne Nercessian, and Constantin Zuckerman, 45–94. Réalitiés Byzantines, no. 7. Paris: Éditions P. Lethielleux.

———. 2008. "Herrschaftsbildung und Machtausübung: Die Anfänge der ar-Rus (Rus') ca. 500–1000 n. Chr." In *Bereit zum Konflikt. Strategien und Medien der Konflikterzeugung*, edited by Oliver Auge, Felix Biermann, Matthias Müller, and Dirk Schultze, 103–30. Ostfieldern: Thorbecke.

———. 2013. "At the Watershed between the Baltic and the Pontic before Gnezdovo." In *From Goths to Varangians. Communication and Cultural Exchange between the Baltic and the Black Sea*, edited by Line Bjerg, John H. Lind, and Søren M. Sindbæk, 39–85. Aarhus: Aarhus University Press.

Callmer, Johan, Ingrid Gustin, and Mats Roslund, eds. 2017. *Identity Formation and Diversity in the Early Medieval Baltic and Beyond*. Leiden: Brill.

Caspar, Erich, ed. 1928. *Epistulae Karolini aevi V*. MGH Rerum Germanicarum medii aevi epistolarum, no. 7. Berlin: Weidmannos.

Chaliand, Gerard 2005. *Nomadic Empires. From Mongolia to the Danube*, translated by A. M. Berett, 2nd ed. New Brunswick: Transaction Publishers.

Chekhov, Anton. 1992. "The Steppe." In *The Steppe and Other Stories*, 1–81. Oxford: Oxford University Press.

Chenery, Carolyn, Angela Lamb, Jane Evans, Hilary Sloane, and Carlyn Stewart. 2014. "Appendix 3: Isotope Analysis of Individuals from the Ridgeway Hill Mass Grave." In *'Given to the Ground': A Viking Age Mass Grave on Ridgeway Hill, Weymouth*, edited by Louis Loe, Angela Boyle, Helen Webb, and David Score, 259–84. Dorchester: Oxford Archaeology.

Christiansen, Eric. 2006. *The Norsemen in the Viking Age*. Malden: Blackwell.

Ciggaar, Nelly Krijna. 1974. "L'émigration anglaise a Byzance aprés 1066." *Revue des etudes Byzantines* 32: 301–42.

———. 1996. *Western Travellers to Constantinople: The West and Byzantium, 962–1204: Cultural and Political Relations*. Leiden: Brill.

Constantine Porphyrogenitus. 1967. *De Administrando Imperio*, edited by Gyula Moravcsik, translated by R. J. H. Jenkins, Vol. 1. CFHB, no. 1. Washington: Dumbarton Oaks.

Constantinus Porphyrogenitus. 1830. *De Cerimoniis Aulae Byzantinae*, edited by Johann Jakob Reiske, Vol. 2. CSHB, no. 17. Bonn: Weber.

Cook, Robert. 1986. "Russian History, Icelandic Story, and Byzantine Strategy in Eymundar Þáttr Hringssonar." *Viator* 17: 65–89.

Corbett, Noël L. ed. 1977. *La Vie de Saint Louis: Le Témoignage de Jehan, Seigneur de Joinville*. Sherbrooke: Naaman.

Cross, Alan S. C., ed. and trans. 1981. *The Terfinnas and Beormas of Ohthere*. London: Viking Society for Northern Research.

Cross, Samuel Hazzard. 1946. "Primitive Civilization of the Eastern Slavs." *The American Slavic and East European Review* 5, no. 1: 51–87.

Cross, Samuel H., and Olgerd P. Sherbowitz-Wetzor, eds. and trans. 1953. *The Russian Primary Chronicle. Laurentian Text*. Cambridge, MA: Medieval Academy of America.

Csáky, Veronika, Dániel Gerber, Bea Szeifert, Balázs Egyed, Balázs Stégmár, Sergei Gennad'evich Botalov, Ivan Valer'evich Grudochko, Natalia Petrovna Matveeva, Alexander Sergejevich Zelenkov, Anastasiia Viktorovna Sleptsova, Rimma Dmitrievna Goldina, Andrey Vasilevich Danich, Balázs Gusztáv Mende, Attila Türk, and Anna

Szécsényi-Nagy. 2020. "Early medieval genetic data from Ural region evaluated in the light of archaeological evidence of ancient Hungarians." *Scientific Reports* 10: 19137.

Cunliffe, Barry. 2015. *By Steppe, Desert & Ocean. The Birth of Eurasia*. Oxford: Oxford University Press.

Curta, Florin. 2007. "Some Remarks on Ethnicity in Medieval Archaeology." *Early Medieval Europe* 15: 159–85.

Damgaard, Peter de Barros, Nina Marchi, Simon Rasmussen, Michaël Peyrot, Gabriel Renaud, Thorfinn Korneliussen, J. Víctor Moreno-Mayar, Mikkel Winther Pedersen, Amy Goldberg, Emma Usmanova, Nurbol Baimukhanov, Valeriy loman, Lotte Hedeager, Anders Gorm Pedersen, Kasper Nielsen, Gennady Afanasiev, Kunbolot Akmatov, Almaz Aldashev, Ashyk Alpaslan, Gabit Baimbetov, Vladimir I. Bazaliiskii, Arman Beisenov, Bazartseren Boldbaatar, Bazartseren Boldgiv, Choduraa Dorzhu, Sturla Ellingvag, Diimaajav Erdenebaatar, Rana Dajani, Evgeniy Dmitriev, Valeriy Evdokimov, Karin M. Frei, Andrey Gromov, Alexander Goryachev, Hakon Hakonarson, Tatyana Hegay, Zaruhi Khachatryan, Ruslan Khaskhanov, Egor Kitov, Alina Kolbina, Tabaldiev Kubatbek, Alexey Kukushkin, Igor Kukushkin, Nina Lau, Ashot Margaryan, Inga Merkyte, Ilya V. Mertz, Viktor K. Mertz, Enkhbayar Mijiddorj, Vyacheslav Moiyesev, Gulmira Mukhtarova, Bekmukhanbet Nurmukhanbetov, Z. Orozbekova, Irina Panyushkina, Karol Pieta, Václav Smrčka, Irina Shevnina, Andrey logvin, Karl-Göran Sjögren, Tereza Štolcová, Angela M. Taravella, Kadicha Tashbaeva, Alexander Tkachev, Turaly Tulegenov, Dmitriy Voyakin, Levon Yepiskoposyan, Sainbileg Undrakhbold, Victor Varfolomeev, Andrzej Weber, Melissa A. Wilson Sayres, Nikolay Kradin, Morten e. Allentoft, ludovic Orlando, Rasmus Nielsen, Martin Sikora, Evelyne Heyer, Kristian Kristiansen, and Eske Willerslev. 2018. "137 Ancient Human Genomes From Across the Eurasian Steppes." *Nature* 557: 369–74.

Davidan, O. I. 1986. "Etnokul'turnyye kontakty Staroy Ladogi VIII – IX vv [Ethnocultural Contacts of Old Ladoga 8–9th Century]." *Arkheologicheskiy sbornik Gosudarstvennogo Ermitazha. Materialy i issledovaniya po arkheologii SSSR* 27: 99–105.

Davidson, Hilda Roderick Ellis. 1968. *The Road to Hel. A Study of the Conception of the Dead in Old Norse Literature*. New York: Greenwood Press.

———. 1976. *The Viking Road to Byzantium*. London: George Allen & Unwin Ltd.

Diaconus, Leo. 1828. *Historiae*, edited by Karl B. Hase. CSHB, no. 11. Bonn: Weber.

Di Cosmo, Nicola. 1994. "Ancient Inner Asian Nomads: Their Economic Basis and Its Significance in Chinese History." *The Journal of Asian Studies* 53, no. 4: 1092–126.

Dienes, István. 1996. "Honfoglalás kori kovácsaink egyik mesterfogásáról [About a Mastertechnique of Hungarian Smiths of the Conquest-Period]." *Folia Archaeologica* 14: 181–99.

Ditten, Hans. 1984. "Zu Germanoi = Derevljane in Leon Diakonos' Gesichtswerk VI 10." *Byzantinoslavica* 45, no. 2: 183–89.

Downham, Clare. 2012. "Viking Ethnicities: A Historiographic Overview." *History Compass* 10, no. 1: 1–12.

Dozy, Reinhart P. A. 1845. *Dictionnaire détaillé des noms des vêtements chez les Arabes*. Amsterdam: Jean Müller.

DuBois, Thomas A. 1999. *Nordic Religions in the Viking Age*. Philadelphia: University of Pennsylvania Press.

Dubov, I. V. 1989. *Velikiy Volzhskiy put' [The Great Volga Way]*. Leninigrad: Izdatelstvo Leninigradskogo Universiteta.

Duczko, Wladyslaw. 1998. "Viking Age Scandinavia and Islam. An Archaeologist's View." In *Byzantium and Islam in Scandinavia. Acts of a Symposium at Uppsala University June 15–16 1996*, edited by Elisabeth Piltz, 107–15. Jonsered: Paul Åströms Förlag.

———. 2004. *Viking Rus. Studies on the Presence of Scandinavians in Eastern Europe.* Leiden: Brill.

Ecsedy, Hilda. 1972. "Tribe and Tribal Society in the 6th Century Turk Empire." *Acta Orientalia Academiae Scientiarum Hungaricae* 25: 245–62.

———. 1982. "The 'Oriental' Background to the Hungarian Tradition about 'Attila's Tomb'." *Acta Orientalia Academiae Scientiarum Hungaricae* 36, no. 1/3: 129–53.

———. 1984. "Ancient Türk (T'u-Chüeh) Burial Customs." *Acta Orientalia Academiae Scientiarum Hungaricae* 38, no. 3: 263–87.

———. 1988. "A Note on 'Slavery' in the Turk Rulers' Burial Customs (Around 649 A.D.)." *Acta Orientalia Academiae Scientiarum Hungaricae* 42, no. 1: 3–16.

Edberg, Rune. 1996. "Vikingar mot strömmen. Några synspunkter på möjliga och omöjliga skepp vid färderi hemmavattnen och i österled." *Fornvännen* 91: 37–42.

———. 2009. "Experimental 'Viking Voyages' on Eastern European Rivers. 1983–2006." *Situne Dei* (yearly issue): 35–46.

Edholm, af Klas. 2016. "Människooffer i fornnordisk religion. En diskussion utifrån arkeologiskt material och källtexter." *Chaos* 65: 125–47.

———. 2020. *Människooffer i myt och minne. En studie av offerpraktiker i fornnordisk religion utifrån källtexter och arkaeologiskt material.* Åbo: Åbo Akademi University Press.

Efthymiadis, Stephanos. 2013. "Byzantine History-Writers and Their Representation of History." In *Chronicon. Medieval Narrative Sources. A Chronological Guide with Introductory Essays*, edited by János M. Bak and Ivan Jurković, 69–79. Turnhout: Brepols.

Ekrem, Inger, and Lars Boje Mortensen, eds. 2006. *Historia Norwegie*. Translated by Peter Fisher. Copenhagen: Museum Tusculanum Press.

Eliade, Mircea. [1964] 1972. *Shamanism. Archaic Techniques of Ecstasy*. Bollingen Series, no. 76. Princeton: Princeton University Press.

Engström, Johan. 1997. "The Vendel Chieftains – A Study of Military Tactics." In *Marital Aspects of Scandinavian Society in a European Perspective, AD 1–1300*, edited by Anne Nørgård Jørgensen and Birthe L. Clausen, 248–55. The National Museum Studies in Arhcaeology and History, no. 2. Copenhagen: PNM.

Eniosova, Natalia and Veronica Murashova. 1999. "Manufacturing Techniques of Belt and Harness Fittings of the 10th Century AD." *Journal of Archaeological Science* 26: 1093–100.

Erdal, Marcel. 2007. "The Language of the Khazars." In *The World of the Khazars. New Perspectives*, edited by Peter B. Golden, Haggai Ben-Shammai, and András Róna-Tas, 76–108. Leiden: Brill.

Fabech, Charlotte. 1991. "Offerfundene fra Sösdala, Fulltofta og Vennebo. Eksempler på rytternomadiske riter og ceremonier udført i sydskandinaviske jernaldersamfund." In *Nordisk hedendom – et symposium*, edited by Grø Steinsland, Ulf Drobin, Juha Pentikäinen, and Preben Meulengracht Sørensen, 103–12. Odense: Odense Universitesforlag.

Fadlân, Ibn. 1988. *Voyage Chez les Bulgares de la Volga*, translated by Marius Canard. Paris: Sindbad.

Fadlán, Ibn. 2007. *Beszámoló a Volgai Bulgárok Földjén Tett Utazásról [Ibn Fadlan. Report on the Voyage on the Land of the Volga Bulghars]*, translated by Róbert Simon. Budapest: Corvina.

Fehértói Katalin. 1997. "Eltérő nézetek legrégebbi személyneveink eredetéről [Differing Views on the Origin of Our Earliest Personal Names]." In *Honfoglalás és nyelvészet*, edited by László Kovács and László Veszprémy, 235–46. Budapest: Balassi Kiadó.

Fettich, Nándor. 1931. "Adatok a honfoglaláskor archaeologiájához [Data to the Archaeology of the Conquest Era]." *Archaeologiai Értesítő* 45: 48–112.

———. 1933. "A levediai magyarság a régészet megvilágításában. I – II [The Levedian Magyars in Light of Archaeology I – II.]." *Századok* 67: 250–76, 369–99.

———. 1937. *Die Metallkunst der landnehmenden Ungarn*. Budapest: Magyar Történeti Múzeum.

Fiedler, Uwe. 2004. "Bulgars in the Lower Danube Region. A Survey of the Archaeological Evidence and of the State of Current Research." In *The Other Europe in the Middle Ages. Avars, Bulgars, Khazars and Cumans*, edited by Florin Curta and Roman Kovalev, 151–236. Leiden: Brill.

Findley, Carter Vaughn. 2005. *The Turks in World History*. Oxford: Oxford University Press.

Fodor, István. 1986. "On the Contacts of Hungarians with the Baltic area in the 9th – 11th centuries. From an Archaeologist's Point of View." *Hungarian Studies* 2, no. 2: 217–26.

———. 1994. "Leletek Magna Hungariától Etelközig [Finds from Magna Hungaria to Etelköz]." In *Honfoglalás és régészet. A honfoglalásról sok szemmel*, edited by László Kovács, Vol. 1, 39–46. Budapest: Balassi Kiadó.

———. 2007. "Olmin dvor. Bemerkungen zu einem Ortsnamen der Russischen Urchronik." *Folia Archaeologica* 53: 193–99.

———. 2017a. "Honfoglalás kori tarsolylemezeink és keleti párhuzamaik [Conquest Period Sabretaches and Their Eastern Analogies]." *Magyar Tudomány* 178, no. 6: 723–31.

———. 2017b. "Régi szomszédaink a vikingek [Our Old Neighbours: The Vikings]." *Határtalan Régészet* 2, no. 4: 22–25.

———. 2017c. "Honfoglalás kori temető Jászberény határában [A Burial Ground of the Conquest Period (10th Century) on the Outskirts of Jászberény]." *Communicationes Archælogicæ Hungariæ* (yearly issue): 237–54.

Fodor, István, László Révész, Mária Wolf, and Ibolya M. Nepper, eds. 1996. *The Ancient Hungarians. Exhibition Catalogue*. Budapest: Hungarian National Museum.

Font, Márta. 2007. "A magyar kalandozások és a kelet-európai viking terjeszkedés [The Magyar Incursions and the East-European Viking Expansion]." In *Állam, hatalom, ideológia. Tanulmányok az orosz történelem sajátosságairól*, edited by Márta Font and Endre Sashalmi, 35–47. Budapest: Pannonica.

———. 2010. "Druzhina." In *The Oxford Encyclopedia of Medieval Warfare and Military Technology: Mercenaries – Zürich, Siege of: 596 S*, edited by Clifford J. Rogers, 549–50. Oxford: Oxford University Press.

———. 2015. "A Poveszty vremennih let mint történeti forrás [The Povest' Vremennykh Let as a Historical Source]." In *Régmúlt idők elbeszélése. A Kijevi Rusz első krónikája*, edited by László Balogh and Szilvia Kovács, translated by István Ferincz, 249–78. Magyar Őstörténeti Könyvtár, no. 30. Budapest: Balassi Kiadó.

Font, Márta, and Balázs Sudár. 2019. *Honfoglalás és államalapítás. 9–10. század. A törzsszövetségtől a keresztény királyságig [Conquest and State Formation. Ninth – Tenth Century. From Tribal Union to Christian Kingdom]*. Budapest: Kossuth Kiadó.

Foote, G. Peter, and David M. Wilson. 1970. *The Viking Achievement: A Survey of the Society and Culture of Early Medieval Scandinavia*. New York: Praeger.

Forand, Paul G. 1971. "The Relation of the Slave and the Client to the Master or Patron in Medieval Islam." *International Journal of Middle East Studies* 2, no. 1: 59–66.

Franklin, Simon, trans. 1973. *Sermons and Rhetoric of Kievan Rus'*. Cambridge: Harvard University Press.

Franklin, Simon, and Jonathan Shepard. 1996. *The Emergence of Rus 750–1200*. London: Longman.

Friis-Jensen, Karsten, ed. 2015. *Saxo Grammaticus, Gesta Danorum. The History of the Danes*. Translated by Peter Fisher, Vol. 1–2. Oxford: Clarendon Press.

Froianov, Isaev I. 1986. "Large-scale Ownership of Land and the Russian Economy in the Tenth to Twelfth Centuries." *Soviet Studies in History* 24, no. 4: 9–82.

Frye, Richard N., trans. 2005. *Ibn Fadlan's Journey to Russia: A Tenth-Century Traveler from Baghdad to the Volga River*. Princeton: Markus Wiener.

Füredi, Ágnes, Ágnes Király, Dániel Pópity, Szabolcs Rosta, Attila Türk, and Bertalan Czigány Zágorhidi. 2017. "Baltaalakú amulettek a Kárpát-medence 10–11. századi hagyatékában. Régészeti megfigyelések a miniatürizált tárgyakról, valamint a kora Árpád-kori rusz – magyar kapcsolatok kérdéséről [Axe-Shaped Amulets Among the 11th- and 12th-Century Finds in the Carpathian Basin. Archaeological Observations on Miniature Objects and on the Issue of Early Árpád-era Rus – Hungarian) Relations]." In *A népvándorláskor fiatal kutatóinak XXIV. konferenciája Esztergom 2014. november 4–6*, edited by Attila Türk Attila, Csilla Balogh and Balázs Major, Vol. 2, 403–48. Budapest: Magyar Őstörténeti Témacsoport Kiadványok.

Gaimar, Geffrei. 2009. *Estoire des Engleis. History of the English*, edited and translated by Ian Short. Oxford: Oxford University Press.

Gardeła, Leszek. 2015. "Vikings in Poland. A Critical Overview." In *Viking Worlds. Things, Spaces and Movement*, edited by Marianne Hem Eriksen, Unn Pedersen, Bernt Rundberget, and Irmelin Axelsen, 213–34. Oxford: Oxbow Books.

———. 2018. "Lutomiersk Unveiled. The Buried Warriors of Poland." *Medieval Warfare* 8, no. 3: 42–50.

Garipzanov, Ildar H. 2006. "The Annals of St. Bertin (839) and Chacanus of the Rhos." *Ruthenica* 5: 7–11.

Gavin, K. A. 1996. "Nomadism." In *Encyclopedia of Cultural Anthropology*, edited by David Levinson and Melvin Ember, Vol. 3, 859. New York: David Brown Book Company.

Geary, Patrick. 2012. "Ethnic Identity as a Situational Construct in the Early Middle Ages." In *Writing History: Identity, Conflict, and Memory in the Middle Ages*, edited by Florin Curta and Cristina Spinei, 1–18. Bucharest: Editura Academiei Române.

Gedai, István. 1980. "The Circulation and the Imitation of Hungarian Coins in North Europe." In *Proceedings of the International Numismatic Symposium*, edited by Gedai István and Katalin B. Sey, 133–35. Budapest: Akadémiai Kiadó.

Georg, Jacob. 1927. *Arabische Berichte von Gesandten an germanische Fürstenhöfe aus dem 9. und 10. Jahrhundert*. Berlin: Walter de Gruyter.

Gieysztor, Aleksander. 2008. "Trade and Industry in Eastern Europe before 1200." In *The Cambridge Economic History*, edited by Michael M. Postan and Edward Miller, Vol. 2, 474–524. Cambridge: Cambridge University Press.

Gillmor, Carroll. 1988. "War on the Rivers: Viking Numbers and Mobility on the Seine and Loire, 841–886." *Viator* 19: 79–109.

Gippius, A. Aleksey. 2017. "Vor und nach dem Načal'nyj svod: Die altrussische Anfangschronistikals Gegenstand der textkritischen Rekonstruktion." In *Die Rus' im 9. – 10. Jahrhundert. Ein archäologisches Panorama*, edited by Nikolaj A. Makarov, 44–70. Studien zur Siedlungsgeschichte und Archäologie der Ostseegebiete, no. 14. Kiel: Wachholtz Murmann Publishers.

Glazyrina, Galina. 1991. "Information about Eastern Europe in Old Norse Sagas and its Adaptation for the Nordic Audience by Saga-Authors." In *The Eighth International Saga Conference, Göteborg 11–17 August 1991. The Audience of the Sagas*, edited by Lars Lönnroth, Vol. 1, 123–31. Gothenburg: Gothenburg University.

de Goeje, Michael. Jan 1871. "Die Istakhri-Balkhi Frage." *Zeitschrift der Deutschen Morgenländische Gesellschaft* 25: 42–58.

———, ed. 1877. *Descriptio Imperii Moslemici Auctore Al-Mokaddasi. Bibliotheca Geographorum Arabicorum*, Vol. 3. Lugdunum Batavorum: Brill.

———, ed. 1885. *Compendium Libri Kitâb Al-Boldän Auctore Ibn al-Fakih al-Hamadhänî. Bibliotheca Geographorum Arabicorum*, Vol. 5. Lugdunum Batavorum: Brill.

———, ed. 1889. *Kitâb Al-Masälik Wa'l-Mamãlik auctore Abu'l-Kâsim Obaidallah ibn Abdallah Ibn Khordädhbeh, Accedunt Excerpta e Kitâb Al-Kharâdj Auctore Kodâma ibn Dja'far. Bibliotheca Geographorum Arabicorum*, Vol. 6. Lugdunum Batavorum: Brill.

———, ed. 1892. *Kitâb Al-A'Lâk An-Nafisa VII Auctore Abû Alî Ahmed ibn Omar Ibn Rosteh et Kitâb Al-Boldân Auctore Ahmed ibn Jakûb ibn Wadhih al-Kâtib Al-Jakûbi. Bibliotheca Geographorum Arabicorum*, Vol. 7. Lugdunum Batavorum: Brill.

———, ed. 1927. *Viae Regnorum Descriptio Ditionis Moslemicae Auctore Abu Isḥák al-Fárisi al-Istakhrí. Bibliotheca Geographorum Arabicorum*, Vol. 1, 2nd ed. Lugdunum Batavorum: Brill.

Göckenjan, Hansgerd, and István Zimonyi, eds. 2011. *Orientalische Berichte über die Völker Osteuropas und Zentralasiens im Mittelalter. Die Ǧayhānī-Tradition*, Veröffentlichungen der Societas Uralo-Altaica, no. 54. Wiesbaden: Harrasowitz Verlag.

Goehrke, Carsten. 1992. *Frühzeit des Ostlaventums*. Darmstadt: Wissenschaftliche Buchgesellschaft.

Goffart, Walter. 2005. "Jordanes's 'Getica' and the Disputed Authenticity of Gothic Origins from Scandinavia." *Speculum* 80, no. 2: 379–98.

Golb, Norman, and Omeljan Pritsak. 1982. *Khazarian Hebrew Documents of the Tenth Century*. Ithaca: Cornell University Press.

Golden, Peter Benjamin. 1972. "The Migrations of the Oğuz." *Archivum Ottomanicum* 4: 68–84.

———. 1982. "The Question of the Rus' Qaganate." *Archivum Eurasiae Medii Aevi* 2: 85–97.

———. 1992. *An Introduction to the History of the Turkic Peoples. Ethnogenesis and State-Formation in Medieval and Early Modern Eurasia and the Middle East*. Wiesbaden: Otto Harrassowitz.

———. 1995. "Rūs." In *Encyclopaedia of Islam*, edited by P. Bearman, Th. Bianquis, C. E. Bosworth, E. van Dozel, and W. P. Heinrich, 2nd ed., 618–29. Leiden: Brill.

———. 1998–99. "The Nomadic Linguistic Impact on Pre-Činggisid Rus' and Georgia." *Archivum Eurasiae Medii Aevi* 10: 72–97.

———. 2001. "Some Notes on the Comitatus in Medieval Eurasia with Special Reference to the Khazars." *Russian History/Histoire Russe* 28: 153–70.

———. 2003. "Aspects of the Nomadic Factor in the Economic Development of the Kievan Rus'." In *Nomads and their Neighbours in the Russian Steppe. Turks, Khazars and Qipchaqs*, edited by Peter Benjamin Golden, 58–101. Cornwall: Ashgate.

———. 2006. "The Khazar Sacral Kingship." In *Pre-Modern Russia and Its World. Essays in Honor of Thomas S. Noonan*, edited by Kathryn L. Reyerson, Theofanis G. Stavrou, and James D. Tracy, 79–102. Wiesbaden: Harrasowitz Verlag.

———. 2009. "Review of The Headless State: Aristocratic Orders, Kinship Society, and Misrepresentations of Nomadic Inner Asia." *Journal of Asian Studies* 68, no. 1: 293–6.

———. 2011. *Central Asia in World History*. Oxford: Oxford University Press.

Golden, Peter B., Clifford E. Bosworth, Pierre Guichard, and Mohamed Meouak. 1995. "al-Sakaliba." In *Encyclopaedia of Islam*, edited by C. E. Bosworth, E. van Donzel, W. P. Heinrichs, and G. Lecomte, 2nd ed., Vol. 8, 872–81. Leiden: Brill.

Golovnov, A. V. 2009. *Antropologiya dvizheniya (drevnosti Severnoy Yevrazii) [The Anthropoology of Movement (Antiquities of Northern Eurasia)]*. Yekaterinburg: Uro RAN: Volot.

Golubovskiy, P. V. 1884. *Pechenegi, torki i polovtsy do nashestviya tatar. Istoriya yuzhno-russkikh stepey IX – XIII vv. [Pechenegs, Torks and Polovtsians Before the Tatar Invasion. History of the South Russian Steppes in the 9th – 13th Centuries]*. Kiev: Universitetskaya tipografiya I.I. Zavadskogo.

Gräslund, Anne-Sofie. 1981. *Birka IV. The Burial Customs. A Study of the Graves on Björkö*. Stockholm: Almqvist & Wiksell.

Grekov, B. D., L. V. Cherepnin, and V. T. Pashuto, eds. 1953. *Ocherki istorii SSSR IX – XIII. vv. [Essays of the History of the CCCP]*, Vol. 3, No. 1. Moscow: Izd-vo Akademii Nauk.

Grierson, Hamilton J. P. 1903. *The Silent Trade. A Contribution to the Early History of Human Intercourse*. Edinburgh: Willian Green & Sons.

Gruszczyński, Jacek, Marek Jankowiak, and Jonathan Shepard, eds. 2021. *Viking-Age Trade. Silver, Slaves and Gotland*. Routledge Archaeologies of the Viking World, no. 3. London: Routledge.

Guichard, P., and Mohamed Meouak. 1995. "al-Sakaliba." In *Encyclopaedia of Islam*, edited by C. E. Bosworth, E. van Donzel, W. P. Heinrich, and G. Lecomte, 2nd ed., Vol. 8, 879–81. Leiden: Brill.

Gumilyov, L. N. 1989. *Drevnyaya Rus' i Velikaya step' [Old Rus' and the Great Steppe]*. Moscow: Mysl'.

Gunnell, Terry. 1995. *The Origins of Drama in Scandinavia*. Cambridge: D. S. Brewer.

———. 2009. "Ansgar's Conversion of Iceland." *Scripta Islandica* 60: 105–18.

Guðmundsson, Finnbogi, ed. 1965. *Orkneyinga saga*. Íslenzk fornrit, no. 24. Reykjavík: Hið Íslenzka Fornritafélag.

Guðnason, Bjarni, ed. 1982. *Knýtlinga saga*. In *Danakonunga sögur*, 91–321. Íslenzk fornrit, no. 35. Reykjavík: Hið íslenzka fornritafélag.

Gustavsson, Helmer. 2002. "Runmonumentet i Rytterne." In *Nya Anteckningar om Rytterns Socken*, edited by Olle Ferm, 145–53. Västmanlands läns museum: Västerås.

Gyllensvärd, Bo. 2004. "The Buddha Found at Helgö." In *Excavations at Helgö XVI. Exotic and Sacral Finds from Helgö*, edited by Helen Clarke and Kristina Lamm, 10–27. Stockholm: Almqvist and Wiksell.

Gyóni, Gábor. 2016. "Egy Ugrin nevű személy a 11. században Novgorodban [A Man Named Ugrin in Eleventh-Century Novgorod]." In *Hadak Útján. A népvándorláskor fiatal kutatóinak XXIV. konferenciája Esztergom 2014. november 4–6*, edited by Attila Türk, Csilla Balogh, and Balázs Major, Vol. 2, 379–88. Budapest: Magyar Őstörténeti Témacsoport Kiadványok.

Györffy, György. 1959. *Tanulmányok a magyar állam eredetéről. A nemzetségtől a vármegyéig, a törzstől az országig. Kurszán és Kurszán vára [Studies on the Origin of the Hungarian State. From the Hungarian Genus to the County, from the Tribe to the Country. Kurszán and His Castle]*. Budapest: Akadémiai Kiadó.

———. 1966–98. *Az Árpád-kori Magyarország történeti földrajza [Historical Geography of Hungary in the Árpád Age]*, Vol. 1–4. Budapest: Akadémiai Kiadó.

———. 1970. "A honfoglaló magyarok települési rendjéről [About the Settlement Structure of the Conquering Magyars]." *Archaeologiai Értesítő* 97: 191–242.

———. 1984. "Államszervezés [State Organization]." In *Magyarország története. Előzmények és magyar történet 1242-ig*, edited by Antal Bartha, Vol. 1, 717–834. Budapest: Akadémiai Kiadó.

———. 1990. "A magyar-szláv érintkezések kezdetei és Etelköz múltja [Beginnings of Hungarian-Slavic Interactions and the Past of Etelköz]." *Századok* 124, no. 1: 3–24.

———. 1994a. "Dual Kingship and the Seven Chieftains of the Hungarians in the Era of the Conquest and the Raids." *Acta Orientalia Academiae Scientiarum Hungaricae* 47, no. 1: 87–104.

———. 1994b. "Vezéri szálláshelyek emlékei [Remnants of Princely Accommodations]." In *Honfoglalás és régészet*, edited by László Kovács, 129–50. A honfoglalásról sok szemmel, no. 1. Budapest: Balassi Kiadó.

———. [1977] 2013. *István király és műve [King Stephen and His Work]*. Budapest: Balassi Kiadó.

Hadley, Dawn M., and Julian D. Richard. 2021. *The Viking Great Army and the Making of England*. London: Thames and Hudson.

Hägg, Inga. 1984. "Birkas orientaliska praktplagg." *Fornvännen* 78: 204–23.

Halbach, Uwe. 1985. *Der Russische Fürstenhof vor dem 16. Jahrhundert: eine vergleichende Untersuchung zur politischen Lexikologie und Verfassungsgeschichte der alten Rus'*. Stuttgart: Franz Steiner Verlag.

Halsall, Guy. 2003. *Warfare and Society in the Barbarian West, 450–900*. London: Routledge.

———. 2011. "Ethnicity and Early Medieval Cemeteries." *Arqueología y Territorio Medieval* 18: 15–27.

Hanak, Walter K. 1995. "The Infamous Svjatoslav: Master of Duplicity in War and Peace?" In *Peace and War in Byzantium: Essays in Honor of George T. Dennis, S. J*, edited by Timothy S. Miller and John Nesbitt, 138–51. Washington: The Catholic University of America Press.

Hansen, Valerie. 2020. *The Year 1000. When Explorers Connected the World – and Globalization Began*. New York: Viking Penguin.

Haussig, Hans-Wilhelm. 1987. "Die Praxis des Warenaustausches im Warägerhandel mit den chasarischen Märkten Sarkel und Itil." In *Untersuchungen zu Handel und Verkehr der vor- und frühgeschichtlichen zeit in Mittel- und Nordeuropa. Vol. 4. Der Handel der Karolinger- und Wikingerzeit*, edited by Klaus Düwel, Herbert Jankuhn, Harald Siems and Dieter Timpe, 528–44. Göttingen: Vandenhoeck & Ruprecth.

Hårdh, Birgitta. 2010. "Viking Age Uppåkra." In *Från romartida skalpeller till senvikingatida urnesspännen*, edited by Birgitta Hårdh, 247–314. Uppåkrastudier, no. 11. Kristianstad: Kristianstads Boktryckeri.

Härke, Heinrich. 1997. "Material Culture as Myth: Weapons from Anglo-Saxon Graves." In *Burial and Society. The Chronological and Social Analysis of Archaeological Burial Data*, edited by Claus Kjeld Jensen and K. Høilund Nielsen, 119–27. Aarhus: Aarhus University Press.

Heather, Peter. 1996. *The Goths*. The Peoples of Europe Series. Oxford: Blackwell.

Heck, Paul L. 2002. *The Construction of Knowledge in Islamic Civilization*. Leiden: Brill.

Hedenstierna-Jonson, Charlotte. 2009a. "Magyar – Rus – Scandinavia. Cultural Exchange in the Early Medieval Period." *Situne Dei*: 47–56.

———. 2009b. "Rus', Varangians and Birka Warriors." In *The Martial Society. Aspects of Warriors, Fortifications and Social Change in Scandinavia*, edited by Lena Holmquist Olausson and Michael Olausson, 159–78. Stockholm: Archaeological Research Laboratory Stockholm University.

———. 2012. "Traces of Contacts: Magyar Material Culture in the Swedish Viking Age Context of Birka." In *Die Archäologie der frühen Ungarn. Chronologie, Technologie und Methodik. Internationaler Workshop des Archäologischen Instituts der Ungarischen Akademie der Wissenschaften und des Römisch-Germanischen Zentralmuseums Mainz in Budapest am 4. und 5. Dezember 2009*, edited by Tobias Bendeguz, 29–46. Mainz: Schnell & Steiner.

———. 2015. "Close Encounters with the Byzantine Border Zones: On the Eastern Connections of the Birka Warrior." In *Scandinavia and the Balkans. Cultural Interaction with Byzantium and Eastern Europe in the First Millenium AD*, edited by Oksana Minaeva and Lena Holmquist, 158–73. Cambridge: Cambridge Scholars Publishing.

———. 2017. "Creating a Cultural Expression. On Rus' Identity and Material Culture." In *Identity Formation and Diversity in the Early Medieval Baltic and Beyond*, edited by Johan Callmer, Ingrid Gustin, and Mats Roslund, 91–106. Leiden: Brill.

———. 2020a. "With Asia as Neighbour: Archaeological Evidence of Contacts Between Scandinavia and Central Asia in the Viking Age and the Tang Dynasty." *Bulletin of the Museum of Far Eastern Antiquities* 81: 43–64.

———. 2020b. "Interactions and Infrastructure – Driving Forces and Organisation Behind the Viking Age Trade Networks in the Baltic and Beyond." In *Iron and the Transformation of Society. Reflexion of Viking Age Metallurgy*, edited by Catarina Karlsson and Gert Magnusson, 187–222. Stockholm: Jernkontoret.

———. 2020c. "Warrior Identities in Viking-Age Scandinavia." In *Vikings Across Boundaries: Viking-Age Transformations*, edited by Hanne Lovise Aannestad, Unn Pedersen, Marianne Moen, Elise Naumann, and Heidi Lund Berg, Vol. 2, 179–94. London: Routledge.

Hedenstierna-Jonson, Charlotte, and Lena Holmquist Olausson. 2006. *The 'Oriental' Mounts from Birka's Garrison. An Expression of Warrior Rank and Status*. Antikvarist arkiv, no. 81. Stockholm: Kungl. Vitterhets Historie och Antikvitets Akademien.

Heide, Eldar. 2005. "Víking – 'rowershifting'? An Etymological Contribution." *Arkiv för nordisk filologi* 120: 41–54.

Hellmann, Manfred, 1987. "Die Handelsverträge des 10. Jahrhunderts zwischen Kiev und Byzanz." In *Untersuchungen zu Handel und Verkehr der vor- und frühgeschichtlichen zeit in Mittel- und Nordeuropa. Vol. 4. Der Handel der Karolinger- und Wikingerzeit*, edsited by Klaus Düwel, Herbert Jankuhn, Harald Siems, and Dieter Timpe, 643–66. Göttingen: Vandenhoeck & Ruprecth.

Heppell, Muriel, trans. 1989. *The Paterik of the Kievan Cave Monastery*. Cambridge: Harvard University Press.

Hermansson, Halldor. 1954. "Tyrkir, Leif Eiriksson's Foster-Father." *Modern Language Notes* 69, no. 6: 388–93.

Hermes, Nizar F. 2012. *The [European] Other in Medieval Arabic Literature and Culture: Ninth-Twelfth Century AD*. New York: Palgrave MacMillan.

Hillerdal, Charlotta. 2006. "Vikings, Rus, Varangians. The 'Varangian Problem' in View of Ethnicity in Archaeology." *Current Swedish Archaeology* 14: 87–108.

Holck, Per. 2006. "The Oseberg Ship Burial, Norway: New Thoughts on the Skeletons From the Grave Mound." *European Journal of Archaeology* 9, no. 2–3: 185–210.

Holtzmann, Robert, ed. 1935. *Thietmar Merseburgensis Episcopi Chronicon*, MGH Scriptores rerum Germanicarum Nova Series 9. Berlin: Weidmannsche Buchhandlund.

Hopkins, J. F. P. 1990. "Geographical and Navigational Literature." In *Religion, Learning and Science in the 'Abbasid Period*, edited by M. J. L. Young, J. D. Latham, and R. B. Serjeant, 301–27. The Cambridge History of Arabic Literature, no. 3. Cambridge: Cambridge University Press.

Hoppál, Mihály. 2007. "Shamanism and the Belief System of the Ancient Hungarians." In *Shamans and Traditions*, edited by Mihály Hoppál and Juha Pentikäinen, 77–81. Budapest: Akadémiai Kiadó.

Howard-Johnston, James. 1998. "Trading in Fur, from Classical Antiquity to the Early Middle Ages." In *Leather and Fur. Aspects of Early Medieval Trade and Technology*, edited by Eshter Cameron, 61–79. London: Archetype Publications.

———. 2000. "The *De administrando imperio*: A Re-examination of the Text and a Re-evaluation of Its Evidence about the Rus." In *Les centres proto-urbain russes entre Scandinavie, Byzance et Orient*, edited by Michel Kazanski, Anne Nercessian and Constantin Zuckerman, 301–36. Paris: Éditions P. Lethielleux.

Hraundal, Þórir Jónsson. 2013. "The Rus in the Arabic sources: Cultural Contacts and Identity." Ph.D dissertation. University of Bergen, Bergen.

———. 2014. "New Perspectives on Eastern Vikings/Rus in Arabic Sources." *Viking and Medieval Scandinavia* 10: 65–97.

Hreinsson, Viðar, ed. 1977. "The Saga of the Greenlanders." In *The Complete Sagas of Icelanders. Including 49 tales*, Vol. 1, 19–32. Reykjavík: Leifur Eiríksson Publishing.

Hultgård, Anders. 2001. "Menschenopfer." In *Reallexikon der Germanischen Altertumskunde*, edited by Heinrich Beck, Vol. 9, 533–46. Berlin: De Gruyter.

Hultkrantz, Åke. 1973. "A Definition of Shamanism." *Temenos* 9: 25–37.

———. 1992. "Aspects of Saami (Lapp) Shamanism." In *Northern Religions and Shamanism*, edited by Mihály Hoppál and Juha Pentikäinen, 138–46. Helsinki: Finnish Literature Society.

Huszár, Lajos. 1967. "Der Umlauf ungarischer Münzen des XI. Jahrhunderts in Nordeuropa." *Acta Archaeologica Academiae Scientiarium Hungaricae* 19: 175–200.

Irons, William. 2003. "Cultural Capital, Livestock Raiding, and the Military Advantage of Traditional Pastoralists." In *Nomadic pathways in social evolution*, edited by Nikolay N. Kradin, Dmitri N. Bondarenko, and Thomas J. Barfield, 63–72. Civilizational dimension, no. 5. Moscow: Russian Academy of Sciences.

Isfandiyar, Muhammad B. Al-Hasan B. 1905. *A History of Tabaristan*, edited by Edward G. Browne. Leiden: Brill.

Isoaho, Mari. 2018. "Shakhmatov's Legacy and the Chronicles of Kievan Rus'." *Kritika: Explorations in Russian & Eurasian History* 19, no. 3: 637–48.

Istvánovits, Eszter. 2003. *A Rétköz honfoglalás és Árpád-kori emlékanyaga [The Conquest and Árpád Period Remains of Rétköz]*. Nyíregyháza: JAM-MNM-MTA.

Ivanov, S. A. 1981. "Bolgary i russkiye v izobrazhenii L'va Diakona [Bulgars and Russians in Leo the Deacon's Representation]." In *Formirovaniye rannefeodal'nykh slavyanskikh narodnostey*, edited by V. D. Korolyuk, V. V. Ivanov, G. G. Litavrin, N. I. Tolstoy, B. N. Florya, and L. V. Zaborovskiy, 203–15. Moscow: Nauka.

Ivanov, V. V., and V. N. Toporov. 2000. "O drevnikh slavyanskikh etnonimakh. (Osnovnyye problemy i perspektivy) [About Old Slavic Ethnonyms (Main Problems and Perspectives)]." In *Iz istorii russkoy kul'tury. Vol. 1. Drevnyaya Rus'*, edited by V. J. Petrukhin, 413–40. Moscow: Yazyki russkoy kul'tury.

Ivantchik, Askold I. 2011. "The Funeral of Scythian Kings: The Historical Reality and the Description of Herodotus (IV, 71–72)". In *The Barbarians of Ancient Europe. Realities and Interactions*, edited by Larissa Bonfante, 71–106. New York: Cambridge University Press.

Izmailov, Iskander L. 2000. "Balymerskiy kurgannyy mogil'nik i yego istoriko-kul'turnoye znacheniye [The Burial Mound of Balymer and Its Historical-Cultural Significance]." In *Slavyane, finno-ugry, skandinavy, volzhskiye bulgary. Doklady mezhd. nauchnogo simpoziuma po voprosam arkheologii i istorii 11–14 maya 1999 g. Pushkinskiye gory*, edited by Anatoliy N. Kirpichnikov, E. N. Nosov, and A. I. Saksa, 70–86. Saint Petersburg: IPK Vesty.

———. 2003. "Balymerskii kurgannyi mogil'nik i 'rusy' na Volge: Problemy i diskussii [The Balymer Burial Mound and the Rus' on the Volga: Problems and Discussions]." In *Velikii volzhskii put'. Materialy II-go etapa mezhdunarodnoi nauchno-prakticheskoi konferencii "Velikii Volzhskii put'", Sankt-Petersburg, Stockholm, 5–14 avgusta 2002 goda*, edited by R. N. Musina, 50–69. Kazan': Institut istorii Akademii Nauk Respubliki Tatarstane.

Jackson, Tatjana. 2019. *Eastern Europe in Icelandic Sagas*. Amsterdam: ARC Humanities Press.
Jancsik, Balázs, András Gulyás, Ádám Strohmayer, Judit Szigeti, and Attila Türk. 2019. "Adatok a 10. századi poncolt süvegcsúcsok és a csövecskés merevítésű tarsolyok elterjedéséhez [Data for the Spread of Tenth-Century Embellished Cap-Ends and Tube-Braced Sabretaches]." In *Hadak Útján. A népvándorláskor fiatal kutatóinak XXIX. konferenciája Esztergom 2019. november 15–16*, edited by Balázs Sudár and Attila Türk, 68–76. Budapest: Martin Opitz.
Jakobsson, Ármann. 2007. "Masculinity and Politics in Njáls saga." *Viator* 38: 191–215.
Jakobsson, Sverrir. 2006. "On the Road to Paradise: 'Austrvegr' in the Icelandic Imagination." In *The Fantastic in Old Norse/Icelandic Literature. Sagas and the British Isles: preprint papers of the 13th International Saga Conference Durham and York, 6th – 12th, August, 2006*, edited by Donata Kick, David Ashurst, and John McKinnel, 935–43. Durham: Centre for Medieval and Renaissance Studies.
———. 2016a. "Saracen Sensibilities: Muslims and Otherness in Medieval Saga Literature." *The Journal of English and Germanic Philology* 115, no. 2: 213–38.
———. 2016b. "The Varangian Legend: Testimony from the Old Norse Sources." In *Byzantium and the Viking World*, edited by Fedir Androshchuk, Jonathan Shephard, and Monica White, 345–62. Uppsala: Uppsala Universitet.
———. 2020. *The Varangians. In God's Holy Fire*. Cham: Palgrave Macmillan.
Jansson, Ingmar. 1975–77. "Ett rembeslag av orientalisk typ funnet på Island. Vikingatidens orientaliska bälten och deras euroasiska sammanhang." *Tor* 17: 383–421.
———. 1987. "Communications between Scandinavia and Eastern Europe in the Viking Age: The Archaeological Evidence." In *Untersuchungen zu Handel und Verkehr der vor- und frühgeschichtlichen Zeit*, edited by Düwel Klaus, Vol. 4, 773–807. Göttingen: Vandenhoeck und Ruprecht.
———. 1988. "Wikingerzeitlicher orientalischer Import in Skandinavien." *Bericht der Römisch-Germanischen Kommission* 69: 564–647.
———. 1997. "Warfare, Trade or Colonization? Some General Remarks on the Eastern Expansion of the Scandinavians in the Viking Period." In *The Rural Viking in Russia and Sweden*, edited by Pär Hansson, 9–64. Örebro: Örebro kommuns bildingförvaltning.
Jansson, Ingmar, and Evgenij N. Nosov. 1992. "The way to the East." In *From Viking to Crusader. The Scandinavians and Europe 800–1200*, edited by Else Roesdahl and David M. Wilson, 74–83. New York: Rizzoli.
Jansson, Sven B. F. 1964. *Västmanlands runinskrifter*. Uppsala: Almqvist & Wiksells.
Jarman, Cat. 2021. *River Kings. A New History of the Vikings from Scandinavia to the Silk Roads*. Dublin: Harper Collins.
Järve, Mari, Lehti Saag, Christiana Lyn Scheib, Ajai K. Pathak, Francesco Montinaro, Luca Pagani, Rodrigo Flores, Meriam Guellil, Lauri Saag, Kristiina Tambets, Alena Kushniarevich, Anu Solnik, Liivi Varul, Stanislav Zadnikov, Oleg Petrauskas, Maryana Avramenko, Boris Magomedov, Serghii Didenko, Gennadi Toshev, Igor Bruyako, Denys Grechko, Vitalii Okatenko, Kyrylo Gorbenko, Oleksandr Smyrnov, Anatolii Heiko, Roman Reida, Serheii Sapiehin, Sergey Sirotin, Aleksandr Tairov, Arman Beisenov, Maksim Starodubtsev, Vitali Vasilev, Alexei Nechvaloda, Biyaslan Atabiev, Sergey Litvinov, Natalia Ekomasova, Murat Dzhaubermezov, Sergey Voroniatov, Olga Utevska, Irina Shramko, Elza Khusnutdinova, Mait Metspalu, Nikita Savelev, Aivar Kriiska, Toomas Kivisild, and Richard Villems. 2019. "Shifts in the Genetic Landscape of the Western Eurasian Steppe Associated with the Beginning and End of the Scythian Dominance." *Current Biology* 29, no. 14: 2430–41.

Jenkins, David, Stefanos Alexopoulos, David Bachrach, Jonathan Couser, Sarah Davis, Darin Hayton, and Andrea Sterk, trans. 2001. *Life of St. George of Amastris*. Notre Dame. Accessed February 17, 2017. https://library.nd.edu/byzantine_studies/documents/Amastris.pdf.

Jesch, Judith. 2001. *Ships and Men in the Late Viking Age: The Vocabulary of Runic Inscriptions and Skaldic Verse*. Woodbridge: The Boydell Press.

———. 2009. "Constructing the Warrior Ideal in the Late Viking Age." In *The Martial Society. Aspects of Warriors, Fortifications and Social Change in Scandinavia*, edited by Lena Holmquist Olausson and Michael Olausson, 71–8. Stockholm: Stockholm University.

———. 2015. *The Viking Diaspora*. London: Routledge.

Johnsen, Albert, and Jón Helgason, eds. 1941. *Saga Óláfs konungs hins helga: Den store saga om Olav den hellige efter pergamenthåndskrift i Kungliga Biblioteket i Stockholm nr. 2 4to med varianter fra andre håndskrifter (1–2)*. Oslo: Jacob Dybwad.

Jones, Prudence, and Nigel Pennick. 1995. *A History of Pagan Europe*. London: Psychology Press.

Jonsson, Anne-Beate. 1954. "Några forntida uppländska stigbygeltyper." *Fornvännen* 4: 234–40.

Jónsson, Guðni, ed. 1954. "Yngvars saga viðförla." In *Fornaldarsögur Norðurlanda*, Vol. 2, 423–59. Reykjavik Íslendingasagnaútgáfan.

Kainov, S. Yu. 2018. "Pogrebeniya s predmetami vooruzheniya Gnozdovskogo nekropolya [Weapon Burials of the Gnezdovo Necropolis]." In *Gnozdovskiy arkheologicheskiy kompleks. Materialy i issledovaniya*, edited by S. Yu. Kainov, Vol. 1, 212–41. Moscow: Istoricheskiy muzey.

———. 2019. " 'Bol'shoy' mech iz Chornoy mogily (predvaritel'nyye itogi novogo etapa izucheniya) [The 'Big' Sword from the Black Grave (Preliminary Results of a New Phase of Investigation)]." In *Zemlya nasha velika i obil'na . . . Sbornik statey, posvyashchennyy 90-letiyu A.N. Kirpichnikova*, edited by S. V. Beletskiy, 125–39. Saint-Petersburg: Knizhnaya Tipografiya.

Kainov, S. Yu., and A. S. Shchavelev. 2005. "Izobrazheniye kresta na nakonechnike kop'ya iz Chornoy mogily (Tekhnologiya i semantika) [Image of a Cross on the Tip of a Spear from the Black Grave (Technology and Semantics)]." In *Drevneyshiye gosudarstva Vostochnoy Yevropy. 2003 god. Mnimyye real' – nosti v antichnykh i srednevekovykh tekstakh*, edited by Elena A. Mel'nikova, 83–90. Moscow: Indrik.

Kaldellis, Anthony. 2010. "The Corpus of Byzantine Historiography. An Interpretative Essay." In *The Byzantine World*, edited by Paul Stephenson, 211–22. London: Routledge.

———. 2013a. "The Original Source for Tzimiskes' Balkan Campaign (971 AD) and the Emperor's Classicizing Propaganda." *Byzantine and Modern Greek Studies* 37, no. 1: 35–52.

———. 2013b. *Ethnography after Antiquity. Foreign Lands and People in Byzantine Literature*. Philadelphia, PA: University of Pennsylvania Press.

Kalinke, Marianne E. 1983. "The Foreign Language Requirement in the Medieval Icelandic Romance." *The Modern Language Review* 78, no. 4: 850–61.

Kalmring, Sven. 2010. "Of Thieves, Counterfeiters, and Homicides. Crime in Hedeby and Birka." *Fornvännen* 105: 281–90.

———. 2014. "A Conical Bronze Boss and Hedeby's Eastern Connection." *Fornvännen* 109: 1–11.

Kantor, Marvin. 1983. *Medieval Slavic Lives of Saints and Princes*. Michigan: Ann Arbor. Accessed January 31, 2020. http://macedonia.kroraina.com/en/kmsl/kmsl_1.htm.

Kaplan, I. Fredercik. 1954. "The Decline of the Khazars and the Rise of the Varangians." *The American Slavic and East European Review* 13, no. 1: 1–10.

Karwasińska, Jadwiga, ed. 1973. "Epistola Brunonis ad Henricum Regem." In *Monumenta Poloniae Historica. Series Nova*. Vol. 4/3, 97–106. Warsaw: Państwowe Wydawn.

Katona, Csete. 2017a. "Vikings in Hungary? The Theory of the Varangian-Rus Bodyguard of the First Hungarian Rulers." *Viking and Medieval Scandinavia* 17: 23–60.

———. 2017b. "Rusz-varég kereskedelmi útvonalak a IX – X. századi Kelet-Európában és a Kárpát-medence [Varangian-Rus Commercial Routes in Ninth-Tenth Century Eastern Europe and Their Relation to the Carpathian Basin]." *Jósa András Múzeum Évkönyve* 59, no. 2: 233–52.

———. 2019a. "A viking, aki magyar király ölt. Egy középkori izlandi saga magyar vonatkozásai [The Viking, Who Killed a Hungarian King. The Relevance of a Medieval Icelandic Saga for Hungary History]." *Századok* 153, no. 6: 1207–32.

———. 2019b. " 'Magyars and Vikings in the same boat.' Public Archaeology and Experimental Re-enactment in Hungary." *Hungarian Archaeology* 8, no. 4: 46–50.

———. 2020. "Otherness along the Austrvegr: Cultural Interaction between the Rus' and the Turkic Nomads of the Steppe." In *Margins, Monsters, Deviants. Alterities in Old Norse Literature and Culture*, edited by Rebecca Merkelbach and Gwendolyne Knight, 189–213. NAW, no. 3. Turnhout: Brepols.

———. 2021a. "Scandinavian/Rus' Captives and Slave Soldiers: An Eastern Perspective." In *Viking Wars. Special Vol. 1,* edited by Frode Iversen and Karoline Kjesrud, 255–74. Oslo: Norsk Arkeologisk Selskap.

———. 2021b. "Exotic Encounters: Vikings and Faraway Species in Motion." In *Medieval Animals on the Move: Between Body and Mind*, edited by László Bartosiewicz and Alice M. Choyke, 167–77. Cham: Palgrave Macmillan.

Kazanski, Michel, and Anna Mastykova. 2017. "The Sösdala Finds in the Perspective of Central and South-Eastern Europe." In *The Sösdala Horsemen and the Equestrian Elite of Fifth Century Europe*, edited by Charlotte Fabech and Ulf Näsman, 297–311. Aarhus: Aarhus University Press.

Kazanski, Michel, Anne Nercessian, and Constantin Zuckerman, eds. 2000. *Les Centres Proto-Urbain Russes Entre Scandinavie, Byzance et Orient*. Paris: Éditions P. Lethielleux.

Kekaumenos. n. d. "Strategikon." Accessed February 4, 2020. www.acad.carleton.edu/curricular/mars/kekaumenos.pdf.

Kennedy, Hugh. 2002. *Mongol, Huns and Vikings. Nomads at War*. London: Cassell.

Keyser, Rudolf, Peter Andreas Munch, and Carl Rikard Unger, eds. 1848. *Speculum Regale. Konungs-skuggsjá*. Christiania: Carl C. Werner & Company.

Khazanov, Anatoly M. 1981. "Myths and Paradoxies of Nomadism." *European Journal of Sociology* 22, no. 1: 141–53.

———. 1994. *Nomads and the Outside World*, 2nd ed. Wisconsin: University of Wisconsin Press.

Kirpichnikov, Anatolij. 1966a. *Drevnerusskoe oruzie. Vol. 1. Mechi i sabli [Ancient Rus Weapons. Vol. 1. Swords and Sabres]*. Moscow: Nauka.

———. 1966b. *Drevnerusskoe oruzie. Vol. 2. Kop'ya, sulitsy, boyevyye topory, bulavy, kisteni. IX – XIII vv [Ancient Rus Weapons. Vol. 2. Spears, Arrows, Battle Axes, Clubs, Maces. 9th – 13th Century]*. Moscow: Nauka.

———. 1970. "Connections between Russia and Scandinavia in the Ninth and Tenth Centuries, as Illustrated by Weapon Finds." In *Varangian Problems. Scando – Slavica Supplementum I*, edited by Knud Hannestad, Knud Jordal, Ole Klindt-Jensen, Knud Rahbek Schmidt, and Carl Stief, 50–76. Copenhagen: Munskgaard.

———. 1977. "Vooruzheniye Voinov Kiyevskoy Derzhavy v Svete Russko-Skandinavskikh Kontaktov [Warrior Armaments of the Kievian State in Light of Russian-Scandinavian Contacts]." *Skandinavskom Sbornike* 22: 159–73.

Kirpichnikov, Anatolij, and Iskander Izmailov. 2000. "Karolingskie mechi iz Bulgarii (iz fondov Gosudarstvennogo ob'yedinennogo muzeya Respubliki Tatarstan) [Carolingian Swords from Bulgaria (from the Finds of the State United Museum of the Republic of Tatarstan]." In *Srednevekovaia Kazan': Vozniknovenie i razvitie. Materialy Mezhdunarodnoi nauchnoi konferencii, Kazan', 1–3 iunia 1999 goda*, edited by K. Sh. Iskhakov, R. S. Khakimov, M. A. Usmanov, and F. Sh. Khuzin, 207–18. Kazan: Master Lain.

Kleingärtner, Sunhild, and Michael Müller-Wille. 2008. "Zwei Kammergräber des 10. Jahrhunderts aus der Stadt Izjaslavs und Vladimirs in Kiev." *Acta Archaeologica Academiae Scientiarum Hungariae* 59, no. 2: 367–86.

Klejn, S. Leo. 2013. "The Russian controversy over the Varangians." In *From Goths to Varangians. Communication and Cultural Exchange between the Baltic and the Black Sea*, edited by Line Bjerg, John H. Lind, and Søren M. Sindbæk, 27–38. Aarhus: Aarhus University Press.

Klingenberg, Heinz. 1993. "Odin und die Seinen. Ältischlandischer Gelehrter Urgeschichte anderer Teil." *Alvíssmál* 2: 31–80.

Kliutschewskij, Wassili. 1925. *Geschichte Russlands*, Vol. 1. Berlin: Obelisk.

Kokovtsov, P. K. 1932. *Yevreysko-khazarskaya perepiska v X veke [The Jewish-Khazar Correspondence in the Tenth Century]*. Leningrad: Izd. Ak. Nauk.

Kolev, Konstantin Jr. 2015. "Visual-Material Evidence of Viking Presence in the Balkans." *Hiperboreea Journal* 2, no. 1: 53–73.

Komar, Oleksiy. 2014. "Mechi Dneprostroya (k istorii nakhodki 1928 g.) [Swords from Dnieprostroi (on the History of a Find Made in 1928)]." In *Rus' v IX – XII vekakh: obshchestvo, gosudarstvo, kul'tura*, edited by N. A. Makarov and A. E. Leontiev, 47–61. Moscow: Drevnosti Severa.

———. 2017a. "Černigov und das Gebiet der unteren Desna." In *Die Rus' im 9. – 10. Jahrhundert. Ein archäologisches Panorama*, edited by Nikolaj A. Makarov, 342–73. Studien zur Siedlungsgeschichte und Archäologie der Ostseegebiete, no. 14. Kiel: Wachholtz – Murmann Publishers.

———. 2017b. "Kiev und das rechtsufrige Dneprgebiet." In *Die Rus' im 9. – 10. Jahrhundert. Ein archäologisches Panorama*, edited by Nikolaj A. Makarov, 308–41. Studien zur Siedlungsgeschichte und Archäologie der Ostseegebiete, no. 14. Kiel: Wachholtz – Murmann Publishers.

———. 2018. *A korai magyarság vándorlásának történeti és régészeti emlékei [The Historical and Archaeological Relics of the Early Magyar Migration]*. Budapest: Martin Opitz.

Konovalova, I. G. 2000. "Pokhod Svyatoslava na vostok v kontekste bor'by za 'khazarskoye nasledstvo' [The 'Oriental' Policy of Svjatoslav in the Context of International Struggle for 'Khazarian Heritage']." *Stratum Plus* 5: 226–35.

Köpke, Rudolf, ed. 1868. *Herbordi Dialogus de Vita Ottonis Episcopi Babenbergensis*. MGH Scriptores rerum Germanicarum in usum scholarum, no. 33. Hannover: Hahn.

Kovács, László. 1970a. "Die Budapester Wikingerlanze. Geschichtsabriss der Ungarischen Königslanze." *Acta Archaeologica Academiae Scientlarum Hungaricae* 22: 324–39.

———. 1970b. "A Honfoglaló Magyarok Lándzsái és Lándzsástemetkezésük [The Spears and Spearburials of the Conquering Hungarians]." *Alba Regia* 11: 81–108.

———. 1986. "Über Einige Steigbügeltypen der Landnahmezeit." *Acta Archaeologica Academiae Scientlarum Hungaricae* 38: 195–227.

———. 1989. *Münzen aus der ungarischen Landnahmezeit. Archäologische Untersuchung der arabischen, byzantinischen, westeuropäischen und römischen Münzen aus dem Karpatenbecken des 10. Jahrhunderts*. Budapest: Akadémiai Kiadó.

———. 1994. "Fegyverek és pénzek [Weapons and Coins]." In *Honfoglalás és régészet,* edited by László Kovács, 181–94. A honfoglalásról sok szemmel, no. 1. Budapest: Balassi Kiadó.

———. 1995. "Előkelő rusz vitéz egy Székesfehérvári sírban. A rádiótelepi honfoglalás kori A. sír és kardja [High Status Rus Warrior in a Grave from Székesfehérvár. The 'A' Grave from Rádiótelep in the Conquest Period, and Its Sword]." In *Kelet és Nyugat között. Történeti tanulmányok Kristó Gyula tiszteletére*, edited by László Koszta, 291–308. Szeged: Szegedi Középkorász Műhely.

———. 2003. "Beregszász-Birka: Beiträge zu den Mützen mit Blechspitze des 10. Jahrhunderts." *Acta Archaeologica Academiae Scientiarum Hungaricae* 54: 205–42.

———. 2008. "Muslimische Münzen im Karpatenbecken des 10. Jahrhunderts." *Anateus* 29–30: 479–533.

Kovalenko, V., A. Motsya, and Yu. Syty. 2012. "Noveyshiye nakhodki v pogrebeniyakh Shestovitsy [The Newest Finds in the Burials in Shestovitsa]." In *Scandinavian Antiquities of Southern Rus'. A Catalogue*, edited by Fedir Androshchuk and Volodymyr Zotsenko, 322–50. Paris: The Ukrainian National Committee for Byzantine Studies.

Kovalev, K. Roman. 2000–01. "The Infrastructure of the Northern Part of the 'Fur Road' between the Middle Volga and the East during the Middle Ages." *Archivum Eurasiae Medii Aevi* 11: 25–64.

———. 2005a. "Commerce and Caravan Routes along the Northern Silk Road (Sixth – Ninth Centuries). Part I: The Western Sector." *Archivum Eurasiae Medii Aevi* 14: 55–105.

———. 2005b. "Creating Khazar Identity through Coins: The Special Issue Dirhams of 837/8." In *East Central & Eastern Europe in the Early Middle Ages*, edited by Florin Curta, 220–53. Ann Arbor: University of Michigan Press.

———. 2011. "Khazaria and Volga Bulğāria as Intermediaries in Trade Relations between the Islamic Near East and the Rus' Lands During the Tenth to Early Eleventh Centuries: The Numismatic Evidence I." *Archivum Eurasiae Medii Aevi* 18: 43–156.

———. 2013. "Were There Direct Contacts between Volga Bulğāria and Sweden in the Second Half of the Tenth Century? The Numismatic Evidence." *Archivum Eurasiae Medii Aevi* 20: 67–102.

———. n.d. "What Role Did the Rus' and the Volga Bulğârs Play in the Import of Northern Iranian Dirhams into Northern Europe during the Second Half of the Tenth – Early Eleventh Centuries?" Accessed November 9, 2021. <https://www.academia.edu/15667012>

Kovalevskiy, A. P., trans. 1956. *Kniga Akhmeda Ibn Faḍlāna o ego puteshestvij na Volgu 921–2 [The Book of Ahmed Ibn Fadlan and His Voyages to the Volga 921–2]*. Kharkiv: Izdatelstvo Gos. Universiteta.

Krachkovskiy, I. Yu. 1957. *Izbrannyye sochineniya. Vol. 4. Arabskaya geograficheskaya literatura*. Moscow: Akademiya Nauk SSSR.

Kradin, Nikolay N. 2015. "Ponyatiye 'Plemya' v Sovremennoy Antropologii [The Concept of 'Tribe' in Modern Anthropology]." *Peterburgskiye Slavyanskiye i Balkanskiye Issledovaniya* 2: 4–12.

———. 2016. "Nomads." In *The Encyclopedia of Empire*, edited by John M. MacKenzie, 1–6. Hoboken, NJ: Wiley & Sons. https://doi.org/10.1002/9781118455074.wbeoe171

Kradin, Nikolay N., Dmitri N. Bondarenko, and Thomas J. Barfield, eds. 2003. *Nomadic Pathways in Social Evolution*. Civilizational dimension, no. 5. Moscow: Russian Academy of Sciences.

Kramers, Johannes H., ed. 1939. *Opus Geographicum. 'Liber Imaginis Terrae'. Abu al-Kasim Ibn Haukal al-Nasibi*. Bibliotheca Geographorum Arabicorum, Vol. 2. Leiden: Brill.

Kristiansen, Kristian, and Thomas B. Larsson. 2005. *The Rise of Bronze Age Society. Travels, Transmissions and Transformations*. New York: Cambridge University Press.

Kristó, Gyula. 1983. "Oroszok az Árpád-kori Magyarországon [Russians in Árpád-Age Hungary]." In *Tanulmányok az Árpád-korról*, 191–208. Budapest: Magvető Kiadó.

———. 1996. *Hungarian History in the Ninth Century*. Szeged: Szegedi Középkorász Műhely.

Kristó, Gyula, and H. Tóth Imre. 1996. "Az Orosz Évkönyvek néhány magyar vonatkozásáról [Some Hungarian-related Issues of the Russian Annals]." *Acta Universitatis Szegediensis Acta historica* 103: 21–29.

Krylaszova, N. B., A. M. Belavin, and Attila Türk. 2014. "Újabb adatok a honfoglalás kori tarsolyok és tűzkészségek klasszifikációjához Volga-Káma vidéki analógiák fényében [New Data for the Classification of Conquest-period Sabretaches and Fire Tools in Light of the Volga-Kama Analogies]." In *Avarok pusztái. Régészeit tanulmányok Lőrincz Gábor 60. születésnapjára*, edited by Anders Alexandra, Csilla Balogh, and Attila Türk, 457–96. Budapest: Martin Opitz.

Krzewińska, Maja, Gro Bjørnstad, Pontus Skoglund, Pall Isolfur Olason, Jan Bill, Anders Götherström, and Erika Hagelberg. 2015. "Mitochondrial DNA Variation in the Viking Age Population of Norway." *Philosophical Transactions of the Royal Society B: Biological Sciences* 370: 20130384.

Kuleshov, Viacheslav, 2021. "Coin Circulation in Early Rus and the Dynamics of the Druzhinas." In *Viking-Age Trade. Silver, Slaves and Gotland*, edited by Jacek Gruszczyński, Marek Jankowiak, and Jonathan Shepard, 155–82. Routledge Archaeologies of the Viking World, no. 3. London: Routledge.

Kurze, Friedrich, ed. 1890. *Regionis Abbatis Prumiensis Chronicon cum Contiunatione Treverensi*. MGH Scriptores Rerum Germanicarum in Usum Scholarum, no. 50. Hannover: Hahn.

Lane, Edward William. 1872. *An Arabic-English Lexicon*, Vol. 4. London: Williams and Norgate.

Langó, Péter. 2017. *Turulok és Árpádok. Nemzeti Emlékezet és Koratörténeti Emlékek [Turuls and Árpáds. National Memory and Early Historical Mementoes]*. Budapest: Typotex.

Lappenberg, Johann Martin, ed. 1868. *Helmoldi presbyteri chronica Slavorum*. MGH Scriptores rerum Germanicarum in usum scholarum, no. 7. Hannover: Hahn.

Larsson, Gunilla. 2011. "Early Contacts between Scandinavia and the Orient." *Silk Road* 9: 122–42.

Larsson, G. Mats. 1986–89. "Yngvarr's Expedition and the Georgian Chronicle." *Saga-Book* 22: 98–108.

Lavrov, Petr Alekseyevich, ed. 1930. *Materialy po Istorii Vozniknoveniya Drevneyshey Slavyanskoy Pis'mennosti [Material on the History of the Emergence of Ancient Slavic Writings]*. Leningrad: Akademiya Nauk SSSR.

Lebedev, G. S. 2005. *Epokha vikingov v Severnoy Yevrope i na Rusi [The Epoch of the Vikings in Northern Europe and Rus']*. Saint-Petersburg: Yevraziya.

Lebsak, Michael. 2021. *"Eastern" Imports in Hedeby/Schleswig – Selected Archaeological Finds and Their Socio-Historic Significance*. Unpublished MA Thesis. Kiel: Prähistorische und Historische Archäologie.

Lepahin, Valerij. 2009. "Magyar Szent Mózes a történelemben és az irodalomban [The Hungarian Saint Moses in History and Literature]." In *Szent Orsolyától Iszaak Babelig*, edited by Gyula Szvák, 41–86. Budapest: Ruszisztikai Intézet.

Lewis, M. Stephen. 2006. "Salt and the Earliest Scandinavian Raids in France: Was There a Connection?" *Viking and Medieval Scandinavia* 12: 103–36.

Likhachev, D. S., A. Yu. Chernov, A. V. Dybo, and S. K. Rusakov, intr., ed. and trans. 2006. *Slovo o polku Igoreve [The Lay of Igor's Campaign]*. Saint-Petersburg: Vita Nova.

Likhachev, D. S., trans. 1966. *Povest' Vremennykh Let [The Tale of Bygone Years]*, edited by V. P. Adrianova-Peretts and M. B. Sverdlov Revis, 2nd ed. Saint-Petersburg: Nauka.

Lind, John. 1984. "The Russo-Byzantine Treaties and the Early Urban Structure of Rus'." *The Slavonic and East European Review* 62, no. 3: 362–70.

———. 2014. "Tissø – Kiev – Konstantinople: Danske netværk i øst?" In *Vikingetidens aristokratiske miljøer*, edited by Henriette Lyngstrøm and Lasse Christian Arboe Sonne, 69–76. Copenhagen: Saxo Institute.

Lindner, Rudi Paul. 1982. "What Was a Nomadic Tribe?" *Comparative Studies in Society and History* 24, no. 4: 689–711.

Ljubarskij, Jakov. 1998. "Quellenforschung and/or Literary Criticism. Narrative Structures in Byzantine Historical Writing." *Symbolae Osloenses* 73, no. 1: 5–22.

Lönnroth, Lars. 2008. "The Icelandic Sagas." In *The Viking World*, edited by Stefan Brink and Neil Price, 304–10. London: Routledge.

Lopatin, Nikolaj V. 2017. "Izborsk." In *Die Rus' im 9. – 10. Jahrhundert. Ein archäologisches Panorama*, edited by Nikolaj A. Makarov, 130–45. Studien zur Siedlungsgeschichte und Archäologie der Ostseegebiete, no. 14. Kiel: Wachholtz – Murmann Publishers.

LSJ. "The Online Liddle-Scott-Jones Greek-English Lexicon." Accessed November 30, 2020. http://stephanus.tlg.uci.edu/lsj/#eid=1.

Lübke, Christian. 2001. *Fremde im östlichen Europa. Von Gesellschaften ohne Staat zu verstaatichten Gesellschaften (9. – 11. Jahrhundert)*. Ostmitteleuropa in Vergangenheit und Gegenwart, no. 23. Köln: Böhlau Verlag.

Ludwig, Dieter. 1982. "Struktur und Gesellschaft des Chazaren-Reiches im Licht der schriftlichen Quellen." Ph.D dissertation. Philosophischen Fakultät, Münster.

Luján, Eugenio R. 2008. "Procopius De bello Gothico III 38.17–23: A Description of Ritual Pagan Slavic Slayings?" *Studia Mythologica Slavica* 11: 105–12.

Lund, Julie. 2010. "At the Water's Edge." In *Signals of Belief in Early England. Anglo-Saxon Paganism Revisited*, edited by Martin Carver, Alexandra Sanmark, and Sarah Semple, 49–66. Oxford: Oxbow Books.

Lunde, Paul, and Caroline Stone, eds. 2012. *Ibn Fadlān and the Land of the Darkness: Arabic Travellers in the far North*. London: Penguin.

Lundström, Fredrik, Charlotte Hedenstierna-Jonson, and Lena Holmquist Olausson. 2009. "Eastern Archery in Birka's Garrison." In *The Martial Society. Aspects of Warriors, Fortifications and Social Change in Scandinavia*, edited by Lena Holmquist Olausson and Michael Olausson, 105–16. Stockholm: Archaeological Research Laboratory.

Lushin, V. G. 2019. "K voprosu o date Chornoy Mogily [To the Question of Dating the Black Grave]." In *Istoriya Arkheologiya Kul'tura. Materialy i issledovaniya*, edited by M. G. Moiseyenko and Ye. P. Tokareva, 21–33. Zimovniki: Zimovnikovskiy krayevedcheskiy muzey.

Maçoudi. 1861. *Les Praires d'or*, translated by C. Barbier de Meynard, and Pavet de Courteille, Vol. 1. Collection d'ouvrages orientaux publiées par le Société Asiatique. Paris: A L'imprimerie Impériale.

———. 1863. *Les Praires d'or,* translated by C. Barbier de Meynard, and Pavet de Courteille, Vol. 2. Collection d'ouvrages orientaux publiées par le Société Asiatique. Paris: A L'imprimerie Impériale.

Madgearu, Alexandru. 2005. "Salt Trade and Warfare: The Rise of the Romanian-Slavic Military Organization in Early Medieval Transylvania." In *East Central & Eastern Europe in the Early Middle Ages*, edited by Florin Curta, 103–20. Ann Arbor: University of Michigan Press.

Mägi, Marika. 2018. *In Austrvegr: The Role of the Eastern Baltic in Viking Age Communication Across the Baltic Sea*. Leiden: Brill.

Makarov, A. Nikolaj, ed. 2017. *Die Rus' im 9. – 10. Jahrhundert. Ein archäologisches Panorama*. Studien zur Siedlungsgeschichte und Archäologie der Ostseegebiete, no. 14. Kiel: Wachholtz – Murmann Publishers.

Makk, Ferenc. 1999. *Ungarische Aussenpolitik (896–1196)*. Herne: Tibor Schäfer Verlag.

Malingoudi, Jana. 1994. *Die russisch-byzantinischen Verträge des 10. Jhds. aus diplomatischer Sicht*. Vivliothēkē Slavikōn meletōn, no. 5. Thessaloniki: Vanias.

———. 1998. "Der rechtshistorische Hintergrund einiger Verordnungen aus den russisch-byzantinischen Verträgen des 10. Jhds." *Byzantinoslavica* 59, no. 1: 52–64.

Mango, Cyril, ed. and trans. 1985. *The Homilies of Photius Patriarch of Constantinople*. Cambridge: Harvard University Press.

Margoliouth, D. Samuel. 1918. "The Russian Seizure of Bardha'ah in 943 A.D." *Bulletin of the School of 'Oriental' Studies University of London* 1, no. 2: 82–95.

———, trans. 1921. "Miskawaihi." In *The Concluding Portion of the Experiences of the Nations. Vol. 2. The Eclipse of the 'Abbasid Caliphate*. Original Chronicles of the Fourth Islamic Century, no. 5. Oxford: Blackwell.

Márkiné, Poll Katalin. 1934. "A zsennyei kincs [The Treasure from Zsennye]." *Archaeológiai Értesítő* 46: 62 84.

Markopoulos, Athanasios. 2003. "Byzantine History Writing at the End of the First Millenium." In *Byzantium in the Year 1000*, edited by Paul Magdalino, 183–97. The Medieval Mediterranean. Peoples, Economies and Cultures, 400–1500, no. 45. Leiden: Brill.

Markov, G. Ye. 1976. *Kochevniki Azii. Struktura khozyaystva i obshchestvennoy organizatsii [Nomads of Asia. Economic Structure and Social Organization]*. Moscow: Moskovskogo Universiteta.

Marquart, Josef. 1903. *Osteuropäische und Ostasiatische Streifzüge. Ethnologische und historisch-topographische Studein zur Gesichte des 9. und 10. Jahrhunderts (ca. 840–940)*. Leipzig: Dieterich'sche Verlagbuchhandlung.

Marsina, Richard, ed. 1971. *Codex diplomaticus et epistolaris Slovaciae I*. Bratislava: Academiae Scientiarum Slovacae.

Martinez, Arsenio P. 1982. "Gardīzī's Two Chapters on the Turks." *Archivum Eurasiae Medii Aevi* 2: 109–217.

Mason, Richard A. E. 1995. "The Religious Beliefs of the Khazars." *The Ukrainian Quarterly* 51, no. 4: 383–415.

Mavrodina, R. M. 1983. *Kiyevskaya Rus' i kochevniki (pechenegi, torki, polovtsy) [The Kievan Rus' and the Nomads (Pechenegs, Torks and Polovtians)]*. Leningrad. Nauka.

McCormick, Michael. 2001. *Origins of the European Economy. Communications and Commerce AD 300–900*. Cambridge: Cambridge University Press.

McDougall, Ian. 1986–89. "Foreigners and Foreign Languages in Medieval Iceland." *Saga-Book* of the Viking Society 22: 180–233.

McGrath, Stamatina. 2007. "The Battles of Dorostolon (971): Rhetoric and Reality." In *Byzantine Warfare*, edited by John Haldon, 347–62. London: Routledge.

Mehren, August Ferdinand, ed. 1866. *Chems-ed-Din Abdallah Mohammed ed-Dimichqui. Cosmographie*. Saint-Petersburg: Académie impériale des sciences.

Mel'nikova, Elena A. 1996. "Retinue Culture and Retinue State." In *The Eastern World of the Vikings: Eight Essays about Scandinavia and Eastern Europe in the Early Middle Ages*, 61–72. Gothenburg: Litteraturvetenskapliga Institutionen.

———. 2003. "The Cultural Assimiliation of Varangians in Eastern Europe from the Point of View of Language and Literacy." In *Runica – Germanica – Mediaevalia*, edited by Wilhelm Heizmann and Astrid van Nahl, Vol. 37, 454–65. Berlin: De Gruyter.

———. 2004. "The List of Old Norse Personal Names in the Russian – Byzantine Treaties of the Tenth Century." *Studia anthropomynica scandinavica: Tidskrift för nordisk personnamsforskning* (yearly issue): 5–27.

———. 2011. "Obrazovaniye Drevnerusskogo gosudarstva: sostoyaniye problemy Istochnik [Formation of the Old Rus State: The State of Source Problems]." *Vostochnaya Yevropa v drevnosti i srednevekov'ye* 13: 188–97.

———. 2012. "The 'Varangian problem'. Science in the Grip of Ideology and Politics." In *Russia's Identity in International Relations*, edited by Raymond Taras, 42–52. London: Routledge.

———. 2014a. "Igor'" [Igor]. In *Drevnyaya Rus' v srednevekovom mire. Entsiklopediya*, edited by Elena A. Mel'nikova and Vladimir J. Petrukhin, 313–14. Moscow: Ladomir.

———. 2014b. "Oleg" [Oleg]. In *Drevnyaya Rus' v srednevekovom mire. Entsiklopediya*, edited by Elena A. Mel'nikova and Vladimir J. Petrukhin, 571–73. Moscow: Ladomir.

———. 2014c. "Ryuryk, Syneus, Truvor [Rurik, Sineus, Truvor]." In *Drevnyaya Rus' v srednevekovom mire. Entsiklopediya*, edited by Elena A. Mel'nikova and Vladimir J. Petrukhin, 702–4. Moscow: Ladomir.

———. 2016. "Rhosia and the Rus in Constantine VII Porphyrogennetos' De administrando imperio." In *Byzantium and the Viking World*, edited by Fedir Androshchuk, Jonathan Shephard, and Monica White, 315–36. Studia Byzantina Upsaliensia, no. 16. Uppsala Universitet: Uppsala.

Mel'nikova, E. A., A. B. Nikitin, and A. V. Fomin. 1984. "Graffiti na kuficheskikh monetakh Petergofskogo klada nachala IX v [Graffiti on Kufic Coins of the Peterhof's Treasure from the Beginning of the Ninth Century]." *Drevneyshiye gosudarstva na territorii SSSR. Materialy i issledovaniya 1982*: 26–47.

Mel'nikova, Elene A., and Vladimir J. Petrukhin. 1990–91. "The Origin and Evaluation of the Name Rus'. The Scandinavians in Eastern European Ethno-Political Processes Before the 11th Century." *Tor* 23: 203–34.

Mel'nikova, E. A., V. J. Petrukhin, and T. A. Pushkina. [1984] 2011. "Drevnerusskiye vliyaniya v kul'ture Skandinavii rannego srednevekov'ya (k postanovke problemy) [Old Russian Influences in the Culture of Scandinavia in the Early Middle Ages (to the Statement of Problem)]." In *Drevnyaya Rus' i Skandinaviya: Izbrannyye trudy*, edited by Galina V. Glazyrina and Tatjana N. Jackson, 279–98. Moscow: Dmitriy Pozharskiy University.

Mesterházy Károly. 1981. "Karoling-normann típusú kengyel a honfoglaló magyaroknál [Carolingian-Norman Type of Stirrup of the Conquest Period Magyars]." *Folia Archaeologica* 32: 211–22.

———. 1989–90. "A felső-tisza-vidéki ötvösműhely és a honfoglalás kori emlékek időrendje [The Goldsmith Workshop of the Upper-Tisza Region and the Chronology of the Conquest Period Remains]." *Agria* 25/26: 235–74.

———. 1993. "Régészeti adatok Magyarország 10–11. századi kereskedelméhez [Archaeological Data for the Commerce of Tenth-Eleventh Century Hungary]." *Századok* 127, no. 3–4: 450–68.

Michailidis, Melanie. 2013. "Samanid Silver and Trade Along the Fur Route." *Medieval Encounters* 18, no. 4–5: 315–38.

Michel, Francisque, and Thomas Wright, eds. 1839. "Voyage en Orient du Frère Guillaume de Rubruk." *Recueil de Voyages et de Mémoires publié de la Société de Geographie* 4: 205–396.

Mikhajlov, Kirill A. 2005. "A Scandinavian Cemetery at Plakun (Notes on its Geography and Topography)." *Russian History/Historie Russe* 32, no. 3/4: 419–32.

———. 2007. "Uppland – Gotland – Novgorod. Russian-Swedish relations in the Late Viking Age on the Basis of Studies of Belt Mountings." In *Cultural Interaction between East and West. Archaeology, Artefacts and Human Contacts in Northern Europe*, edited by Ulf Fransson, Marie Svedin, Sophie Bergerbrant, and Fedir Androshchuk, 205–11. Stockholm: Stockholm University.

———. 2011. "Chamber-Graves As International Phenomenon of the Viking Age: From Denmark to Old Rus'." In *Wolińskie Spotkania Mediewistyczne I. Eksluzywne życie – dostojny pochówek w kręgu kultury elitarnej wieków średnich*, edited by Mariana Rebkowski, 205–21. Wolin: MKiDN.

Mikhailov, Kirill A., and Sergej Yu. Kainov. 2011. "Finds of Structural Details of Composite Bows from Ancient Rus." *Acta Archaeologica Academiae Scientiarum Hungaricae* 62: 229–44.

Mikkelsen, Egil. 2008. "The Vikings and Islam." In *The Viking World*, edited by Stefan Brink and Neil Price, 543–49. London: Routledge.

Minorsky, Vladimir, trans. 1942. *Sharaf al-Zamān Tāhir Marvazī on China, the Turks and India*. London: The Royal Asiatic Society.

———, ed. and trans. 1958. *A History of Sharvān and Darband in the 10th – 11th Centuries*. Cambridge: W. Heffer & Sons.

Mishin, Dmitrij. 1994–95. "Ibrahim Ibn-Ya'qub At-Turtushi's Account of the Slavs from the Middle of the Tenth Century." *Annual of Medieval Studies at the CEU*: 184–99.

———. 1999. "Ṣaqlabī servants in Islamic Spain and North Africa in the Early Middle Ages." Ph.D dissertation. Central European University, Budapest.

Mocja, Oleksandr. 2000. "Le rôle des élites guerriéres dans la formation des centres urbains de la Rus' kiévienne, d'après la fouille des tombes." In *Les centres proto-urbain russes entre Scandinavie, Byzance et Orient*, edited by Michel Kazanski, Anne Nercessian, and Constantin Zuckerman, 267–82. Paris: Éditions P. Lethielleux.

Moldovan, A. M. 1984. *"Slovo o zakone i blagodati" Ilariona [Ilarion's Sermon on Law and Grace]*. Kiev: Naukova Dumka.

Mommsen, Theodor, ed. 1882. "Iordanes. *De origine actibusque Getarum*." In *Iordanis Romana et Getica*, 53–138. MGH Auctores Antiquissimi, no. 5. Berlin: Weidmann.

Montgomery, James E. 2000. "Ibn Fadlān and the Rūsiyyah." *Journal of Arabic and Islamic Studies* 3: 1–25.

———. 2001. "Ibn Rusta's lack of eloquence." *Edebiyāt* 12: 73–93.

———. 2004a. "Pyrrhic Scepticism and the Conquest of Disorder: Prolegomenona to the Study of Ibn Fadlan." In *Problems in Arabic Literature*, edited by Miklós Maróth, 43–89. Pilicsaba: The Avicenna Institute of Middle East Studies.

———. 2004b. "Travelling Autopsies: Ibn Fadlan and the Bulghar." *Middle Eastern Literatures* 7, no. 1: 3–32.

———. 2008. "Arabic Sources on the Vikings." In *The Viking World*, edited by Stefan Brink and Neil Price, 550–61. London: Routledge.

———. 2010. "Vikings and Rus in Arabic Sources." In *Living Islamic History. Studies in Honour of Professor Carole Hillenbrand*, edited by Yasir Suleiman, 151–65. Edinburgh: Edinburgh University Press.

———, trans. 2014. "Aḥmad ibn Faḍlān. *Mission to the Volga*." In *Two Arabic Travel Books*, edited by Philip F. Kennedy and Shawkat M. Toorawa, 165–297. New York: New York University Press.

Moravcsik, Gyula. 1938. "Görögnyelvű kolostorok Szent István korában [Greek Cloisters in the Age of Saint Stephen]." In *Emlékkönyv Szent István király halálának kilencszázadik évfordulóján*, edited by Jusztinián Serédi, Vol. 1, 388–422. Budapest: MTA.

———. 1955. "Zum Bericht des Leon Diakonos über den Glauben an die Dienstleistung im Jenseits." *Studia Antiqua. Antonio Salač septuagenario oblate*: 74–76.

———. 1970. *Byzantium and the Magyars*. Amsterdam: Adolf M. Hakkert Publisher.

———. 1983. *Byzantinoturcica. Die Byzantinischen Quellen der Geschichte der Türkvölker*, Vol. 1. Leiden: Brill.

Motsya, A. P. 2009. "Volga – Dnepr – Dunay: srednevekovyy put' Bulgar – Kiev – Regensburg [Volga – Dnieper – Danube: The Medieval Road between Bulgar – Kiev – Regensburg]." In *Krayeugol'nyy kamen' Arkheologiya, istoriya, iskusstvo, kul'tura Rossii i sopredel'nykh stran*, edited by T. N. Dzhakson, M. M. Kazanskiy, A. Ye. Musin, A. I. Saksa, and N. V. Khvoshchinskaya, Vol. 1, 523–29. Saint-Petersburg: Rossiyskaya Akademiya Nauk Institut Istorii Material'noy Kul'tury.

Movchan, Ivan. 2007. "A 10th-century Warrior's Grave from Kiev." In *Kiev – Cherson – Constantinople. Ukrainian Papers at the XXth International Congress of Byzantine Studies (Paris, 19–25 August 2001)*, edited by Alexander Abiabin and Hlib Ivakin, 221–23. Kiev: Ukrainian National Committee for Byzantine Studies.

Mühle, Eduard. 1991. *Die städtischen Handelszentren der nordwestlichen Ruś. Anfänge und frühe Entwicklung altrussischer Städte (bis gegen Ende des 12. Jahrhunderts)*. Quellen und Studien zur Geschichte des östlichen Europa, no. 32. Stuttgart: Franz Steiner Verlag.

Müller-Boysen, Carsten. 1990. *Kaufmannsschutz und Handelsrecht im frühmittelalterlichen Nordeuropa*. Kiel: Karl Wachholtz Verlag.

Mundal, Else. 2000. "Coexistence of Saami and Norse Culture – Reflected in and Interpreted by Old Norse Myths." In *Old Norse Myths, Literature and Society. Papers of the 11th International Saga Conference 2–7 July 2000, University of Sydney*, edited by Geraldine Barnes and Margaret Clunies Ross, 346–55. Sydney: Centre for Medieval Studies.

Murasheva, Veronika. 2006. "Kompositgürtel altrussischer Krieger aus dem 10. und dem Beginn des 11. Jahrhunderts." *Eurasia Antiqua* 12: 353–68.

———. 2016. " 'Ia videl Rusov, kogda oni pribyli po svoim torgovym delam i raspolozhilis' u reki Atyl' [I Saw the Rus', When They Came to do Their Trade Business and Settled on the River Atil]." In *Puteshestvie ibn Fadlana: Volzhskii put' ot Bagdada do Bulgara. Katalog vystavki*, edited by A. I. Torgoev and I. R. Akhmedov, 474–511. Moscow: Izdatel'skii dom Mardzhani.

———. 2019. "In den Osten. Die Wallburg von Supruty." In *Die Wikinger. Entdecker und Eroberer*, edited by Jörn Staecker and Matthias Toplak, 262–72. Berlin: Propyläen.

Murasheva, V. V., A. V. Panin, A. O. Shevtsov, N. N. Malysheva, E. P. Zazovskaya, and N. Ye. Zaretskaya. 2020. "Vremya Vozniknoveniya Poseleniya Gnozdovskogo Arkheologicheskogo Kompleksa po Dannym ra Diouglerodnogo Datirovaniya [The Time of the Emergence of the Settlement of the Gnezdovo Archaeological Complex According Data from Radiocarbon Dating]." *Rossiyskaya Arkheologiya* 4: 70–86.

Murasheva, V. V., O. V. Orfinskaya, and A. Yu. Loboda. 2019. "'Novaya istoriya"idola' iz kurgana Chernaya mogila (X. v.) [A New History of the Idol of the Chernigov Black Kurgan (10th century)]." *Rossiyskaya Arkheologiya* no. 1: 73–86.

Musin, A. Ye. 2012. "Skandinavskoye yazychestvo na Vostoke po dannym arkheologii: obshcheye i osobennoye [Scandinavian Paganism in East Europe in the Light of Archaeology: Commonalities and Specificities]." *Rossiyskiy arkheologicheskiy yezhegodnik* 2: 555–602.

Naimushin, Boris. 2003. "Khazarskiy Kaganat i Vostochnaya Yevropa: stolknoveniya mezhdu 'kochevnikami stepey' i 'kochevnikami rek' [The Khazar Kaghanate and Eastern Europe: Collision between the 'Nomads of the Steppe' and the 'Nomads of the Rivers']." In *Bŭlgari i khazari prez Rannoto srednovekovie*, edited by Tsvetelin Stepanov, 142–58. Sofia: Tangra.

Nazarenko, A. V. 2001. *Drevnyaya Rus' na mezhdunarodnykh putyakh: Mezhdistsiplinarnyye ocherki kul'turnykh, torgovykh, politicheskikh svyazey IX – XII vv [Ancient Rus' on International Routes: Interdisciplinary Essays on Cultural, Commercial and Political Relations in the 9th – 12th Centuries]*. Moscow: Yazyki russkoy kul'tury.

Nazmi, Ahmad. 1998. *Commercial Relations between Arabs and Slavs (9th – 11th centuries)*. Warsaw: Dialog.

Nelson, Janet L. 1997. "The Frankish Empire." In *The Oxford Illustrated History of the Vikings*, edited by Peter Sawyer, 19–47. Oxford: Oxford University Press.

Németh, Gyula. 1958. "Zur Geschichte des Wortes tolmács 'Dolmetscher'." *Acta Orientalia Academiae Scientiarum Hungaricae* 8, no. 1: 1–8.

Nevizánsky, Gabriel, and Jiří Košta. 2009. "Výskum staromaďarského jazdeckého pohrebiska v Strede nad Bodrogom v rokoch 1926 a 1937 [Excavation of the Old Magyar Rider Grave in Strede at the Bodrog between 1926 and 1937]." *Slovenská Archaeológia* 57, no 2: 301–54.

Noonan, Thomas S. 1986. "Why the Vikings First Came to Russia?" *Jahrbücher für Geschichte Osteuropas* 34, no. 3: 321–48.

———. 1990. "Scandinavian-Russian-Islamic Trade in the Ninth Century." *Wosinszky Mór Múzeum Évkönyve* 15: 53–63.

———. 1991. "The Vikings and Russia: Some New Directions and Approaches to an Old Problem." In *Social Approaches to Viking Studies*, edited by Ross Samson, 201–6. Glasgow: Cruithne Press.

———. 1992. "Rus', Pechenegs and Polovtsy: Economic Interaction along the Steppe Frontier in the pre-Mongol Era." *Russian history/Historie Russe* 19, no. 1/4: 301–26.

———. 1997. "Scandinavians in European Russia." In *The Oxford Illustrated History of the Vikings*, edited by Peter Sawyer, 134–55. New York: Oxford University Press.

———. 2000–01. "The Tenth-Century Trade of Volga Bulghāria with Sāmānid Central Asia." *Archivum Eurasiae Medii Aevi* 11: 140–219.

———. 2007. "Some Observations on the Economy of the Khazar Khaganate." In *The World of the Khazars. New Perspectives Selected Papers from the Jerusalem 1999 International Khazar Colloqium*, edited by Peter B. Golden, Haggai Ben-Shammai, and András Róna-Tas, 207–44. Leiden: Brill.

Nordal, Sigurður, ed. 1979. *Egils saga Skallagrímssonar*. Íslenzk fornrit, no. 2. Reykjavík: Hið íslenzka fornritafélag.

Nordberg, Andreas. 2002. "Vertikalt placerade vapen i vikingatida gravar." *Fornvännen* 97: 15–24.

———. 2012. "Continuity, Change and Regional Variation in Old Norse Religion." In *More than Mythology. Narratives, Ritual Practices and Regional Distribution in Pre-Christian Scandinavian Religions*, edited by Catharina Raudvere and Jens Peter Schjødt, 119–51. Lund: Nordic Academic Press.

Nosov, Evgenij N. 1994. "The Emergence and Development of Russian Towns: Some Outline Ideas." *Archaeologia Polona* 32: 185–96.

———. 2017. "Das Novgoroder Land: Das nördliche Ilmenseegebiet und das Volchov-Gebiet." In *Die Rus' im 9. – 10. Jahrhundert. Ein archäologisches Panorama*, edited by Nikolaj A. Makarov, 100–29. Studien zur Siedlungsgeschichte und Archäologie der Ostseegebiete, no. 14. Kiel: Wachholtz – Murmann Publishers.

Nylén, Erik. 1983. *I österled. Med vikingaskepp mot Miklagård. Uppströms gennom Polen.* Visby: Risbergs Tryckeri.

———. 1987. *Vikingaskepp mot Miklagård. Krampmacken i Österled.* Stockholm: Carlsson.

Obolensky, Dimitri. 1982. "The Byzantine Sources on the Scandinavians in Eastern Europe." In *The Byzantine Inheritance of Eastern Europe*, 149–64. London: Variorum.

Oikonomidés, Nicolas. 1972. *Les listes de préséance byzantines des IXe et Xe siècles.* Paris: CNRS.

Olajos Terézia. 1998. "Egy felhasználatlan forráscsoport a 11. századi magyar-bizánci kapcsolatok történetéhez [An Unused Group of Sources to the History of the Eleventh-Century Hungarian-Byzantine Connections]." *Századok* 132: 215–22.

Ólason, Vésteinn. 2007. "The Icelandic Saga as a Kind of Literature with Special Reference to its Representation of Reality." In *Learning and Understanding in the Old Norse World: Essays in Honour of Margaret Cluny Ross*, edited by Judy Quinn, Kate Heslop, and Tarrin Wills, 27–47. Turnout: Brepols.

Olausson, Lena Holmquist, and Slavica Petrovski. 2007. "Curious Birds – Two Helmet (?) Mounts with a Christian Motif from Birka's Garrison." In *Cultural Interaction between East and West. Archaeology, Artefacts and Human Contacts in Northern Europe*, edited by Ulf Fransson, Marie Svedin, Sophie Bergerbrant, and Fedir Androshchuk, 231–37. Stockholm: Stockholm University.

Olson, Emil, ed. 1912. *Yngvars saga víðförla. Jämte ett bihang om Ingvarsinskrifterna.* København: S. L. Møllers.

Ostrogorsky, George. 1940. "L'expédition du prince Oleg contre Constantinople en 907." *Annales de l'Institut Kondakov* 11: 47–62.

Ostrowski, Donald, David Birnbaum, and Horace G. Lunt, eds. 2003. *The Pověst' vremennykh lět. An Interlinear Collation and Paradosis.* Cambridge: Harvard University Press.

Pálóczi, Horváth András. 1989. *Pechenegs, Cumans, Iasians. Steppe Peoples in Medieval Hungary.* Gyomaendrőd: Corvina.

Pálsson, Hermann. 1999. "The Sami people in Old Norse Literature." *Nordlit Arbeidstidsskrift i Litteratur* 5: 29–53.

Pape, Wilhelm. 1914. *Handwörterbuch der griechischen Sprache*, Vol. 2. Braunschweig: F. Vieweg.

Paroń, Aleksander. 2021. *The Pechenegs: Nomads in the Political and Cultural Landscape of Medieval Europe. East Central and Eastern Europe in the Middle Ages*, 450–1450, no. 74. Leiden: Brill.

Pashuto, V. T. 1968. *Vneshnyaya politika Drevney Rusi [The Foreign Policy of Old Rus'].* Moscow: Nauka.

Paulsen, Peter. 1933. *Wikingerfunde aus Ungarn im Lichte der Nord- und Westeuropäischen Frühgeschichte.* Budapest: Magyar Nemzeti Múzeum.

Peel, Christine, ed. 1999. *Guta Saga. The History of the Gotlanders.* London: Viking Society for Northern Research.

Petkes, Zsolt. 2006. "Fokosok és balták a honfoglaló és kora Árpád-kori magyarság régészeti hagyatékában [Adzes and Axes in the Archaeological Heritage of the Conquering and Early Árpád Age Hungarians]." Ph.D dissertation. ELTE, Budapest.

Petrukhin Vladimir. 1998. "Bol'shiye kurgany Rusi i Severnoy Yevropy. K probleme etnokul'turnykh svyazey v rannesrednevekovyy period [Big Burial Mounds of Russia and Northern Europe. On the Problem of Ethnocultural Ties in the Early Medieval Period]." In *Istoricheskaya arkheologiya. Traditsii i perspektivy. K 80-letiyu so dnya rozhdeniya D. A. Avdusina*, edited by V. L. Yanin and T. A. Pushkina, 361–69. Moscow: Pamyatniki istoricheskoy mysli.

———. 2006. "The Dnieper Rapids in 'De Administrando Imperio': The Trade Route and its Sacrificial Rites." In *The Significance of Portages. Proceedings of the First International Conference on the Significance of Portages, 29 Sept – 2nd Oct 2004*, edited by Christer Weesterdahl, 187–89. Kristiansand: Archaeopress.

———. 2007. "Khazaria and Rus': An Examination of their Historical Relations." In *The World of the Khazars. New Perspectives Selected Papers from the Jerusalem 1999 International Khazar Colloqium*, edited by Peter B. Golden, Haggai Ben-Shammai, and András Róna-Tas, 245–68. Leiden: Brill.

———. 2009. "Migratory Mechanism. Rus' and Magyars in the Ninth Century." In *Ancient Human Migrations: A Multidisciplinary Approach*, edited by Peter N. Peregrine, Ilia Peiros, and Marcus Feldman, 229–48. Santa Fé: University of Utah Press.

———. 2015. "Rus', Scandinavians and the Balkans in the Ninth and Tenth Centuries." In *Scandinavia and the Balkans: Cultural Interactions with Byzantium and Eastern Europe in the First Millennium AD*, edited by Oksana Minaeva and Lena Holmquist, 55–67. Cambridge: Cambridge Scholars Publishing.

———. 2016. "Vikingi i step': k probleme vozdeystviya Vostoka na Shvetsiyu v rannem srednevekov'ye [Vikings and the Steppe: To the Problem of Eastern Impact in Sweden in the Early Middle Ages]." *Divnogorskiy sbornik* 6: 126–37.

Phelpstead, Carl. 2013. "Hair Today, Gone Tomorrow: Hair Loss, the Tonsure, and Masculinity in Medieval Iceland." *Scandinavian Studies* 85, no. 1: 1–19.

Photius. 1883. "De Rossorum Incursione Homoliæ duæ." In *Fragmenta Historicorum Graecorum*, edited by Carl Müller, Vol. 5, 162–73. Paris: Firmin-Didot.

Piltz, Elisabeth, ed. 1998. *Byzantium and Islam in Scandinavia. Acts of a Symposium at Uppsala University June 15–16 1996*. Jonsered: Paul Åströms Förlag.

Pintescu, Florin. 2001. "Presences de l'element viking dans l'espace de la romanité orientale en contexte méditerranéen." *Studia Antiqua et Archaeologica. Centrul Interdisciplinar de Studii Arheoistorice* 8: 257–72.

Pipes, Daniel. 1981. *Slave Soldiers and Islam. The Genesis of a Military System*. New Haven: Yale University Press.

Pires, Helio. 2011. "Money for Freedom: Ransom Paying to Vikings in Western Iberia." *Viking and Medieval Scandinavia* 7: 125–30.

Pivány, Jenő. 1903. "Magyar volt-e a Heimskringla Tyrker-je? [Was Heimskringla's Tyrker a Hungarian?]." *Századok* 43, no. 7: 571–77.

Platonova, Nadezhda I. 2017. "Elite culture of Old Rus': New Publications and Discussions (A Review of IHMC Ras Studies in 2015–2016)." *Archaeologica Baltica* 24: 123–30.

Pletnjeva, S. A. 1978. *Die Chasaren. Mittelalterliches Reich an Don und Wolga*. Leipzig: Koehler & Amelang.

———. 2003. *Kochevniki yuzhnorusskikh stepey v epokhu srednevekov'ya IV – XIII veka [Nomads of the South Russian Steppe in the Epoch of the Middle Ages 4th – 13th Centuries]*. Voronezh: Voronezhskogo gosudarstvennogo universiteta.

Pohl, Walter. 1998. "Conceptions of Ethnicity in Early Medieval Studies." In *Debating the Middle Ages: Issues and Readings*, edited by Lester K. Little and Barbara H. Rosenwein, 13–24. Malden: Blackwell Publishers.

———. 2018. "Ethnicity and Empire in the Western Eurasian Steppes." In *Empires and Exchanges in Eurasian Late Antiquity. Rome, China, Iran, and the Steppe, ca. 250–750*, edited by Nicola di Cosmo and Michael Maas, 189–205. Cambridge: Cambridge University Press.

Polgár, Szabolcs. 2000. "Kereskedelem a Fekete-tenger északi partvidékén a 9–10. században (A Ğayhānī-féle leírás adatai a magyarok és a De Administrando imperio értesülései a besenyők kereskedelméről) [Trade on the North coast of the Black Sea (Data from

Ğayhānī's Description on the Magyars' and That of the De administrando Imperio on the Pechenegs' Commerce]." In *A népvándorláskor kutatóinak kilencedik konferenciája*, edited by Petercsák Tivadar, 194–206. Heves Megyei Régészeti Közlemények, no. 2. Eger: Dobó István Vármúzeum.

———. 2002. "A Volga-vidékről a Kárpát-medencéig vezető utak említése egy muszlim forrásban és a magyar fejedelmi székhely a 10. század első évtizedeiben [A Muslim Source's Mention of the Routes from the Volga Area to the Carpathian Basin and the Question of the Magyar Princely Headquerter in the First Decades of the Tenth Century]." In *Központok és falvak a honfoglalás és kora Árpád-kori Magyarországon*, edited by Julianna Cseh Kisné, 217–30. Tatabánya: Tatabányai Múzeum.

———. 2004. "Kora középkori (9–12. századi) kelet-európai fegyverkereskedelemre utaló feljegyzések az írott forrásokban [Notes in the Early Medieval (9th – 12th-Century) Written Sources on Eastern European Weapontrade]." In *Fegyveres nomádok, nomád fegyverek*, edited by László Balogh and László Keller, 92–101. Magyar Őstörténeti Könyvtár 21. Budapest: Balassi Kiadó.

Price, Neil. 2002. "The Viking Way. Religion and War in Late Iron Age Scandinavia." Ph.D dissertation. University of Uppsala, Uppsala.

———. 2008. "Dying and the Dead. Viking Age mortuary behaviour." In *The Viking World*, edited by Stefan Brink and Neil Price, 257–73. London: Routledge.

———. 2014. "Ship-Men and Slaughter-Wolves. Pirate Polities in the Viking Age." In *Persistent Piracy. Maritime Violence and State-Formation in Global Historical Perspective*, edited by Stefan Eklöf Amirell and Leos Müller, 51–68. Basingstoke: Palgrave Macmillan.

———. 2020. *The Children of Ash & Elm. A History of the Vikings*. London: Allen Lane.

Price, T. Douglas, Jüri Peets, Raili Allmäe, Liina Maldre, and Neil Price. 2020. "Human Remains, Context, and the Place of Origin of the Salme, Estonia, Boat Burials." *Journal of Anthropological Archaeology* 58: 1–13.

Price, T. Douglas, Karin Margarita Frei, Andres Siegfried Dobat, Niels Lynnerup, and Pia Bennike. 2011. "Who Was in Harold Bluetooth's Army? Strontium Isotope Investigation of the Cemetery at the Viking Age Fortress at Trelleborg, Denmark." *Antiquity* 85, no. 328: 476–89.

Pritsak, Omeljan. 1970. "An Arabic Text on the Trade Route of the Corporation of ar-Rūs in the Second Half of the Ninth Century." *Folia Orientalia* 12: 241–59.

———. 1975. "The Pechenegs: A Case of Social and Economic Transformation." *Archivum Eurasiae Medii Aevi* 1: 211–35.

———. 1977. "The Origin of Rus'." *The Russian Review* 36, no. 3: 249–73.

———. 1981. *The Origin of Rus'. Old Scandinavian Sources Other Than the Sagas*, Vol. 1. Cambridge: Harvard University Press.

———. 1982. "An Eleventh-Century Turkic Bilingual (Turko-Slavic) Graffito from the St. Sophia Cathedral in Kiev." *Harvard Ukrainian Studies* 6, no. 2: 152–66.

Procopius. 1919. *History of the Wars. Books V and VI*, edited by E. Capps, T. E. Page, and W. H. D. Rouse, translated by H. B. Dewing. London: William Heinemann.

Psellos, Michel. 1967. *Chronographie ou Histoire d'un Siècle de Byzance (976–1077)*, edited by Émile Renauld, Vol. 1, 2nd ed. Paris: Société d'édition "Les Belles Lettres".

Pushkina, Tamara. 2004. "Viking-period Pre-Urban Settlements in Russia and Finds of Artefacts of Scandinavian Character." In *Land, Sea and Home. Settlement in the Viking Period*, edited by John Hines, Alan Lane, and Mark Redknap, 41–53. Maney: Northern Universities Press.

———. 2007. "Khazarian Souvenirs." In *Cultural Interaction between East and West. Archaeology, Artefacts and Human Contacts in Northern Europe*, edited by Ulf Fransson, Marie Svedin, Sophie Bergerbrant, and Fedir Androshchuk, 149–51. Stockholm: Stockholm University.

———. 2020. "K Probleme Vozdeystviya Vostoka na Skandinaviyu i Rus' v Rannem Srednevekov'ye [To the Problem of Eastern Impact on Scandinavia and Rus' in the Early Middle Ages]." *Khazarskiy Al'manakh* 17: 228–42.

Pushkina, Tamara, Veronika V. Murasheva, and Natalja V. Eniosova. 2017. "Der archäologische Komplex von Gnezdovo." In *Die Rus' im 9. – 10. Jahrhundert. Ein archäologisches Panorama*, edited by Nikolaj A. Makarov, 250–81. Studien zur Siedlungsgeschichte und Archäologie der Ostseegebiete, no. 14. Kiel: Wachholtz – Murmann Publishers.

Raffensperger, Christian. 2017. *The Kingdom of Rus'*. Amsterdam: ARC Humanities Press.

Raffield, Ben. 2016. "Band of Brothers: A Re-Appraisal of the Viking Great Army and its Implications for the Scandinavian Colonization of England." *Early Medieval Europe* 24, no. 3: 308–37.

Raffield, Ben, Claire Greenlow, Neil Price, and Mark Collard. 2016. "Ingroup Identification, Identity Fusion and the Formation of Viking Warbands." *World Archaeology* 48, no. 1: 35–50.

Raffield, Ben, Neil Price, and Mark Collard. 2017. "Polygyny, Concubinage and the Social Life of Women in Viking-Age Scandinavia." *Viking and Medieval Scandinavia* 13: 165–209.

Rafn, Carl Christian, ed. 1829a. "Saga af Ragnari Konungi Lodbrok ok Sonum Hans." In *Fornaldar Sögur Nordrlanda*, Vol. 1, 235–99. Copenhagen: Hardvig Fridrek Popp.

———, ed. 1829b. "Örvar Odds saga." In *Fornaldar sögur Nordrlanda*, Vol. 2, 159–322. Copenhagen: Hardvig Fridrek Popp.

Rasovskiy, D. A. [1933] 2012. *Polovtsy. Chernyye klobuki. Pechenegi, torki i berendei na Rusi i v Vengrii [Polovtsians. Black Hoods. Pechenegs, Torks and Berendeys in Russia and Hungary]*. Moscow: Tsivoi.

Renaud, Jean. 2000. *Les Vikings en France*. Rennes: Ouest-France.

Révész, László. 1999. *Emlékezzetek utatok kezdetére . . . Régészeti kalandozások a magyar honfoglalás és államalapítás korában [Remember the Start of Your Journey . . . Archaeological Adventures in the Age of the Hungarian Conquest and State Formation]*. Budapest: Timp.

Roesdahl, Else, and David M. Wilson, eds. 1992. *From Viking to Crusader. The Scandinavians and Europe 800–1200*. New York: Rizzoli.

Rolle, Renate. 1979. *Totenkult der Skythen. Vol. 1. Das Steppengebiet*. Berlin: Walter de Gryuter.

Romenskiy, A. A. 2017. "Nachal'naya Rus' bez nachal'noy letopisi: novyy vitok spora o ranney istorii Vostochnoy Yevropy [Primary Rus' without the Primary Chronicle: New Round of Debate about the Early History of Eastern Europe]." *Maiask* 9: 541–52.

Róna-Tas András. 1987. "Materialien zur alten Religion der Türken." In *Synkretismuis in den Religionen Zentralasiens*, edited by Walther Heissig and Hans-Joachim Klimkeit, 33–45. Wiesbaden: Otto Harrassowitz.

———. 1999. *Hungarians and Europe in the Early Middle Ages. An Introduction to Early Hungarian History*. Budapest: CEU Press.

Roux, Jean-Paul. 1963. *La Mort chez les peuples altaïques anciens et mediévaux*. Paris: Libraire d'Amérique et d'Orient.

———. 1984. *La religion des Turcs et des Mongols*. Paris: Payot.

———. 2005a. "Tengri." In *Encyclopedia of Religion*, edited by Lindsay Jones, Vol. 13, 2nd ed, 9080–2. Detroit: Macmillan Reference USA.

———. 2005b. "Turkic Religions." In *Encyclopedia of Religion*, edited by Lindsay Jones, Vol. 14, 2nd ed, 9397–404. Detroit: Macmillan Reference USA.

Różycki, Łukasz. 2014. "Description de l'Ukraine in light of De Administrando Imperio: Two Accounts of a Journey Along the Dnieper." *Byzantinoslavica* 72, no. 1–2: 122–35.

Rybakov, B. A. 1982. *Kiyevskaya Rus' i russkiye knyazhestva XII – XIII vv [The Kievan Rus' and Russian Principalities 12th – 13th Century]*. Moscow: Nauka.

Said, Edward. 1978. *Orientalism*. London: Routledge & Kegan Paul.

Sakharov, A. N. 1980. *Diplomatiya Drevney Rusi [The Diplomacy of Old Rus']*. Moscow: Mysl'.

———. 1986. "Orosz-magyar szövetségi kapcsolatok a 9–10. században [Russian-Hungarian Alliances in the Ninth-Tenth Centuries]." *Századok* 120: 111–22.

Samokvasov, D. Ya. 1916. *Mogil'nyye drevnosti severyanskoy Chernigovshchiny [Grave Antiquities of the Severyans of the Chernigov Region]*. Moscow: Sinodal'naya tipografiya.

Sawyer, Peter. 1982. *Kings and Vikings. AD 700–1100*. London: Methuen.

Schäfer, Tibor. 2004. "Lovasnomád hatás a keleti germán népekre [Equastrian Nomadic Impact on the Eastern Germanic People]." In *Fegyveres nomádok, nomád fegyverek*, edited by László Balogh and László Keller, 20–25. Magyar Őstörténeti Könyvtár, no. 21. Budapest: Balassi Kiadó.

Scheel, Roland. 2015. *Skandinavien und Byzanz. Bedingungen und Konsequenzen mittelalterlicher Kulturbeziehungen*, Vol. 1–2. Göttingen: Vandenhoeck & Ruprecht.

Schjødt, Jens Peter. 2007. "Ibn Fadlan's Account of a Rus funeral: To What Degree Does it Reflect Nordic Myths?" In *Reflections on Old Norse Myths*, edited by Pernille Hermann, Jens Peter Schjødt, and Rasmus Tranum Kristensen, 133–49. Turnhout: Brepols.

———. 2011. "The Warrior in Old Norse Religion." In *Ideology and Power in the Viking and Middle Ages*, edited by Gro Steinsland, Jón Viðar Sigurðson, Jan Erik Rekdal, and Ian Beuerman, 269–95. Leiden: Brill.

Schmeidler, Bernhard, ed. 1917. *Magister Adam Bremensis Gesta Hammaburgensis Ecclesiae Pontificum*, 3rd ed. MGH Scriptores rerum Germanicarum in usum scholarum, no. 2. Hannover: Hahniani.

Schmidt, Knud Rahbek. 1970. "The Varangian Problem. A Brief History of the Controversy." In *Varangian Problems. Scando – Slavica Supplementum I*, edited by Knud Hannestad, Knud Jordal, Ole Klindt-Jensen, Knud Rahbek Schmidt, and Carl Stief, 7–20. Copenhagen: Munskgaard.

Schramm, Gottfried. 2007. "Viel Lärm um vier Buchstaben. Der Name Rus' als Beispiel für die Rückständigkeit einer historischen Hilfswissenschaft." *Jahrbücher für Geschichte Osteuropas (Neue Folge)* 55, no. 1: 67–79.

Shandrovskaia, S. Valentina. 2016. "The Seal of Michael, Grand Interpreter of the Varangians." In *Byzantium and the Viking World*, edited by Fedir Androshchuk, Jonathan Shephard, and Monica White, 305–12. Uppsala: Uppsala Universitet.

Shaw, Denis J. B. 2006. "Russia's Geographical Environment." In *The Cambridge History of Russia. Vol. 1. From Early Rus' to 1689*, edited by Maureen Perrie, 19–43. Cambridge: Cambridge University Press.

Shchavelev, A. S. 2007. "Izvestiye Ipat'yevskoy letopisi o Chornoy mogile (k voprosu ob imeni pogrebonnogo knyazya) [News from the Ipatyev Chronicle on the Black Grave (to the Question of the Name of the Buried Knyaz]." In *Chernihiv u seredn'ovichniy ta rann'omoderniy istorii tsentral'no-skhidnoi Evropy*, edited by O. B. Kovalenko, 100–5. Chernihiv: Desnyans'ka Pravda.

———. 2013. "Dve 'kar'yery' funktsionerov rannego gosudarstva: voyevoda Svenel'd i khevding Torol'v Kvel'dul'vsson [Two 'Careers' of Early State Functionaries: Voevoda Sveneld and Höfðing Þórolfr Kveldúlfsson]." *Vestnik NNGU* 4, no. 3: 72–78.

Shepard, Jonathan. 1973. "The English and Byzantium: A Study of Their Role in the Byzantine Army in the Later Eleventh Century." *Traditio* 29: 53–92.

———. 1984–85. "Yngvarr's Expedition to the East and a Russian Inscribed Stone Cross." *Saga-Book* 21: 222–92.

———. 2005. "Conversions and Regimes Compared: The Rus' and the Poles, ca. 1000." In *East Central & Eastern Europe in the Early Middle Ages*, edited by Florin Curta, 254–82. Ann Arbor: University of Michigan Press.

———. 2008. "The Viking Rus and Byzantium." In *The Viking World*, edited by Stefan Brink and Neil Price, 496–516. London: Routledge.

———. 2009. "'Mists and Portals': The Black Sea's North Coast." In *Byzantine Trade, 4th – 12th Centuries. The Archaeology of Local, Regional and International Exchange*, edited by Marlia Mundell Mango, 421–41. Society for the Promotion of Byzantine Studies, no. 14. Farnham: Ashgate.

———. 2010. "From the Bosporus to the British Isles: The Way from the Greeks to the Varangians." In *Drevnejshhie gosudarstva Vostochnoj Evropy 2009 god*, edited by Tatjana N. Jackson, 15–42. Moscow: Institut vseobshhej istorii PAH.

———. 2015. "Things, Persons and Practices in Circulation between Byzantium and the British Isles in the Viking Age: A Role for Rus?" In *Goroda i vesi srednevekovoy Rusi: arkheologiya, istoriya, kul'tura: k 60-letiyu Nikolaya Andreyevicha Makarova*, edited by L. A. Belyayev, P. G. Gaydukov, I. Ye. Zaytseva, S. D. Zakharov, N. V. Lopatin, V. V. Sedov, A. N. Fedorina, and A. V. Engovatova, 274–85. Moscow: Drevnosti Severa.

———. 2017. "Photios' Sermons on the Rus Attack of 860: The Questions of His Origins, and of the Route of the Rus." In *Prosopon Rhomaikon. Ergänzende Studien zur Prosopographie der mittelbyzantinischen Zeit*, edited by Alexander Beihammer, Bettina Krönung, and Claudia Ludwig, 111–28. De Gruyter: Berlin.

Sielicki, Stanislaw. 2015. "Saxo Grammaticus on pre-Christian Religion of the Slavs. The Relevant Fragments from Book XIV of Gesta Danorum." 1–17. Accessed February 23, 2017. www.academia.edu/11345671/Saxo_Grammaticus_on_pre-Christian_religion_of_the_Slavs_the_relevant_fragments_from_book_XIV_of_Gesta_Danorum_final_draft_.

Sigurðsson, Gísli. 2004. *The Medieval Icelandic Saga and Oral Tradition*. Cambridge: Milman Parry Collection.

Simek, Rudolf. 2006. "Totenreiche." In *Reallexikon der Germanischen Altertumskunde*, edited by Heinrich Beck, Dieter Geuenich, and Heiko Steuer, Vol. 31, 89–92. Berlin: Walter de Gruyter.

Simpson, Jacqueline. 1967. *Everyday life in the Viking Age*. London: Batsford.

Sindbæk, Søren M. 2003. "Varægiske vinterruter. Slædetransport i Rusland og spørgsmålet om den tidlige vikingetids orientalske import i Nordeuropa." *Fornvännen* 98, no. 3: 179–93.

———. 2007. "Networks and Nodal Points: The Emergence of Towns in Early Viking Age Scandinavia." *Antiquity* 81: 119–32.

———. 2008. "Local and Long-Distance Exchange." In *The Viking World*, edited by Stefan Brink and Neil Price, 150–58. London: Routledge.

Sinor, Denis. 1981. "The Inner Asian Warriors." *Journal of the American 'Oriental' Society* 101, no. 2: 133–44.

———. 1997. "Interpreters in Medieval Inner Asia." In *Studies in Medieval Inner Asia*, 293–320. Ashgate: Variorum.
———, ed. [1990] 2008. *The Cambridge History of Early Inner Asia*. Cambridge: Cambridge University Press.
Sitzmann, Alexander. 2003. *Nordgermanisch-ostslavische Sprachkontakte in der Kiever Rus' bis zum Tode Jaroslavs des Weisen*. Vienna: Praesens Verlag.
Słupecki, Leszek. 2013. "Slavic Religion." In *The Handbook of Religions in Ancient Europe*, edited by Lisbeth Bredholt Christensen, Olav Hammer, and David A. Warburton, 339–58. Durham: Acumen.
Smedt, de Charles, Guillaume van Hooff, and Joseph de Backer, eds. 1883. "Translatio S. Germani Parisiensis anno 846, secundum primævam narrationem." In *Analecta Bollandiana*, Vol. 2, 69–98. Brusells: Société des Bollandiste.
Smyser, Hamilton Martin. 1965. "Ibn Fadlan's Account of the Rus with Some Commentary and Some Allusions to Beowulf." In *Franciplegius: Medieval and Linguistic Studies in Honor of Francis Peabody Magoun*, edited by Jess B. Bessinger and Robert P. Creed, 92–119. New York: New York University Press.
Sneath, David. 2007. *The Headless State. Aristocratic Orders, Kinship Society, & Mispresentations of Nomadic Inner Asia*. New York: Columbia University Press.
Soloviev, A. V. 1960. "Die angebliche ungarische Herrschaft in Kiev im 9. Jahrhundert." *Jahrbücher für Geschichte Osteuropas* 8: 123–29.
Solov'yov, S. M. 1896. *Istóriya Rossíi s drevnéyshikh vremon [The History of Russia from Ancient Times]*, Vol. 1, 2nd ed. Saint-Petersburg: Tovarishchestvo obshchestvennaya pol'za.
Sorokin, Petr. 2006. "Staraya Ladoga: a seaport in Medieval Russia." In *Connected by the Sea. Proceedings of the Tenth International Symposium on Boat and Ship Archaeology Roskilde 2003*, edited by Lucy Blue, Fred Hocker and Anton Englert, 157–62. Oxford: Oxbow Books.
Sourdel, Dominique, C. E. Bosworth, P. Hardy, and Halil Inalcik. 1991. "Ghulām." In *Encyclopaedia of Islam*, edited by B. Lewis, Ch. Pellat and J. Schacht, Vol. 2, 1079–91. Leiden: Brill.
Spinei, Victor. 2009. *The Romanians and the Turkic Nomads North of the Danube Delta from Tenth to the Mid-Thirteenth Century*, Leiden: Brill.
Spitzer, J. Shlomo, and Komoróczy Géza, eds. 2003. *Héber kútforrások Magyarország és a magyarországi zsidóság történetéhez a kezdetektől 1686-ig [Hebrew Sources for the History of Hungary and the Hungarian Jewry from the Beginnings to 1686]*. Budapest: Osiris Kiadó.
Stalsberg, Anne. 1982. "Scandinavian Relations with Northwestern Russia During the Viking Age: The Archaeological Evidence." *Journal of Baltic Studies* 13, no. 3: 267–95.
———. 1988. "The Scandinavian Viking Age Finds in Rus'. Overview and Analysis." *Bericht der Romisch-Germanischen Kommission* 69: 448–71.
———. 2001. "Scandinavian Viking-Age Boat Graves in Old Rus'." *Russian History/Histoire Russe* 28, no. 1–4: 359–401.
Standen, Naomi, and Monica White. 2018. "Structural Mobilities in the Global Middle Ages." *Past & Present* 238, no. 13: 158–89.
Stefanovich, Petr C. 2012. *Boyare, otroki, druzhiny. Voyenno-politicheskaya elita rusi v X – XI vekakh [Boyars, Otroks and Druzhinniks. Military-Political Elite of the Rus in the 10th – 11th Centuries]*. Moscow: Indrik.
Stein-Wilkeshuis, Martina. 1991. "A Viking-Age Treaty between Constantinople and Northern Merchants, with its Provisions on Theft and Robbery." *Scando-Slavica* 37: 35–47.

———. 2002. “Scandinavians Swearing Oaths in Tenth-Century Russia: Pagans and Christians.” *Journal of Medieval History* 28: 155–68.

Stender-Petersen, Adolf. 1931–32. “Zur Bedeutungsgeschichte des Wortes vǽringi, Russ. vaŕag.” *Acta Philologica Scandinavica. Tidsskrift for nordisk sprogforskning* 6: 26–38.

———. 1953. “The Varangian Problem.” In *Varangica*, 5–20. Aarhus: B. Lunos.

Stephenson, Paul. 2004. *Byzantium's Balkan Frontier. A Political Study of the Northern Balkans, 900–1204*. Cambridge: Cambridge University Press.

Steuer, Heiko. 1975. “Eine dreieckige Bronzeschale aus Haithabu bei Schleswig.” *Archäologisches Korrespondenzblatt*, no. 3: 89–93.

———. 2014. “Mittelasien und der Wikingerzeitliche Norden.” In *Die Wikinger und das Frankische Reich. Identitäten zwischen Konfrontation und Annäherung*, edited by Kerstin P. Hofmann, Hermann Kamp, and Matthias Wemhoff, 217–38. Paderborn: Wilhelm Fink.

Stillman, Yedida Kalfon. 2003. *Arab Dress. A Short History. From the Dawn of Islam to Modern Times*. Leiden: Brill.

Stjerna, Niklas. 2004. “En stäppnomadisk rustning från Birka.” *Fornvännen* 99: 27–32.

Struminski, Bohdan. 1996. *Linguistic Interrelations in Early Rus': Northmen, Finns and East Slavs (Ninth to Eleventh Centuries)*. Edmonton: Canadian Institute of Ukrainian Studies Press.

Sturluson, Snorri. 2002a. “Hákonar Saga Góða.” In *Heimskringla*, edited by Bjarni Aðalbjarnarson, Vol. 1, 150–97. Íslenzk Fornrit, no. 26. Reykjavík: Hið íslenzka fornritafélag.

———. 2002b. “Haralds Saga Sigurðarsonar.” In *Heimskringla*, edited by Bjarni Aðalbjarnarson, Vol. 3, 68–202. Íslenzk fornrit, no. 28. Reykjavík: Hið íslenzka fornritafélag.

———. 2002c. “Magnússona Saga.” In *Heimskringla*, edited by Bjarni Aðalbjarnarson, Vol. 3, 238–77. Íslenzk Fornrit Vol. 28. Reykjavík: Hið Íslenzka Fornritafélag.

Sudár, Balázs. 2019. “A turbános morvák esete a korai magyar szállásokkal. A Hudúd al-álam és a magyar őstörténet [The Case of the Turbaned Moravians and the Early Hungarian Settlements. The Hudud al-‘Alam and Hungarian Prehistory].” *Századok* 153, no. 1, 75–100.

Suleymenov, R. B. 1989. “Formatsionnaya priroda kochevogo obshchestva: problema i metod [The Nature of the Formation of Nomadic Society: Problem and Method].” In *Vzaimodeystviye kochevykh kul'tur i drevnikh tsivilizatsiy*, edited by A. N. Turkmenskoy, V. M. Masson, A. N. Kazakhskoy, R. B. Suleymenov, K. A. Akishev, K. M. Baypakov, S. M. Akhinzhanov, and L. B. Yerzakovich, 89–102. Almaty: Nauka.

Sundkvist, Anneli. 2001. *Hästarnas land: aristokratisk hästhållning och ridkonst i Svealands yngre järnålder*. Occasional Papers in Archaeology, no. 28. Uppsala: Uppsala Universitet.

Svane, Gunnar. 1989. “Vikingetidens nordiske låneord i russisk.” In *Ottende tværfaglige vikingesymposium*, edited by Thorben Kisbye and Else Roesdahl, 18–32. Aarhus: Hiruni.

Sveinsson, Einar Ól., ed. 1934. *Laxdœla saga*. Íslenzk fornrit, no. 5. Reykjavík: Hið íslenzka fornritafélag.

———, ed. 1939. “Kormáks saga.” In *Vatnsdœla saga*, 201–302. Íslenzk fornrit, no. 8. Reykjavík: Hið íslenzka fornritafélag.

Sveinsson, Einar Ól., and Matthias Þórðarson, eds. 1935a. “Grœnlendinga saga.” In *Eyrbyggja saga*, 238–69. Íslenzk fornrit, no. 4. Reykjavík: Hið íslenzka fornritafélag.

———, eds. 1935b. “Eiríks saga rauða.” In *Eyrbyggja saga*, 193–237 and 401–34. Íslenzk fornrit, no. 4. Reykjavík: Hið íslenzka fornritafélag.

Sverdlov, M. B. 2003. *Domongol'skaya Rus': Knyaz' i knyazhes vlast' na Rusi VI-pervoy treti XIII vv [Pre-Mongol Rus: Prince and Princely Power in Rus' from the 6th to the First Third of the 13th Century]*. Saint-Petersburg: Akademicheskiy proyekt.

Szabados, György. 2011. *Magyar Államalapítások a IX–XI. Században [Hungarian State Foundations in the 9th to 11th Centuries]*. Szegedi Középkortörténeti Könyvtár, 26. Szeged: Szegedi Középkorász Műhely.
———. 2019. "The Origins and Transformation of the Early Hungarian State." In *Reform and Renewal in Medieval East and Central Europe: Politics, Law and Society*, edited by Suzana Miljan, Éva B. Halász, and Alexandru Simon, 9–30. Cluj-Napoca: Romanian Academy Center for Transylvanian Studies.
Székely, György. 1975. "Hungary and Sweden – Historical Contacts and Parallels in the Middle Ages." In *Hungary and Sweden. Early Contacts, Early Sources*, edited by Folke Lindenberg and György Ránki, 9–36. Budapest: Akadémiai Kiadó.
Szentpétery, Emericus, ed. [1938] 1999. *Scriptores Rerum Hungaricarum*, Vol. 2. Budapest: Nap Kiadó.
Taaffe, Robert N. 1990. "The Geographic Setting." In *The Cambridge History of Early Inner Asia*, edited by Denis Sinor, 19–40. Cambridge: Cambridge University Press.
Tacitus. 1914. *Dialogus, Agricola, Germania*, edited by T. E. Page and W. H. D. Rouse. London: William Heinemann.
Tagán, Galimdzsán. 1941. "Honfoglaláskori magyar sír Kijevben [A Conquest Period Hungarian Grave in Kiev]." *Folia Archaeologica* 3–4: 311–13.
Talbot, Alice-Mary, and Denis F. Sullivan, eds. and trans. 2005. *The History of Leo the Deacon. Byzantine Military Expansion in the Tenth Century*. Dumbarton Oaks Studies, no. 41. Washington, DC: Dumbarton Oaks.
Tarras, Victor. 1965. "Leo Diaconus and the Ethnology of Kievan Rus'." *Slavic Review* 24, no. 3: 395–406.
Taylor, Timothy. 2002. *The Buried Soul. How Humans Invented Death*. London: Fourth Estate.
Teuntiuc, Ion. 2018–19. "On the Viking Enclaves and Their Relations with the Inhabitants of the Carpathian – Dniester Region between the 9th and the 11th Centuries." *Dacia. Revue d'archéologie et d'histoire ancienne* 62–63: 249–86.
Theophanes. 1883. *Chronographia*, edited by Karl De Boor, Vol. 1. Leipzig: B.G. Teubneri.
Thörnqvist, Clara. 1948. *Studien über die nordischen Lehnwörter im Russischen*. Uppsala: Almqvist & Wiksells.
Thurn, Hans, ed. 1973. *Ioannis Scylitzae Synopsis historiarum*. CFHB Series Berolinensis, no. 5. Berlin: De Gruyter.
Tibbets, Gerald. 1992. "The Balkhi School of Geographers." In *The History of Cartography: Cartography in the Traditional Islamic and South Asian Societies*, edited by John B. Harley and David Woodward, 108–36. Chicago: University of Chicago Press.
Timberlake, Alan. 2001. "The Redactions of the Primary Chronicle." *Russkii jazyk v nauchnom osveshchenii* 1: 196–218.
Togan, Zeki Validi Ahmed. 1939. *Ibn Fadlan's Reisebericht*. Leipzig: Kommissionsverlag F. A. Brockhaus.
Tolochko, I. Oleksiy. 2008. "The Primary Chronicle's 'Ethnography' Revisited: Slavs and Varangians in the Middle Dnieper Region and the Origin of the Rus' State." In *Franks, Northmen, and Slavs: Identities and State Formation in Early Medieval Europe*, edited by Ildar H. Garipzanov, Patrick Geary, and Przemyslaw Urbanczyk, 169–88. Cursor Mundi, no. 5. Turnhout: Brepols.
———. 2011. "Christian Chronology, Universal History, and the Origin of Chronicle Writing in Rus'." In *Historical Narratives and Christian Identity on a European Periphery: Early History Writing in Northern, East-Central, and Eastern Europe (c. 1070–1200)*, edited by Ildar H. Garipzanov, 205–27. Medieval Texts and Cultures of Northern Europe, no. 26. Turnhout: Brepols.

———. 2015. *Ocherki nachal'noi Rusi [Studies of Early Rus']*. Kiev: Laurus.

Tolochko, P. P. 1987. *Drevnyaya Rus'. Ocherki sotsial'no-politicheskoy istorii [Old Rus'. Essays about Socio-Political History]*. Kiev: Naukova dumka.

———. 2017. *Kochevyye narody stepey i Kiyevskaya Rus' [Nomadic People of the Steppe and the Kievan Rus']*. Saint-Petersburg: Aleteyya.

Tortika, A. A. 2006. *Severo-Zapadnaya Khazariya v kontekste istorii Vostochnoy Yevropy (vtoraya polovina VII – tret'ya chetvert' X v.) [Northwestern Khazaria in the Context of Eastern European history (from Second Half of the Seventh- to the Third Quarter of the Tenth Century)]*. Harkov: KHGAK.

Tóth, Zoltán. 1988. "A Botond-monda eredete s az anonymusi Botond-hagyomány [Origins of the Botond Legend and the Botond Tradition at Anonymus]." *Hadtörténeti Közlemények* 35: 467–83.

Townend, Matthew. 2000. "Viking Age England as a Bilingual Society." In *Cultures in Contact. Scandinavian Settlements in England in the Ninth and Tenth Centuries*, edited by Dawn M. Hadley and Julian D. Richards, 89–105. Turnhout: Brepols.

Treadgold, Warren. 2013. *The Middle Byzantine Historians*. Basingstoke: Palgrave MacMillan.

Türk, Attila. 2012. "The New Archaeological Research Design for Early Hungarian History." *Hungarian Archaeology* (yearly summer issue): 1–6.

———. 2016. "10. századi magyar jelenlét a Kárpátokról keletre [Tenth-century Magyar Presence to the East of the Carpathians]." In *Honfoglalás és megtelepedés*, edited by Balázs Sudár and Zsolt Petkes, 84. Magyar őstörténet, no. 4. Budapest: Helikon.

Unterländer, Martina Friso Palstra, Iosif Lazaridis, Aleksandr Pilipenko, Zuzana Hofmanova, Melanie Groß, Christian Sell, Jens Blöcher, Karola Kirsanow, Nadin Rohland, Benjamin Rieger, Elke Kaiser, Wolfram Schier, Dimitri Pozdniakov, Aleksandr Khokhlov, Myriam Georges, Sandra Wilde, Adam Powell, Evelyne Heyer, Mathias Currat, David Reich, Zainolla Samashev, Hermann Parzinger, Vyacheslav I. Molodin, and Joachim Burger. 2017. "Ancestry and Demography and Descendants of Iron Age Nomads of the Eurasian Steppe." *Nature Communications* 8: 14615.

Upham, Tonicha. 2019. *Equal Rites. Parsing Rus' Gender Values Through an Arabic Lens*. Unpublished MA Thesis in Viking and Medieval Norse Studies. Reykjavík: University of Iceland.

Urbańczyk, Przemysław. 2014. "Who Were the Early Rus'?" In *Rus' v IX – XII vekakh: obshchestvo, gosudarstvo, kul'tura*, edited by N. A. Makarov and A. E. Leontiev, 228–33. Moscow: Drevnosti Severa.

Validi, A. Zeki. 1936. "Die Schwerter der Germanen, nach arabischen Berichten des 9–11. Jahrhunderts." *Zeitschrift der Deutschen Morgenländischen Gesellschaft* 9, no. 1: 19–37.

Vandkilde, Helle. 2007. *Culture and Change in Central European Prehistory 6th – 1st Millenium BC*. Aarhus: Aarhus University Press.

Vásáry, István. 1993. *Geschichte des frühen Innerasiens*. Studia Turcica, no. 1. Herne: Tibor Schäfer.

Vasiliev, Alexander A. 1946. *The Russian attack on Constantinople in 860*. Cambridge: The Medieval Academy of America.

Vasilievskii, V. G. 1908. "Variago-russkaia i variago-angliiskaia druzhina [Varangian-Russian and Varangian-English Druzhina]." *Trudy* 1: 355–78.

Vasmer, Max. 1953. *Russiches Etymologisches Wörterbuch*, Vol. 1. Heidelberg: Carl Winter.

Vasyuta, Oleh. 2016. "Kurhan Chorna Mohyla v istorychnykh doslidzhennyakh mynuloho ta suchasnosti [The Kurgan of the Black Mound in Historical Studies of the Past and Present]." *Siveryans'kyy litopys* 132, no. 6: 3–18.

Vékony, Gábor. 2004. "Sókereskedelem a Kárpát-medencében az Árpád-kor előtt [Salt Trade in the Carpathian Basin before the Árpád Age]." In *Quasi liber et pictura. Tanulmányok Kubinyi András hetvenedik születésnapjára*, edited by Gyöngyi Kovács, 655–62. Budapest: ELTE Régészettudományi Intézet.

Vernadsky, George. 1939. "Lebedia Studies on the Magyar Background of Kievan Russia." *Byzantion* 14, no. 1: 179–203.

———. 1959. *The Origins of Russia*. Oxford: Clarendon Press.

Veszprémy, László, and Frank Schaer, eds. and trans. 1999. *Simonis de Kéza Gesta Hungarorum/Simon of Kéza. The Deeds of the Hungarians*. Budapest: CEU Press.

Vigfússon, Guðbrandur, and Carl Rikard Unger, eds. 1862. "Eymundar þáttr Hringssonar." In *Flateyjarbok. En samling af norske konge-sagaer*, Vol. 2, 118–34. Christiania: P. T. Malling.

———, eds. 1868a. "Snegluhalla þáttr." In *Flateyjarbok. En samling af norske konge-sagaer*, Vol. 3, 415–28. Christiania: P. T. Mallings.

———, eds. 1868b. "Saga hins heilaga Edvardar." In *Flateyjarbók: En Samling af norske Konge-Sagaer med indskudte mindre Fortælinger om Begivenheder i og undenfor Norge samt Annaler*, Vol. 3, 461–72. Christiania: P. T. Malling.

Vysotskiy, S. A. 1966. *Drevnerusskiye graffiti Sofii Kiyevskoy XI – XIV vv [Old Rus graffities of the Kievan Sophia 11th – 14th century]*, Vol. 1. Kiev: Naukova Dumka.

Vukovich, Alexandra. 2018. "Enthronement in Early Rus: Between Byzantium and Scandinavia." *Viking and Medieval Scandinavia* 14: 211–39.

Waitz, Georg Isidore, ed. 1878. *Annales Hildesheimenses*. MGH Scriptores rerum Germanicarum in usum scholarum, no. 8. Hannover: Hahn.

———, ed. 1883. *Annales Bertiniani*. MGH Scriptores rerum Germanicarum in usum scholarum, no. 5. Hannover: Hahn.

Wallace, Birgitta. 2008. "The Discovery of Vínland." In *The Viking World*, edited by Stefan Brink and Neil Price, 604–12. London: Routledge.

Warmind, Morten Lund. 1995. "Ibn Fadlan in the Context of his Age." In *The Ship as Symbol in Prehistoric and Medieval Scandinavia. Papers from an International Research Seminar at the Danish National Museum, Copenhagen, 5th-7th May 1994*, edited by Ole-Crumlin Pedersen and Birgitte Munch Thye, 131–35. Copenhagen: PNM.

Watson, Burton, trans. 1993. *Records of the Grand Historian: Han Dynasty*. Vol. 2. Revised ed. New York: Columbia University Press.

Wenska, Izabella. 2015. "Sacrifices among the Slavs: Between Archaeological Evidence and 19th Century Folklore." *Analecta Archaeologica Ressoviensia* 10: 271–313.

Wielhorsky, Mikhail M., trans. 1857. "The Travels of Athanasius Nikitin of Twer." In *India in the Fifteenth Century*, edited by Richard H. Mayor, 1–32. London: Hakluyt Society.

Wikander, Stig. 1978. *Araber, Vikingar, Väringar*. Lund: Svenska Humanistiska Förbundet.

Williams, Alan. 2012. *The Sword of Crucible. A History of the Metallurgy of European Swords up to the 16th Century*. History of Warfare, no. 77. Leiden: Brill.

Williams, Gareth. 2019. *Weapons of the Viking warrior*. Oxford: Osprey.

Wilson, Nigel G. ed. 2015. *Herodoti Historiae. Tomvs Prior: Libros I–IV Continens*. Oxford: Oxford University Press.

Wolfram, Herwig. [1979] 1990. *History of the Goths*. Translated by Thomas J. Dunlap. Berkeley: University of California Press.

Yotov, Valeri. 2015. "Traces of Scandinavian Warriors' Presence in the Balkans." In *Scandinavia and the Balkans. Cultural Interaction with Byzantium and Eastern Europe in the First Millenium AD*, edited by Oksana Minaeva and Lena Holmquist, 187–204. Cambridge: Cambridge Scholars Publishing.

Yule, Henry, ed. and trans. 1871. *The Book of Ser Marco Polo, the Venetian. Concerning the Kingdoms and Marvels of the East*, Vol. 2. London: John Murray.

Zadeh, Travis. 2017. "Ibn Faḍlān." In *Encyclopaedia of Islam THREE*, edited by Kate Fleet, Gudrun Krämer, Denis Matringe, John Nawas, and Everett Rowson, 121–28. Brill Online.

Zaliznyak, A. A. 2004. *Drevnenovgorodskiy dialekt [Old Novgorodian Dialect]*. Moscow: Yazyki slavyanskoy kul'tury.

Zanchi, Anna. 2008. "'Melius abundare Quam Deficere': Scarlet Clothing in Laxdaela Saga and Njals Saga." In *Medieval Clothing and Textiles*, edited by Robin Netherton and Gale R. Owen-Crocker, Vol. 4, 21–37. Woodbridge: The Boydell Press.

Zhivkov, Boris. 2015. *Khazaria in the Ninth and Tenth Centuries*. East Central and Eastern Europe in the Middle Ages, 450–1450, no. 30. Leiden: Brill.

Zhuravlev, D. V., and V. V. Murasheva, eds. 2012. *Mech i zlatnik. K 1150-letiyu zarozhdeniya Drevnerusskogo gosudarstva [Sword and zlatnik. To the 1150th Anniversary of the Old Russian State]*. Moscow: Kuchkovo pole.

Zimonyi, István. 1989. "The Origins of the Volga Bulghars." Ph.D dissertation. Studio uralo-altaica. University of Szeged, Szeged.

———. 1998. "Wolgabulgaren." In *Lexikon des Mittelalters*, edited by Robert Auty and Charlotte Bretscher-Gisiger, Vol. 9, 315–17. Munich: Artemis Verlag.

———. 2001. "Why Were the Hungarians Referred to as Turks in the Early Muslim Sources?" In *Néptörténet – Nyelvtörténet: A 70 éves Róna-Tas András köszöntése*, edited by László Károly and Éva Nagy Kincses, 201–12. Szeged: SZTE BTK Altajisztikai Tanszék.

———. 2016. *Muslim Sources on the Magyars in the Second Half of the 9th Century. The Magyar Chapter of the Jayhānī Tradition*. Leiden: Brill.

Zuckerman, Constantin. 1995. "On the Date of the Khazars' Conversion to Judaism and the Chronology of the Kings of the Rus Oleg and Igor. A Study of the Anonymous Khazar Letter from the Genizah of Kairo." *Revue des études byzantines* 53: 237–70.

# Index